Metropolitan Governance:
American/Canadian
Intergovernmental Perspectives

Metropolitan Governance: American/Canadian Intergovernmental Perspectives

Edited by
Donald N. Rothblatt
and Andrew Sancton

Institute of Governmental Studies Press
University of California, Berkeley
Institute of Intergovernmental Relations
Queen's University
1993

Volume One of the North American Federalism Project
Victor Jones, Project Coordinator

Library of Congress Cataloging-In-Publication Data

Metropolitan governance : American/Canadian intergovernmental perspectives / Donald
   N. Rothblatt, Andrew Sancton, editors.
       p. cm.
   Includes bibliographical references.
   ISBN 0-87772-334-6
    1. City planning--United States. 2. City planning--Canada. 3. Metropolitan
government--United States. 4. Metropolitan government--Canada. I. Rothblatt,
Donald N. II. Sancton, Andrew, 1948- .
HT167.M48 1993
307.1'6'0973--dc20
                                                92-43736
                                                  CIP

*This series on Canadian-American federalism is dedicated to
Ronald Watts and Daniel Elazar.*

Contents

FOREWORD

An old saying among political scientists is that foreigners are more likely than natives to understand a country's political culture. They may even give respectability to or be the originator of facile, untested legends. But the principal contribution of an outsider is to raise questions, often embedded in sweeping assertions, that move insiders to confirm, modify, or refute the visitor's findings and conclusions.

We do not aspire to the role of Toqueville, Lord Bryce, or Lord Durham. We hope, however, that our collaborative examination of three specific aspects of Canadian and American federalism at work will bring to each participant, as well as to our readers, a clearer appreciation of Canadian and American government and politics. The give and take of our collaboration over the past five years has given us a clearer picture and a sharper background for observing the formation of new, and the total or partial dissolution of old, federal bonds all over the world.

The generic problem is the structuring and restructuring of conflict and controversy so that center, region, and locality participate effectively (not necessarily efficiently) and with at least a modicum of satisfaction to parochial and superparochial interests. In this sense, unitary governments are faced with similar conflicting interests without the formal admission of territorial constraints in their resolution. We are still faced with Harold Laski's question: what difference does federalism in any of its organizational manifestations make? We need more penetrating and detailed comparisons of interest articulation, policymaking, and policy implementation along a continuum from totalitarian central management to anarchy.

I hope that our transnational collaboration extending from the selection of topics and participants through collegial discussion and criticism of individual papers and their editing into a book (a process not at all unusual in academia), which we have enjoyed in the Canadian-American Federalism Project, can be continued. There are dozens of topics that need to be explored arising from Canada's ongoing search for an acceptable constitutional order. Likewise, in the supposedly stable American federal system, we are faced with the systemic strains and opportunities of our unstable intergovernmental relations (national, state, and local) as we move cyclically from the more passive (at least

---

Note: Each author spells and measures in accord with his or her respective national custom, e.g., labour/labor, kilometres/miles, Canadian dollars/U.S. dollars.

ideologically) Reagan-Bush role of government to the promise of a more active role under Clinton and undoubtedly back again, but never to the *status quo ante*. All of this is occurring in both countries in the context of a globalization we cannot yet fully comprehend.

For the past five years, 18 Canadians and 21 Americans from 14 American and 11 Canadian universities have been exploring the differences and similarities in intergovernmental relations under the two neighboring federal systems. In fact, even more scholars have been involved since the workshops for the federalism project have been held back-to-back with the annual University of California seminars on federalism under the leadership of Professor Harry N. Scheiber.[1] Three independent critics have also been present at each workshop. We are grateful to the following for intellectual and social stimulation and for specific criticism of the papers: Jean-Pierre Gaboury (University of Ottawa), Thomas Anton (Brown), Ronald Watts (Queen's), Bruce Cain (Berkeley), Deil Wright (North Carolina), L. J. Sharpe (Nuffield College, Oxford), John Kincaid (U.S. Advisory Commission on Intergovernmental Relations), Peter Leslie (Queen's), and Henry Keith (U.S.-Canada Business Institute, San Francisco State University).

This series consists of three volumes. The first volume, *Metropolitan Governance: American/Canadian Intergovernmental Perspectives*, edited by Andrew Sancton (Western Ontario) and Donald N. Rothblatt (San Jose State University), examines the governance of metropolitan regions under the Canadian and American federal systems. Volume two, *States and Provinces in the International Economy*, is edited by Douglas M. Brown (Queen's) and Earl H. Fry (Brigham Young). Volume three, *Representation and Policy Formation in Federal Systems: Canada and the United States*, edited by C. E. S. Franks (Queen's) and David Olson (University of North Carolina at Greensboro), studies representation of regional and other interests in the two federal systems.

The Canadian-American Federalism Project was initiated and conducted by the Canadian Studies Program of the University of California, Berkeley. The cochairmen of the Canadian Studies Program,

---

[1] The proceedings of these seminars on federalism have been published by IGS Press as *Perspectives on Federalism* (1987); *Federalism: Studies in History, Law, and Policy* (1988); *Power Divided: Essays on the Theory and Practice of Federalism* (1989); *Federalism and the Judicial Mind: Essays on American Constitutional Law and Politics* (1992); and *North American & Comparative Federalism: Essays for the 1990s* (1992).

Professor Thomas G. Barnes (History and Law), and Professor Nelson Graburn (Anthropology), have been supportive, encouraging, and demanding. We needed all three elements of oversight and are thankful to Professors Barnes and Graburn for their kindness and persistence.

The Canadian Studies Program for most of its life was part of the Institute of International Studies. It was a pleasure to work with its director, Professor Carl Rosberg, its assistant director, Harry Kreisler, and its managing officer, Karen Beros. The Canadian Studies Program continues under the university's International and Area Studies, headed by Dean Albert Fishlow. Literally, the project would not have survived without the 24-hour assistance and guidance of Peggy Nelson. Rita Ross, administrative assistant for the Canadian Studies Program, has been a capable and friendly successor.

The Canadian Studies Program has profited from the participation of scholars from other colleges and universities in the Bay Area. We are grateful to Ted Thomas (Professor of Sociology and Provost of Mills College), Donald Rothblatt (chair, Department of Urban and Regional Planning, San Jose State University), and Calvin Massey (Professor of Law at Hastings College of Law), for participation in the federalism project.

The Institute of Governmental Studies (IGS), both under its former director Eugene C. Lee and its current director Nelson W. Polsby, has served *de facto* as a second home for the federalism project and in fact for the entire Canadian Studies Program. Without its in-kind support (paper clips, office spaces, xerox, telephones, library, etc.) I should not have been able to formulate and manage the Canadian-American Federalism Project.

I have lived in the IGS Library off and on since 1938. I thank past and present librarians for their tolerance, help, and friendship. Our federalism project is indebted to Jack Leister, former head librarian, Terry Dean, current head librarian, Kathleen Burgess, Ron Heckart, Marc Levin, Diana Neves, and Susi Schneider. Since I have never been allowed to browse in the stacks, I salute the many pages who over the years have retrieved books for me.

Equally important has been IGS' support of the annual seminars on federalism under Harry N. Scheiber of the Boalt Hall School of Law. IGS Associate Director Bruce Cain and Assistant Director Adrienne Jamieson continue to be delightful and supportive colleagues.

The three project reports are being published by IGS Press and marketed in Canada by the Institute of Intergovernmental Relations of

Queen's University (Douglas Brown, Director) and in the United States and elsewhere by IGS. We are deeply indebted to the IGS Director of Publications, Jerry Lubenow, and his associates, Maria Wolf (Publications Editor), Pat Ramirez (Publications Coordinator), and Catherine West (Publications Marketing Coordinator). I personally accept responsibility for all my procrastination, which makes Maria Wolf's continued good nature both extraordinary and appreciated.

The IGS Press has also assumed from the University of California Press the publication of the Franklin K. Lane series of books on major metropolitan regions. Three of the nine published volumes are on Canadian metropolitan regions: Albert Rose (University of Toronto) on Toronto, Andrew Sancton (Western Ontario) on Montreal, and Meyer Brownstone (University of Toronto) and T. J. Plunkett (Queen's) on Winnipeg. IGS Press will also publish this year, jointly with the Canadian Urban Institute, *The Changing Canadian Metropolis: A Public Policy Perspective,* edited by Frances Frisken (York).

We are especially indebted to several people at Queen's University: Ronald Watts, Douglas Brown, Richard Simeon (now at the University of Toronto), Peter Leslie, C. E. S. (Ned) Franks, and T. J. Plunkett. Similar assistance, encouragement and criticism has come from Peter Oberlander and Alan Cairns at the University of British Columbia and from Patrick Smith of Simon Fraser University.

The Canadian government has also been closely involved in developing the idea of a joint venture and in furnishing financial assistance to support the research of several participants. The encouragement and assistance of the following are especially appreciated: Alan Unger, Public Affairs Officer, Consul Stuart Hughes, and Andrew Thompson, Academic Affairs Officer, at the Canadian Consulate-General in San Francisco. From the beginning of our efforts to go forward with Canadian-American collaboration Norman London, Academic Relations officer at the Canadian Embassy in Washington, D.C., has constantly shown the deepest interest in our work. We are grateful to him and to the Canadian government for a close professional friendship.

The Honorable James D. Horsman, Deputy Premier of Alberta and Minister of Federalism and Intergovernmental Affairs has taken time frequently to visit with the Canadian Studies Program and to discuss events leading to and following from Meech Lake and the national and Quebec referenda of 1992.

We would also like to acknowledge the advice, stimulation, and criticism at various times and in various ways from Stanley Scott

(Berkeley); Martin Landau (Berkeley); Randy Hamilton (Berkeley and Golden Gate University); Don Chisholm (UCLA); James Desveaux (Texas A&M); Evert Lindquist (Toronto); Peter Lyden (visiting scholar at IGS); John Sproul, Roger Thompson and David McLean of the Advisory Group to our Canadian Studies Program; Malcolm Taylor (York); David Elton (University of Letheridge and Canada West Foundation); Alan Artibise and David Elkins (University of British Columbia); Lloyd Brown-John (University of Windsor); Charles Doran (Johns Hopkins-SAIS); Daniel Elazar (Bar Ilan University and Temple University); Stephen Schecter (Russell Sage College); David Walker (University of Connecticut); Lyle C. Fitch (Institute of Public Administration); Carl Stenberg (University of Virginia); Bruce McDowall (U.S. Advisory Commission on Intergovernmental Relations); and Kent Mathewson, a leader in the reconstruction of intergovernmental relations in metropolitan regions.

This magnificent experience for all participants and the publication of some of our findings and conclusions have been possible only because the William H. Donner Foundation decided to fund our efforts. We salute William T. Alpert for his trust backed by the generosity of the foundation. Other people and institutions have contributed equally generously with grants to match the foundation's support. Robert H. Gayner, executive director of the Business Fund for Canadian Studies in the U.S., made it possible to complete the project. The Pacific Gas Transmission Company, The McLean Group of Vancouver, the Canadian Embassy, the Province of Alberta, and Marathon U.S. Realtors, Inc. were equally generous throughout the life of the project.

Victor Jones
Canadian-American Federalism Project
Project Coordinator

Policymaking for Urban Development in American and Canadian Metropolitan Regions

Andrew Sancton
University of Western Ontario

In 1990-91 there were 51 metropolitan areas in the United States with populations of over 800,000. In Canada there were five. (See Table 1.) This research project looks at policymaking for urban development in nine metropolitan regions in the two countries: five in the United States and four in Canada. Even with fewer cities, the coverage of Canada is relatively much more comprehensive. This is especially obvious when it is realized that the two largest American metropolitan areas, New York and Los Angeles, are not included in the project at all. Respectively, they are more than four and three times more populous than Toronto, which is Canada's largest metropolitan area. Given such wide differences in scale, it seemed appropriate for them to be excluded.

Even Chicago, which is included in the project, has more than twice the population of Toronto. San Francisco, Boston, and Houston are also included, but their population levels are much closer to those of Toronto and of Montreal, which is Canada's second-largest metropolitan area. Minneapolis, Vancouver, and Edmonton round out the study but, even among this group, the American metropolitan area is by far the largest.

The central object of this collection of papers is to determine the extent to which we can characterize American and Canadian metropolitan regions as each having distinctive policymaking processes and patterns of intergovernmental relations with respect to regional planning and the provision of major urban infrastructure. We are particularly interested in the policymaking role of metropolitan governments and/or other mechanisms whereby municipalities can collaborate with each other in approaching intermunicipal issues relating to urban development. In the

Table 1. *Metropolitan Regions with Populations over 800,000 in the United States and Canada, 1990-91*

		Population of Region (000s)	Population of Central City (000s)	Ratio of Central City to Region
1	New York	18,087	7,323	.40
2	Los Angeles	14,532	3,485	.24
3	CHICAGO	8,066	2,784	.35
4	SAN FRANCISCO	6,253	724	.12
5	Philadelphia	5,899	1,586	.27
6	Detroit	4,665	1,028	.17
7	BOSTON	4,172	574	.14
8	Washington	3,924	607	.15
9	TORONTO	3,893	635	.16
10	Dallas	3,885	1,007	.26
11	HOUSTON	3,711	1,631	.44
12	Miami	3,193	359	.11
13	MONTREAL	3,127	1,018	.33
14	Atlanta	2,834	394	.14
15	Cleveland	2,760	506	.18
16	Seattle	2,559	516	.20
17	San Diego	2,498	1,111	.44
18	MINNEAPOLIS	2,464	368	.15
19	St. Louis	2,444	397	.16
20	Baltimore	2,382	736	.31
21	Pittsburgh	2,243	370	.16
22	Phoenix	2,122	983	.46
23	Tampa	2,068	280	.14
24	Denver	1,848	468	.25
25	Cincinnati	1,744	364	.21
26	Milwaukee	1,607	628	.39
27	VANCOUVER	1,603	472	.29
28	Kansas City	1,566	435	.28
29	Sacramento	1,481	369	.25
30	Portland	1,478	437	.30
31	Norfolk	1,396	261	.19
32	Columbus	1,377	633	.46
33	San Antonio	1,302	936	.72
34	Indianapolis	1,250	742	.59
35	New Orleans	1,239	497	.40

36	Buffalo	1,189	328	.28
37	Charlotte	1,162	396	.34
38	Providence	1,142	161	.14
39	Hartford	1,086	140	.13
40	Orlando	1,073	165	.15
41	Salt Lake City	1,072	160	.15
42	Rochester	1,002	232	.23
43	Nashville	985	488	.49
44	Memphis	982	610	.62
45	Oklahoma City	959	445	.46
46	Louisville	953	269	.28
47	Dayton	951	182	.19
48	Greensboro	942	184	.20
49	Ottawa	921	314	.34
50	Birmingham	908	266	.29
51	Jacksonville	907	635	.70
52	Albany	874	101	.12
53	Richmond	866	203	.23
54	West Palm Beach	864	68	.08
55	EDMONTON	840	617	.73
56	Honolulu	836	365	.44

Notes: Metropolitan regions in UPPER-CASE letters are treated in separate essays in this collection; underlined ones are in Canada. American metropolitan regions are Metropolitan Statistical Areas or, where applicable, Consolidated Metropolitan Statistical Areas. Canadian metropolitan regions are Census Metropolitan Areas.

Sources: For the United States, 1990 census figures as reported in United States Department of Commerce, *Statistical Abstract of the United States 1991* (Washington, D.C.: United States Government Printing Office, 1991), 29-36; For Canada, Statistics Canada, *A National Overview* (Ottawa: Supply and Services Canada, 1992). 1991 Census of Canada, Catalogue number 93-301.

collection's concluding essay Donald N. Rothblatt examines some of the implications of the differences between the two countries both for understanding policymaking and for attempting to come to grips more effectively with each country's urban development problems.

The United States and Canada are both federations and in each case the federal, or national government, has no constitutional jurisdiction over municipal or local government. As the essays in this collection will show, such a lack of jurisdiction has not prevented either federal government from having a profound influence on the nature of urban development. But the ways in which this influence have been exercised has been significantly different in each country.

In both countries, federal governments have always been major urban landowners, primarily as a result of their need for centrally located facilities for both military and civilian purposes. The Canadian government tended to become more involved in the direct ownership of ports, railways, and airports, but American federal law and spending policies were determining factors in how many vital elements of the urban infrastructure developed in the United States. Indeed, for urban expressways, the American federal government became virtually the direct provider, a role in urban policymaking never even contemplated by its Canadian counterpart.

During the 1930s both federal governments became actively involved in arranging the financing of new housing. The postwar construction of North American suburbia was in many ways a direct result (Doucet and Weaver 1991). But it was not until the 1960s that the two federal governments launched direct and massive interventions across a wide array of policy areas that had hitherto traditionally been the preserve of state/provincial or local governments. In the United States, federal initiatives resulted from the civil rights movement and President Johnson's War on Poverty. Prime Minister Pearson borrowed Johnson's rhetoric and introduced a series of social measures, including universal medicare, that probably had more lasting influence on the quality of urban life in Canada than any of Johnson's measures had in the United States.

During this period both federal governments were active sponsors of massive downtown urban redevelopment. The new cabinet positions of Secretary of Housing and Urban Development in the United States and Ministry of State for Urban Affairs in Canada were supposed to help ensure that federal intervention in urban areas was coordinated, controlled, and responsive to local wishes. One such wish was that massive federally sponsored downtown redevelopment schemes cease—and eventually they did.

In both countries during the 1970s and 1980s, direct federal involvement in policies relating to urban development and urban problems was dramatically reduced, but for quite different reasons. In the United States, more conservative federal administrations attempted to block the flow of conditional federal funds so as to reduce overall government expenditures on redistributive programs (Kantor 1988, Ch. 10). In Canada, opposition to federal involvement, led mainly by

Quebec, came from the provinces. They preferred to control urban policy themselves and were generally successful in forcing the federal government to retreat. The Ministry of State for Urban Affairs was abolished in 1979 (Oberlander and Fallick 1987). In the constitutional agreement of August 22, 1992, all governments agreed that any province could, if it wished, take control over its share of all federal money spent on urban affairs and housing, thereby eliminating the federal presence in these fields within its territory.

In practical terms, the Canadian federal government's formal retreat means very little to individual municipal governments. The government of Canada has virtually no ongoing programs to channel funds directly to municipal and other local governments. This contrasts with the American federal government, which, even after the Reagan cutbacks, still supplies funds to cities for urban transit, public housing, senior citizens' programs, and other related functions.

Observers walking the inner-city streets of cities in the two countries might well take issue with the notion that there is less federal involvement in Canadian cities than in American ones. Vancouver has its federally sponsored Granville Island, Toronto has Harbourfront, and Montreal and Quebec City are seeing old port areas rejuvenated by federal agencies. Although similar projects can be found in American cities, few, if any, are under the direct control of the federal government. Rather than turning its surplus land over to others, the Canadian government has itself developed new amenities in many of Canada's larger cities. Its physical presence in urban areas is significant—and likely to remain so—but its presence in the day-to-day operation of local government is nonexistent.

In the United States there are meaningful sets of relationships between both the federal governments and the states and between the federal government and local governments. In Canada, the federal government interacts only with the provinces. This means that, for a Canadian municipality, its provincial government is more significant to it than a state government is to an American municipality, especially since, as the essays in this collection will show, Canadian provinces are much more interventionist in local affairs than their American counterparts.

American and Canadian political institutions are more similar to each other at the municipal level than at any other (Munro 1929, 99). In both countries the origins of municipal institutions can be traced to Britain. In the mid-nineteenth century—first in the United States and then in

Canada—they were increasingly subject to democratic control. Unlike Britain, mayors in both countries began to be directly elected. Canadians, however, generally resisted Jacksonian pressure for the direct election of other local officials. Progressive reformers at the turn of the century had profound influences in both countries: nonpartisan municipal elections became the norm; city manager schemes were introduced; special-purpose bodies were established for certain sensitive functions considered inappropriate for direct control by municipal politicians; the rationalization of municipal boundaries so as to facilitate comprehensive planning was urged almost everywhere (Schiesl 1977; Weaver 1977). During the Great Depression municipalities on both sides of the border were unable to cope with demands for unemployment relief. The result was that most welfare functions were generally taken over by the federal and state and provincial governments (Leman 1980, 21-42).

In the period immediately after World War II, major metropolitan areas in both countries experienced an explosion in suburban growth. In both countries academics and planners urged further governmental consolidation so as to bring central city and suburb under some kind of common planning and taxing authority. In Canada these proposed reforms were generally implemented. In the United States they were not. Explanations of these contrasting outcomes are plentiful (Teaford 1979; Magnusson 1981). This collection is more concerned, however, with the impact of the different institutional arrangements. Does it matter much that Canadian metropolitan regions generally have some form of multifunctional metropolitan government while American ones generally do not?

With the exception of those particularly interested in metropolitan reorganization, American scholars have shown little interest in Canadian cities. Given the content of Table 1, this is scarcely surprising. However, there has been at least one occasion in the recent past when attention by an American to the Canadian experience would have added a great deal to the American analysis. The work in question is Paul Peterson's acclaimed and controversial work, *City Limits* (1981). In his concluding chapter Peterson proposes three reforms aimed at increasing the capacity of American local governments to adopt and implement policies that redistribute resources from the wealthy to the poor. One of them is that "The federal government should institute a revenue-sharing plan that would attempt to equalize per capita fiscal resources available to each state and local government" (219). Such a plan is not only federal policy in Canada, it is now entrenched in the constitution.

Furthermore, each province has some form of municipal fiscal equalization scheme performing the same function internally (Auld and Eden 1987). These policies—combined with other Canadian municipal regulatory practices likely to win Peterson's favour—ensure that financially weak municipalities in Canada are not in the same objectively subordinate position in relation to their creditors and large businesses as Peterson argues is the case in the United States.

Peterson makes reference to local government equalization schemes in Britain, but not in Canada. This is unfortunate, because federalism and the absence of strong socialist parties in local politics makes the Canadian setting much more useful for contemplating the possible effects of implementing Peterson's proposed reforms in the United States. What he would discover from the Canadian experience is that such policies do indeed reduce the influence of creditors and local big businesses on municipal politics. Since local taxation and service levels are not likely to vary much (by American standards at least) within a given province, the stakes of municipal politics in Canada for community elites are generally much lower. Freeing municipal councils from what some would see as economic reality does not, however, usher in a new era of local autonomy and democracy. Control by provincial government is substituted for the control by banks and big businesses (Keating and Mehrhoff 1992; Garber and Imbroscio 1992)—a substitution of which Peterson would doubtless approve but one that he might have better understood by looking to Canada.

Canadian scholars who have compared American and Canadian cities have developed two opposing positions. Not surprisingly, some consider that there are meaningful distinctions to be made between American and Canadian cities and others that there are not. Much of the debate depends on one's perspective (Linteau 1987). If one is looking at cities of the world, Canadian and American ones appear quite similar. If comparisons are restricted to the two countries, there can be considerable debate about which variables are relevant. Goldberg and Mercer (1986) focused on those that appeared to be different in the two countries and arrived at the predictable conclusion that Canadian cities have recognizable, distinct, and quantifiable characteristics that set them apart from American cities collectively and any particular subset of American cities. Certain of the Goldberg and Mercer findings seem beyond dispute. Central areas of Canadian cities are more densely populated than equivalent areas in American cities; Canadian city-dwellers make more use of public transit; and there is more disparity between central city and suburban mean incomes in the United States than in Canada.

The most serious challenge to the Goldberg and Mercer case has come from Frances Frisken (1986). She claims that in recent years Canadian provincial governments have begun to relax previous efforts to bolster the economic and political strength of central cities and have instead catered more to the needs of peripheral suburban municipalities. "In this respect at least the situation of Canada's larger cities is now very like that in which the large cities of the northern and eastern United States had begun to find themselves by the 1920s" (376). Frisken agrees with Goldberg and Mercer that Canadian and American cities are different but disagrees with them about the explanation. For Goldberg and Mercer there is a whole range of social, economic, and political variables that mutually reinforce the differences. For Frisken, the differences result primarily from political decisions taken mainly in the 1950s and 1960s by Canadian provincial governments. The policies seem to be changing; if the trend continues, Canadian urban distinctiveness in relation to the United States will inevitably decline.

A third possible hypothesis is that in advanced western democracies urban public policy is increasingly determined by global socio-economic factors over which national governments—let alone regional or local ones—have little control. As the world economy becomes more open and competitive, diseconomies of urban concentration (e.g., overburdened infrastructure, high housing costs, pollution, crime) make established urban centers less desirable and encourage continued decentralization of development to outlying areas (Hall and Hay 1980; Rothblatt and Garr 1986; Levine 1989). This line of reasoning suggests that urban development in Canada and the United States is simply a reflection of world trends. Their cities, and those in western Europe and Japan, are indeed becoming more similar, but not as the result of actions taken by government.

For the moment, however, we are concerned with the urban differences between the two countries, notwithstanding the possibility that they might be eroding. Since Goldberg and Mercer aim more to document these differences than to explain them, they need not be especially concerned about confusing cause and effect. For example, they include in their book a chapter on urban local government which shows that Canadians have been much more likely than Americans to establish multifunctional governments for metropolitan regions. It remains unclear, however, whether or not these governments are theorized as relatively independent variables that help create and maintain the differences or whether their existence is a result of the differences. For Frisken the existence of such governments reflects provincial policy; it is the provincial policy that is the main independent variable.

Let us assume that the main differences to be explained relate in one way or another to the demonstrated healthier state of Canadian central cities, i.e., more diversity of land use, better public services, less urban poverty, etc. One line of argument is fundamentally political. As a result of political values embedded in their society, Canadians have made decisions that, in comparison to those made by Americans, have limited the rights of individuals to pursue wealth through the exploitation of urban land. Instead they have protected certain collective interests that may or may not be subject to explicit definition. This appears to be Frisken's approach; she is worried that Canadian political values (and hence ultimately public policies) are becoming more American or market-oriented and that, as a result, Canadian central cities will suffer.

Another explanation relates to the social realities of the two countries. Until the mid-nineteenth century black slave labour in the South was an integral part of the American economy. The formal abolition of slavery had little immediate effect on American cities. It was not until the mechanization of agriculture in the South and the industrial boom in the North caused by World War II that southern blacks migrated to the major cities of the North. Such cities had been renowned for their capacities to assimilate wave after wave of European immigrants. For whatever reasons, similar assimilation of blacks did not occur. Those who stress the importance of the racial issue in understanding the politics of American cities (Banfield and Wilson 1963, 44) would no doubt argue, if asked to assess the relevance of the Canadian experience for the United States, that the increasing presence of a black underclass in American central cities has so dramatically changed the nature of American urban life that such innovations as metropolitan government, municipal fiscal equalization, and centrally imposed minimum standards for public services are now politically and financially impossible and/or irrelevant, even if at some time in the past they might have been at least conceivable. Had Canadian cities been subject to the same kind of migration from the descendants of black slaves, the argument goes, their central cities would now be indistinguishable from those of the United States, notwithstanding the implementation of the distinct Canadian policies referred to above.

This collection is not meant to catalogue similarities and differences in urban form and public services in the two countries. The focus is the political process, especially within intermunicipal institutions whose territories cover substantial portions of the relevant metropolitan areas. How and why are decisions made, or not made, about the nature of urban growth? In attempting to answer this question we aim to learn not just about urban political power in the two countries but about the role of the public sector in shaping our urban physical environment.

REFERENCES

Auld, D. A. L., and L. Eden. 1987. A Comparative Evaluation of Provincial-Local Equalization. *Canadian Public Policy* 13: 515-28.

Banfield, E. C., and J. Q. Wilson. 1963. *City Politics.* Cambridge: M.I.T. Press.

Doucet, M., and J. Weaver. 1991. *Housing the North American City.* Montreal and Kingston: McGill-Queen's University Press.

Frisken, F. 1986. Canadian Cities and the American Example: A Prologue to Urban Policy Analysis. *Canadian Public Administration* 29: 345-76.

Garber, J. A., and D. Imbroscio. 1992. Growth Politics in Canadian and American Cities: The Myth of the North American City Reconsidered. Paper presented to the annual meeting of the Canadian Political Science Association, Charlottetown, Prince Edward Island.

Goldberg, M. A., and J. Mercer. 1986. *The Myth of the North American City: Continentalism Challenged.* Vancouver: University of British Columbia Press.

Hall, P., and D. Hay. 1980. *Growth Centers in the European Urban System.* Berkeley: University of California Press.

Kantor, P., with S. David. 1988. *The Dependent City: The Changing Political Economy of Urban America.* Glenview, Illinois: Scott Foresman.

Keating, M., and A. Mehrhoff. 1992. Canadian Provincial and U.S. State Roles in Urban Planning and Development: A Study of London, Ontario and St. Cloud, Minnesota. *Environment and Planning C: Government and Policy* 10: 173-87.

Leman, C. 1980. *The Collapse of Welfare Reform: Political Institutions, Policy, and the Poor in Canada and the United States.* Cambridge: M.I.T. Press.

Levine, Marc V. 1989. Urban Redevelopment in a Global Economy: The Cases of Montreal and Baltimore. In *Cities in a Global Society,* ed. R. V. Knight and G. Gappert, Newbury Park, Calif.: Sage, 141-52.

Linteau, P. A. 1987. Canadian Suburbanization in a North American Context - Does the Border Make A Difference. *Journal of Urban History* 13: 252-74.

Magnusson, W. 1981. Metropolitan Reform and the Capitalist City. *Canadian Journal of Political Science* 14: 557-85.

Munro, W. B. 1929. *American Influences on Canadian Government.* Toronto: Macmillan.

Oberlander, H. P., and A. L. Fallick, eds. 1987. *The Ministry of State for Urban Affairs: A Courageous Experiment in Public Administration* Vancouver B.C.: Center for Human Settlements, University of British Columbia.

Peterson, P. E. 1981. *City Limits.* Chicago: University of Chicago Press.

Rothblatt, D. N., and D. J. Garr. 1986. *Suburbia: An International Assessment.* London and New York: Croom Helm and St, Martin's Press.

Schiesl, M. J. 1977. *The Politics of Efficiency: Municipal Administration and Reform in America, 1880-1920.* Berkeley: University of California Press.

Teaford, J. C. 1979. *City and Suburb: The Political Fragmentation of Metropolitan America, 1850-1970.* Baltimore: The Johns Hopkins University Press.

Weaver, J. C. 1977. *Shaping the Canadian City: Essays on Urban Politics and Policy, 1890-1920.* Toronto: Institute of Public Administration of Canada.

Chapter 1

Development Policy in Metropolitan Boston

Mark I. Gelfand
Boston College

INTRODUCTION

More than any other U.S. city, modern Boston is the product of a long and rich history, and the structure of metropolitan institutions in the region reflects this. The same heritage of local self-government and central city-suburban antagonism that led the Boston metropolitan area to pioneer in the regional delivery of essential urban services at the close of the nineteenth century has also stymied the development of vigorous metropolitan political and planning institutions at the close of the twentieth century. More than 350 years after the Puritans embarked on their "errand into the wilderness," metropolitan Boston remains enthralled with its uniqueness, which is both its greatest strength and its greatest weakness.

This paper is divided into six sections. The first is an overview of the Boston region's geographic and governmental setting. The second section offers a historical discussion of the Boston metropolitan area's political fragmentation and the abortive efforts during the past century at re-integration. The following two sections examine water and sewerage and transportation. The background and current status of metropolitan planning are the focus of the fifth section. A concluding section presents some impressions of the parts played by local, state, and national governments in the policymaking process of the Boston metropolitan region.

GEOGRAPHIC AND GOVERNMENTAL SETTING

Boston is both the capital of and largest city in the Commonwealth of Massachusetts.   Although the Hub (from Oliver Wendell Holmes' characterization of nineteenth century Boston as "The Hub of the Universe") ranks (1990) but twentieth in population (574,000) among U.S. municipalities, the Boston-Lawrence-Salem (N.H.) Consolidated Metropolitan Statistical Area (CMSA), extending over five counties in eastern Massachusetts and part of one in southern New Hampshire, is the seventh largest CMSA (4,025,000). Confining the borders of the Boston region to the limits of the 101 cities and towns that are members of the state-established Metropolitan Area Planning Council (MAPC) (see Map 1.1) reduces the population figure to 2,922,000 but does not alter the underlying relationship between the central city and its environs. Boston may account only for slightly less than 20 percent of the planning district's population, but it is about six times as big as the next largest city in the region (Cambridge). (See Table 1.1.) Of the metropolitan area's many newspapers, only the Hub's two dailies circulate throughout the whole region, and all four VHF television stations licensed in eastern Massachusetts are based in Boston. (There are also VHF stations in Rhode Island and New Hampshire whose signals can be received in different parts of the region.) Although Boston no longer holds the global spotlight the city once did, within its immediate surroundings it still casts a giant shadow.

Similarly, the Boston metropolitan region dominates the state demographically, economically, and politically. The MAPC district, covering about 18 percent of the Commonwealth's land area, contains more than half of its residents. The state's largest employers are located in the region and, with the advent of statewide banking in the past decade, the power of Boston's financial community—always a major element in the Commonwealth's economy—has grown even larger. Five of the six men elected governor since 1960 have been residents of the region; significantly, however, none lived in Boston itself. Because the Commonwealth does not provide its chief executive with an official mansion, these governors continued to live in their suburban communities and to experience on a daily basis the opportunities and frustrations awaiting the typical metropolitan citizen.

Despite the metropolitan region's towering presence, the state's political leaders, who have adopted generally liberal philosophies regardless of party affiliation, have not made metropolitan issues a focus

Map 1.1. *Metropolitan Area Planning Council District*

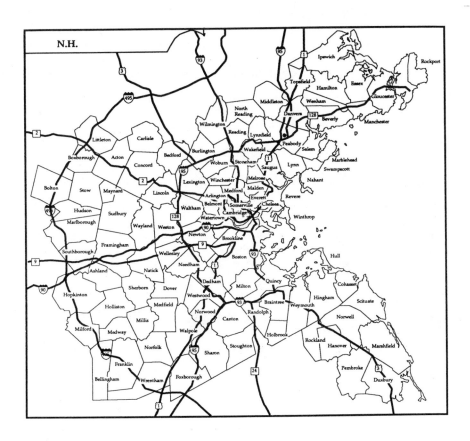

Table 1.1. *Cities and Towns in the Metropolitan Area Planning Council; Showing Population (1990) and Membership in Special-Purpose Districts.*

Community	Population	MWRA Water	MWRA Sewage	MBTA (Transit)	MDC (Parks)
Acton	17,872				
Arlington	44,630	X	X	X	X
Ashland	12,066		X	X	
Bedford	12,996		X	X	
Bellingham	14,877				
Belmont	24,720	X	X	X	X
Beverly	38,195			X	
Bolton	3,134				
Boston	574,280	X	X	X	X
Boxborough	3,343				
Braintree	33,836		X	X	X
Brookline	54,718	X	X	X	X
Burlington	23,302		X	X	
Cambridge	95,802	X	X	X	X
Canton	18,530	X	X	X	X
Carlisle	4,333				
Chelsea	28,710	X	X	X	X
Cohasset	7,075			X	
Concord	17,076			X	
Danvers	24,174			X	
Dedham	23,782		X	X	X
Dover	4,915			X	X
Duxbury	13,895			X	
Essex	3,260				
Everett	35,701	X	X	X	X
Foxborough	14,637				
Framingham	64,989	X	X	X	
Franklin	22,095				
Gloucester	28,716				
Hamilton	7,280			X	
Hanover	11,912			X	
Hingham	19,821		X	X	X
Holbrook	11,041		X	X	
Holliston	12,926				

Hopkinton	9,191				
Hudson	17,233				
Hull	10,466			X	X
Ipswich	11,873				
Lexington	28,974	X	X	X	
Lincoln	7,666			X	
Littleton	7,051				
Lynn	81,245	X		X	X
Lynnfield	11,274	X		X	
Malden	53,884	X	X	X	X
Manchester	5,286			X	
Marblehead	19,971	X		X	
Marlborough	31,813				
Marshfield	21,531			X	
Maynard	10,325				
Medfield	10,531			X	
Medford	57,407	X	X	X	X
Medway	9,931				
Melrose	28,150	X	X	X	X
Middleton	4,921			X	
Milford	25,355				
Millis	7,613			X	
Milton	25,725	X	X	X	X
Nahant	3,828	X		X	X
Natick	30,510		X	X	
Needham	27,557	X	X	X	
Newton	82,585	X	X	X	X
Norfolk	9,270			X	
North Reading	12,002			X	
Norwell	9,279			X	
Norwood	28,700	X	X	X	
Peabody	47,039	X		X	
Pembroke	14,544			X	
Quincy	84,985	X	X	X	X
Randolph	30,093		X	X	
Reading	22,539		X	X	
Revere	42,786	X	X	X	X
Rockland	16,123			X	
Rockport	7,482				
Salem	38,091			X	
Saugus	25,549	X		X	X
Scituate	16,786			X	
Sharon	15,517			X	

Sherborn	3,989			X	
Somerville	76,210	X	X	X	X
Southborough	6,628	X			
Stoneham	22,203	X	X	X	X
Stoughton	26,777		X		
Stow	5,328				
Sudbury	14,358			X	
Swampscott	13,650	X		X	X
Topsfield	5,754			X	
Wakefield	24,825	X	X	X	X
Walpole	20,212		X	X	
Waltham	57,878	X	X	X	X
Waltertown	33,284	X	X	X	X
Wayland	11,874			X	
Wellesley	26,615	X	X	X	X
Wenham	4,212			X	
Weston	10,200	X		X	X
Westwood	12,557		X	X	X
Weymouth	54,063		X	X	X
Wilmington	17,651		X	X	
Winchester	20,267	X	X	X	
Winthrop	18,127	X	X	X	X
Woburn	35,943	X	X	X	
Wrentham	9,006				
Totals:	2,922,934	38	43	78	35
21 Cities, 80 Towns					

Cities in Bold Type
Population data are either preliminary 1990 census results or Metropolitan Area Planning Council estimates.
MWRA = Massachusetts Water Resources Authority
MBTA = Massachusetts Bay Transportation Authority
MDC = Metropolitan District Commission

of their campaigning or legislative programs. Only once (in 1970) has a regional matter—involving the construction of an Interstate high-way—intruded into an election contest, but its potential as a catalyst for sparking discussion of metropolitan areawide problems was quickly neutralized by statements from both the incumbent Republican governor and his leading Democratic challenger pledging that the road would not be built.

That the Boston metropolitan area remains more an artificial statistical and cartographic construct than a popularly perceived economic, social, and political entity is revealed in both the organization of state government and the outlook of private groups. Neither the executive nor legislative branches are set up to look at metropolitan issues in a comprehensive way. Committees of the Great and General Court are arranged along functional lines and, while they may on occasion propose metropolitan solutions to problems, their tendency is to concern themselves with statewide matters. Several boards and authorities have been created during the past century to supply regional services (water and sewerage, parks, mass transit, harbor and airport), but these agencies operate not only within different geographic boundaries but also independently of one another. The agency with the largest purview, both in terms of territory and mission, the Metropolitan Area Planning Council, has only advisory power and lies outside the regular state governmental structure.

Private groups have mirrored—one might even say generated—the state government's hesitant approach to metropolitan issues. Most of the business and public interest associations in the Commonwealth are either statewide or local in organization. Whether the controversy in recent years has been taxes, the handling of solid waste, or the allocation of state aid to localities, the context of debate has been the Commonwealth as a whole or the community, not the metropolitan area. It has been almost two decades since the Greater Boston Chamber of Commerce, one of the few groups with a metropolitan focus to its membership, took a strong stand on a metropolitan question. The Boston College Citizens' Seminars, inaugurated in the mid-1950s to bring businessmen and academics together in an effort to revive the region's foundering economy, were instrumental in both paving the way for Boston's urban renewal boom in the 1960s and gaining state approval for the Metropolitan Area Planning Council in 1963. But in the decades since, the Citizens' Seminars have lacked the will or power to generate public discussion on metropolitan issues. A recently formed organization, 1,000 Friends of Massachusetts, which counts among its members some of the region's leading businessmen and civic activists, seeks to promote controlled-growth policies, but its political effectiveness has yet to be demonstrated.

An environmental group, the Conservation Law Foundation, has relied mainly on the courts to push its program. Besides forcing a massive cleanup of Boston harbor, the foundation has attempted to curb further development of Boston's business district, citing the inadequacy of mass transit facilities and violations of federal air pollution laws. The Sierra Club, which generally has had a low profile in this part of the country, recently gained local headlines with its legal challenge to the state- and business-backed $4 billion plan to tear down the elevated interstate highway that has disfigured Boston's downtown since the 1950s and replace it with a tunnel. The club's suit raised questions about the air quality around the proposed tunnel's exhaust vents.

But if Boston has become a battleground between groups with competing visions of its future, there has been scant consideration of how development of the other parts of the metropolitan area is to be handled. Although the Commonwealth recently authorized the imposition of strict land-use controls on Cape Cod, a popular vacation peninsula just south of the metropolitan region, there has been little agitation for similar controls within the region itself. The gutting of MAPC's MetroPlan 2000 in the spring of 1990 is indicative of the lack of consensus on even whether, much less how, the various elements of the metropolitan area should to be coordinated.

Also instructive on this point has been the fate of a 1969 statute commonly known as the "Anti-Snob Zoning Act." Passed at a time when the Commonwealth's social conscience had been raised by the civil rights struggle and the war on poverty, the law allowed the state to overrule local zoning codes when communities with less than 10 percent of their housing in the "affordable category" used their zoning powers to block construction of low- and moderate-income housing. In the 20 years the act has been in force, this power has been invoked infrequently, despite the fact that only a handful of communities (mostly older cities with an aged housing stock) are in compliance with the 10 percent standard (*Boston Globe* 1989).

As will be discussed in the following section, the Boston region has always been marked by a dispersal of population, but this scattering of people, as elsewhere, gained momentum in the past half-century. The construction in the 1940s and 1950s of the circumferential Route 128, on an arc about 10 miles from downtown Boston, and the building in the 1960s and 1970s of Interstate 495, on an arc of about 25 miles, dramatically increased mobility within the region and provided the focus for linear development only marginally related to the central city. (See Table 1.2.) Much of the economic vitality of the Boston area since the 1960s has been associated with the rise of high technology firms, first along Route 128 and then along I-495. The city of Boston enjoyed an urban

Table 1.2. *Metropolitan Region: Population Distribution and Population Change, 1980-1990**

Subregion (Number In Category)	Share of Region Population (1990) (Percent)	Population Change (1980-1990) (Percent)
Central City (1)	19.6	+2
Core Suburbs (27)	39.2	-1
Intermediate Suburbs (32)	22.2	+0.8
Outer Suburbs (41)	19.0	+6

*101 Cities and Towns in the Metropolitan Area Planning Council District.

renaissance of its own during this period, resulting largely from its reputation among young professionals as a livable community, but if the downtown core made a rapid adjustment to the modern service economy, other parts of the city and many of Boston's neighbors were not so fortunate. The Boston region had long been characterized by numerous small manufacturing units spread throughout the area. Although the individual closings of these facilities were not as dramatic as the shutting down of huge industrial plants in the Rustbelt, the cumulative effect was almost as severe.

State politics over the past 15 years have been dominated by economic development issues. The Commonwealth suffered badly during the national economic malaise of the 1970s, hurt not only by the general shift to the Sunbelt but also by its reputation as a high-tax state ("Taxachusetts"). In 1980 the voters adopted Proposition 2½, which imposed severe limitations on local property taxes. In conjunction with the dramatic growth of the computer industry and the higher defense spending of the Reagan administration, Prop. 2½ is usually credited with fostering the "Massachusetts Miracle" that almost carried Governor Michael Dukakis to the White House. Although Dukakis directed most of the increased state revenues resulting from the boom times of the 1980s into social services and additional local assistance, he also worked to keep the business community happy. In one of the more controversial decisions of his 12-year tenure as governor, Dukakis, over the vehement protests of preservationists, approved construction of a company headquarters building on one of the few remaining extensive open spaces within the inner suburban belt. In the spring of 1990 the building was vacant, a victim of corporate reorganization and a slackening regional economy.

Now that the Massachusetts Miracle is history, the pressures for creating a positive climate for business have intensified. Much of this has, so far, been directed at cutting state taxes; leading the fight has been the Massachusetts High Technology Council, a lobbying group for the large computer-related firms. Although the economic slowdown has led to declines in housing prices, which had been among the highest in the nation, and curbed new housing construction, thereby easing the strong pressures during the 1980s for suburban development, the renewed focus on business opportunity and job creation may make metropolitan planning and regional land-use controls even less palatable than they were in the past.

The absence of a metropolitan vision in the Boston area has its roots deep in the region's history. The major contribution of Massachusetts to the American polity has been the autonomous local community governing itself through the town meeting. Already a political icon by the time of the Revolution, the town meeting remains more than 200 years later the fulcrum of local government in 80 of the planning district's communities. Whether it be an open town meeting (which all voters in the town may attend, speak, and vote) or a representative one (members elected on a district basis—Brookline, which has one-tenth the population of Boston, has a representative town meeting of 251 members, whereas Boston, which like 20 other communities in the district functions under a municipal charter similar to that of most U.S. cities, has a council of 13 members), community decisions regarding appropriations and land use are made by a comparatively large segment of the local population. With a long tradition of local self-government to fall back on, Massachusetts towns have generally been successful in resisting state efforts to encroach on their powers. Aberrations such as the "Anti-Snob Zoning Act" have been both extremely rare and of limited effectiveness.

The dichotomy between state and local government has been heightened by the weakness of Massachusetts county government. Indeed, in the commonly accepted use of the term, the Commonwealth's 14 counties (of which six—in whole or in part—lie in the planning district) are not units of government at all, but rather administrative arms of the state. Besides lacking the authority to tax directly (they are financed by assessments on the communities within their borders), counties in Massachusetts do not have a power usually possessed by their counterparts elsewhere in the U.S., namely, control over "unincorporated areas." There are no "unincorporated areas" in Massachusetts—every square inch of land in the Commonwealth is within one or another of the state's 351 cities and towns and therefore subject to the jurisdiction of local government. Because counties *per se* are so inconsequential and also because they split up the metropolitan region, they have not figured in the various schemes for regional government and planning that have been considered over the past century (Legislative Research Council 1970).

A CENTURY OF FRUSTRATION

Three different plans for reorganizing local and regional government have been offered to the citizens of the Boston metropolitan area during the past 100 years. Each was rejected, as the combination of seventeenth century Puritan theology, eighteenth century Republican political theory, and nineteenth and twentieth century sociology proved too strong for the self-proclaimed advocates of modernization.

The political history of the region between 1630 (date of the first settlement at Shawmut, i.e., Boston) and the 1890s was an almost uninterrupted story of fragmentation. Geography, population growth, the Puritan concept of independent churches, and the Republican faith in local self-government worked in unison to divide and subdivide the territory not only of Boston, but of its neighbors as well. While the towns of Brookline, Chelsea, Quincy, Revere, and Winthrop were being carved out of Boston, other communities also saw peripheral areas spun off into separate towns; in the most extreme case, 12 towns—either in whole or in part—were formed from the original Dedham. Not until 1897, with the creation of Westwood, was this process finally brought to a close (McCaffrey 1937).

For a short period in the 1860s and 1870s an opposite trend took hold. Pursuing what historians have labeled a policy of "urban imperialism," Boston's business and civic leaders held out the allure of better and more economical municipal services in appealing to their neighbors to consolidate with the central city. This promise of improved water supply, sewerage, schools, police, and lower tax rates proved attractive to the "streetcar suburbs" of Roxbury, Dorchester, Charlestown, Brighton, and West Roxbury. Between 1867 and 1873, Boston expanded from 8 square miles to 40 and, for the first time since the Revolution, held more than half the metropolitan area's population.

But if these working- and lower-middle-class towns were prepared to give up independence to enjoy the benefits of more efficient administration, Boston's prosperous neighbors were not. In 1873, the same year that Charlestown, Brighton, and West Roxbury voters accepted Boston's invitation, Brookline's citizens spurned it by a better than 2-to-1 margin. This affluent suburb preferred to keep control of its physical and social environment firmly in its own hands and was able and willing to bear the burden that the decision to go it alone entailed. With Brookline's rejection, the campaign to widen the political borders of Boston ran out of steam. There would be one additional annexation in 1912 (Hyde Park, a working-class town), but even with that Boston would remain geographically the smallest (45 square miles) of the nation's major cities (Jackson 1985).

Widening social and cultural fissures between the central city and its suburbs played an important role in keeping Boston and its neighbors apart. Until the middle of the nineteenth century, the inhabitants of the metropolitan area had been fairly homogeneous, but with the coming of the Irish in the 1840s, the bonds were broken. Forced by poverty to remain in Boston, the Irish gave their new home a totally different tone. Although old-line families still maintained control of Boston's economy, on the political and social fronts they were in sharp retreat. What had once been a Yankee, Protestant, and Republican city, was increasingly an Irish, Catholic, and Democratic city. Facing the loss of this citadel of western civilization to those they considered barbarians, the Yankees set up defensive positions in the suburbs from which they would counter-attack.

The anti-Boston forces also maintained an outpost in the heart of the enemy camp—the State House. Alone of the nation's big cities in the nineteenth century, Boston was its state's capital, and the propinquity of State House and City Hall fostered the use of state power to deal with what rural and suburban legislators saw as the dangers of urban life. Both literally and figuratively, the State House on top of Beacon Hill looked down on the city.

State intervention as a remedy for urban ills surfaced as early as the 1860s. Distressed by the unwillingness of municipal officials in Boston and some of its heavily populated neighbors to enforce the state temperance law, the Massachusetts Senate in 1865 passed a bill combining the police forces of Boston, Chelsea, Cambridge, Charlestown, and Roxbury into a single unit under state direction. In recommending this step a committee report had declared:

It is necessary to adopt the *metropolitan principle* (emphasis added) in order to prevent the elements which are destructive of property and laws from keeping practical control of the city; and so, from the size and wealth of Boston, and the intimacy of its relations with the whole state, undermining the prosperity and peace of the commonwealth.

This intrusion into local authority proved too much for the House to accept, but out of this concern came establishment of the state police. Two decades later, following election of the first Irish Democratic mayor of Boston, the state legislature took the power of appointing the city's police commissioner away from the mayor and gave it to the governor. This authority would not be restored to the mayor until the 1960s (Blodgett 1984).

If provincial assertions of cultural supremacy lay behind these efforts to employ state power, a different type of threat associated with urban life would create the setting for a more enlightened and innovative exercise of state authority. In 1869, Massachusetts established a statewide Board of Health, the first in the nation, and in its annual report for 1873 the board focused on the sewage problems of the Boston region. Finding that the situation was beyond the capacity of individual communities to cope with, the board pointed to the need for a metropolitan approach. The state legislature took no action on this recommendation, nor on similar reports issued in 1880, 1883, and 1884. Finally, in 1889, the legislature created the Metropolitan Sewerage Commission to construct and maintain a comprehensive waste-water disposal system for Boston and 17 additional communities. The Metropolitan Sewerage District is usually accorded the honor of being the first modern special-purpose district in the United States. Within a decade there were also formed a Metropolitan Park Commission (serving Boston and 35 communities) and a Metropolitan Water Board (Boston and 12 communities) (Merino 1968).

These special-purpose districts performed spectacularly well in their early years, but they had their critics. While conceding that much good had been done, these critics argued that supporters of these state boards and commissions had made a Faustian bargain. If the suburban communities had successfully avoided political consolidation with Boston, they had fallen into the trap of turning over their long-held and cherished power to tax and spend to outside and unrepresentative authorities. With an influential Republican Boston newspaper editorializing along these lines, the legislature agreed to the appointment of a special commission to investigate alternative approaches to metropolitan organization.

The commission's report, issued in 1896, urged a federal plan similar to one recently adopted for the London metropolitan area. Local initiative and local autonomy would be maintained in all matters where the service could be carried on by the individual communities working within their own borders. Larger and more general undertakings (i.e., water, sewerage, parks, highways, and mass transit) would be the responsibility of a council elected by the voters of the 29 communities in the region (covering 273 square miles and having a population of nearly 1 million—of which about half lived in Boston). But the proposal never had a chance. Suburbanites feared that the council scheme was simply a ruse to pave the way for consolidation with Boston, and that even if formal annexation was avoided, Boston's great strength on the council would politicize and corrupt its operations (Wakstein 1972).

The decisive rejection of the metropolitan council proposal at the turn of the twentieth century stifled consideration of alternative designs for regional government until the mid-1940s. The New England region in general, and the Boston area in particular, had known economic hard times long before the Great Depression, and business, government, and academic leaders recognized that unprecedented levels of planning and cooperation were necessary if war-time prosperity was to be maintained in the postwar period. To stimulate thinking along these lines, the governor, the mayor of Boston, and the presidents of Harvard, M.I.T., and the Boston Chamber of Commerce sponsored the Boston Contest of 1944. Entrants were asked to prepare specific proposals for improving the political, economic, social, and physical environments for residents of the metropolitan area.

The winning entry, prepared by a team of Harvard professors led by political scientist Carl J. Friedrich, and including sociologist Talcott Parsons and economist Seymour Harris, began by stressing the importance of the historical record:

> Boston is hemmed in by the heritage of the past. No plan for the metropolitan area . . . can overlook this tradition-bound substructure, for it is not only physical, but social, economic, governmental, and cultural in its impact.

Working from this premise, the Harvard group proposed enlarging the definition of the metropolitan region from the customary radius of 10-15 miles from the State House to 20-25 miles. By this step, the population balance would be clearly shifted away from the central city and "the outlying communities would not have to fear being dominated by Boston."

A specialist in federalism, Friedrich devised a plan that he believed compatible with both the region's history and its need for metropolitan government. He criticized the special-purpose-district approach, which the 1896 report also had, for lacking "firm, democratic foundations" and urged that these districts be "democratized, expanded and constituted as a federation of all the local governmental authorities in the area." This new entity, which Friedrich proposed calling the Boston Metropolitan Authority, would "exercise those joint functions which are clearly metropolitan in nature," including water supply, sewerage, parks, fire, police, health, sanitation, welfare, economic development, transportation, and planning. The policymaking power of this authority would reside in a council whose members would be elected directly by the residents of the metropolitan region from districts corresponding to the existing cities and towns. This council could levy taxes (but not real estate taxes, which have been the mainstay of local budgets) and select a professional administrator to oversee the authority's operations (Boston Contest of 1944).

The Friedrich plan was unveiled with great hoopla at a December 1944 gathering at historic Faneuil Hall. With characteristic hyperbole, *Life* magazine wrote, "In the future history of Boston this Boston Contest meeting may be considered as important as the Tea Party of 1773 or the founding of the Anti-Slavery Society in 1832." But the plan went nowhere. The political and cultural divide that separated Boston and its suburbs was as wide, or perhaps even wider, in the 1940s than it had been in the 1890s. Less than a year after the Faneuil Hall session, James Michael Curley was back in Boston City Hall for a fourth term; more than anyone else in twentieth century Massachusetts politics, Curley's career personified for Yankee suburbanites all that was evil about Boston. With this buccaneering and Yankee-baiting politician running the city, any hopes for metropolitan cooperation were dashed. Thirty years would pass before metropolitan government would receive another serious hearing.

This most recent effort was inspired by the federal government. As part of the Nixon administration's espousal of a new federalism, Secretary of Housing and Urban Development (HUD) George Romney approached his fellow Republican, Governor Francis W. Sargent, with an offer of HUD funds to finance a study of novel approaches to metropolitan development. Although a Yankee, Sargent represented the new breed of Massachusetts politician who reached out across ethnic lines and combined "good government" reform passion for efficiency with a liberal belief in the efficacy of government action. (By the time the report was ready in June 1975, Sargent had been defeated by Michael Dukakis, whose background and party affiliation were quite different, but whose outlook was virtually identical.) To head the task force, Sargent chose Robert Wood, an academic with substantial government experience. Wood, author of the widely acclaimed *Suburbia* (1959) and architect of many of the Great Society's urban programs, was quite familiar with the Commonwealth, having been on the faculty of M.I.T. in the 1950s and early 1960s, and president of the University of Massachusetts since 1969.

Like the winners of the Boston Contest of 1944, Wood and his associates began their report with a bow to the past. There has been a "firm tradition" in Massachusetts, the report declared, "of communities resolving their own difficulties and problems, and a strong sense that this makes for the most effective, responsive, and satisfying government." Schemes devised elsewhere for metropolitan integration were not transferable here because the "special New England tradition of participatory local government requires a unique solution for Boston." Indeed, the 1960s had given additional meaning to the role of "participatory local government":

> We have strong reservations about any metropolitan approach that would create a bureaucracy. We would be greatly distressed about any new mechanism which would undercut gains in neighborhood-based participation and power that have been achieved at so much cost in the last decade and a half.

> The basic job we are about is the reaffirmation of localism and neighborhood—the capacity of a large metropolitan community to govern itself and to maintain over-the-fence living in central city as well as suburb. The basic job we have is not to abdicate to state or national authority. We need to build a regional structure, not from the "top down," as higher authority preempts local responsibilities, but from the "bottom up" when existing neighborhoods, cities and towns contribute to the regional policy and achieve greater control over their collective destiny.

To reconcile these seemingly contradictory aspirations, the task force urged not a metropolitan government of general jurisdiction, but rather "a representationally constructed entity that would have the power to review developmental decisions of key regional importance." This new entity would have: (1) oversight powers in regard to the state agencies supplying water, sewerage, parks, public transit, and airport and harbor facilities for the metropolitan area; (2) authority to block state projects (e.g., highways, land disposal, higher education, solid waste disposal, health care, air and water quality plans, allocation of state housing funds) when inconsistent with regional plans, subject only to gubernatorial override; (3) authority to review local requests for federal aid and to block the granting of local requests for state aid, this latter power again subject only to gubernatorial override; (4) authority to override local land-use decisions when the sites involved were of strategic importance to the region. The governing board would comprise the top elected officials (e.g., mayor or chairman of the board of selectmen) of each member community, who would cast weighted votes linked to the population of the city or town they represented (Governor's Task Force 1975).

Variations on the task force suggestion for a strong planning agency with service responsibilities came from other sources (notably the Greater Boston Chamber of Commerce) in the early and mid-1970s, but none of them including that of the task force itself came to fruition. Ethnic and political (the state was now overwhelmingly Democratic) hostilities may have been muted by the migration of Boston's Irish into the suburbs and the arrival of newcomers to the region, but the long-standing divisions within the region had not dissolved. When Boston faced a severe financial crisis in the early 1980s, Democratic legislators from the suburbs would not come to the assistance of the Democratic mayor of Boston until they had been guaranteed that their constituents would not be taxed to bail out the city. Giving the central city-suburban split even greater intensity in recent decades has been the emergence of racial diversity. Compared to most of the nation's major cities, Boston had a small black population in the century following emancipation, but beginning in the 1950s the African-American share of the city's population began to climb as the white middle-class moved out. In 1963, Boston's segregated school system became the focus of black protests and, in 1974, court-ordered integration, which required large-scale busing, generated considerable violence in the city's streets and big headlines in the national media. Although some of Boston's suburbs had been enrolling, on a voluntary basis, ghetto children in their excellent school systems, the spectre of a racially torn Boston killed any chance of greater metropolitan cooperation. There has been no serious discussion of regional governance—of any type—for more than a decade.

WATER AND SEWERAGE

The Boston region's nineteenth century path-setting approach to providing metropolitan services became an issue in the 1988 presidential campaign. Ninety-nine years after creation of the Metropolitan Sewerage Commission, George Bush traveled to the home state of his Democratic opponent and, standing in a boat in the middle of Boston Harbor, labeled the Harbor an environmental disaster. Whatever the validity of Bush's efforts to tag Michael Dukakis with responsibility for polluting the harbor's waters, there was no denying that the harbor was a pestilential mix of sewage and toxic waste and that it would cost area residents $6 billion to clean up. The governor's claim to managerial competence never recovered from this assault, and the garbage that had been accumulating in Boston Harbor for more than three centuries claimed its first political casualty.

Central city-suburban political animosity had played a key role in the formation of the Metropolitan Sewerage Commission in 1889 (and of the Metropolitan Park Commission in 1892 and the Metropolitan Water Board in 1895), but for the first quarter-century or so of their operations, these state agencies overcame the divisions and provided their member communities with an excellent set of services. Although the park system, with its imaginative mix of forest preserves, beaches, and scenic corridors drew the most attention from outside observers, the water and sewerage systems were equally impressive. Construction of the Wachusett Reservoir, 40 miles west of Boston, with a capacity of 65 billion gallons, multiplied sevenfold the water supply available to Boston and its neighbors. Less glamorous, but just as important, was the completion of a comprehensive sewer network for each of the three major drainage basins in the region.

Consolidation of the three agencies into the Metropolitan District Commission (MDC) in 1919 opened a period of general decline. Most of the prominent civic leaders who had spearheaded the movement for special-purpose metropolitan districts had passed from the scene, their positions as commissioners taken by patronage-hungry politicians. And while MDC was still capable of such large-scale construction projects as the Quabbin Reservoir (65 miles west of Boston), built in the 1930s and having a capacity of 412 billion gallons, it became increasingly bogged down in the mechanics of running playgrounds, supplying clean water and carrying away the dirty. By mid-century, the commission was widely perceived as unresponsive to the region's growing needs and uninvolved in its newer problems. As the metropolitan region expanded, the additional communities now within its orbit avoided becoming members of MDC for reasons strikingly similar to those that had halted the annexation movement 75 years before (Wakstein 1972).

Indicative of MDC's failure to command confidence and provide direction was the abortive effort in the early 1950s to move the commission into the field of solid waste disposal. Legislation enacted in 1952 authorized MDC to build and operate a refuse disposal plant to serve 17 communities. But MDC and the cities and towns were unable to agree on terms, and the bond issuing power lapsed. Not since then has MDC been considered as a worthy vehicle for new metropolitan endeavors (Legislative Research Council 1976).

Critics of MDC have identified at least two weaknesses in its structure. Unlike the metropolitan transit agencies, MDC never had any mechanism for local input toward its decisions. A 1938 legislative committee noted proposals for an advisory body but, without explanation, simply dismissed them as "not expedient at this time." Apparently nothing has made them expedient in the 50 years since, because MDC continues to function without benefit of counsel from locally elected officials. This resistance to change stems from the legislature's desire to keep the commission tightly under its control. With thousands of jobs to hand out, MDC became "a place that employed everybody's cousin." The location of MDC skating rinks and pools were an integral element of the bargaining that characterized decision making on Beacon Hill. But the State House politicians were not content merely to exploit the commission for its pork-barrel possibilities—they also intruded on its rate-setting authority for the water and sewer services MDC provided, imposing limits that forced the commission to operate at a loss and to issue bonds to cover the deficits. By such action the legislature was able to hide the real costs of providing water and sewerage and pass them along as part of general increases in the local property tax (Birkhead 1972).

MDC lived off its illustrious past for about a half-century, but in recent decades the toll of abuse and neglect began to mount so noticeably that it could no longer be ignored. Construction of the Quabbin Reservoir was intended to meet the water needs of the region through the 40-year planning period from 1940 to 1980. As the 1980s ended, however, the system's designed yield of approximately 300 million gallons per day was outpaced by an average demand of 343 million gallons per day; on some hot summer days consumption soared to 440

million gallons.   Although there has been recurring discussion about
tapping additional watersheds, opposition from the Connecticut River
valley communities that would be affected, and the high costs that such
a project would entail, have blocked action. Consequently the focus in
recent years has been on demand management, including metering, leak
detection, system rehabilitation, and pricing policy. The effectiveness of
these is limited somewhat by the fact that each community retains a large
measure of autonomy, especially in regard to rate structure (Massachusetts Water Resources Authority 1987). In the spring of 1989, following
several years of low precipitation, a water emergency was declared,
restricting consumption by homeowners and municipalities. By early
summer, however, heavier than normal rainfall permitted the lifting of
these rules.

Uncertain as the last decade has been for the adequacy of the region's
water supply, it has been almost tranquil compared to the turmoil
surrounding the sewerage system. Not only was MDC's sewer operations
the oldest of its functions, but it was also the one serving the largest
number of communities (43, compared to 38 in the water district [see
Maps 1.2 and 1.3] and 35 in the park district). Like the water division,
the sewer division did not completely stagnate after MDC's creation in
1919, but its efforts did not keep up with needs or rising expectations.
Towns and cities were responsible for sewers to serve individual homes
and businesses, while MDC built the large collecting sewers. An early
decision to combine waste-water sewers and storm sewers into a single
system would come back to haunt the region when in the 1960s MDC
built a primary treatment plant on an island in Boston Harbor. On days
of heavy rainfall, the combined flow of water exceeded the capacity of
the treatment plant and dumped raw sewage into the harbor. Such
activity had been going on for centuries, but by this time the federal
government was committed to ending pollution of the nation's waters.
In the early 1970s, following passage of the Clean Water Act of 1970,
the Environmental Protection Agency (EPA) began pressuring MDC to
do something about the combined sewer overflows and to upgrade its
plant from primary to secondary treatment. Between 1973 and 1983
more than 100 consultants' reports were prepared for MDC and EPA on
how untreated sewage could be kept out of Boston Harbor, but nothing
was done. MDC would not risk the political fallout that would be
generated by going to the legislature for the estimated (1976) $750
million it would take to carry out the EPA proposals. For its part, EPA
showed little inclination to force the issue. When the Dukakis adminis-

Map 1.2. *Massachusetts Water Resources Authority—Sewerage District*

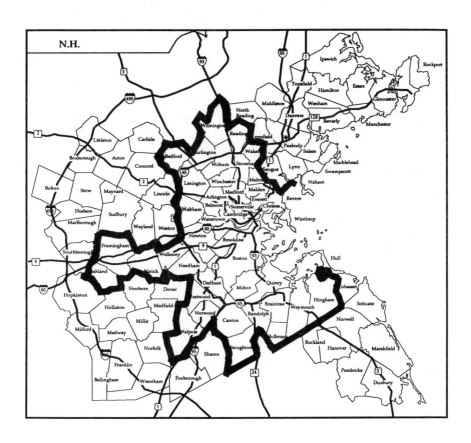

Map 1.3.   *Massachusetts Water Resources Authority—Water District*

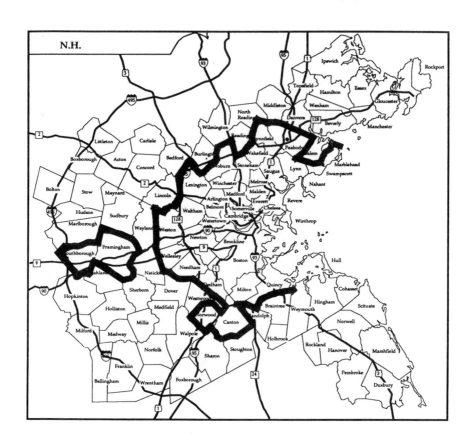

tration requested a waiver from the Clean Water Act, the matter sat on the agency's docket for five years. Only after the Conservation Law Foundation announced in the spring of 1983 that it intended to file a federal suit against both MDC and EPA "to force them to act, to end this federal-state, Alphonse-Gaston approach," was EPA's rejection of the application announced (*Boston Globe* 1983a).

Helpful as the Law Foundation's action had been in moving things along, the real drama occurred in a state court in suburban Dedham. In July 1983 a judge began hearing a case brought by the city of Quincy against MDC demanding an end to fouling of the harbor and despoiling of Quincy's beaches. The judge, who in a different capacity had put the Boston Housing Authority under court receivership for its failure to serve its tenants adequately, turned down a plea by MDC to defer to the political branches on this matter, calling the history of political efforts "bleak." By fall, the idea of a separate sewerage authority, with the power to set its own rates, to write its own budget and issue its own bonds, and the ability to hire a new staff of professional engineers and managers, was gaining support (*Boston Globe* 1983b).

Although Governor Dukakis endorsed the proposal (broadened to include both sewerage and water supply) in his State of the State Message in January 1984, it would be December before the bill was on his desk for signature. The struggle on Beacon Hill brought out into the open the fissures that had characterized efforts to deal with metropolitan problems since the 1880s. Legislators from the western part of the state feared the new agency would have the power to divert the Connecticut River and disrupt the recreational opportunities residents of the area had traditionally enjoyed around Quabbin Reservoir. More generally, legislators from outside the 43 cities and towns to be serviced by the authority were afraid that their constituents would end up being taxed for the water and sewerage district's deficits, just as they were already being taxed to pay for the fiscal shortfalls of the metropolitan transit system. And legislators from the Boston region looked for ways to shield their voters from the much higher user rates that would be necessary to finance the massive construction projects. After much negotiating, and a forceful nudge from the judge who ordered a ban on new sewer hookups (thereby threatening to bring home and office building in the region to a halt), the Massachusetts Water Resources Authority (MWRA) was created (*Boston Globe* 1984).

MWRA represents yet another effort by the Commonwealth to find a proper mix of state and local responsibility for providing metropolitan services. The authority, with its own rate-setting, bond-issuing, and pay-scale powers is, unlike MDC (now left only with its parks division—but including responsibility for the areas around the Quabbin and Wachusett reservoirs) largely free from legislative influence. Although the authority is required by statute to assess communities at a level sufficient to cover operating and capital costs, the individual communities still determine how the costs are passed along to consumers. Direction of the authority is vested in an 11-member board, five of whom are appointed by the governor, three by the mayor of Boston, and three by the cities and towns through an MWRA Advisory Board. For the first five years of its activities, MWRA was viewed as following the managerial policies and political preferences of Governor Dukakis.

Although predictions of huge rate increases were fulfilled (rates have tripled since 1985 and are expected to triple again in the next decade), the major controversies surrounding MWRA have been over the siting of its facilities. The MWRA board chose locations for secondary waste treatment, sludge processing, and solid-debris landfills recommended by its professional staff (Massachusetts Water Resources Authority 1988). Despite having been given considerable financial concessions to accept the sludge-processing plant, Quincy's unhappiness with the deal prompted a major fracas between the legislature and the governor. In the spring of 1989, after much public discussion, the MWRA board, under pressure from Governor Dukakis and Mayor Flynn, agreed to place the authority's headquarters in a building to be constructed on a parcel of land targeted for redevelopment in one of Boston's most depressed minority neighborhoods. Arguing that fairness as well as lower cost should have sent the MWRA offices to Quincy, representatives from that city and other South Shore towns persuaded the legislature to pass a measure mandating that MWRA locate its staff in Quincy. Dukakis vetoed the bill and the legislature, after keeping the measure in limbo for over six months, eventually upheld the governor's action, but by then MWRA had already renewed the expiring lease on its offices in Charlestown.

Still another battle over siting occurred in the winter and spring of 1991. Walpole, 25 miles southwest of Boston and home to the Commonwealth's maximum security prison, had been named in 1989 as the location for the landfill to accept solid debris created by MWRA operations. Although the state already owned the property in question, the legislature, ignoring the pleas of Governor Dukakis, refused to enact a law transferring title to MWRA. When William Weld, who assumed the governorship in January 1991, withdrew executive support for the

Walpole site and called for further studies, the federal judge supervising the harbor clean-up slapped a ban on all new sewer hook-ups in the MWRA region. With his hands full trying to cope with the state's serious financial woes and depressed economy, Weld backed off from a confrontation with the court and submitted a bill giving the ownership to the MWRA. The legislature gave it its reluctant approval.

TRANSPORTATION

Because of the central city's small geographic area, transportation issues in the Boston region have had a metropolitan character since the earliest days of mass transit. The first horsecar route in 1856 went from Central Square in Cambridge to Bowdoin Square at the foot of Beacon Hill. When electric trolley service started in 1889, the first line went from the Allston neighborhood of Boston through the town of Brookline to Park Street alongside the Boston Common. Boston built the nation's first subway in the late 1890s, and over the next two decades extended its rapid transit system to Cambridge and Everett.

Even before the subway, the Commonwealth had started recognizing the metropolitan nature of public transportation. Legislation enacted in 1887 gave the state Board of Railroad Commissioners, which oversaw the finances of street railway companies, the power to pass on requests for new routes in Boston, Cambridge, and Brookline. The commissioners had opposed this broadening of their responsibilities, fearing that the board "may be brought into conflict with the city authorities upon matters which they have, after a public hearing, previously acted, and which have always been deemed to be within their special province" (Board of Railroad Commissioners 1888). Although their advice had been rejected, the commissioners exercised the discretion granted them; in 1893, for example, the board overturned Cambridge's decision to have a new electric trolley line constructed on elegant Brattle Street and ordered it built on Mt. Auburn Street instead. In 1898 the legislature further strengthened the board's role by giving it the power, statewide, to issue a franchise for a connecting line desired by a transit company despite objections of the locality involved.

But even as the Board of Railroad Commissioners was gaining power at the expense of communities, the Boston metropolitan region had begun the process of replacing private ownership of mass transportation with public control. Until 1887 Massachusetts had followed a policy of encouraging competition among private transit companies as the best means of providing coverage and service. But lured by the promise of swift adoption of the new technology offered by electric trolleys, the Commonwealth consented in 1887 to formation of the West End Street Railway Company, which consolidated seven of the horsecar companies linking Boston and its neighbors. West End delivered on its pledges, giving the region one of the country's first unified metropolitan surface transportation systems, but when the company owners proved hesitant about plowing their hefty profits into rapid transit (subway and elevated) construction, the legislature in 1897 allowed West End to be taken over by yet another firm, the Boston Elevated Railway Company. In return for this permission, Elevated agreed not only to finance the rapid transit improvements, but also to hold the fare at 5 cents for 25 years (Cheape 1980).

By 1917 the mass transit system was on the verge of breakdown. Higher than expected wage costs and the heavy expenses of new construction left inadequate funds for replacement of rolling stock. The following year the legislature took over the property of the Boston Elevated Railway Company by guaranteeing the corporation's stockholders a 5-6 percent return on their investment. The company's rapid transit and trolley operations were to be run by five trustees appointed by the governor. Fares were set at levels that covered the cost of service. Deficits flowing from other sources were to be paid for by assessments on the 14 cities and towns directly served by Elevated; these assessments were based on the degree to which citizens of each community used the system.

New legislation enacted in 1931 continued the key features of the existing arrangement and made a few alterations. In order to supply the financing to retire Elevated's preferred stock, the 1931 law created a Metropolitan Transit District, a body politic and corporate comprising the 14 cities and towns. This district, administered by a board made up of four gubernatorial appointees and one appointee chosen by the mayor of Boston, could issue tax-exempt bonds that were to be paid off by assessments on the communities. The measure also established a Metropolitan Transit Council to bring together the mayors and chairmen of the boards of selectmen of the 14 cities and towns. The council was to determine whether the annual operating deficits were to be dealt with through fare hikes or assessments. Deficits continued to climb during the next decade, and in the mid-1940s the legislature appointed a study commission to recommend steps for improving mass transit in the metropolitan region. In two reports, issued in 1945 and 1947, this commission emphasized the importance of extending the geographic boundaries of the transit district and of expanding service throughout the region. It was the commission's contention that decline in transit patronage could be attributed to the movement of population beyond the limits of the existing transit network and, by extending that network farther into the suburbs, that ridership would reach levels that would put the transit system back in the black.

The legislature rejected the commission's proposals. Not buying the commission's argument that mass transit was a much better public investment than new highways, the legislature was not prepared to enlarge the transit district against the wishes of the 15 communities the commission had targeted for inclusion. Any expansion of the transportation network beyond the 14 cities and towns would have to be approved by residents of the individual communities to which service might be provided. In 1948, when it was suggested that the transit district take over commuter lines being abandoned by the New Haven Railroad, voters in Quincy and Braintree defeated the proposal by overwhelming margins.

The new transit law (whose most important provision was public purchase of all remaining Boston Elevated stock) passed in 1947 reflected this suburban resistance to metropolitan cooperation on transportation matters. Not only was the new Metropolitan Transit Authority (MTA) confined to the same area as its predecessor, but it was also less representative than the previous arrangement. Gone was the Metropolitan Transit Council and its power to set fares and assessments. This authority rested with a board of gubernatorial appointees whose selection was more often a function of political patronage than of executive talent or knowledge of mass transit issues.

MTA's inability during the 1950s to halt the decline of patronage and the increasing flow of red ink made it even less attractive to suburban communities, but the 14 cities and towns in its operating area did have some of their power restored by mid-decade. The legislature agreed to the establishment of an MTA Advisory Board identical in composition to the old Metropolitan District Council. Board approval was required for appointment of the MTA's general manager, changes in fares, and the issuance of new bonds. MTA members cast weighted votes tied to the share of the MTA's assessments (based on usage) their communities paid; a majority of 85 percent (reflecting the large vote cast by Boston) was necessary for the board to act (Deem 1953).

Although given national publicity by a popular song of the 1950s (Kingston Trio, *The Man Who Never Returned* [Charlie on the MTA]),

MTA was turning into a local disaster by the early 1960s. Operating deficits were running at about $16 million annually, the 14 cities and towns were complaining about burdens on their property tax rates, and the region seemed likely to lose the last of its commuter railroads. With Boston business interests screaming for action, Governor Endicott Peabody in 1964 endorsed a major restructuring of the metropolitan transit framework. A new Massachusetts Bay Transportation Authority (MBTA) was to be created, covering the original 14 cities and towns and 64 additional communities. (See Map 1.4.) This breakthrough in the district's geographical dimensions (1,022 square miles compared to MTA's 123 square miles) was accompanied by an equally important change in the Commonwealth's role—for the first time state funds would be appropriated for capital expenses. (Federal funds for mass transit construction and purchase of equipment also became available in the mid-1960s.) Having already started moving in this direction on its own, the legislature quickly approved the major points of the governor's program.

Passage of the MBTA legislation was just one indication of the Commonwealth's developing interest in and growing sophistication about metropolitan transportation issues. In 1959 the legislature had established a Mass Transportation Commission (MTC) to explore the coordination of highway, mass transit, and land-use policies in the metropolitan region. As one element of its work, MTC received federal grants for a demonstration program to determine how commuters could be enticed to relinquish their cars for public transportation. MTC's recommendations also played a role in the creation of MBTA. In conjunction with the state Department of Public Works, MTC also received federal funds for the Boston Regional Planning Project, later renamed the Eastern Massachusetts Regional Planning Project (EMRPP), which was to prepare a comprehensive transportation and land-use plan. Originally scheduled to be completed by late 1964, this plan would not be ready until mid-1969.

By the time the EMRPP report appeared, the Commonwealth's love affair with the automobile had begun to sour. Like most states, Massachusetts had gone on a highway-building spree in the postwar decades, with most of the construction concentrated in the metropolitan area. A Master Highway Plan put together in 1948 by the Department of Public Works, the State Planning Board, and the Metropolitan District Commission, had envisioned an inner belt around the core of Boston, a circumferential route (Route 128) on an arc about 10 miles from the State House, and six radial expressways from the central city into various parts

Map 1.4. *Massachusetts Bay Transportation Authority*

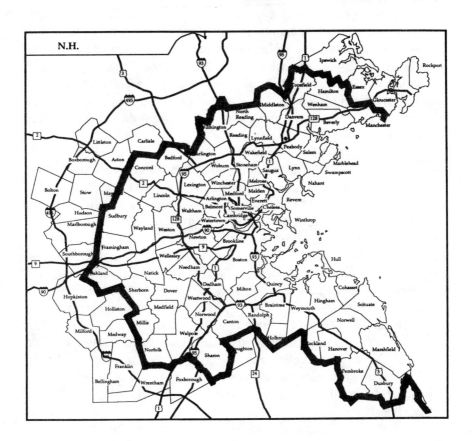

of the hinterland. By the late 1960s, all but the inner belt and one of the radials (the Southwest Expressway, I-95) were largely completed. Neighborhood opposition to construction of the remaining links in the system gained strength in Cambridge and Boston during the latter part of the decade as part of a growing movement for citizen participation in government decisions, and when the EMRPP report finally appeared in mid-1969 with the inner belt and I-95 on its maps, the plan was immediately denounced as the handiwork of highway engineers who had no appreciation of the social, economic, and environmental consequences of their proposals.

With Boston and Cambridge activists joining forces with suburban opponents of I-95, the highway issue entered the political arena. In May 1969, Governor Sargent, who in an earlier capacity as Commissioner of Public Works had helped end the veto power localities had enjoyed over interstate highways within their borders, announced the formation of a task force to review transportation planning in the state. In December 1969, Mayor Kevin White of Boston, who was preparing to challenge Sargent for the governorship in the following year's elections, announced his support for a moratorium on all new highway construction. The next month the governor's task force recommended that Sargent impose a moratorium, a step he took in February 1970. Sargent went on to defeat White in November and subsequently ordered that the inner belt and I-95 be deleted from state planning maps (Lupo, Colcord, and Fowler 1971).

The highway battle led to a new focus on mass transportation. Massachusetts politicians put partisan labels aside to work together for federal legislation permitting transfer of the highway funds originally slated for the inner belt and I-95 to mass transit construction projects. Their success made $1.1 billion available, enough for significant extension of one of the subway lines and the total rebuilding of another in the right-of-way that had been cleared for I-95. The state also began assuming a share of MBTA's operating deficit—at present it absorbs almost 70 percent of the authority's $400 million annual loss.

Under the reorganization of state government carried out in the 1970s, MBTA is part of the Executive Office of Transportation and Construction. With MBTA and the Department of Public Works now under the same administrative roof, coordination between highway and mass transit programs has been substantially improved. An MBTA Advisory Board similar to that which functioned under MTA remains operational, but important initiatives are largely the product of the governor, his Secretary of Transportation and Construction, and the

MBTA General Manager, who is a gubernatorial appointee. Because of the region's heavy reliance on public transit (the MBTA system is the fifth largest in the U.S.) and its inability to meet federal clean air standards, MBTA has been very sensitive to the issue of fares. Despite an increase in the late 1980s in the cost of subway tokens from 60 to 75 cents and a further rise to 85 cents in 1991, mass transit in Boston remains a bargain compared to the rest of the nation. Nonetheless, as failure to extend one of the subway lines to Route 128 because of community opposition demonstrates, more enlightened state management in Massachusetts does not always translate into measures beneficial to the metropolitan region as a whole.

PLANNING

Although the Puritan visions of a "city upon a hill" and of a model Christian commonwealth looked toward a planned society where the good of the whole took precedence over the interests of the individual, the Boston experience—from almost the very start—has been quite different. Economic opportunity overwhelmed religious conviction, and the process of urban development from the colonial period to the present, as elsewhere, has largely been driven by the engine of private enterprise, which, in turn, has been fueled by public action.

Local government has had the key promotional role, but the state has also been an important participant—most dramatically in the filling in of Boston's Back Bay. Lying immediately west of Beacon Hill and northwest of the Common, this was a 580-acre area of mudflats that were covered and uncovered daily by the tidal ebb and flow of the Charles River. Because it presented both an obstacle to access with Boston's western neighbors and the convenience of being located near downtown, the Back Bay became the subject of several proposals for turning it into usable land. In the 1850s, the Commonwealth, rejecting the city's request for permission to fill in the mudflats, decided to assume the task itself, and over the next two decades a special state agency managed the massive operation. Reclamation of the Back Bay returned a hefty profit to the state from the sale of land and provided Boston with an upper-class residential neighborhood that has one of few systematic street-naming and grid arrangements in the entire city. Unfortunately for Boston, however, the planners of the Back Bay made no effort to integrate these street patterns with the adjacent South End, which was being developed with city assistance. With the state taking steps to ensure the exclusivity of the Back Bay, the South End quickly lost its attraction for the well-to-do and went into a long period of decline (Kennedy 1988).

The Back Bay experience provided a precedent for the sewerage, park, and water boards of the 1890s, but with the new focus now on the metropolitan area. In 1911, with the Progressive movement at its height, the legislature authorized the formation of a commission to develop proposals for a metropolitan planning agency. Completing their work the following year, the commissioners urged establishment of a permanent and salaried Metropolitan Planning Board of five members (three to be appointed by the governor, two by the mayor of Boston) that which would prepare a comprehensive plan for Boston and 37 neighboring communities.   Once this plan was in place, the board would have the power to review all local projects that affected the plan and to suspend for one year those local projects in conflict with it. To encourage local cooperation with the board, the commissioners also recommended that the state contribute to the financing of metropolitan area projects. Notwithstanding this inducement, suburban legislators killed the scheme (Scott 1969).

Another decade would pass before the Commonwealth took a first small step down the planning road: creation of a Metropolitan Planning Division in 1923 within the recently reorganized Metropolitan District Commission (MDC). Placing the planning unit within MDC was more a matter of administrative necessity than appreciation of the importance of linking service delivery to planning; the Massachusetts constitution imposed a limit on the number of executive branch agencies and the new planning division had to be placed somewhere. The division had its own board, composed of four members chosen by the governor, plus representatives of the state departments of Public Works and Public Utilities, MDC, and the Boston Transit Department. Like MDC, however, the planning division was financed not out of state funds but from assessments on the communities of the metropolitan region. Its purview confined to transportation issues, the division devoted itself almost exclusively to laying out new suburban parkways. In 1941 its staff was transferred, in the name of "simplification and economy," to the State Planning Board, which granted the metropolitan region no special recognition (Wakstein 1972).

Action on the national level in the 1950s and 1960s prompted renewed state attention to metropolitan planning. Section 701 of the Housing Act of 1954 made federal grants available to metropolitan planning agencies, and the following year Massachusetts passed legislation enabling contiguous communities to form regional planning districts, with purely advisory powers, on their own accord. None of the cities and towns in the Boston region took advantage of this opportunity. Business and civic leaders in the region began mobilizing support in the mid-1950s for special state legislation creating a Boston metropolitan planning agency, and by 1963 three successive governors of the Commonwealth had endorsed the idea. The major hurdle to be surmounted was the opposition of William F. Callahan, chairman of the Massachusetts Turnpike Authority. Callahan, who was as close as the state ever came to having a power broker like Robert Moses of New York, had for years been seeking legislative approval to extend the Turnpike from its eastern terminus in the suburbs into the heart of Boston. When the legislature finally gave Callahan what he wanted (the alternative to his toll road was a freeway with 90 percent financing by the federal government as part of the Interstate Highway System), Callahan, no longer fearing that the planning agency might block his project, withdrew his objections. In the summer of 1963 the Metropolitan Area Planning Council (MAPC) was established.

What ultimately emerged from the legislature was a planning body that was a unit of the state government. The council was to consist of one representative (appointed by the mayor or board of selectmen of the municipality) from each of the 47 cities and towns specified by the law, 21 private citizens chosen by the governor (a 1970 amendment to the law would require the governor to include "sufficient representation of minority and low-income groups so as to substantially represent these viewpoints"), and *ex-officio* members from nine state agencies (Metropolitan Transit Authority, Metropolitan District Commission, Department of Public Works, Department of Public Safety, Department of Commerce, Massachusetts Port Authority, Massachusetts Turnpike Authority, Mass Transportation Commission, and State Housing Board) and two Boston agencies (Redevelopment Authority and Department of Public Works). Although control over the council's policies rested with the cities and towns, direction of MAPC fiscal affairs remained in state hands. Council operations were paid for out of state appropriations, which the state recovered by population-based assessments on the communities.

If the council structure reflected the peculiar features of Massachusetts' 75 years of experience in dealing with metropolitan Boston, the council's responsibilities were fairly conventional. MAPC was authorized to conduct research and prepare such reports as might be helpful or necessary to improve the physical, social, and economic conditions of the metropolitan district; to provide technical planning assistance to member communities; and to "prepare comprehensive plans . . . with respect to the optimum use of the land areas and the most efficient provisions for the utilities serving" the region. Such plans, when adopted by the council, were to be only advisory in character (MAPC 1989a).

MAPC's geographic boundaries expanded significantly in its first decade. The 1963 legislation specified that the 47 communities receiving at least one of the services provided by the MDC were to be members of the council. It also opened up membership as a matter of right to any community contiguous to the MDC area that desired it, and allowed any other community to join, subject to consent of a majority of MAPC cities and towns. By 1965, membership under these provisions had increased to 51 but, in that same year, the legislature jumped the total to 79. This was done in order to have the MAPC district conform to the Bureau of the Budget's definition of the Boston metropolitan area, a step necessary to make the council eligible for federal planning grants. Then in 1970, as part of a general reorganization of the various regional planning units set up across the state, the legislature placed 99 cities and towns within MAPC. One community would subsequently receive legislative approval to quit MAPC, but three others would seek and gain MAPC consent to join. Since the mid-1970s, MAPC has covered 101 cities and towns in a 1,422 square mile territory with a population (1990) of nearly 3 million. (See Map 1.1.)

The 1970 legislation, in response to calls from council representatives, also removed MAPC (and the other regional planning agencies) from the state governmental structure. The practical effect of this step was to give the council greater control over its budget. No longer would MAPC have to get legislative approval every time it wanted to increase the per capita assessments levied on members, although the 1970 law set a cap of 5 cents. The ceiling was raised to 15 cents in 1974, but with the proviso that MAPC could go even higher if two-thirds of the representatives of the cities and towns agreed to the hike. For fiscal year 1989 the assessment was slightly more than 19 cents, bringing in just under $550,000, about 45 percent of the council's regular budget.

It was the lure of federal money that led to MAPC's creation in the 1960s, and the council has remained heavily dependent on federal and state grants to carry on its work. Funds from the federal highway and urban mass transit agencies, as well as from various state departments, have supported the council's transportation, land-use, economic development, and environmental quality studies. Severe cutbacks in federal spending in the 1980s put a crimp in council activities, although the state did step up its assistance. In 1986 the Commonwealth appropriated funds directly out of the state budget for MAPC and other regional planning agencies, but the legislature has not repeated this action and is unlikely to do so in the near future, given the state's current financial problems (MAPC 1964-1988).

The unsettled condition of MAPC funding reflects the fundamental weakness of the council during its quarter-century of operations: MAPC's inability to generate enthusiasm for or commitment to its purposes. Despite several changes of leadership and of approaches to exerting influence, MAPC has not been an active player in the Byzantine maneuvering that characterizes decision making in highly politicized Massachusetts. On a technical level, MAPC is included in the interagency studies that supposedly inform legislative or executive action on metropolitan issues, but when deals are struck behind closed doors the council's representatives are not present. Neither the council's elected spokesmen, typically civic-minded suburbanites, nor its professional staff, have demonstrated that they speak for anyone but themselves, and thus they have yet to find a way to transform MAPC's advisory authority into a strong bargaining chip. Even Governor Dukakis, who was temperamentally inclined toward planning, adopted a distinctly low-level profile on metropolitan issues. Political power in Massachusetts flows out of the locality, and in his last eight years as governor, Dukakis did not challenge that fact of life. In the absence of a metropolitan consciousness among the 101 cities and towns, the officials on Beacon Hill are not about to act on their own.

Conspicuous among MAPC past failures was its inability to prepare the "comprehensive plan" called for in the 1963 legislation. Although the council made some progress in encouraging subregional cooperation on local problems, over its first quarter-century MAPC could never find the will to translate its many research studies into a blueprint for the region's future. In 1987, however, under the lead of a new executive director, MAPC started moving toward that goal. Unveiled in the spring of 1990, MetroPlan 2000 adopted as its "basic tenet" the belief that "concentrating development is economically and environmentally more practical than our current mode of scattered development." According to this concept, development would be directed toward two types of areas in the region: (1) the urban core (roughly within the arc of Route 128); and (2) subregional growth centers—areas currently experiencing growth or where growth is anticipated (a total of seven, with all but two lying west of Boston). The plan envisioned a major saving of infrastructure costs by stressing conservation measures and enhancements to existing water and sewer systems before new water supply sources or new sewer systems are developed, and by creating a network of high occupancy vehicle lanes on existing major highways rather than building new roads. MetroPlan 2000 also included a laundry list of specific recommendations in seven categories (economic development, housing, land resources, transportation, water/wastewater, solid waste, and facility siting) to deal with regional problems (MAPC 1990).

Although the MAPC Council approved MetroPlan 2000 in May 1990, it did so only after eliminating the proposal's designation of specific communities and areas as subregional growth centers. Some of the towns were unhappy at being selected, while others were dissatisfied for being left off the list. The notion of such centers remained alive, but MAPC's aspirations to be a vigorous planning agency were dealt a serious set-back.

CONCLUSION

Writing in the mid-1940s, soon after the celebration of the fiftieth anniversary of the Metropolitan Sewerage Board, a proponent of regional cooperation observed that the "state has been the one solvent capable of containing the conflicting elements of the Boston area" (Atkins 1944). Nearly a half-century later, with the board's centennial all but ignored, this statement remains valid. Although the ethnic divisions that had exacerbated the cleavage between central city and suburbs have eased, and while the federal government has altered the playing field with the imposition of new rules, the state still occupies the central role in meeting the service needs of metropolitan Boston.

It is a role the state has accepted both willingly and by default. Reviewing a proposal from the U.S. Advisory Commission on Intergovernmental Relations that metropolitan residents "on their own initiative" establish metropolitan study commissions, a report prepared for the Massachusetts legislature dismissed the idea as "completely alien to Massachusetts tradition" (Legislative Research Council 1964). Thus, with communities showing no inclination to cooperate voluntarily, the state found itself obliged to act   It might have imposed metropolitan government upon the region, but chose not to do so because this would have created a major rival to its own authority. Hence, the creation of a set of state agencies that functioned for decades as patronage havens as much as suppliers of essential services.

Growing national involvement forced the state to start cleaning up its act. Federal highway and environmental laws broke the state Department of Public Works' monopoly over road construction and paved the way for a more comprehensive treatment of the region's transportation requirements. With money from Washington available for transit subsidies, MBTA was both obliged to operate more efficiently and given the opportunity to extend its system. Federal legislation and court action led to the dismemberment of MDC and inauguration of the largest public works program in the history of the Commonwealth. Because Massachusetts waited so long to do something about Boston Harbor, most of the funds for this job will have to come out of state coffers—federal aid that was previously available for this purpose is drying up. Additional large expenditures also loom if federal administrators ratify a preliminary finding that national water quality rules demand improvement in the region's purification facilities for drinking water.

Metropolitan government for Boston in the absence of an absolute federal mandate is not likely during the foreseeable future, but federal planning regulations might act as the catalyst to bring the region's development under areawide control. Although federal authorities have been lax about enforcing their own rules, the Metropolitan Area Planning Council proposes to take them seriously. The council's record is not encouraging, but if it can discover the means to convince local, state, and federal officials that its MetroPlan 2000 is necessary and workable, then the future of the Boston region may yet be different from its past.

REFERENCES

Atkins, Richard A. 1974. Half-Century—Half Measures. *National Municipal Review* 33 (March): 117-22.

Birkhead, Guthrie S. 1972. *Massachusetts Substate Government.* Occasional Paper No. 7, Metropolitan Studies Program, Maxwell School, Syracuse University.

Blodgett, Geoffrey. 1984. Yankee Leadership in a Divided City, 1860-1910. In *Boston 1700-1980: The Evolution of Urban Politics,* ed. Ronald P. Formisano and Constance K. Burns, Westport, Conn.: Greenwood Press.

Board of Railroad Commissioners. 1888. *Nineteenth Annual Report, Boston Contest of 1944.* Boston: Boston University Press.

Boston Globe. 1983a. April 7, May 16, June 30.

_____. 1983b. July 9, September 7, 15.

_____. 1984. January 25, October 11, 14, November 9, December 13, 18.

_____. 1989. January 1.

Cheape, Charles W. 1980. *Moving the Masses.* Cambridge: Harvard University Press.

Deem, Warren H. 1953. *The Problem of Boston's Metropolitan Transit Authority.* Mimeographed. Bureau of Research in Municipal Government, Graduate School of Public Administration, Harvard University.

Governor's Task Force on Metropolitan Development. 1975. *Report.* Offset. State House Library.

Jackson, Kenneth T. 1985. *Crabgrass Frontier: The Suburbanization of the United States.* New York: Oxford University Press.

Kennedy, Lawrence. 1988. *Shaping Boston: A History of Planning and Growth.* Typescript. Boston Redevelopment Authority.

Legislative Research Council. 1964. *State Compliance with Proposals of the Federal Advisory Commission on Intergovernmental Relations.* Senate Document 860.

_____. 1970. *Regional Government.* House Document 4988.

_____. 1976. *Establishing a Metropolitan Services Financing District in the Boston Metropolitan Area.* Senate Document 1680.

Lupo, Alan, Frank Colcord, and Edmund P. Fowler. 1971. *Rites of Way: The Politics of Transportation in Boston and the U.S. City.* Boston: Little Brown.

MAPC. 1964-1988. Metropolitan Area Planning Council, *Annual Reports.*

_____. 1989a. Metropolitan Area Planning Council, *Handbook.*

_____. 1990. Metropolitan Area Planning Council, *MetroPlan 2000: Action Recommendations for Future Growth.*

Massachusetts Water Resources Authority. 1987. *Long Range Water Supply Program.*

_____. 1988. *Annual Report.*

McCaffrey, George H. 1937. The Political Disintegration and Reintegration of Metropolitan Boston. Unpublished Ph.D. dissertation, Harvard University.

Merino, James A. 1968. A Great City and Its Suburbs: Attempts to Integrate Metropolitan Boston, 1865-1920. Unpublished Ph.D. dissertation, University of Texas.

Scott, Mel. 1969. *American City Planning Since 1890.* Berkeley: University of California Press.

Wakstein, Allen M. 1972. Boston's Search for a Metropolitan Solution. *Journal of the American Institute of Planners* 38 (September): 285-96.

Wood, Robert. 1959. *Suburbia, Its People and their Politics.* Boston: Houghton Miffin.

Chapter 2

Metropolitan Government in the Montreal Area

Marie-Odile Trépanier
University of Montreal

THE MONTREAL REGION: A BRIEF PRESENTATION

Changing Economic Structure

There are many reasons to believe that Montreal is at a crossroads. Its economic and cultural domination over Canada has been challenged by Toronto. The quality of its economic links with the rest of Quebec has been questioned. It has now entered a process of restructuring its economy and redefining its role within Quebec, Canada, and the entire world. What is the link between these profound changes and land-use planning? What is the role of the various levels of government in confronting these changes? What kind of metropolitan governance system is already in place? These are some of the questions addressed in this paper.

Montreal vs. Toronto

During the 19th century, Montreal served as the main port of entry to Canada for the British Empire. Technology would not allow an easy crossing of the Lachine Rapids, so goods had to be trans-shipped in Montreal. Mass arrivals of immigrants from Europe and the high birth rate of French Canadians provided a wealth of cheap labor that facilitated industrial development.

Many studies have shown that, since World War II, Montreal has been declining in relation to Toronto. The reduction in trade with Britain, combined with economic growth in western Canada and increasing economic integration with the United States, has strengthened

Ontario's economic role, particularly with the development of the automobile and chemical industries (Léveillée 1978; Québec, OPDQ 1977). Decisions by the Canadian government concerning the St. Lawrence Seaway, the Canada-U.S. Auto Pact, and oil pipelines have favored the development of Ontario and the western provinces while necessarily diminishing Montreal's influence over Canada as a whole (Québec, OPDQ 1977). Traditional sectors of the Montreal economy, such as textiles, garment-making, and food processing, have been adversely affected by various international economic developments such as the increasing manufacturing strength of some developing countries, especially in Asia.

The decline of Montreal has been well documented. Professor Benjamin Higgins' book, *The Rise and Fall of Montreal* (1986), presents one of the most recent and provocative pictures of Montreal's past and present. The decline of Montreal is noticeable in the manufacturing and financial sectors as well as in relative population growth.

Table 2.1.   ***Decline of the Manufacturing Sector in Montreal***

Year	Number of Jobs	Percent of Total Employment
1971	284,000	30.6
1981	305,700	24.1
1986	282,000	20.6

Source: Lemelin et Morin, 13; Ville de Montréal, 1990, 13.

The most dramatic examples of manufacturing decline were the closing down of petrochemical industries in Montreal East and of old industrial plants along the Lachine Canal. In both cases vast amounts of derelict land were left.

Because of the loss of highly skilled jobs, the departure of corporate head offices to Toronto was of great concern in Montreal throughout the 1970s. Higgins, however, has gathered figures to show that this process started a long time ago and that the shift of Canada's financial center to

Toronto was already a reality by 1970, even though it did accelerate in the 1970s, especially after the Quebec elections of 1976 (p. 58).

As Higgins indicates, in terms of population, after 1970 "the picture is one of stagnation in Montreal and vigorous growth in Toronto" (p. 54). For instance, "Toronto's metropolitan region grew three times as fast as Montreal's during the 1971-1976 period." With low population growth (see Table 2.4) and stagnation in employment at the end of the 1970s, commercial activity was also bound to decline.

Restructuring the Economy

Governments at all levels responded to this critical situation by establishing study committees and announcing action plans. In 1981, the government of Quebec held a regional summit in Montreal. In 1986, the city of Montreal organized one on downtown development. The federal government created a committee on development in the Montreal region that presented an impressive report in 1986 (Canada, Rapport Picard 1986). In some cases local workers badly hit by plant closures instigated the establishment of experimental joint committees aimed at public-private collaboration in economic redevelopment: the CREEM (*Comité pour la relance de l'économie et de l'emploi de l'Est de Montréal*) and the CREESOM (*Comité de relance de l'économie et de l'emploi du Sud-Ouest de Montréal*). They involved every level of government, unions, local citizens' groups, and local business people. More recently, the city of Montreal, after acknowledging unemployment rates between 15 and even 30 percent in many areas, prepared a strategy for local development in partnership with local groups, and enterprises (Ville de Montréal 1990). All of these came out with more or less specific proposals, many of which have already been implemented. In short, people are getting together to tackle the important economic development challenges that Montreal is facing. There is a great number of interesting ideas in circulation, although implementation is not as easy.

On the other hand, tertiarization is increasing in Montreal, as in most western countries. The 1982 recession dealt a further blow to Montreal's manufacturing sector, but in so doing it created further opportunity for diversification.

Map 2.1.   *Montreal Census Metropolitan Area, 1971 and 1991*

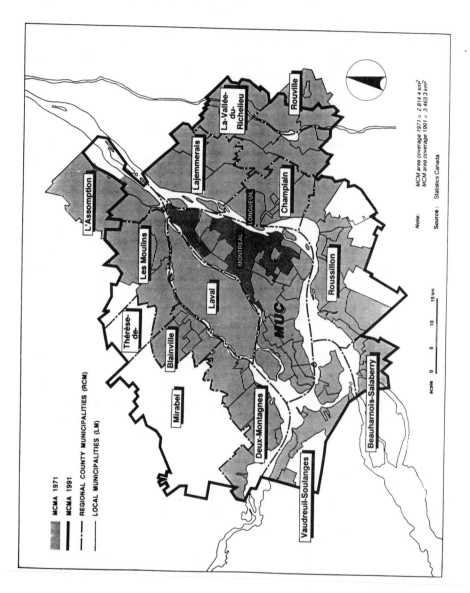

Table 2.2. *Tertiarization in Montreal (number of workers)*

Year	Number of Jobs	Percent of Total Employment
1971	585,000	63
1986	989,000	74

Source: Lemelin et Morin, 15.

While the tertiary sector in Montreal has steadily developed, it has been noted (Canada, Rapport Picard 1986, 20) that its growth during the '70s was much stronger in Toronto and Vancouver. As a result, there is a danger that Montreal will become only a regional center and a satellite of Toronto (*Id.* 23), thereby squandering its apparent potential as an international metropolis. Even as a regional center, however, Montreal still has its problems. Its economic links with the rest of Quebec are weak, and it lacks the strong network of nearby urban centers that characterizes metropolitan Toronto (Québec, Groupe de travail sur l'urbanisation 1976; Higgins, Martin, Raynauld 1970).

Montreal vs. the Suburbs

While the central parts of Montreal were declining, much of the new growth was occurring in the suburbs. New industries were developing to replace old ones, but they tended to locate outside the central area. In 1971, 185,000 or 65 percent of manufacturing jobs could be found in central Montreal. That number dropped to 116,000 or 41 percent in 1986; in the other parts of the metropolitan area, they rose from 95,000 to 164,000 during the same period (Lemelin et Morin 1989; Ville de Montréal 1990). Table 2.3 examines in more detail the distribution of these changes during the seventies.

Similarly, but to a lesser degree, tertiary employment increased more rapidly in the suburbs than in the center. In 1971 central Montreal was the location of 69 percent of the tertiary employment in the metropolitan area; by 1986 the figure was only 52.5 percent (Lamonde 1989). Given the rather slow growth rate for the entire region (Table 2.4), these figures are worrisome; they imply a simple transfer of tertiary employment from the central area to the urban periphery.

Table 2.3. *Evolution of Manufacturing Employment by Planning Sector in MUC and in the Suburban Ring, 1971-1981*

	1971 Number	%	1981 Number	%	1971-1981 Number	%
West	6,800	2.4	12,300	4.0	5,500	80.9
West-Central	21,200	7.5	38,000	12.4	16,800	79.2
Southwest	19,500	6.9	21,300	7.0	1,800	9.2
Central	184,800	65.0	138,600	45.4	-46,200	-25.0
East	16,100	5.7	36,300	11.9	20,200	125.5
MUC	248,400	87.5	246,500	80.7	-1,900	-0.8
Suburban Ring	35,600	12.5	58,800	19.2	23,200	65.2
MCMA	284,000	100.0	305,000	100.0	21,300	7.5

Source: MUC Development Plan (1986), and INRS-Urbanisation (1984).
Note: See Map 2.2. *Planning Sectors.*

Geography and Demography in Montreal

Montreal's geographical setting has always been a matter of considerable importance. It was chosen for settlement because of its location at the foot of the then impassable Lachine Rapids on the St. Lawrence River. Furthermore, Montreal is itself a vast island some 30 miles long. On its north side, the island of Montreal is bordered by the Rivière-des-Prairies and by two large islands, Ile-Jésus and Ile-Bizard, themselves separated from the north shore by the Rivière-des-Mille-Iles (see Maps 2.1 and 2.6). All this forms an impressive archipelago comprising more than 300 smaller islands, two large lakes as well as many rapids. In terms of development, this has posed tremendous transportation problems. Montreal cannot be reached by land except by bridge or tunnel. Victoria Bridge, the first, was built in the early nineteenth century. There are now some 14 bridges and one tunnel, the majority of which were built or greatly redesigned since 1945.

Until that period, settlement in Montreal was very much concentrated around the old central core. Occupation densities were high: in 1976, the central area still registered a density of 84.2 units/hectare compared to 11.2 in the western sector, according to the Montreal Urban Community

Map 2.2. *Montreal Urban Community: Planning Sectors, 1986*

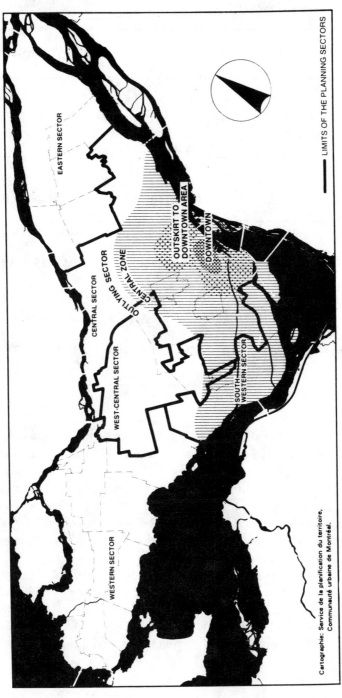

Certographie: **Service de la planification du territoire,**
Communauté urbaine de Montréal.

Source: MUC Development Plan, 1986, p. 16.

Table 2.4. *Demographic Trends in the Montreal Census Metropolitan Area (1966-1991)*

	1966		1971		1976	
		% MUC		% MUC		% MUC
Montreal	1,298,648	67.5	1,218,120	62.2	1,083,372	57.9
Suburbs	624,530	32.5	741,023	37.8	786,269	42.1
		% MCMA		% MCMA		% MCMA
Total MUC	1,923,178	74.8	1,959,140	71.5	1,869,640	66.5
		% MCMA		% MCMA		% MCMA
Outer Suburbs	647,804	25.2	784,065	28.5	944,425	33.5
		%MCMA		% MCMA		% MCMA
Montreal Census Metropolitan Area	2,570,982	100.0	2,743,205	100.0	2,814,065	100.0

Development Plan (MUC 1986, 19). The city of Montreal is also notable by Canadian standards for having more tenants (68 percent in 1981, *id.*) than owner-occupiers.

Changes in transportation and industrial technology have dramatically reversed this pattern. Since 1951, most of the population increase occurred outside the central area (Map 2.2). According to an MUC study, when the population increase in the central area was only 1.77 percent for the period 1951-56, it was 6.46 percent for the other parts of Montreal Island, and 7.74 percent for the outer suburbs, even though in absolute numbers, the central area was still much more heavily populated: 1,196,127 against 311,526 for the island and 322,579 for the outer suburbs (Communauté Urbaine de Montréal [CUM] 1985). Yet, Table 2.4 shows that as the years passed, this trend persisted; in 1966 Montreal's

Table 2.4. *(continued)*

	1981		1986		1991	
		% MUC		% MUC		% MUC
Montreal	982,339	55.8	1,015,420	58	1,017,666	57.3
Suburbs	777,695	44.2	737,162	42	758,205	42.6
		% MCMA		% MCMA		% MCMA
Total MUC	1,760,034	62.2	1,752,582	60	1,775,871	56.7
		% MCMA		% MCMA		% MCMA
Outer Suburbs	1,068,315	37.7	1,168,775	40	1,351,371	43.2
		% MCMA		% MCMA		% MCMA
Montreal Census Metropolitan Area	2,828,349	100.0	2,921,357	100	3,127,242	100

Metropolitan area coverage: $1981 = 2,814.43 \text{ km}^2$
$1986 = 3,508.89 \text{ km}^2$

Source: MUC Development Plan 1986, p. 20 and Statistics Canada

population started to decline in absolute numbers as well and was superseded by the rest of the metropolitan area. (See also Figure 2.1.)

This fact may have been underestimated following the creation of the metropolitan government (MUC) in 1970, because we now tend to compare figures between MUC territory and the rest of the metropolitan area. Yet, in terms of settlement patterns, central Montreal and other parts of MUC appear quite different, as indicated by the density figures in Table 2.5.

The MUC territory covers the entire island of Montreal plus the much smaller Ile-Bizard and the tiny Dorval Island. This division has been said to be a very logical approach politically (Sancton 1985). But the definition of administrative boundaries following the lines of the unusually triangular island of Montreal did cause some problems.

Figure 2.1. *Population Evolution in the Montreal Area 1951-1986*

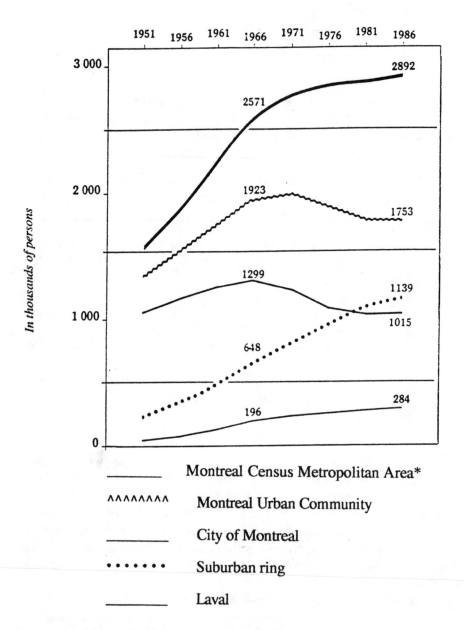

Source: Statistics Canada; OPDQ, Montreal region, 1988
*Territorial basis: 1971 Census

Table 2.5. *Housing Density on MUC Territory by Planning Sector (housing unit per hectare)*

	1976	1981
West	11,2	12,3
West-Central	27,9	29,9
South-West	55,4	55,1
Central	84,2	82,8
East	34,4	36,5

Source: MUC Development Plan, 1986, 19.

Development in Montreal has always been related to the St. Lawrence River. Many smaller towns also developed along the river, particularly near rapids, such as Lachine, Laval-des-Rapides, or Longueuil. Although Montreal originally developed as a trading and transportation center, the island also had very good farm lands and the best agricultural climate in Quebec. Rural villages developed all along the riverside, north and south of the island. These were not typical suburbs. Incorporation of some of them (like Ste-Anne-de-Bellevue, Ste-Geneviève, Senneville) into metropolitan bodies was accidental, mainly due to their location within the island of Montreal. For that matter, the presence of Ile Bizard within the MUC is not logical; it remains even today mainly rural.

Until recently urban development all over the island was seen as normal. Typical suburban development occurred beside old villages and on good farm lands, with very little public concern in either case. Currently, 75 percent of the 500 km² of MUC territory is urbanized (376,6 km²). Between 1961 and 1981, according to the MUC Development Plan (MUC 1986, 15), 60 km² were developed at an unprecedented pace. However, attempts to preserve the last open spaces have recently become important public issues. But, as we shall see later, development and its demographic repercussions also have a political impact because votes on the MUC Council are distributed according to population. As Table 2.4 has shown, Montreal still has the majority of the MUC population, but the suburbs are now getting closer to equality.

On the south shore of the St. Lawrence River small towns such as Longueuil, St-Lambert, and Boucherville had existed for long periods of time. But during the 1950s and '60s they were surrounded by new

suburbs, like Brossard, all of which were quite close to Montreal's downtown. South-shore municipalities, however, were never incorporated into
Montreal's metropolitan bodies (except for Longueuil, which had a metro
station built in 1967 to facilitate entrance to the Expo '67 site from the
south and which was consequently linked to the Montreal Transit
Commission). Although politically understandable, this fact had important
consequences in relation to the difficulties of planning future urban
development around Montreal. In this regard, as we shall see, the
existence of the island has been a powerful barrier to the territorial
expansion of metropolitan government.

Most of the 300 other islands in the Montreal Archipelago are too
small to have been connected to the others and thus are still very much
undeveloped. The most important exception is Ile-Jésus. This island,
about half the size of the Montreal Island, has undergone tremendous
development since the last world war. It has not, however, been
incorporated into the MUC. Instead, the 14 small rural villages that had
slowly developed on Ile-Jésus were amalgamated in 1965 by way of a
special Quebec law that was the result of a proposal of the Lemay
committee study on the island's intermunicipal relations. The new city,
called Laval, has become the second largest city in the province, with a
population of 284,164 (Québec, Ministère des Affaires Municipales
1988). Yet, as powerful as it is, it is a typical suburb, with little industrial
infrastructure and no central area, unless we can accept as a center the
four or five shopping malls that developed along the main north-south
highway.

Outer suburban development is becoming more and more significant.
In 1991 it comprised 43.2 percent of the metropolitan area's total population. There is an unlimited reserve of available land for future development. As the population of these suburbs grows, so does their demand for
infrastructure and services. But the real problem, as has been pointed out
in recent studies, is that, since the overall development of the metropolitan area is now rather slow, there is a danger that the periphery is
growing solely at the expense of the center (Lamonde 1989; Lemelin et
Morin 1989; Conseil des Affaires Sociales 1989).

Compared with other North American cities, the core city of
Montreal, mostly populated by middle- and lower-class workers, mainly
francophones and immigrants, has always been considered as a safe and
lively area bursting with a strong cultural life. Recent demographic
trends, however, show increasingly worrisome figures. The birth rate in
Quebec has fallen to 1.4 in 1986 and is said to be even lower in Montreal

(Lemelin et Morin 1989, 4). The population decline in the center is not only quantitative; it is also qualitative. There is a general tendency for older people to be left in the center, because families with children are fleeing to the suburbs. Family units in the center are smaller, have fewer children, and are more at risk (unemployed or welfare persons, handicapped persons, immigrants, etc.) (Conseil des Affaires Sociales 1989; Lemelin et Morin 1989; Ville de Montréal, 1990). Criminality and drug problems are becoming more prevalent.

Some important conclusions may be drawn from these trends. First, it has become clear that suburban development is not only residential but also economic; thus it is in competition with downtown development and vitality. This will be an important issue during debates over the MUC development plan. Second, the central area has become more than ever a focus for social problems, mainly because of massive closures of traditional industries. Large numbers of jobless people have appeared in central Montreal in a relatively short period. Governments became seriously aware of these issues in recent years and started to develop special programs. But what kind of relationship has evolved between these policies and land-use planning? That remains to be seen.

GOVERNMENTS IN THE MONTREAL REGION

Who governs the Montreal region? Before addressing this question, it is important to remember that Montreal is not a capital city, which implies that it has no special attraction for major public investments, and moreover, that it is relatively remote from decision makers at both the provincial and federal levels. However, the Montreal metropolitan area contains about half the population of Quebec and is the location of more than half its economic activity (Québec, OPDQ 1988, 1-2). The dominance of Montreal within the province has ensured that the Quebec government has always been cautious about establishing a rival to itself in the form of a powerful metropolitan institution. But there are also more profound causes for the Quebec-Montreal tension. They are rooted in Montreal's unique socio-economic structure. Higgins summarizes the problem this way: "Montreal may be 'a primate city' within Quebec as a geographically and politically defined entity; but Montreal is not linked primarily to the Quebec economy. The city operates in a worldwide 'economic space'" (p. 116). Faced with the perspective of Montreal as a neo-colonial enclave, an "appendage to the American, West European and Middle-East economies" (p. 115), decision makers have been confronted with a double dilemma concerning Montreal's economic role in Quebec development: (1) Should energies be devoted to reinforcing the Montreal region or to sustaining the underdeveloped regions? Would investing in Montreal be detrimental to the rest of Quebec, considering its weak links with the "hinterland"? (2) Should and how can these links be reinforced? To many analysts, the solution was to be found in the development of indigenous entrepreneurs and in asserting Quebec's control over major economic decisions (see Higgins 1986).

This, of course, is part of the Quebec nationalistic project, or Quiet Revolution, and has been explained in more detail elsewhere. While the purpose of this paper is not to develop these aspects at length, it is important to keep them in mind as contextual circumstances that make governance so particularly difficult in the Montreal region. It could easily be argued that in many fields it might be preferable for the Quebec government (from the nationalistic point of view) to keep some kind of control over issues and policies rather than to decentralize power to ambivalent local governments. Still, if only because of Quebec's remoteness, there was a need for some sort of regionally based institution(s) in the Montreal area.

Yet, on the local scene, these tensions also colored the relationships between the city of Montreal and other municipalities. Unequal wealth distribution and language divisions seriously hampered attempts to define new metropolitan institutions (Sancton 1985). Thus, to define functional institutional arrangements in this environment was no easy task.

According to the 1991 census (see Table 2.4), the Montreal metropolitan area comprised roughly 3,500 km² of land and 3,127,242 people. Regional governance in that area is divided between one urban community and about a dozen regional county municipalities (see Map 2.1). Although it may look like a metropolitan government, the Montreal Urban Community in reality is quite weak, as this paper will try to demonstrate. In recent years it has become apparent that even its territory of influence is minimal, and that regional governance and planning is still very fragile. The MUC itself covers only 500 km² and has a population of 1,775,871, or 56.7 percent of the total metropolitan area. As in many other cities, urban development at the fringe is threatening the central area. How is each level of government coping with this situation? This evolving context is an interesting setting for an analysis of intergovernmental relations. What role has each been playing in this process of adaptation . . . or resistance?

Federal Influence

While federal attempts to develop a national urban policy failed, the federal government's influence on regional development has always been considerable (Léveillée 1978). Its constitutional powers over specific activities (international and interprovincial transportation, including navigation, ports, airports; military installations; Indian affairs; etc.) have given it direct tools over development. In the Montreal region, the federal government thus controls the port and the St. Lawrence Seaway, some important bridges, Dorval and Mirabel airports, and the Indian reserves or settlements of Kahnawake and Kanasetake (Oka). In 1989 it established a new Canadian space agency in the region but was criticized for locating it in the urban fringe at St. Hubert instead of on the island of Montreal.

The Quiet Revolution and the First Repercussions of Quebec Government Modernization on Metropolitan Governance in the Montreal Area

The Canadian constitution gives the provinces all powers over local institutions; there is no such thing as local, self-determined charters. The province alone creates, modifies, or abolishes local governments, with or without local consultation. It also determines what is a local matter and what is not. Among the most important reforms of the Quiet Revolution were the reforms of the education system and later of health and social services. The new system put in place in the '60s and '70s not only transformed a clergy-run system into a public and secular system but also put it under the complete control of the Quebec government. Regional and local democratic institutions were indeed created to manage local schools, hospitals, and other services, but they relate to the Ministry of Education and to the Ministry of Social Affairs; they are totally independent from one another or from the more traditional local municipalities. Briefly, the municipal organizations have no power nor responsibility concerning most social and educational issues.

One other important aspect of the modernization of Quebec government is that during the '60s and '70s, it also started to develop policies and establish agencies for planning and land-use issues. The province created in 1967 the *Office de Planification et de Développement du Québec* (OPDQ), which was to be responsible for preparing a provincial development plan. Ten administrative regions were designated where regional branches of every provincial department were to get together to coordinate their activities at the regional level. OPDQ was also to prepare regional development plans to further the national plan, but such a plan never appeared. At the regional level, the system did not work either. Many studies were carried out, but they had little immediate operational impact, although they may have been quite useful in the long run in reaching a better understanding of important land-use issues. At the end of the 1970s, OPDQ more or less fell into disuse as a central planning agency. Other means of coordination were developed, particularly various cabinet committees organized on a sectoral basis.

"Regional summits" were also introduced by the Quebec government at about the same time. These were opportunities for local and regional decision makers to get together in a collaborative approach to prepare regional plans and projects for presentation to the government. Preparatory and follow-up activities were very important. Several provincial agencies were involved, but the coordination team would vary from one region to another (see Quebec, Gendron 1983). As already mentioned, the first such summit for Montreal took place in 1981.

In the meantime, provincial ministries developed stronger instruments for controlling land use. The province itself became much more directly involved in housing, heritage preservation, parks, and environmental protection. Sectoral planning by each ministry proved much more effective than the comprehensive approaches considered in the 1960s.

In 1967, the Quebec Housing Corporation was established so as to implement new federal-provincial agreements concerning the decentralization of federal housing programs. The law provided for local housing offices to be established by interested local municipalities.

An Environmental Protection Branch was created in 1972 and transformed into a ministry in 1980. It is responsible for water management, air pollution, and related issues. The Environmental Impact Assessment Board, established in 1978, played an important role in overseeing several issues of special importance to Montreal, including proposals to build a new system of dams on the various rivers surrounding Montreal and to dump snow from the city's roads in the St. Lawrence River during the winter.

In the 1970s, several pieces of legislation were adopted concerning parks, ecological reserves, and natural historic areas. The adoption of the Agricultural Land Preservation Act in 1978 completed this set of legislative tools. It was one of the most powerful tools over land use that the government ever developed. It gave the Agricultural Preservation Commission power to designate agricultural zones in which nonagricultural activities would be severely controlled. In particular, land subdivision in these zones was considerably restrained.

In 1972 a Cultural Property Act was adopted and a heritage preservation department was established within the Ministry of Cultural Affairs. It was made responsible for historic districts such as Old Montreal and Old Laprairie, both within the Montreal region. It could also designate natural areas and preserve specific sites or buildings. A Montreal regional heritage branch was set up to manage these areas. In the late '70s, a joint agreement was adopted between the ministry and the city of Montreal for the management of Old Montreal.

In the 1960s, at the same time as important reforms were enacted concerning public education and health, attempts were also made to reform the municipal system and to implement mandatory planning at the local level. A study commission formed in 1963 presented a report in 1968 proposing a thorough planning system integrating planning at provincial, regional, and local levels (Québec, Commission Provinciale d'Urbanisme, 1968). But the whole scheme was too intricate to be implemented directly. It was modelled on the French system and did not take into account Quebec's hitherto limited experience with land-use planning. It took 10 more years to develop a simpler and more realistic system. Finally, the adoption of the Land Use Planning and Development Act in 1979, which provided for the establishment of Regional County Municipalities (RCM) all over the province, was to complete this reform. Each RCM was mandated to adopt a development plan within seven years. Such plans were supposed to specify boundaries for local urban development and to identify resulting infrastructure objectives for both the local and provincial levels of government. This appeared a promising formula because it meant that there was to be an effort towards coordination through an intensive negotiation process between Quebec and the RCMs (Trépanier 1982).

MONTREAL URBAN COMMUNITY:
A METROPOLITAN GOVERNMENT?

When the Montreal Urban Community bill was adopted in 1969, it seemed an impressive reform. But in reality the MUC developed into quite a weak form of metropolitan government. Its territory and powers may have been sufficient for the mission it was then expected to accomplish; but they were limited in relation to the problems of the region as a whole. As time went by, it became clear to both the member municipalities and the province that the MUC was not much more than an administrative organization to help achieve better intermunicipal coordination. Political power still rested entirely in the hands of local rather than regional representatives, and the MUC has had little, if any, political clout.

Historical Background

The City of Montreal, a Product of Annexations

Between 1881 and 1921, the city of Montreal increased its population more than fourfold (148,747 in 1881 to 618,506 in 1921). Much of this was achieved through the annexation of some 30 municipalities (in total or in part). However, most of these annexations were the result of bankruptcies caused by extravagant public expenses instigated by influential land developers (Sancton 1985, 26). Yet, while the financial burden of Montreal citizens was increasing, other more fortunate municipalities were able to resist annexation, thereby preventing the central city from achieving financial equilibrium. Indeed, wealthier inner suburbs like Westmount, Outremont, Montreal West, Hampstead, and Mount Royal have successfully maintained their municipal independence to this day.

By 1920 solutions other than annexation had to be found for bankrupt suburbs so as to prevent Montreal itself from developing serious financial difficulties. Faced with a provincial government proposal of total amalgamation of the entire island, suburbs had no alternative but to accept a compromise to establish a Montreal Metropolitan Commission in 1921. The commission's functions were essentially to manage these financial problems and redistribute the bankrupts' debts among all central and eastern island municipalities (Sancton 1985).

The commission's establishment came too late to prevent the city of Montreal from completely dominating in size and population the other municipalities on the island. In 1921, the total population of the Montreal and Bizard Islands was 720,502. Ranking behind the city of Montreal, in descending order by population, were Verdun (25,001), Westmount, Lachine, and Outremont. Verdun and Lachine were populated mainly by the French-speaking working class. Westmount and Outremont, on the other hand, were dominated by the wealthy; the former was very much English-speaking, while the latter comprised people of both linguistic groups. Both municipalities were perhaps already big enough to resist annexation, but too small to become equal partners with Montreal. So they developed conservative, protectionist attitudes against the Montreal giant. This situation has been a serious handicap facing all subsequent metropolitan reformers.

Establishing the Montreal Urban Community

From 1960 to 1986 Montreal's mayor was Jean Drapeau, a strong, imaginative, yet authoritarian municipal leader. His first task had been to reorganize the city's administration. He strengthened his authority by establishing an executive committee, which he controlled with the help of Lucien Saulnier, who served as the committee's chair for 10 years before becoming the MUC's first chief executive.

Mayor Drapeau envisioned Montreal as a great international city. He successfully promoted it as the site of the 1967 World Exhibition and, later, of the 1976 Olympics. These were occasions for grandiose designs and ingenious infrastructures, such as the "Métro" subway system and the artificial islands for "Expo '67." But he also wanted to extend his territorial authority throughout the island of Montreal, using the slogan "one Island, one City." In the early 1960s, he launched a new annexation campaign. Although mainly unsuccessful, he was able to add three municipalities: Rivière-des-Prairies, Saraguay, and St. Michel.

Many of the reasons for the MUC's creation are common to all metropolitan areas. In the case of Montreal, however, the sharing of costs seemed particularly important. For instance, metropolitan services had started to be developed by the city itself, as part of Drapeau's grand metropolitan strategy (Sancton 1985, 95). Because Montreal shaped these first metropolitan services, the suburbs were even more suspicious than usual. Two services were particularly controversial: public transit and police. Montreal had built a very modern underground transit system; it was bound to extend eventually into the suburbs. But where and at what cost? Montreal's police services had become increasingly expensive during the 1960s, in part due to a wave of nationalistic terrorism. Undoubtedly, suburbs were benefiting from the work of the Montreal police. Further, a police strike in October 1969 created a crisis that needed a fast solution.

Meanwhile, the Quebec government had been endeavoring to undertake a vast local-government reform throughout the province. Local municipalities were quite reluctant. But the crisis in the Montreal area gave the government an opportunity to move. At the same time, there were important regional problems around Quebec City and Hull (across the river from Ottawa). So in 1969 the government created simultaneously two urban communities in Montreal and Quebec, and one regional community for the Outaouais area. They were to be the three metropolitan pillars of the future reform.

The MUC was a forced compromise that satisfied no one entirely. Decision making within its institutions was very difficult; on many occasions no decision was preferred to any other solution. So stagnation was frequent, as we will see through the case studies. Finally, in 1982, after intensive discussions, an agreement was made on a set of reforms to enliven the MUC. We will examine this evolution first in terms of power distribution, second in terms of functions.

Power Distribution in the Montreal Urban Community

Institutional arrangements for the MUC combined recognition of the principle of local autonomy with the imperative of developing important regional services. More than anything else, the MUC is a federation of municipalities to which a certain number of tasks have been entrusted.

Originally, in 1971, Montreal's population of 1,218,120 represented 62.2 percent of the total MUC population of 1,959,143 (Québec, Ministère des Affaires Municipales 1981). The remaining 37.8 percent was distributed among 28 municipalities; the most populous being Montreal North with 89,139. Eleven municipalities had a population of less than 10,000. Although the 1969 MUC Act stated that "within five years . . . the Community shall prepare and submit to the Minister a project for rearranging the territorial limits of the municipalities" (s. 195), this was never done. Many proposals were considered in the 1970s, but it was not possible to come to an agreement; according to Sancton (1985), any new arrangement would disrupt the fragile equilibrium between French and English.

This problem was so sensitive that it was generally not dealt with directly. Political accommodations had to be found within the MUC. We shall see that the original arrangements gave a predominant role to the city of Montreal, but, as demographic changes occurred, the suburbs redressed the balance.

Map 2.3. *Montreal Urban Community and Local Municipalities*

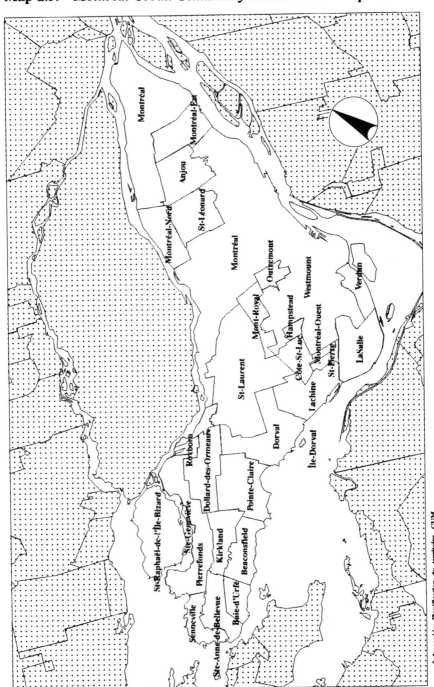

Infographie: Planification du territoire, CUM

Table 2.6. *Local Municipalities in the Montreal Urban Community, Population and Area Coverage*

Municipality	Population	Area (km²)
Anjou	37,500	13.64
Baie-d'Urfé	3,630	6.70
Beaconsfield	19,600	10.64
Côte-Saint-Luc	29,500	7.18
Dollard-des-Ormeaux	43,800	15.20
Dorval	17,600	20.64
Hampstead	7,500	1.76
Kirkland	15,700	10.28
Lachine	35,400	17.31
LaSalle	76,400	16.42
L'Île-Dorval	3	0.18
Montréal	1,030,900	176.78
Montréal-Est	3,690	12.38
Montréal-Nord	89,000	11.03
Montréal-Ouest	5,500	1.63
Mont-Royal	18,100	7.43
Outremont	22,700	3.67
Pierrefonds	44,000	24.47
Pointe-Claire	27,500	19.16
Roxboro	6,000	2.07
Sainte-Anne-de-Bellevue	4,220	15.11
Sainte-Geneviève	2,640	1.24
Saint-Laurent	68,700	46.28
Saint-Léonard	77,100	13.63
Saint-Pierre	4,820	2.15
Saint-Raphaël-de-l'Île-Bizard	9,900	22.68
Senneville	1,050	7.84
Verdun	61,200	8.07
Westmount	20,000	3.96
Total	*1,783,653*	*499.53*

Source: Répertoire des municipalités du Québec, 1992

MUC Council

On the MUC council, Montreal was represented by all of its 55 city councillors, while all of the other municipalities were represented by only one person, the mayor. This meant that Montreal had an overwhelming majority of 66.2 percent in terms of representation while the suburbs were left with 33.7 percent. However, votes were weighted according to population. This gave a little more strength to the suburbs (37.8 percent/62.2 percent). As time went by, suburban population increased more than Montreal's, thus giving them relatively more votes on the council. But the original 1969 act contained another mechanism that proved to be the most important element in the voting procedure: every decision had to be approved by a majority of Montreal votes and a majority of suburban votes. In practice, this double majority system gave a veto power to the suburbs provided that they presented a common front. They did not take long to understand. In 1975 they formed a suburban alliance, the Conference of Montreal Suburban Mayors. According to Divay and Collin, this enabled them to develop and present alternative proposals instead of adopting merely defensive positions. However, as Sancton suggested, their main goal still is to maintain "the fundamental assumption that every municipality has the right to exist" (Sancton 1985, 148). In any case, they were able not only to block any Montreal proposal that might infringe upon their autonomy, but given this basic principle, to practically transform this voting mechanism into a veto power for every individual municipality, at least politically if not legally.

MUC Executive Committee

As in the city of Montreal, the executive committee was the MUC's most important structural element. It not only controlled the administration, but it was the sole initiator of every bylaw and budgetary proposal. Under the 1969 act, the executive committee was composed of the seven members of the city of Montreal's own executive committee, plus five suburban mayors chosen by their colleagues. Such an arrangement was an important concession obtained by the city of Montreal in order to keep control over the services it had itself previously administered (Trépanier 1975). While the suburbs had learned how to use the voting mechanism at the council, they were not happy with the composition of the executive committee. When, at the beginning of the 1980s, it became clear that population increases were favoring the suburbs, they asked for a revision of the composition of the executive committee in order to bring parity between Montreal and the suburbs. They obtained that in the 1982 reform of the MUC Act.

Since then the MUC is said to be working better. Montreal has, however, lost much of its control. It now has to negotiate everything with the suburbs. In the 1982 reform, the government endeavored to clarify MUC functions and to encourage more commitment from MUC members to a regional perspective. This was done through establishing five permanent commissions whose chairs and vice-chairs became members of the executive committee. Chairs and vice-chairs must be distributed on an equal basis between Montreal and the suburbs. Thus, each member of the executive committee is attributed a specific mandate (like a cabinet minister) and becomes more responsible. Further, each main function is under the responsibility of two elected officials, one from Montreal and one from the suburbs. Therefore, important problems are being discussed jointly sooner in the process, with the expectation that negotiation will become easier.

MUC Functions and Achievements

Originally, the MUC was charged with such tasks as: property assessment, traffic regulation, data processing, construction standards, public transit, coordination and integration of police services, regional planning, air pollution, drinking water supply, waste disposal, public health, and intermunicipal sewers and water purification works (MUC Act, s. 112). It might also, after an affirmative vote of the two majorities, get involved in other matters, such as: recreation and parks, subsidized housing, fire services integration, and libraries (MUC Act, s. 114). At the eve of the 1982 reform, the MUC had effectively been active in: property assessment, regional planning, air pollution, public health, coordination and integration of police services, public transit, recreation and parks, and water purification works (Québec, Ministère des Affaires Municipales 1981). One other field of activity has been added: economic promotion.

While police and transit were the most important issues in the early years, environmental matters became more significant later on. But some important matters such as water supply and waste disposal were never dealt with by MUC because Montreal and the suburbs were not able to come to an agreement. Integrating police services was not easy: it needed provincial intervention to force it in 1971. In the field of environment, the most notable achievements were the building of main sewage collectors and of a major water treatment plant; the adoption of important regulations concerning air pollution and industrial waste; and the food inspection service. Yet, most of these activities had already been started by the city of Montreal. Very few new activities were agreed upon within the MUC; they were possible only with some help or push from the province, such as regulation of industrial waste. Such was also the case to a great extent with parks and with planning, which will be examined in the case studies.

Agreement within the MUC was usually only reached on issues that were mainly technical, such as the building of sewage collectors. Unlike the case in suburban Toronto, major sewers were not an important factor in the location of new suburban development. In Montreal they were built simply to replace existing systems that had previously emptied their contents directly into the surrounding rivers. The new MUC sewage-collector system was more of an engineering and financial issue, rather than one that was crucial to the future pattern of the island's land use. Within the MUC, such broader issues were rarely addressed.

The 1982 reform proposals regarding functions were dictated by pragmatism. The provincial government simply eliminated from MUC jurisdiction those matters that had never been dealt with. Waste disposal was a notable exception: in this case, the government hoped that the MUC would in the near future concern itself with waste recycling while leaving more traditional waste collection and disposal to local municipalities. Only one new field was added: financial assistance to artistic and cultural activities. The rest was left open to future intermunicipal agreements. This meant that the province agreed to leave the MUC's future development to the good will of the local municipalities, bringing it closer to the model provided by councils of governments in the United States (Léveillée 1980).

The 1982 Reform in Context

Sancton has suggested that only strong interventions by the provincial government could change the MUC from a weak coordinating body to a real regional authority. However, the 1982 reform cannot be seen as a strong intervention by the province. Indeed, the province acted more like a neutral mediator between the conflicting parties. If anything, it accepted the suburbs' arguments by slightly reducing Montreal's influence. Many factors may be advanced in explanation. For one thing, Mayor Drapeau's prestige had been declining since the financial disaster of the 1976

Olympics; in any case, he was getting older and less impressive. On the other hand, the *Parti Québécois* government was not in a very strong position itself because of the failure of its 1980 referendum on sovereignty and because of the dramatic impact on the provincial economy of the worldwide recession.

Another reason for the provincial government's caution concerning the MUC was that it was simultaneously engaged in convincing all the province's municipalities to implement a more general reorganization (Léveillée and Trépanier 1982; Divay and Léveillée 1981). For more than 15 years the government had been working on such a plan. The municipal associations had successfully resisted all radical reforms throughout this period. The reforms that were finally agreed on were a compromise (Léveillée 1982). They dealt with local fiscal arrangements, local democracy, and planning. In structural terms, instead of reorganizing the municipal system by eliminating a great number of the 1,300 municipalities with a population under 3,000, the 1980 reforms simply revised the county system. New regional county municipalities (RCM) replaced the old counties. Local municipalities were left unchanged, except that from now on every one of them (including cities and towns) had to be part of a RCM. These new regional entities were given very few powers: property assessment, waste management, and regional planning. The only significant innovation was that every one of the 95 RCMs was expected to adopt a development plan.

The government presented these reforms under the guise of aiming to reorganize provincial-municipal relations through decentralization (Trépanier 1988). The contention was that, by reinforcing local governments, a better equilibrium would be achieved. Government proposals also suggested that municipalities would learn by themselves, through planning, the importance of more coordination. The idea was that the government should withdraw from a lot of detailed, local-management matters; it should rather concentrate on major provincewide goals and issues (Trépanier 1988). The government made a commitment to invest in environmental protection, public transit, the preservation of farm land, and housing. Other more local matters were left for municipal initiative. Therefore, it cannot be said that the government was withdrawing from the urban field; on the contrary, it designed a number of special programs that were to have a major impact on urban development. For the Montreal region, this was presented as the *Option préférable pour Montréal,* which will be discussed later in this paper. But one idea that recurred frequently was that structural reforms were no longer the only solution.

From this point of view, the MUC was seen as an old-fashioned, "hard" structure, while RCMs were the new "soft" devices. This approach also explains partly why the 1982 reform did not force the MUC into new fields of activity, but simply provided for mechanisms for better debates between local representatives through the standing commissions and through a reformed planning process.

From the Island to the Metropolitan Region?

Within the MUC, city and suburban population figures are converging (see Table 2.4). Montreal's gains in 1986 are due to the annexation in 1982 of the east-end municipality of Pointe-aux-Trembles. Without the annexation, the city's population would have fallen below the suburbs'. An attempt to annex Verdun in 1986 was unsuccessful. That year a new Montreal government was elected with views differing from Mayor Drapeau's; it does not intend to follow Drapeau's steps on this matter and has taken a more conciliatory and cooperative approach toward the suburbs.

Table 2.4 shows that since 1971 total MUC population has steadily decreased, while the outer suburbs increased. The latter now comprise 43 percent of the total metropolitan population, and the proportion still seems to be growing, although at a slower pace than in the 1970s. These figures support the contention made by Divay and Collin in 1977 that the debate is bound to move from "the *central City to the central Island*" (the translation of their book's title).

In its *Explanatory Notes on the 1982 Reform*, the Quebec government made a distinction for institutional purposes between the Montreal Island and the region. It contended that one single coordinating agency for the whole region would be unrealistic, especially since there were now new regional county municipalities with planning powers for the area around the island of Montreal. The document admitted that cooperation would be needed among these regional municipalities, the MUC and the government; yet, it did not intend to deal with this matter within the legislation reforming the MUC. There are now more than 13 RCMs involved in the Montreal metropolitan area; no coordinating device has yet been established.

The growth of the outer suburbs implies that municipalities within the MUC may develop a self-protective bond among themselves. This process is presently underway for many important issues, especially transportation. On many of these matters, the teaming of suburban and Montreal representatives has strengthened the MUC position. The MUC commissions' chairs and vice-chairs have become political spokespersons on subjects within their respective fields of jurisdiction. This was one aspect of the 1982 reform that can be considered a success.

REGIONAL PLANNING IN THE MONTREAL AREA

As in many other metropolitan areas, Montreal underwent rapid development in the 1950s and 1960s. Downtown development boomed, with Place Ville-Marie as its new center. Expo '67 was the occasion for major public investments, particularly in transportation. New airports, highways and bridges or tunnels were built or planned to link the island of Montreal with the rest of the world. An innovative subway system was opened just a few months before the World Exhibition's opening day. Federal housing policies stimulated urban development, while highways opened up new territory for development. However, urban planners were critical about the lack of direction given to these new developments. As early as 1966 a city of Montreal planning study noted that dispersion and discontinuity resulted from these massive investments; vast amounts of farm lands had been abandoned due to land speculation (Gaudreau 1988).

This boom period did not last long after Expo '67. The economic deterioration of Montreal became apparent in the 1970s. Part of it was due to the generalized financial crisis throughout the industrial world; part of it was more specifically related to economic restructuring in North America and in Canada; and part of it resulted from a redefinition of Montreal's role in Canada and in Quebec (Martin 1979). In any case, Montreal's industrial structure was decaying; many important activities were moving west, leaving behind vast stretches of derelict industrial land. Housing in Montreal was also very old and needed special attention. In short, the region desperately needed new strategies for redevelopment.

After the recession of the early 1980s, the rhythm of redevelopment started to accelerate. But growth was territorially selective: Montreal's downtown, the West Island, Laval, and the South Shore have known rapid and intense development; but the old industrial areas south and east of Montreal are still dragging behind. Planning strategies needed to be designed not only to stimulate but also to channel new development in order not to amplify problems in the inner industrial and residential fringe. At the same time, environmental consciousness became more acute and demanded more policies to reduce pollution, to clean up old areas, and to preserve the last green oases on the island of Montreal.

Except for the city, individual municipalities were generally unable or unwilling to control these different stages of development from a broad regional perspective. Many were rapidly transforming themselves from old rural settlements into new urban suburbs. Both the federal and Quebec governments had difficulty understanding regional issues because they were physically distant from Montreal. Further, the provincial government, which should have provided municipalities with better tools for land-use planning, was too busy in the 1960s and '70s modernizing its own structure. Before it could deal with Montreal metropolitan development, it had to go through different phases of planning experimentation.

Horizon 2000: First Attempts at Regional Planning

The first studies on regional planning in the Montreal area came from the city's planning department. In 1967, it prepared an impressive audio-visual presentation on urban development in the Montreal region called *Horizon 2000*. The document presented an image of what the region might look in the year 2000, assuming adequate planning and management. It was the first attempt at contemplating a vast metropolitan region that would contain seven million people by the year 2000. It suggested an urban structure with subregional satellites and related infrastructures, linked with a complete transportation system. It also provided for a balanced distribution of urban functions, farm lands, and recreation sites (Marsan 1974, 333). Although intellectually very stimulating, *Horizon 2000* did not (and probably was not intended to) have immediate practical effects. It was more of a plea in favor of public planning and coordination. It showed that Montreal had visions for the future, and it provided ammunition to Mayor Drapeau for the pursuit of his metropolitan ambitions. As was the case for many other structure plans prepared in those days, growth predictions were far too optimistic; therefore, many of the proposed investments were quite unrealistic.

First Planning Efforts in MUC

The MUC's initial planning powers were limited. Its plan was not meant to have real binding effect on local municipalities. More important still, because it was restricted to the islands of Montreal and Bizard, it could not deal with many real regional issues. Therefore, on the one hand, the MUC could only deal with intermunicipal matters but not regional nor local matters; on the other hand, main transportation infrastructures such as bridges, highways, and the first subway lines had already been decided upon, if not already built.

Planning issues as presented in the first planning documents in 1972 and 1973 concerned the preservation of the few natural areas (wooded areas and river banks) left on MUC territory; controlling development in fringe areas where farming was still active; reorganizing land use or eliminating land-use conflicts in some areas (industrial relocation, pollution); strengthening public transportation systems (main intermunicipal roads, subway extensions, and commuting services); and creating two subcenters for mixed office and commercial development east and west along the Metropolitan Highway (Highway 40). Consensus on many of these issues was hard to reach, especially concerning the subcenters and any other proposal that involved a limitation on local development (Sancton 1985). Many suburbs also saw the planning documents as simply another means of imposing on them Montreal's infrastructures and costs (Ducas 1987, 84).

As time went by, many committees examined the planning proposals and their financial implications (Ducas 1987), but on the eve of the 1982 MUC reform, they had still not been adopted. Indeed, they probably never would have been had the provincial government not forced it.

Quebec's Involvement in Regional Planning in Montreal

Quebec's involvement was eventually much more than forcing the adoption of the MUC development plan. Yet, during the first stages of the Quiet Revolution, in terms of land-use planning, the Montreal region was not considered much differently than other parts of the province. True, a regional branch of the OPDQ had been set up in the early 1970s, which prepared many studies on the Montreal region, but it had no operational authority within the government nor over the municipalities; its studies nevertheless substantiated many of the prevailing regional problems and thus helped to raise the level of consciousness on these matters (Québec, OPDQ 1977). The election in 1976 of the *Parti Québécois*, many of whose members were influential and knowledgeable Montrealers, triggered at the provincial level real concern over planning and development issues in the Montreal region. Indeed, the *Parti Québécois* was particularly strong in eastern Montreal; it had, in contrast with previous governments in Quebec, a strong urban base.

The "Preferable Option for the Montreal Region"

As soon as it took power, the *Parti Québécois* cabinet decided to re-examine all of the government's financial investments in the region and to shape them into a comprehensive strategy; this was presented in 1978 as the "Preferable Development Option for the Montreal Region" (*Option Préférable D'Aménagement*). It stated that the future goals were the: "Consolidation of the urban tissue inside the present urbanized perimeter and accelerated redevelopment of the Montreal Island in terms of quality of life" (author's translation from Quebec, 1984). These general goals were in accord with the growing awareness concerning the economic slowdown and the decaying central area. They implied a limitation on infrastructure expenses outside the already urbanized area, including a moratorium on new highways, bridges, and water-supply systems. Instead, emphasis was put on investment within the urbanized area in public transit, environmental infrastructures such as water-treatment and waste-management systems, and infill housing. Other goals involved protecting farm land in fringe areas and preserving regional open spaces.

Specific policies were subsequently adopted in accordance with these goals. The province concluded an agreement with the MUC to take over all capital investments related to the subway extension and to establish a special committee to study public transit in the metropolitan area (COTREM, *Comité des Transports dans la Région de Montréal*). In 1979 this committee recommended an integrated transportation plan that emphasized public transit. The government renegotiated financial arrangements with the MUC regarding its sewage-treatment program, while at the same time deciding to launch a $6-billion program for water quality throughout the province. It also adopted a strong piece of legislation, the Agricultural Land Preservation Act of 1978, to control urban sprawl and to protect the farming industry. New housing programs were created, including one aimed at restoration. The Ministry of Cultural Affairs took action concerning heritage preservation and improvement in the Old Montreal area. The province also contributed some money to help municipalities within the urbanized area develop better industrial parks and traditional commercial districts. An important and innovative project was also designed to deal with water management in an integrated manner for the entire Montreal archipelago, including protecting flood areas, building dams, and developing recreation areas.

In 1983 the government reassessed the option and amended some of the details. The aim was to assist the MUC and the RCMs in the region in the preparation of their development plans in accordance with the 1979 Land Use Planning and Development Act (Québec 1984).

Regional Planning and the Land Use Planning and Development Act

The option was meant to help coordinate government investments and policies. It was not directly addressed to local and regional municipalities nor to the MUC. According to the 1979 Land Use Planning and Development Act, each such regional body had seven years to adopt its own development plan. At the beginning of that period, the act provided that the government was to send each of the 95 RCMs and the urban communities an individual statement concerning its intentions within the relevant area (s. 11). This document was not formally binding on the regional bodies, but development plans were required to identify government infrastructures and projects. The government retained authority to review the plans and hence could ultimately ensure that its projects were included, but only after lengthy negotiations (ss. 16, 27).

The Option and the MUC's Development Plan

The 1982 MUC reform included a redefinition of the community's planning powers so as to make them consistent with the provisions of the Planning Act of 1979. This meant that the content of the plan would have to be slightly different: it would describe an urbanization perimeter; it would identify areas of special interest and areas of restricted development for reasons of public safety, such as flood zones; it would also include provincial government projects (Land Use Planning and Development Act 1979, as amended in 1982, ss. 5 and 264.1). Once the plan was adopted, municipalities would be compelled to adopt local plans and by-laws consistent with its objectives (s. 33). The plan therefore was to become more significant than under previous MUC legislation.

There was no contradiction between the option and the MUC's general positions. On the contrary, the option was a commitment in favor of reinforcing development within the MUC. Moreover, the option involved financial arrangements that relieved municipalities from much of the capital investments foreseen in the plan (e.g., transit and water treatment). In effect, the option, together with the new version of the plan, was a recognition of a new distribution of responsibilities between the province and the municipalities. As one MUC committee put it, it was now a government responsibility "to channel urban development trends and to prefer a certain urban form at the level of the Montreal Metropolitan Area" (author's translation), while the MUC plan would define main urban infrastructures, and local municipalities would be solely responsible for land-use policies within their territory (CUM 1978). This left little for the MUC. The development plan was adopted in 1986 but raised little public debate.

Understandably, critics have said that the MUC's plan was nothing more than a recognition of the present land-use patterns; that it had no vision, presented no discussion, no alternative; that it did not relate issues to socio-economic trends; that it did not discuss Montreal's role in Quebec and in Canada; that it was too vague and presented very little operational instrumentation (Gaudreau and Veltman 1986; Divay and Collin 1977; Ducas 1987). Important issues concerning housing, industrial redevelopment, and open space were considered in general terms, with few specific recommended actions, and were left mainly to local municipalities.

The only serious issue that did cause debate was the recognition of three subcenters in the suburban municipalities of Anjou, Pointe Claire, and St. Laurent, (i.e., east, west, and north of Montreal). In the days of Montreal's *Horizon 2000*, such proposals aiming at creating a stronger urban network had already been worked out in terms of subregional satellites some 30 miles from the island of Montreal. The recognition of subcenters on the island itself was a different story. In Toronto, such subcenters were used to deconcentrate development from an overcrowded downtown. But that was not really a problem in Montreal. In the 1970s, when subcenters were first proposed by MUC planners, development and demographic forecasts were much more optimistic than in the 1980s. By the time the 1981 recession had struck, the city of Montreal was fiercely against such subcenters on the grounds that they might create undesirable competition for Montreal's already threatened central area. The final proposal softened the concept by establishing a clear hierarchy between Montreal's downtown and the subcenters (Gaudreau 1990). Indeed, the recognition of subcenters was merely an acknowledgement of ongoing trends and perhaps an effort to counter the tendency toward strip development along major highways. Nevertheless, the mere mention of the subcenters within the plan can be seen as a compromise by the city of Montreal.

The Option and the Regional County Municipalities' Development Plans

Detailed assessments of the RCMs' development plans are still to come. They have been adopted only recently, mainly in 1988 and 1989. Nevertheless, a recent analysis of the consideration given to the goals of Montreal Preferable Option by the government's statement of intentions for each RCM in the metropolitan area (Land Use Planning and Development Act, s. 16) is quite revealing (Barcelo *et al.* 1990). The general conclusion was that the option was considered more loosely as time passed, as if it had been forgotten or deliberately relaxed. The study also observed that, within the metropolitan area's 13 RCMs, the government's statements were more vague and less compelling in the peripheral RCMs than in Laval and MUC (which were also the first to receive such statements). Thus, although the government had a real opportunity to question the urbanization perimeters adopted by the RCMs and to suggest a stronger control of urban sprawl, it appears to have assumed its responsibility very lightly.

The *Option Préférable* in Question

Many of the individual programs comprising the option were weakened as time went on (see Barcelo *et al.* 1990). Important projects for cultural and arts buildings, such as a museum of science and technology in the central area, were abandoned. So were special programs concerning the renewal of old industrial infrastructures. Only very limited funds were made available to support the redevelopment of heritage areas outside Old Montreal.

The option's rather informal status probably affected its effectiveness (see Barcelo *et al.*). Indeed, part of the difficulty with the policy resided in the fact that the cabinet approved it without provision for the coordination of its implementation and without assigning any staff to monitor it. Moreover, the option was not publicly debated nor negotiated with local and regional leaders. When the new Liberal government came into power in 1985, few cabinet ministers knew anything about the option and fewer still felt bound by it. This government was well known to be closer than its predecessor to business interests and to favor such neoconservative policies as deregulation and privatization. In these circumstances, the option seemed seriously threatened.

In 1987-88 the government decided to dismantle its own Montreal administrative region and hence the Montreal regional branch of the Office de Planification et de Développement du Québec. Instead of one administrative region, there are now five: one for the South Shore, one for Laval, two for the North Shore (Laurentides and Lanaudière), and one corresponding to the territory of the MUC. The only provincial government institution that for many years had been seriously analyzing regional problems was now confined to the Montreal and Bizard Islands. Its new mission involved taking an active part in specific studies concerning redevelopment of old industrial areas in the central part of Montreal, but its role in developing an overall regional strategy was over.

By the end of the eighties, three issues involving the option have caused considerable debate. The first one was the presentation of a new transportation plan for the Montreal area by the Quebec Minister of Transportation (Quebec 1988). This plan proposed an emphasis on new highways outside the MUC. Montreal and other municipalities on the island pointed out that such a plan seemed contrary to the option. They felt that the government was giving in to the outer suburbs' requests for more highways. The issue was linked to the problem of allocating public-transit deficits between Montrealers and north and south suburbanites. After much debate, the MUC, Laval, and the south-shore municipalities reached an agreement containing the following provisions: (1) the outer suburbs will share MUC's annual public-transit deficit on the condition that MUC municipalities raise their financial commitment as well; (2) there will be a regional coordinating structure among the transit corporations for the MUC, Laval, and the South Shore; and (3) the subway system will be developed into Laval (*Le Devoir*, Sept. 22, 1989; *La Presse*, Oct. 14, 1989). As for more highways, many decisions are still pending.

The second issue concerned a changing of policies relating to the preservation of agricultural land. Originally, the legislation imposed stringent controls on property owners and local municipalities. Its implementation was entrusted to a commission having regulatory and quasi-judiciary powers. Under the Liberal government, the nomination of new commissioners, as well as some amendments to the legislation caused a general relaxation of the rules. The amendments allowed for a revision of the limits of the designated agricultural zones in the province following the coming into force of the RCMs development plans. But for a few exceptions, it appears that between 1985 and 1991, all RCMs submitted a request for the exclusion of a certain amount of lands from the agricultural zones.   Furthermore, the commission itself offered additional lands that it considered unfit for farming. The commission invoked four major reasons to allow these exclusions: (1) low bio-physical potential for agriculture; (2) lands already used for other activities; (3) isolated hard to reach areas making agricultural activity too difficult; (4) lands needed for urbanization according to RCMs develop-ment plans. In its final report on the whole operation (CPTAQ 1992), the commission stated that it was not its responsibility to question the opportunity of RCMs aims and land development policies. In every case, it tried to accommodate the expressed needs. Its only concern being the vitality of farming activities, it mainly debated the specific locations of projected land developments and the preservation of the lands best suited for agriculture. At the end of this process, the designated agricultural zones in the whole province were reduced by 206,247 ha or 3.2 percent of the 6,440,463 ha previously protected. The Montreal area, however, was by far the most affected area, with a loss of 73,698 ha (4.6 percent).

Thus, the commission's new direction, by concentrating its concerns on intensive farming, resulted in the handing over to regional municipali-ties of the regulation of urban fringe areas and of conflicts between urban development and farming. This meant not only that farm activity would not be as strongly supported near urban areas, but that urban sprawl might start anew. Considering that this change of policy occurred after the adoption of RCMs development plans, very few RCMs were really prepared to tackle this issue. Specially in the Montreal region, many leaders, planners, and environmentalists expressed serious worries that this would only increase Montreal's downfall and asked for a general debate concerning urban sprawl and growth control.

The third event was a major reform of local fiscality adopted by the Québec Government in June 1991 (Québec Statutes 1991, Bill 145). The purpose of the reform was to redefine the share of public finances between all levels of government in the province so as to make the fiscal burden of the taxpayer more comparable to other Canadian provinces. Particularly, it purported to render local municipalities more accountable for local expenses previously assumed by the province, such as local police services (provided by the Sureté du Québec in rural areas), rural roads and public transit. This meant an estimated additional burden on municipal taxes throughout the province of Cdn $260 million annually. Montreal itself estimated the loss at Cdn $100 million for 1992. The city of Montreal was unable to avoid this new blow on public transit; it pleaded, however, considering its devastating economic problems, for a special status as Quebec's metropolis and as a central city providing special services to the region and the province. It requested that the government adopt a specific urban policy for the Montreal region and that a study commission be put up to examine publicly institutional responsibilities and fiscal resources in the region (La Presse, 14 juin 1991; Le Devoir, 6 juin 1991).

Towards New Regional Strategies?

Quebec's answer to these requests was twofold. In December 1991, a development strategy for Greater Montreal was released by the interministerial committee on development of greater Montreal. This strategy was designed to stimulate the restructuring of Montreal's economic base. It revolved around four axes: (1) high tech innovation, (2) modernization of the industrial structure, (3) human resources training, and (4) market expansion. However, the document recognized a real problem of coordination among regional institutions and municipalities. Therefore, the minister of municipal affairs announced his intention to tackle this specific problem. A study group on Montreal and its region was formed on April 2, 1992, to study the exercise of municipal functions in the region, and to propose a vision for the future followed by recommendations on institutions and public services, fiscality, land-use planning, environment, economic, social and cultural development, and transportation. The study group was given one year to issue its report, starting early summer 1992. The two groups cover the same territory, which comprises the Census Metropolitan Area (102 municipalities) plus a few other municipalities to include entire regional municipalities; the total amounts to 137 local municipalities, 13 regional municipalities and one urban community.

PARKS AND OPEN SPACE IN THE MONTREAL METROPOLITAN AREA

Metropolitan Parks and Open Space in the MUC from 1970 to 1979

When it was created in 1970, the MUC was empowered to take over existing parks of intermunicipal character and to create new intermunicipal parks (MUC Act 1969, ss. 190-91). However, it took some 10 years before any such MUC parks were established. These 10 years have been marked by extreme caution on the part of local politicians combined with rising citizens' expectations regarding open space and the environment. Eventually the Quebec government played a key role as facilitator for new parks and provided some much-needed financial support.

Planning Proposals and Municipal Reluctance

In 1972, preliminary drafts of MUC planning documents proposed designating four of the city's most important parks as metropolitan parks: Mount Royal, Maisonneuve (the eventual Olympic site), the Expo '67 site, and Angrignon. They also suggested the creation of four new parks: Rivière-des Prairies (east end), Bois-de-Liesse, Anse-à-l'Orme, and Cap-St-Jacques (west end). The planning documents also considered other lands under private property, such as golf courses, the Morgan Arboretum (McGill University), and other public property, such as the Lachine Canal (federal government). Some thought was also given to establishing green links between the parks, to designating lakeshore and riverside drives, and to protecting endangered woodlands. These elements would constitute the basis of an open-space system that is still under debate.

Designation of the Montreal parks as intermunicipal was the first proposal to be dropped. Other municipalities were unwilling to contribute to Montreal's maintenance costs, while Montreal resisted placing its most prestigious parks under other municipalities' supervision. Proposals to create new metropolitan parks, even though they seemed quite desirable, were met with much reserve by MUC politicians who thought purchasing costs would be too high. A committee set up to study the financial implications of the Draft Development Plan concluded in 1975 that the MUC needed provincial financial assistance in order to develop new metropolitan parks (CUM 1975). Here again, we see that the traditional tensions among municipalities, their unfamiliarity with planning tools, and their unwillingness to enter into capital investments all contributed to preventing MUC action.

Citizens' Pressures

In the early 1970s, citizens' groups were formed to preserve open space in the region. They formed a coalition that presented briefs urging the MUC to implement its proposals on open space and to create a parks department (Regroupement . . . 1973). They suggested that a metropolitan parks department should also be responsible for many important recre-

Map 2.4. *Draft Proposal for Recreation and Open Space, MUC, 1972*

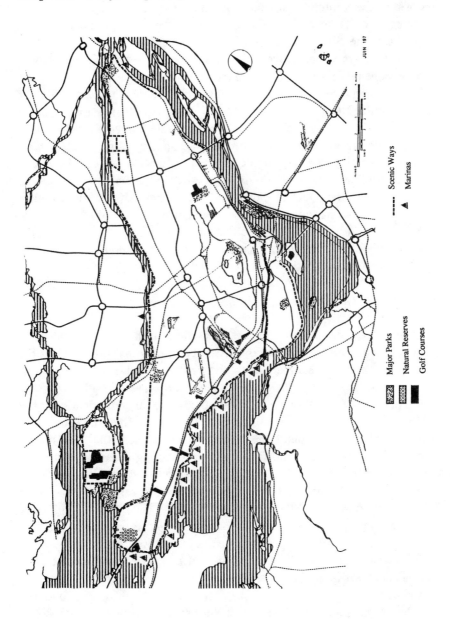

ation facilities such as the Botanical Garden, the Dow Planetarium, the Aquarium, and a future zoological garden, all then under city jurisdiction. Citizens' groups were more successful in preserving specific sites, particularly the Saraguay, Héritage, and Réparation woodlands. In the case of the first one, citizens became worried by a big residential development project in 1977 (Leblanc 1979). They gathered around the *Société d'horticulture et d'écologie du Nord de Montréal* and the *Société d'animation du Jardin et de l'Institut Botanique*. Their main argument was that the Saraguay woodland had been studied since the 1940s as a model of the primitive Montreal forest based on maple and hickory trees; for that reason, it had a very high ecological value (Domon and Bouchard 1981; Dansereau 1978). They finally convinced Montreal's executive committee and the Quebec Minister of Cultural Affairs to designate Saraguay as a natural area according to the Quebec Cultural Property Act. The designation in 1979 had the effect of freezing any development that might impinge on the natural character of the site, thereby buying time for the negotiated acquisition of the woodlands.

Early Quebec Government Commitments

The same year that Saraguay was designated as a natural area, another Quebec minister showed sensitivity to citizens' pressures in the island's east end: the Minister of the Environment, who also represented the area in the Legislative Assembly, Marcel Léger, acquired the Héritage and Réparation woodlands so as to turn them into an ecological center (a rather new concept for the Ministry of the Environment). Then, after having been shown around the Saraguay woodlands, the Minister of Municipal Affairs, Guy Tardif, himself representing a nearby district in the north part of Montreal Island, decided also to get involved. He first found some $10.5 million to help the MUC start to buy lands for parks. Then he sat down with MUC's new chair, Pierre DesMarais II, a former suburban mayor, to work out solutions for the other problems. After a few months, an agreement was reached between both governments. The MUC Act was amended to allow new parks to be created more easily, without necessarily taking over existing parks of metropolitan interest. Consequently, the main cause of tension between Montreal and the suburbs on this issue was eliminated. Sites recently protected by Quebec ministers were transferred to the MUC to become metropolitan parks and a new park, Ile-de-la-Visitation, was added.

The new MUC parks (see Map 2.5) comprised: Cap-St- Jacques, Anse-à-l'Orme, Bois-de-Liesse, Bois-de-Saraguay, Ile-de-la-Visitation, Rivière-des-Prairies, and Bois-de-l'Héritage et de-la-Réparation. Capital costs for the MUC were $31.5 million (Ducas 1987). Some analysts have observed that, even with these new parks, the total area (940 hectares) thus preserved and eventually purchased was still lower in 1984 than the initial 1974 proposals of 1,134 hectares (Ducas 1987; Marsan 1983). The area effectively covered by the parks of Rivière-des-Prairies, Bois-de-Liesse, and Anse-à-l'Orme lost respectively 43, 46, and 70 percent of intended area coverage; indeed, the latter was merely a shadow of its original concept. These losses indicate not just that the land turned out to be expensive to acquire but also that MUC leaders were not entirely committed to the project.

A Growing Regional Parks System for Metropolitan Montreal

While the MUC was slowly moving forward, other governments were much more active concerning urban and regional recreation around Montreal. Both the federal and the provincial governments created new parks and open space specifically for the enjoyment of a mainly urban population.

Federally Owned Open Space in the Montreal Area

The federal government got involved in open-space creation through its activities in transportation. The opening in 1959 of the St. Lawrence Seaway caused the closing of the old Lachine Canal. Transport Canada decided to transform its banks into a cycling path, thus cleaning up portions of the derelict industrial lands along the canal. Funding was also made available to adjoining municipalities for the creation of additional open space: Montreal and Lachine acted accordingly. Other obsolete canals and locks in the area were adapted for leisure boats and tourism; facilities and open space were made available alongside. The St. Lawrence Seaway dike was also opened to the public as a cycling path.

The federal government also purchased a number of islands in the St. Lawrence River for bird sanctuaries, such as Iles-de-la-Paix and Tailhandier. While planning Mirabel Airport, the government expropriated vast areas, too much as it eventually turned out, for much of it was eventually sold back to the farmers. Some woodlands in the area were preserved for recreation, notably the Bois-de-Belle-Rivière. Finally, the

Map 2.5.   *Montreal Urban Community: Regional Parks in 1987*

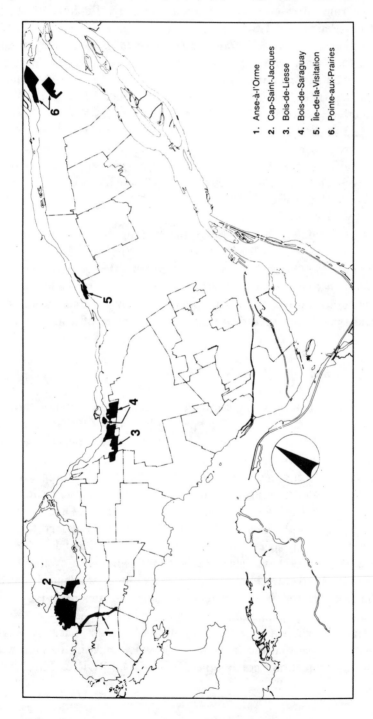

1. Anse-à-l'Orme
2. Cap-Saint-Jacques
3. Bois-de-Liesse
4. Bois-de-Saraguay
5. Île-de-la-Visitation
6. Pointe-aux-Prairies

federal government started to reclaim unused port lands in the central area for recreation or redevelopment. Although some work, such as demolition of old grain elevators, had been done in the 1970s, most of the new developments came much later (Canada, Comité consultatif du Vieux-Port 1985).

Provincial Parks and Open Space in the Montreal Region

While the MUC was quite uncertain about how to deal with parks and open space, many ministries in Quebec became very interested in this region. Apart from the government's involvement in MUC parks as already mentioned, the Ministry of the Environment purchased Ste-Thérèse Island in the St. Lawrence River to be used for environmental education and recreation. The Ministry of Cultural Affairs designated many cultural properties plus two historical areas in Old Montreal and the small town of Laprairie; it also developed a heritage park in Pointe-du-Moulin on Ile Perrot. Finally, the Ministry of Recreation Hunting and Fishing, and Leisure developed a new generation of parks during the 1970s, including six in the Montreal region (see Map 2.6). Many of these parks and open spaces were established as a result of public pressure for the preservation of significant ecosystems, such as hills in the Montreal plain and islands in the St. Lawrence River. By the end of the 1970s, the ministry was preparing a general policy on leisure and another one on parks.

Great Visions But Still More Hesitations

The Archipelago Project

While it was redefining its approach to the Montreal region with the *option préférable*, the Quebec government also launched other important special initiatives for the area, such as the committee on regional transportation. The Archipelago Project was probably the most ambitious of such initiatives. It aimed to develop an integrated approach towards water management in the Montreal region, by pulling together projects concerning hydraulic control, water regulation, and flood control; hydroelectric works; and recreation and conservation management along the river banks. An interministerial committee was created to bring together the relevant expertise; there was also important political supervision by the Quebec cabinet, consultation with local representatives, and public involvement through open meetings.

The technical and financial aspects were quite intricate. Indeed, the project rested on the idea that the Lachine Rapids would be harnessed for hydroelectric power, without endangering the exceptional wildlife in the area or altering its aesthetic value. About 20 scenarios were tested including rerouting water currents around the many islands of the archipelago and building dams accordingly. Impacts on navigation, wildlife, water levels and flooding, etc., were assessed. Thousands of dollars were spent in studies. The financial gains from the project and the changes on the flood zones would allow recovering lands for recreation. However, all this assumed a continuing energy crisis and the competitive capacity of hydroelectricity. By 1985, as energy prices had dropped, the harnessing of the Lachine Rapids became less feasible, and the whole project was abandoned. This ambitious project was not a total loss, however; it generated a considerable mass of important studies on the conditions of the St. Lawrence waters that can still be very useful for future action. Besides, more specific proposals survived on their own. One of the outcomes of the Archipelago Project was the suggestion to create an Archipelago National (Quebec) Park (Décarie 1987).

The Archipelago National Park Proposal

This proposal resulted from two main initiatives: one was the Archipelago Project; the other was the product of a committee established to develop a provincial policy on urban parks. Concerning the latter, an initial study was begun in 1978 to assess what the province was doing in this field, acknowledging that past actions had been quite uncoordinated. An interministerial committee, established in 1983, prepared a diagnosis and drafted a set of objectives, concepts, and potential modalities (Québec, Nov. 1983).

The proposed policy suggested a wider notion of open space, which would include not only parks, but also town squares and ecological reserves; not only green spaces, but also "blue" (for water) and "gray" (for urban areas) spaces. The policy proposed an integrated system of parks and open space linked by networks of paths and trails, or riverside activities. A kind of green thread was proposed to structure this system, starting from the top of Mount Royal, circling it once, then, as a spiral, making another bigger circle along old railways and eventually moving toward the rivers. This open-space system would be developed following

Map 2.6. *Proposal for a National Park in the Montreal Archipelago by the Quebec Government, 1984*

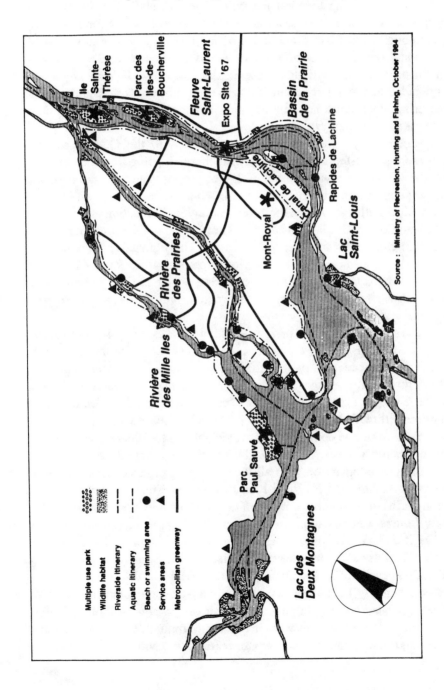

a collaborative approach, under the leadership of a committee or a mixed public corporation. It would count on the cooperation of all public property owners, linking together not only parks but also other institutional properties such as school and university grounds, hospitals and cemeteries, public utilities lands and land owned by other levels of government. Users and private recreation services would also be expected to cooperate in managing this complex system. In other words, the document contended that, without adding much to the public lands base and without requiring much additional funding, it would be possible to achieve a more integrated, flexible system.

When the proposed policy was presented to the Quebec cabinet, ministers suggested it be merged with the archipelago project so as to create a European-style national park. The proposed archipelago park was made public in October 1984 by the Quebec prime minister and four of his cabinet colleagues from the Montreal region. The anticipated cost was $150 million; half this sum to be offered by the province to municipalities participating in the Archipelago park. Unfortunately, the announcement was little more than an election promise by the *Parti Québécois*, which was justifiably worried about losing power in the 1985 elections; they needed to spend money in the region, and this appeared to be a sparkling way to do it.

The proposed national park was indeed quite exciting. It was centered on the "blue spaces" of the archipelago: rivers would be the main links between a collection of parks and open space along the shores. Different networks would be developed: a nautical network, a beach network, a wildlife habitat network, a network of riverside trails and paths, including the green thread developed in the proposed policy on urban parks. The networks would be completed by provincial and local parks, services and interpretation centers. Institutional arrangements were to be developed gradually in cooperation with all the concerned organizations.

The Archipelago National Park had a short life. The 1985 elections brought in a new government committed to reducing public spending. The new Bourassa team had promised to cut public spending, and one of the ways it did so was to terminate the archipelago studies. In April 1986 most of the professional team was dismantled. Some $20 million had already been spent in Montreal, Longueuil, and Laval.

Presumably, the proposed park would have been implemented had the *Parti Québécois* stayed in power. One can never know. Although Quebec politicians and technocrats were impatient to implement it, local organizations and municipalities had been exceptionally cautious throughout the entire process. The proposal was innovative and surprising. To have become a reality, however, it would have needed more time and the mobilization of much more local political support.

The MUC in the '80s: Towards an Open-Space System?

The MUC Development Plan and Open Space

Among the new tasks that were assigned to the MUC by the 1982 reform was the compulsory adoption of interim control during preparation of the development plan. Interim control measures were to last until adoption of local plans and recognition by the MUC of their conformity with its own development plan. Although the Planning Act was not precise about the purpose of these controls, there had been a pressure by the Ministry of Municipal Affairs on all the regional county municipalities to use them to control development in flood zones and other areas subject to high natural risks (Trépanier 1983). After significant damage from spring floods in 1974 and 1976, both the federal and the provincial governments had signed an agreement to map flood zones. In 1977, the province introduced into municipal legislation special powers to forbid development in such zones.

Much of the north shore of the island of Montreal was subject to floods as were many smaller islands in the Rivière des Prairies and the Rivière des Mille-Iles. The MUC adopted its interim control bylaw in September 1983 (MUC, bylaw 65). But the most controversial part of it was that it also included protective measures concerning 15 woodlands. If ecologists were applauding, developers were not, and local politicians were quite uneasy about such measures. They were not used to confronting developers, and many were not eager to lose development opportunities. During the three years that passed before the adoption of the development plan, the question facing municipalities was: who will buy these woodlands or river banks for the purpose of recreation or preservation? Very few answers were given. Neither local municipalities nor the MUC were willing or able to lead on this issue. They all turned once again for help from Quebec. Much was expected from the ongoing provincial studies about the archipelago.

When Quebec finally abandoned the archipelago plan, so did the MUC. Its development plan, as finally adopted in 1986, contained very little about open space. Of the 15 woodlands (770 hectares) identified in the interim control bylaw, eight were dropped; the seven others (550 hectares) would still be protected until adoption and approval of local plans, but no goal, no policy, no strategy was designed for them.

There was one real protective measure that was still in force, the Quebec Agricultural Land Preservation Act. Under that legislation, some 3,300 hectares on MUC territory had been preserved since 1979 from any development other than agricultural. This legislation had priority over any development plan according to the Planning Act. Therefore, the MUC could only acknowledge it. Practically, it was an easy way to wash its hands from that section of its territory on which were located four of the woodlands still under consideration.

Changes Resulting from 1986 Municipal Elections

In November 1986, after 26 years of power, Mayor Drapeau's Civic Party was replaced by a younger, more progressive party, the Montreal's Citizens Movement (MCM), headed by Jean Doré. Citizen activists and environmentalists formed part of the political base of the MCM. During the election campaign, the MCM promised to bring back the proposal of a "green thread" and to redevelop parks and open space in Montreal and the MUC. The new administration began by putting together a team of professionals to work on a plan for the Mount Royal (Montreal 1988), and another one on the Expo '67 site. Another assignment was given to the city planning department for the preparation of an open-space policy to be integrated with a new city master plan.

The MCM also brought change to the MUC. By 1987, most of the sites for the seven regional parks were still inaccessible to the general public. After MCM prodding, the MUC planning commission in December 1987 undertook a public consultation process on the "future of the regional parks." A document was prepared that summarized past actions, proposed more definite policies for the parks network, and explored the possibilities of new partnerships for preserving open space (CUM 1987). In so doing, it also referred to some of the archipelago proposals, notably the "green thread." According to the MUC document, 913 hectares of land had been acquired and preserved, involving provincial and local investments totalling $44 million. Only one park, Ile-de-la-Visitation, was totally developed. Work was partially completed in Rivière-des-Prairies, Bois-de-la-Réparation, and Cap-St. Jacques.

An impressive number of citizen groups responded to the invitation offered by the MUC planning commission. More than 50 briefs were presented. Although a few from municipalities expressed reluctance, the majority of the papers were in favor of the commission's proposals; many insisted on even more vigorous positions, particularly on expanding the open-space system through the purchasing and preserving of many more sites.

Following this important support, the planning commission was able to push through some important decisions. First, $8 million was put aside in June 1988 for the acquisition of new open space (to which another $6 million was added in 1989), and a list of priority sites was established. Further, a new assistant to the director of planning was hired with the specific mandate of preparing an open-space policy. He would also supervise the preparation of development plans for each regional park. In June 1989, three of these plans were adopted, concerning Cap-St. Jacques, Bois-de-Liesse, and Pointe-aux-Prairies (formerly Bois-de-l'Héritage-et-de-la-Réparation). The first draft of the open-space policy discussed at the planning commission in September 1989 (CUM 1989b); suggested that $500 million would be needed to preserve and develop the MUC's remaining open spaces. While this amount was seen as extravagant by many politicians, there was finally, after much debate, an agreement to allocate $200 million over the next 15 years. This was part of a strategic plan for open space adopted by the MUC in December 1989 (CUM 1989c). The plan involved acquisition of 500 hectares more than the 997 already acquired, including woodlands, river shores, and the development of the "green thread." The plan endorsed many of the original archipelago proposals. It went further by introducing the "greening the city" concept and suggesting the idea of green plans for local municipalities.

Protecting farm land also remained an important issue. Contrary to all expectations, a developer had obtained a "dezoning" of 456 hectares on Ile Bizard in August 1988 (*La Presse*, Aug. 6, 1988); this piece of land included an important woodland that citizens were very eager to have established as an MUC regional park. The MUC itself had just identified it as one of its priorities for acquisition. Because it was dezoned by the Agricultural Land Commission, its price went up so much that the MUC found it very difficult to buy it at a reasonable price. After intense negotiations with the developer and the municipality, an agreement was reached that would allow a mixed development including housing, a golf course, and the preservation as a park of a significant part of the woodland. Still, the price the MUC had to offer was very high. Other parcels of protected agricultural land were also threatened in the West Island. Some lands were acquired by MUC to become an agricultural demonstration park. Thus, by 1991, two new parks were added: Bois-de-l'île-Bizard and Parc agricole (see Map 2.7). Another park, Bois-de-Liesse, was consideringly enlarged. Other projects were still under negotiation.

Related to the issue of open space is the question of conformity of local plans with the MUC development plan. According to the Planning Act, local plans must be adopted before 1990. The MUC has the power to reject them if not in conformity with objectives of the development plan. Although these objectives are not very precise, the MUC does have certain instruments at its disposal to induce local municipalities to preserve open space. Furthermore, it can now appeal to its open-space strategic plan. Many municipalities are still reluctant to yield development opportunities, but there is a growing citizens' awareness that might inspire change even in the suburbs, particularly in the West Island.

CONCLUSION

One of the objects of this comparative research project is to determine if the existence of multipurpose metropolitan governments has had any significant effects on urban growth and the distribution of urban services. If so, are such effects likely to continue or are there indications that they are changing, that metropolitan governments are weakening or losing their redistributive capacity? Can they survive without strong support from provincial or state governments?

In dealing with these questions as they relate to Montreal, this paper has first asked if there is a metropolitan government in the Montreal area. The Montreal Urban Community started with many weaknesses. The political tension between the city of Montreal and the 28 much smaller suburbs inhibited MUC in many ways. As a result, MUC functions, except for police and transit, tended to be limited to noncontroversial, technical matters such as sewage collectors or air pollution control. At first, the MUC was little more than an administrative mechanism for delivering a few metropolitan services. The MUC council strongly supported local autonomy and evolved very much like a council of governments. Another reason to consider the MUC as a very mild form of metropolitan government is that its territory is small relative to the entire metropolitan area. The MUC boundaries were not administratively logical even at first, but they became even more obsolete as development accelerated in the outer metropolitan fringe. Expanding the MUC territory

Map 2.7. *Montreal Urban Community: Regional Parks in 1991*

1. Anse-à-l'Orme
2. Cap-Saint-Jacques
3. Bois-de-Liesse
4. Bois-de-Saraguay
5. Île-de-la-Visitation
6. Pointe-aux-Prairies
7. Parc agricole
8. Bois-de-l'Île-Bizard

would be politically difficult. Proposals to do so could be seen as threatening the provincial government itself.

The relative lack of growth within the MUC territory has at least caused the city and suburbs to recognize their common interests. The MUC has been a useful forum for the discussion of common concerns. The 1982 MUC reform promoted more meaningful discussion by ensuring that some local politicians would be seen as having at least some degree of responsibility for specific issues.

Has the MUC significantly dealt with problems related to urban development? Its powers in this regard have been limited. For one thing, most of the growth was occurring outside its territory. Inside its territory, the MUC did not take a leading role in controlling or directing the growth. Its development plan was more of a management plan for intermunicipal infrastructures. The development of the transit system has been a major achievement, but the provincial role in financing has become so important that the role of the MUC seems marginal at best. The regional parks system and the recent "green" strategy are perhaps indications that the MUC is starting to play a new, more constructive role in urban development.

The provincial role with respect to the MUC has been ambiguous. Although it created the MUC, the province has not always been a firm and reliable supporter. Its policies for the MUC have lacked consistency. Its promises have not always been kept; even announced provincial plans have not always been implemented. The provincial government was much influenced by general political considerations in the province as a whole. For example it could not ignore demands from the outer suburbs for provincial funding of improved infrastructure. Overall, provincial support for the MUC has softened in recent years. But this apparently changing position must be considered within the context of the province's general vulnerability in a fast-changing economic environment.

In the past 10 years, the Quebec government proposed a new deal for local governments, involving more autonomy and responsibility. This meant that the province would restrain itself from interfering with local responsibilities, providing local and regional governments took their share of the burden. Accordingly, the provincial role became more of a facilitator and less of a mandator. Similar decentralization trends are apparent in other countries. There are risks in such an approach but there is also much to be gained from increased local involvement. The case study of open space in the Montreal area has been presented as an illustration of this point.

Current issues in Montreal may require new approaches. Traditionally, Montreal was seen as a rich city. Things have slowly changed since World War II. People are just beginning to become aware that, while the outer suburbs are booming, the central area is in serious decline. Both the federal and the provincial government have set up study committees and promised important investments, but significant results are still to be seen. Local people are becoming impatient. Are we beginning to be like American cities? Perhaps we shall soon know.

REFERENCES

Agricultural Land Preservation Act, Quebec Statutes. 1978. c. 10.

Barcelo, Michel, François Charbonneau, et Pierre Hamel. 1990. *Option préférable d'aménagement et étalement urbain, 1978-1988, dans la région de Montréal*, Notes de recherche, Faculté de l'Aménagement, Université de Montréal.

Centre de Recherche Ecologiques de Montréal. 1984. *Evaluation de la valeur écologique de différents bois, ruisseaux et îles du territoire de la CUM*, Montréal.

Communauté Urbaine de Montréal. 1975. *Rapport de la Commission d'étude sur l'évaluation financière et des incidences économiques du schéma d'aménagement*, (Commission Lamarre), Montréal.

_____. 1978. *Rapport du sous-comité des objectifs du schéma d'aménagement*, coprésidé par Mm. Yvon Lamarre et Jean Corbeil, Montréal, Octobre 1978, 52.

_____. 1985. *Etude de l'impact des tendances démographiques actuelles*, mai 1985.

_____. 1986. Service de la planification du territoire, *Schéma d'aménagement*. In English: MUC Development Plan.

_____. 1987. Commission de l'aménagement, *Des parcs régionaux au réseau récréo-touristique*, Consultation sur la mise en valeur et l'avenir des parcs régionaux, Montréal.

_____. 1989a. Service de la planification du territoire. *Impacts des recommandations de l'étude sur l'avenir de la zone rurale dans le territoire de la Communauté urbaine de Montréal sur son schéma d'aménagement*, mai.

_____. 1989b. Service de planification du territoire. *Projet de politique sur les espaces verts*.

_____. 1989c. Service de planification du territoire. *La CUM . . . naturellement*, stratégie d'action pour les espaces naturels.

Conseil des Affaires Sociales. 1989. *Deux Québec dans un: rapport sur le développement social et démographique*, Gaëtan Morin, ed. et Gouvernement du Québec.

Cultural Property Act, Quebec Statutes. 1972. c. 19.

Dansereau, Pierre. 1978. *Un parc urbain dans la forêt de Saraguay*. SAJIB et SHENM.

Décarie, Jean. 1987. *L'archipel après Archipel*. Conférence Hydro-Québec / Faculté de l'Aménagement, Montréal.

Divay, Gérard et Jean-Pierre Collin. 1977. *La Communauté urbaine de Montréal: de la ville centrale à l'île centrale.* Montréal: INRS-Urbanisation, rapports de recherche no. 4.

_____, et Jacques Léveillée. 1981. *La réforme municipale et l'Etat québécois.* Montréal. INRS-Urbanisation, coll. Etudes et documents no. 27.

Domon, Gérald, et André Bouchard. 1981. *La végétation et l'aménagement du parc régional du Bois-de-Saraguay.* Montréal, Ville de Montréal, Jardin botanique.

Ducas, Sylvain. 1987. *La Communauté urbaine de Montréal, 1970-1986: structure métropolitaine et interventions en aménagement.* Mémoire de maîtrise, Institut d'urbanisme, Université de Montréal.

Gaudreau, Marcel. 1988. Considérations exploratoires sur les effets de l'expansion autoroutière et du dézonage agricole sur la forme de l'agglomération montréalaise, in *Actualité immobilière*, vol. 12, no. 3.

_____. 1990. Problématique et enjeux d'une planification intégrée de l'espace métropolitain montréalais, in Richard Morin et al., *Gestion locale et problématiques urbaines au tournant des années 1990.* Montréal, Université du Québec à Montréal, Etudes urbaines.

_____, et Calvin Veltman. 1986. *Le schéma de la CUM, 1970-1982: la difficile recherche d'une rationalité métropolitaine en aménagement.* Montréal: INRS-Urbanisation.

Gouvernement du Canada, Comité consultatif du Vieux-Port de Montréal. 1985. Document d'information et de synthèse pour la consultation publique.

_____. 1986. Comité consultatif au comité ministériel sur le développement de Montréal (Rapport Picard), *Rapport*, novembre 1986.

Gouvernement du Québec, Comité ministériel permanent de développement du Grand Montréal. 1991. *Pour un redressement durable. Plan stratégique du Grand Montréal*, 72p.

_____, Commission de protection du territoire agricole du Québec. 1992. *Révision de la zone agricole. Bilan final.*

_____, Commission provinciale d'urbanisme. 1968. *Rapport.*

_____. Groupe de travail sur l'urbanisation. 1976. *Rapport.*

_____. OPDQ. 1977. *Esquisse de la Région de Montréal.* Evolution et orientation du développement et de l'aménagement.

_____, Ministère des Affaires municipales. 1981. *Une nouvelle communauté. La réforme de la Communauté urbaine de Montréal.* Document explicatif.

_____, François Gendron. 1983. *Le choix des régions*, document de consultation sur le développement des régions.

_____. 1983. *Projet de politique des parcs en milieu urbain pour la région de Montréal.* Rapport principal du comité interministériel, 24 novembre.

_____. 1984. *Option d'aménagement de la région métropolitaine de Montréal.*

_____, Ministère du Loisir, de la Chasse et de la Pêche. 1984. Service *Archipel. Rapport principal*, octobre.

_____, Ministère des Affaires municipales. 1988. *Répertoire des municipalités.*

_____, Ministère des Transports. 1988. *Le transport dans la région de Montréal. Plan d'action: 1988-1998.*

_____. OPDQ. 1988. *Région de Montréal. Bilan socio-économique 1987.*

Higgins, Benjamin. 1986. *The Rise and Fall of Montreal.* The Canadian Institute for Research on Regional Development, Moncton.

_____, F. Martin, A. Raynauld. 1970. *Les orientations du développement économique régional dans la Province de Québec.* Ottawa. Ministère de l'Expansion économique régionale.

Lacharité, Luc. 1990. Montréal, un cas unique, in Richard Morin et al., *Gestion locale et problématiques urbaines au tournant des années 1990.* Montréal Université du Québec à Montréal, Etudes urbaines.

Lamonde, Pierre. 1988. *La transformation de l'économie montréalaise, 1971-1986.* Montréal: INRS-Urbanisation.

_____. 1989. *Développement urbain et stratégie de transport pour Montréal—Horizon 2001.* Etude effectuée pour le Comité technique du transport de la Ville de Montréal, INRS-Urbanisation.

Land Use Planning and Development Act, Quebec Statutes. 1979. c. 51.

Leblanc, Rodrigue. 1979. La Forêt de Saraguay, un parc naturel urbain, in *La foresterie urbaine*, comptes-rendus du symposium international sur la foresterie urbaine, Université Laval, mai.

Lemelin, André, et Richard Morin. 1989. *Le développement économique local et communautaire: éléments d'analyse et pistes de réflexion pour une stratégie municipale*, INRS-Urbanisation.

Léveillée, Jacques. 1978. *Développement urbain et politiques gouvernementales urbaines dans l'agglomération montréalaise, 1945-1975.* Collection Etudes en science politique, Société canadienne de science politique, Montréal.

_____. 1980. Les institutions politiques et administratives des communautés urbaines du Québec: une illustration, la Communauté urbaine de Montréal, in *Le système politique de Montréal*, recueil de textes sous la direction de Guy Bourassa et Jacques Léveillée, Cahiers de l'ACFAS, no 43, 1986.

_____. 1982. *L'aménagement du territoire au Québec, du rêve au compromis*. Montréal: Nouvelle Optique.

_____, et Marie-Odile Trépanier. 1982. Evolution de la législation relative à l'espace urbain, in *Droit et société urbaine au Québec*. Montréal, Université de Montréal, Centre de recherche en droit public.

Loisir-Ville. 1986. *Les espaces verts et la Communauté urbaine de Montréal, 1972-1985*, Montréal, janvier 1986.

Marsan, Jean-Claude. 1974. *Montréal en évolution*. Montréal: FIDES.

_____. 1983. *Montréal, une esquisse du futur*. Montréal: IQRC

Martin, Fernand. 1979. Montréal: les forces économiques en jeu, in Guy Bourassa et Jacques Léveillée, *Le système politique de Montréal*. Montréal: Cahiers de l'ACFAS no. 43, 1986.

Montreal Urban Community Act, Quebec Statutes. 1969. c. 84.

Montreal Urban Community. 1986. Development Plan.

_____, by-law 65, Bylaw respecting interim control of development of the territory of the Montreal Urban Community, adopted on September 21, 1983.

Regroupement pour la Préservation des Espaces Verts. 1973. *Mémoire sur les propositions pour l'aménagement du territoire de la Communauté urbaine de Montréal.*

Sancton, Andrew. 1985. *Governing the Island of Montreal, Languages Differences and Metropolitan Politics*. Berkeley: University of California Press.

Trépanier, Marie-Odile. 1975. Réflexions sur les aspects politico-administratifs des communautés urbaines au Québec, in G. Lord, A. Tremblay, M.-O. Trépanier, *Les communautés urbaines de Montréal et de Québec, premier bilan*. Montréal: Presses de l'Université de Montréal.

_____. 1982. Formes traditionnelles et réforme récente du droit de l'urbanisme au Québec: changement de fond ou changements de formes? in Leveillee, Jacques. *L'aménagement du territoire au Québec, du rêve au compromis*. Montréal: Nouvelle Optique.

_____. 1983. Le contrôle intérimaire dans le cadre de la Loi sur l'aménagement et l'urbanisme: essai d'analyse stratégique, in *Actualité immobilière*, vol. 7 no. 3.

_____. 1988. Local Government Reorganization in Quebec, in Hilda Symonds and H. Peter Oberlander, ed., *Meech Lake: from Center to Periphery.* Vancouver: Centre for Human Settlements, University of British Columbia.

Ville de Montréal et Groupe d'Intervention Urbaine de Montréal. 1988. *La Montagne en question,* 2 volumes.

Ville de Montréal. 1988. *Orientations préliminaires pour la mise en valeur du Mont Royal,* document de concertation, novembre.

_____. 1990. *Partenaires dans le développement économique des quartiers.*

Chapter 3

Planning and Development Decision Making in the Chicago Region

George C. Hemmens
Janet McBride
University of Illinois at Chicago

THE CHICAGO REGION

In 1990 the Chicago metropolitan region was home to 7,261,176 people according to census bureau estimates. They lived in six counties arranged in a semicircle around Chicago on the shore of Lake Michigan in the northeastern corner of Illinois. The region is bounded, somewhat artificially, by the Indiana state line on the east and the Wisconsin state line on the north. The western and southern boundaries lie in the rich agricultural lands of the midwestern heartland (see Map 3.1).

Changes in the region during the 1980s may significantly affect its future and change the policy debate on metropolitan development. Much to the surprise of and disputed by Chicago officials, the 1990 Census showed a continued decline in the city's population. The traditional base of the Chicago economy, manufacturing employment, also continued to decline. However, Chicago experienced considerable growth in employment in the services. This growth was accompanied by a large downtown office building boom and considerable gentrification of some older neighborhoods. Overall, suburban areas continued to grow at a rapid rate with increased employment in both manufacturing and services, but there were major differences in growth between suburban communities. Serious traffic problems and the construction of high rise office buildings demonstrated a qualitative as well as quantitative change in development in the suburbs.

In retrospect the 1980s may be seen as the decade when the region turned the corner in the transition from its traditional economy to a not

Map 3.1.   *Municipalities in the Chicago Metropolitan Region*

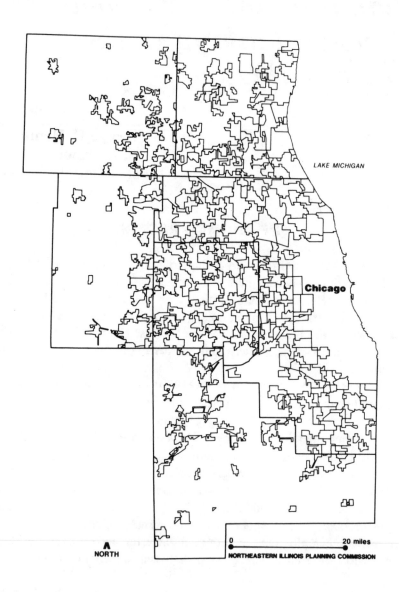

yet fully defined service economy, and from a traditional single-centered region to a multicentered development pattern with accompanying changes in public policy issues and leadership influence. Also during the 1980s Chicago went through major political struggles, electing a reform mayor and the first black mayor. Chicago endured another political corruption scandal, "Operation Greylord" in the judiciary. The traditional political split between the Democratic city and the Republican "collar" counties continued. And the region continued to be one of the most densely governed in the United States with over 1,250 local governments.

To set the context for discussion of regional planning and public infrastructure decisions in the Chicago region we will briefly review the changing and projected population and economic structure of the region and its governance structure.

Population

The Chicago region's population is expected to grow moderately over the 30-year period from 1980 to 2010 to a total of 8.18 million (NIPC 1988a). This is an additional 1 million people and a growth rate of about 15 percent for the period. By comparison, the region grew twice as much during the previous 30 years adding 2 million people. The city of Chicago is expected to grow slowly, adding 150,000 people by 2010. So the city's share of regional population will continue to decline from the 1980 ratio of 42 percent to 39 percent in 2010. The suburbs are expected to grow at a rate of about 23 percent (see Table 3.1).

From a development and planning perspective the changes in structure of the population are as important as the changes in size. For example, demographers expect the average household size in the Chicago region to decline to 2.5 by 2010. This means that the 1 million population growth in the region will be accompanied by almost 728,000 additional households. Chicago is expected to add about 173,000 households (16 percent growth), and the remainder, over a half million (40 percent growth), will be located in the suburbs. At the same time the population age profile will change to reflect the aging of the present population. There will be 130,000 fewer school age (under 20) persons, 250,000 fewer young workers (20-34) and 342,000 more persons over 65 in 2010 than there were in 1980. Almost two-thirds of the elderly will be over 75.

The racial composition of Chicago is changing with population growth. The reported white and black population of the city each de-

Table 3.1. *Chicago Area Population*

	1970	1980	1986	2010	1990*
Chicago	3,369,357	3,005,072	3,009,530	3,155,000	2,783,726
Cook County (except Chicago)	2,124,409	2,248,594	2,288,380	2,350,000	2,321,341
DuPage County	487,966	658,835	727,700	971,000	781,666
Kane County	251,005	278,405	300,800	434,000	317,471
Lake County	382,638	440,372	480,200	599,000	516,418
McHenry County	111,555	147,897	162,400	222,000	183,241
Will County	247,825	324,460	338,400	450,000	357,313
Northeastern Illinois	6,974,755	7,103,624	7,307,400	8,181,000	7,261,176

Source: Northeastern Illinois Regional Planning Commission, 1988.
*U.S. Census, 1991.

clined about one percent during the 1980s to 45 and 39 percent respectively. However, the population of Hispanic origin was 20 percent of the city total compared to 14 percent in 1980 when the census counted Hispanics differently. Whites and blacks, not of Hispanic origin, each accounted for about 38 percent of the city population in 1990, with blacks slightly outnumbering whites. The reported white population of the Chicago area suburbs was 86 percent in 1990, down from 90 percent in 1980. Persons of Hispanic origin accounted for 6.5 percent of the suburban population, while, blacks, not of Hispanic origin, are less than one percent of the suburban population.

Suburban population growth is expected to be distributed unevenly. Sixty-one communities are expected to lose population. These are older suburbs adjacent to Chicago and are fully built up. Major growth is expected to be concentrated northwest and west of Chicago as it has been in the past decade. However, not only outlying suburban communities will benefit from the new growth. Older satellite cities, Elgin and Aurora, that had been manufacturing centers but have experienced significant declines in recent decades will become major growth centers anchoring the western end of development corridors (see Map 3.1).

Regional Economy

The Chicago area regional economy is expected to grow 21 percent between 1985 and 2010 to 4,171,000 jobs (NIPC 1988a). Most of the

770,000 additional jobs will be located in the suburbs. Chicago will likely get 185,200 additional jobs, a 12 percent growth. Almost three-fourths of the remaining additional jobs will be located in suburban Cook County and DuPage County adjacent to Chicago. This rapid, concentrated suburban growth will complete a long-term shift of the major employment centers in the region from Chicago to the inner suburbs of northwest Cook and DuPage counties. In 1985 these suburban areas had drawn even with Chicago in total employment. By 2010 Chicago is expected to have 1,683,000 jobs and suburban Cook and DuPage counties 1,930,000 jobs. DuPage has been the fastest growing county in the region and will continue to be (up 43 percent to 562,000 jobs by 2010). It is home to the region's "High Tech Corridor," which includes the Argonne National Laboratories, Fermi Labs, the AMOCO Research Center, and Bell Laboratories.

The net growth in regional employment masks expected major changes in the structure of the economy that continue long-term trends. Manufacturing employment is expected to decline both in share of the economy (from 25 percent in 1985 to 14 percent in 2010) and in absolute terms (from 841,700 jobs in 1985 to 580,400 jobs in 2010). At the same time employment in finance, insurance, real estate, and services (FIRES) will grow to 1,657,200 and account for 39 percent of all employment in the region. The changes will be even more dramatic in Chicago. Manufacturing employment is expected to fall to 9 percent of all jobs in Chicago as 39 percent of the existing, remaining manufacturing jobs disappear. By 2010, FIRES employment is expected to account for 47 percent of all jobs in Chicago. Manufacturing employment is expected to grow only in DuPage County (up 67 percent) in connection with the research and development activities of the "High Tech" corridor. In all other suburban areas manufacturing employment is expected to decline while FIRES employment grows substantially. Suburban Cook County will increase FIRES employment by 77 percent while losing 20 percent of its manufacturing jobs.

The overall picture that emerges from these estimates is of an economy increasingly dominated by services employment and especially by the advanced services of finance and communications. This is a far different world from the Chicago of legend that many still have as their image—Carl Sandburg's "city of big shoulders," "hog butcher to the world," land of steel mills and smokestacks.

Although the employment estimates suggest a positive outlook for the region, there are some obvious difficulties associated with the particular form of growth expected. First, there will need to be an adjustment of the existing labor force to the new employment opportunities, requiring considerable re-education. The amount of change is actually obscured by looking at the net figures. Recent analysis suggests that the 8.4 percent net job increase in the Chicago region between 1980 and 1986 was the combined result of a job loss rate of 42.7 percent and a job creation rate of 51.1 percent during the period (Austrian and Zlatoper 1988). Thus, there is considerable churning in the regional economy similar to the national economy. Second, the changing geography of employment will continue to cause difficult transportation and housing problems, especially for low-income Chicagoans seeking employment in the suburbs.

Although the region's economy is growing as it shifts to more reliance on services, it is not clear whether the region will gain or lose its relative position in the national economy. A recent study of the export employment (that portion of total employment that supports the production of goods and services sold outside the region) in "broad services" suggests that Chicago is not keeping pace with its national competitors. Broad services include employment in the FIRES and TCUW (transportation, communication, utilities, and wholesale) categories. Between 1974 and 1985 the Chicago region actually lost 8.4 percent of its export employment in broad services and fell from fourth to sixth rank nationally (Austrian and Zlatoper 1988). Los Angeles and Boston moved ahead of Chicago during the period. Overall, Chicago is growing slower than the nation.

The Social Economy of the Region

Changes in population and employment composition in the region are inseparable from changes in social well-being. In Chicago's case the result of recent changes appears to be that "the rich get richer and the poor get poorer." Like other large cities, Chicago has experienced an apparent increased disparity during the 1980s between those worst off and those best off. Generally the suburbs appear to be better off than Chicago. At the same time, within the suburbs there is an increasing gap between those who are doing well and those who are not.

Poverty in Chicago is increasingly concentrated in particular areas and among minority groups. In 1980 only 3 percent of predominately white census tracts had poverty rates over 20 percent; 76 percent of predominately black and 79 percent of predominately Hispanic census tracts had poverty rates over 20 percent. Chicago's social problems have been well documented. They include, among others, a substantial number of persons in poverty, including an undetermined number who experience long-term or persistent poverty, high rates of unemployment for minorities, especially youth, a high rate of adult illiteracy, poor quality public schools, high infant mortality rates, high teen pregnancy rates, rapid increases in the number of AIDS cases, youth gangs, and a substantial number of homeless persons (United Way of Chicago 1988). Increasingly, concern is being raised about the possibility of a permanently impoverished group, an urban underclass, residing in Chicago. In the suburbs there are equally sharp differences between communities, as for example between the wealthy northern suburb of Kenilworth and the nearly bankrupt southern suburb of Harvey. Chicago remains one of the most segregated cities and regions in the country.

Governance Structure

There are now over 1,250 local governments in the Chicago region making it one of the most intensely governed regions in the country. In 1982 there were six counties, 261 municipalities, 113 township governments, 313 school districts, and 503 special districts. In addition, state agencies and a number of special agencies, such as the Northeastern Illinois Regional Planning Commission, play a role in regional governance (Fiske 1989).

One historical reason for the multitude of local governments is that before passage of the 1970 Illinois Constitution, local governing bodies could issue bonds only up to 5 percent of the assessed valuation of property within their boundaries. Special districts, however, could be set up within the same or an overlapping area and could issue bonds on their own. They include park, education, library, transit, sewage, and mosquito abatement districts, among others. These special-purpose districts are established under state law and have only the powers specifically granted.

County government in Illinois traditionally administers health and social services as an agent of the state and provides services to unincorporated areas. However, counties can assume more active roles and some Chicago region counties have begun to do so, taking on more of a policymaking and development role for the county as a whole, sometimes in conflict with municipalities.

Municipalities and counties in Illinois can have limited home-rule powers. In the mid-1980s there were 67 home-rule municipalities and one home-rule county (Cook) in the region. Amendments to the state constitution grant home rule to all counties with an elected chief executive officer; home rule is granted automatically to any municipality with a population of 25,000 or more and by referendum to smaller communities. Article VII, Section 6(a) of the 1970 Illinois Constitution gives home-rule governments broad powers. The legislation and the prevalence of home rule among larger municipalities shows a preference for strong municipal governments rather than strong state, county, or regional governance.

As elsewhere in the United States, local government activities have expanded rapidly in recent years, and the financial pressure on local governments has also been increased by the cutback of federal funds. In the Chicago region municipal revenues have increased 258 percent between 1972 and 1982 while expenditures increased 276 percent (Banovetz 1988). Chicago and some of the older suburbs face more severe problems as revenues have fallen even farther behind expenditures and intergovernmental transfers have declined. Intergovernmental aid from both state and federal governments to the region fell 10 percent between 1977 and 1986 (state transfers down 7.6 percent and federal transfers down 17.4 percent) (Bania and Calkins 1988). Chicago received 58 million dollars less in transfers in 1986 than in 1977 despite an increase of 71 million dollars flowing to the city through the state.

Local planning powers are granted by numerous provisions in Illinois law. The statutes provide for local, county, and multicounty regional planning commissions. The planning statutes encourage greater than local cooperation on planning issues. County and regional planning commissions are instructed to encourage the cooperation of the political subdivisions within their territories on plans. County planning agencies in the Chicago region are required to submit their plans to the regional agency for review prior to adoption. Plans adopted by regional commissions are to be advisory only, unless the plan or a portion of it pertains to a municipality and is adopted separately by it. Between specific enabling legislation and home-rule powers it appears that there is adequate opportunity for local governments in the Chicago region to develop needed mechanisms for local and cooperative planning.

Summary

It would require more than an average crystal ball to predict with any certainty the future of the Chicago region. The estimates reported here are all subject to the usual limitations of such efforts, and some of these estimates are contested. For example, advocates of Chicago's policy efforts to retain manufacturing employment would probably take exception to NIPC's employment forecasts. However, it is clear that changes are coming in the region, and they will have a large cumulative effect. The changes are slow. They have been underway for several decades, so their overall impact is easily underestimated. At the same time traditional regional characteristics continue giving comfort to those who prefer to hold on to the familiar. Some manufacturing sectors are doing well. Community organization and community-based development are very active in Chicago. Chicago continues to be a "melting pot," attracting large numbers of the newest wave of immigrants—Hispanics and Asians. The White Sox decided not to move to Florida after the promise of a large public subsidy. The suburbs mostly vote Republican, and Chicago votes Democratic. All of this seems like the old Chicago.

The changes are real, however. Already there are shortages of low-skilled labor in the suburbs. High housing costs and limited existing low-income housing in the suburbs contribute to the problem. Journey to work commuting from Chicago to western and northern suburbs now matches or exceeds commuting into the city. The revitalization of Chicago's northside neighborhoods is clearly tied to the new, professional employment opportunities in the city *and* the suburbs. How these development pressures eventually get worked out and the resulting structure of the spatial social economy will depend on the policies adopted and implemented by governments in the region, even though the forces creating these pressures largely originate outside the region in national and international business and political decisions. The fields of action will probably be traditional: land-use control, environment (water, sewer, solid waste), transportation, housing, and economic development. There will be some major, high impact issues befitting a large urban region, like the question of whether and where to build a third regional airport, but most of the issues will be small. There will be a lot of them, and when they are decided the region will be different.

ORGANIZATION FOR PLANNING AND DEVELOPMENT DECISIONS

Decisions about infrastructure development in the region are made by municipalities, counties, special districts, and the state government. Planning and negotiation for those area development decisions requiring coordinated action or cooperation can be done in a variety of formal settings. We will briefly review the function and activities of the major agencies that provide some form of development planning for all or large portions of the region to give a general picture of the decision-making environment. Perhaps the key term to describe the situation is variety. There is no monolithic structure for development planning in the region; no central point of coordination. Rather, there are a number of complementary, sometimes competing, ways for areawide issues to be raised and reviewed.   There are two regional planning agencies, both created by the state of Illinois. The Northeastern Illinois Planning Commission (NIPC) is the general agency.   It serves and is governed by area counties, municipalities, and special districts.   The Chicago Area Transportation Study (CATS) is a specialized transportation planning agency that shares responsibility with NIPC for long-range areawide transportation planning. Among the many special districts, two are particularly important because of the size and spatial extent of their operations. The Regional Transportation Authority (RTA) provides public transportation in most of the region. The Metropolitan Water Reclamation District (MWRD) provides sewer services and related flood control for Chicago and the inner suburbs.

Counties in the region can act as subregional planning and development agencies. While they have no power over local planning decisions, counties are in a position to broker local conflicts and provide leadership on general issues. They can also serve as a buffer between the localities and regional decision makers.   Municipalities form associations to promote their mutual interests and to negotiate with the counties and regional and state agencies.   Finally, some of the larger nonprofit organizations have played a limited role in regional planning.

The agencies and some of the programs are referred to by popular acronyms in the text.   A reference guide to these acronyms is given in Table 3.2.

Regional Planning Agencies

Northeastern Illinois Regional Planning Commission (NIPC)

NIPC was created by the State of Illinois in 1957 (chapter 85, Illinois State Statutes).   The enabling legislation stresses the commission's plan-making function, calling for the agency to prepare "a sound and comprehensive general plan . . . to guide and coordinate the development of (water supply, storm water, sewage, transportation, land use, local

Table 3.2: *Government Agency and Program Acronyms*

BACOG	Barrington Area Council on Governments
CATS	Chicago Area Transportation Study
CTA	Chicago Transit Authority
IDOT	Illinois Department of Transportation
Metra	Commuter Rail Service Board of the RTA
MPC	Metropolitan Planning Council
MPO	Metropolitan Planning Organization
MWRD	Metropolitan Water Reclamation District
NIPC	Northeastern Illinois Regional Planning Commission
PACE	Suburban Bus Service Board of the RTA
PZ&EQ	Lake County Department of Planning Zoning and Environmental Quality
RTA	Regional Transportation Authority
TARP	Tunnel and Reservoir Plan
TIP	Transportation Improvement Program
TSD	Transportation System Development (Plan)

governmental services, and improved civic design) . . . and to cooperate with various units of government in comprehensive planning for future growth and development." The legislation is also explicit about how limited the powers of the agency will be: "In the exercise of these powers . . . the Commission shall act solely as an advisory body to units of government. . ." NIPC's recent emphasis is the preparation and dissemination of information and technical assistance to local government. It currently defines its basic mission as threefold: (1) to prepare and disseminate information about the region and its needs; (2) to foster cooperation among units of government; and (3) ultimately, to strive for consensus on policies and plans for action that will promote the sound and orderly development of the northeastern Illinois area.

NIPC is governed by 32 commissioners. The governor of Illinois and the mayor of Chicago each appoints five members. Seven are elected on a quadrennial basis by suburban mayors and presidents. Three are appointed by the president of the board of Cook County, and one each is appointed by the county board chairs of each of the remaining member counties. Finally, the boards of the following each appoint one member: the Regional Transportation Authority; the Metropolitan Water Reclamation District of Greater Chicago; the Illinois Association of Park Districts; the Chicago Park District; The Chicago Transit Authority; Metra; and PACE.

NIPC has neither taxing authority nor any assured source of revenue. Funds can be obtained by contracting for specialized planning services and by contributions.   The commission annually suggests to each governing body a sum that the commission considers a fair and equitable appropriation. In fiscal year 1987, NIPC had a total income of approximately $2.4 million.   Of this total, 51 percent came from the state (mainly federal pass through funds), 38 percent was from local funds and contributions, and 11 percent was direct federal funding.

The current work program indicates that NIPC performs three main activities. First, they provide information and technical assistance. NIPC is a principal source of regional information including aerial photographs, flood hazard maps, generalized soils information, census data, population and employment forecasts, and governmental tax base and expenditure data.   They also provide analyses and publications on land use and natural resource planning, housing, transportation, recreation, energy, water quality, flood/storm water, noise abatement, and other topics. To provide technical assistance to local governments NIPC has nine senior staff who spend part of their time as Local Service Officers assigned to specific geographic areas. In addition eight staff specialists are available on call for special problems. Second, NIPC develops general plans. Its first plans were developed in the 1960s to meet areawide planning requirements for federal capital grants. A Comprehensive General Plan was completed in 1968. This was followed two years later by a Regional Open Space Plan and the Regional Wastewater Plan. Subsequent plans include the 1976 Regional Overbank Flooding and Storm Water Drainage Policy Plan, and a 1977 Residential Policy Plan, a 1980 Regional Open Space and Recreation Policy Plan, a 1979 Water Quality Management Plan, a 1986 update of the Regional Solid Waste Management Policy Plan. These plans set forth the basic ingredients for a regional growth policy. They are relatively concise and heavily policy oriented. Some plans provide recommendations for followup actions or implementation mechanisms.   However, since the plans are advisory, except in the instances where they are prerequisite to state or federal action, their influence is hard to gauge.

NIPC has had a collaborative role with the Chicago Area Transportation Study (CATS) for the past 25 years in the development of long-range transportation plans. The 2010 Transportation System Development Plan was jointly developed in 1989.

Third, NIPC provides plan, grant, and permit review services. Under the federal A-95 review process NIPC was assigned responsibility for review of local plans and related capital grant applications consistency with regional plans. NIPC continues to review local plans for their fit with adopted regional policies and for their compatibility with other locality plans, and attempts to resolve conflicts between local and regional plans as they arise. The Illinois Environmental Protection Agency has designated NIPC as the responsible agency for reviewing wastewater plans and point source proposals for consistency with the state water quality plan.

Chicago Area Transportation Study (CATS)

CATS was formed in 1955 with the mission of developing the first comprehensive long-range transportation plan for the region. The first plan was completed in 1962 and had a target date of 1980. CATS was originally formed as an experiment (hence the word "study" in its title). The perceived value of its first planning effort led to its evolution into a permanent agency and to the expansion of its boundaries. However, almost none of the plan's recommendations for freeway and transit network improvements have since become part of the region's infrastructure. In 1971, the original CATS plan and subsequent subregional studies were combined into an Interim Plan covering the six-county area. The first complete six-county area effort resulted in the 1995 Transportation System Plan, adopted in 1974. In 1974, the CATS Policy Committee was designated by the governor of Illinois as the "Metropolitan Planning Organization" (MPO) for the metropolitan area. The Year 2000 Transportation System Development Plan was adopted in 1980. This plan was updated in 1981 and 1983 and republished in 1984. The 2010 Plan, completed in 1989, is currently the official regional transportation plan.

CATS operates through a series of policy, technical, and advisory committees with support provided by agency staff. The Policy Committee consists of "policy level" representatives of transportation operating and planning agencies in the metropolitan area. The committee is responsible for policy on both long-range planning and short-range improvement programming. The expectation is that once the Policy Committee reaches a decision, "implementation is rapid because all concerned parties with authority to act have participated in it."

The Work Program Committee monitors planning efforts for consistency with the policy decisions. The committee screens recommendations, projects, and proposals before submitting them to the Policy

Committee. It is composed of one member each from member agencies, groups on the Policy Committee, and one participant from other state and regional planning agencies.

The CATS Council of Mayors consists of a representative from each of 11 subregional councils and the city of Chicago. Of the 11 subareas, 6 are in Cook County and 5 are in the "collar" counties. The council represents over 260 municipalities in northeastern Illinois. The goal of the council is "to [allow] groups of municipalities to consider projects of mutual, geographic interest." The council has an executive committee (consisting of two members from each subarea) that meets bimonthly. The council allocates some of the Federal Aid Urban (FAU) funds. These regional councils are the basic mechanisms for linking area transportation decisions to local government.

The CATS' work program contains two major planning efforts: long-range facility planning and short-range improvement programming resulting respectively in the Transportation System Development Plan and the Transportation Improvement Program. CATS considers the Transportation System Development (TSD) plan to be the heart of its efforts. The plan identifies new capital projects and facilities, and maintenance and replacement needs for highways, bridges, and transit equipment. The 2010 Transportation System Development Plan is discussed in detail below as a case study in regional plan making.

The Transportation Improvement Program (TIP) is a five-year program of transportation projects. It presents a prioritization of how the region's federal capital assistance funds will be used to enhance the region's transportation system. Each year, the previously adopted program is reviewed and an operational and fiscal evaluation is conducted for each of the proposed projects. The Work Program Committee then makes recommendations to the Policy Committee on whether to adopt, modify, or reject the Transportation Improvement Program and Annual Element.

CATS is also involved in other transportation issues in the region. There is an Aviation Advisory Committee, which prepared the Regional Airport System Plan (RASP). The plan identifies and characterizes the operations of airports within the region and addresses issues of land use and environmental quality. The Freight Committee works in an advisory capacity to develop and implement goals for freight traffic management in the northeastern Illinois-northwestern Indiana region. Other committees and groups include: the Transportation Operations Committee, which provides guidance for overall Transportation System Management policy and projects; a Taxi Advisory Board; the Air Quality Advisory Committee; the Mobility Limited Advisory Committee; and the Unified Work Program Committee.

Special Districts

Metropolitan Water Reclamation District (MWRD)

The Metropolitan Water Reclamation District celebrated its centennial in 1989. The district was created to address drinking water quality problems experienced due to the dumping of sewage and other pollutants into the Chicago River, which discharged into Lake Michigan, the city's drinking water source. The flow of the Chicago River was reversed by the construction of a series of canals that rerouted the Chicago waterway to eventually connect with the Mississippi River system. Today, the MWRD service area covers over 872 square miles within Cook County and includes the city of Chicago and 124 neighboring municipalities. MWRD has a total of seven wastewater reclamation plants and treats a total of almost 1.5 billion gallons of wastewater per day. MWRD is governed by a nine-member board of commissioners, elected at large within district boundaries to six-year terms (three are elected every two years). The district's 1989 budget was $406.1 million.

MWRD is in the middle of a major construction program, the Tunnel and Reservoir Plan (TARP), building a system of tunnels and reservoirs to accommodate sewage and stormwater overflows. Fifty-three municipalities within MWRD's jurisdiction have combined systems that carry both wastewater and rainwater. During periods of heavy rainfall, there have been problems with sewers backing up in low elevation areas as well as polluted overflow discharge into waterways. The TARP project is described as one of the largest public works projects ever undertaken.

TARP consists of two phases. Phase I is oriented primarily towards pollution control and consists of four tunnel systems including drop shafts, tunnels, and pumping stations. The tunnels range from nine to 33 feet in diameter and are constructed in solid rock up to 350 feet below the surface. Nearly 110 miles of tunnels will be constructed in order to eliminate 85 percent of the combined sewer overflows. About 31 miles of tunnels have been completed thus far. Phase I is expected to cost $2.25 billion. Phase II focuses on flood control and will consist of three reservoirs and 21 miles of tunnels. It will provide flood control protection and will eliminate the remaining 15 percent of pollution from combined sewer overflows. The U.S. Army Corps of Engineers will be responsible for Phase II.

While MWRD does not have a specific statutory responsibility in the area of flood control, it is involved in cooperative efforts with local communities, the U.S. Soil Conservation Service, and the state of Illinois to develop and manage flood control storage reservoirs and stream improvement facilities. MWRD is a principal sponsor of regional floodwater management plans developed by the Soil Conservation Service. In addition, MWRD has an extensive water quality monitoring system for Lake Michigan, the area waterways, and the sewer system.

Regional Transportation Authority (RTA)

The RTA was created in 1974 by the Illinois General Assembly. The aim was to coordinate the diverse mass transportation systems in the six-county region of northeastern Illinois and to provide a consistent level of financial support. The authority is governed by a 13-member board of directors: five from Chicago; three from Cook County; and one from each of the five "collar" counties.

The RTA was extensively restructured under the RTA Amendments adopted in 1983 by the Illinois General Assembly so that primary operating responsibilities were vested with three subsidiary agencies, called Service Boards: PACE, the suburban bus division; Metra, the commuter rail division; and the Chicago Transit Authority (CTA), responsible for bus and rapid transit service within the city of Chicago and adjoining suburbs. The intent of the restructuring was to increase public accountability, and improve local control over fares, service levels, and system performance. RTA is now a smaller body with the responsibility of funding and oversight of the three agencies. In this capacity it is responsible for the integration of transit services in the region, for allocating resources to the different services, and for evaluating performance of the three service boards.

At the time of the 1983 restructuring, RTA received a boost in financial stability by the allotment of a percentage of sales tax within the region. In Cook County one cent out of every dollar is allocated to RTA. In the five remaining counties, one-quarter of one cent goes to RTA. Of the sales tax total, 85 percent is allocated directly to the service boards "according to need" and 15 percent is retained on a discretionary basis. RTA also receives funding from the Illinois' Public Transportation Fund equal to one-quarter of the collected sales tax receipts. Federal transit subsidies are allocated to the service boards by the RTA on the basis of ridership. The state mandates that the agency recover 50 percent of its expenses from fare box revenues. The combined operation budget for RTA's Service boards was estimated at about $1 billion in 1987.

For the past several years the RTA has been developing a strategic plan that was published in January 1989. The plan aims to restore the system to good condition, estimated to cost $600 million over the next 10 years, and guide extension of the system. Five general policies are developed in the plan that focuses primarily on financial issues. Increasingly, system planning is the responsibility of the three service boards.

The Chicago Transit Authority (CTA) is the largest of the service boards. It serves the city of Chicago and 38 suburbs, a service area population of approximately 3.7 million, or 51 percent of RTA's total service population. Bus service is provided on a grid system throughout the service area with express radial service provided along designated corridors for 921,000 route miles. The rapid transit system consists of six radial rail lines providing 215 route miles. Annually, 439.5 million passengers use CTA buses, and 147.0 million passengers use CTA rapid transit, taking 586.5 million trips. CTA's 1988 fiscal year operations budget was $644.8 million. Half of this is accounted for by bus system expenditures, 32 percent by rail, and 18 percent by shared expenses. The proposed 1989 capital program budget is $217.5 million; annual capital expenditures have averaged $120 million in recent years. CTA's estimated fare box revenue in 1988 was $320 million. Total expenses were about $636 million. The recovery ratio was 52.2 percent.

Metra is responsible for system monitoring and coordination of all commuter rail operation within the six-county northeast Illinois region. It operates several formerly private commuter rail services that have been acquired since 1981 through bankruptcy proceedings and direct purchase. The commuter rail network is comprised of over 500 route miles and 1,200 track miles. The network extends throughout northeastern Illinois and also into Indiana and Wisconsin. Metra received an estimated $140 million in fare box revenues in 1988. Estimated expenses were about $259 million. The recovery ratio was about 58 percent.

PACE describes its charge as the administration and provision of all nonrail mass transit service in all of the six-county region with the exception of that portion of Cook County that is serviced by CTA. PACE is governed by a 12-member board of directors. The board is comprised of current and former suburban village presidents and city mayors. PACE's estimated fare box revenues in 1988 were $22 million. Total estimated 1988 expenses were about $70 million. The recovery ratio was 31.1 percent.

County Planning Agencies

County government is another layer of regional planning and development decision making. All six counties have active planning programs. The two most rapidly urbanizing counties, Lake County north of Chicago and DuPage County west of Chicago, have developed very sophisticated planning programs that treat the individual counties as subregions and attempt to coordinate countywide growth and development.

DuPage County

The DuPage County Regional Planning Commission is currently working on an update of the 1985 Countywide Land Use Plan because of the continuing high volume of development requests that are often in conflict with the plan. DuPage County has begun making impact assessments for major new developments in an effort to manage growth and mitigate the serious local traffic problems and overloading of development infrastructure. The county only exercises land-use control in unincorporated areas, and even there its influence is affected by the extraterritorial zoning powers of municipalities. However, the county sees its role as balancing development and assuring efficient use of infrastructure and transportation systems. From the county's perspective each municipality is overly generous in providing opportunities for office and industrial development in the competition to gain the tax benefits from such development. The county identifies seven regional (countywide) issues that define its planning role: conflicts between adjacent land uses; flood and stormwater management; impacts on the local road network; fiscal impacts; recreation and open space needs; impacts on the intercommunity road network; and impacts on the Land Use Plan balance.

To work with municipalities on bringing county and local plans into agreement, the County Planning Commission has formed "regional clusters" of localities, which meet with the county staff for development and review of the plan. Like NIPC, the County Planning Commission sees itself as a regional body and, because of home-rule powers, relies heavily on its role as information and assistance provider to influence land-use decisions. Their regional interests are confined primarily to the county boundaries, however, and they do not have formal intergovern-mental planning arrangements with adjacent counties.

Lake County

Lake County's Department of Planning, Zoning, and Environmental Quality (PZ&EQ) combines long-range planning, community develop-ment, economic development, and development regulation. It staffs separate countywide community development, economic development, and regional planning commissions. The main work of the Regional Planning Commission over the last five years has been the development of a countywide Framework Plan, the most recent update was adopted in November 1987, and a new zoning ordinance to implement it was adopted in April 1989. Like DuPage, Lake County uses information and assistance provision to encourage municipalities to cooperate on planning and development decisions. The county has joined with municipalities in part of the county to create a new water commission to bring Lake Michigan water directly to them. Jointly with DuPage, Lake County was instrumental in establishing the new state legislation requiring countywide stormwater management planning and now has an active planning program jointly governed by county and municipal representatives. Similarly, the county is jointly working with municipalities on solid waste management planning.

Also like DuPage, the Lake County Regional Planning Commission sees itself as a regional body concerned with the county. Lake County contains all the usual elements of a midwestern urban region: an aging, industrial center city (Waukegan); old established suburbs; rapidly developing new suburbs; and rural, estate, and second-home residential areas. And the county experiences the full range of social, economic, and development problems of an urban region. The southern part of the county is home to Chicago commuters, but in many respects the area sees its problems as separate issues requiring county action.

Councils of Government

Councils of Governments are voluntary associations of elected public officials of an area. They are completely advisory in nature. Each governmental unit is represented by its elected chief executive. The Illinois statute grants the councils the following advisory powers: (1) to study such area governmental problems common to two or more members of the council as it deems appropriate, including but not limited to matters affecting health, safety, welfare, education, economic conditions, and regional development; (2) to promote cooperative arrangements and coordinate action among its members; and (3) to make recommendations for review and action to the members and other public agencies that perform functions within the region." Some of the existing associations have been active for a long time, starting as informal associations. Some are quite recent and were stimulated in part by CAT's creation of subregional councils. They vary greatly in population served, budget, staff, and activities.

The Northwest Municipal Conference describes itself as the second oldest intergovernmental organization in the state. It was organized by several municipalities in 1958 to study the future of commuter rail stations along the Chicago and Northwestern Railroad lines. The council has a membership of 33 municipalities and seven townships, representing a population of about one million. The members are in Cook, DuPage, and Lake Counties. Major elements of the current work program include a solid waste management planning and siting effort, the Transportation Partnership (a public-private organization), a joint purchasing program, joint training and education efforts, and legislative liaison.

The West Central Municipal Conference was founded in 1979 on a part-time basis and has been fully active since May 1986. Executive Director Dave Bennet bills the conference as a "trade association for municipalities." The conference currently has 29 members, with a service population of just under 450,000. There are a total of 36 municipalities within the area served, which is western Cook County between Chicago and DuPage County. Some of the major concerns of the conference are transportation planning, intergovernmental funding, state lobbying, economic development, solid waste management, and job training and education.

The Barrington Area Council of Governments (BACOG) began as an informal association in the mid-1960s. It was officially founded in 1970. BACOG serves seven municipalities with a population of approximately 35,000. BACOG differs from other councils in that its mandate includes development of an areawide comprehensive plan with a land-use component. BACOG is involved in planning and growth management, joint services, citizen education, the arts, demographics, school district issues, drug education, and recycling.

The South Suburban Mayors and Managers Association was formed in 1968 as an informal organization of southern Cook County government officials. In 1978 the association first hired full-time professional staff. It serves 38 member municipalities in the southern suburbs of Cook County with a population of more than 550,000. The association provides municipal management assistance through special programs such as joint purchasing and through seminars. It is also active in municipal compliance with the Clean Water Act, support of a third regional airport, federal and state legislative liaison, a public safety program, cooperation with other intergovernmental organization, housing issues, public and media relations, economic development assistance, monitoring of transportation proposals and participation in planning efforts, review of solid waste, and review of flooding issues.

Private/Nonprofit Sector

The private sector can address regional planning and development issues through the activities of nonprofit organizations. Only a few of the many nonprofits in the Chicago region have had such a program focus.

The Metropolitan Planning Council (MPC) is an influential nonprofit in Chicago and, to a lesser extent, the metropolitan area. It was founded in 1934 as the Metropolitan Housing Council, later becoming the Metropolitan Housing and Planning Council and then the MPC. MPC is led by a board of governors drawn from corporations, universities, and consulting firms. It is organized into executive, standing, and ad hoc committees served by a professional full-time staff. Estimated income in 1988 was about $733,650. The standing committees of the council are: Urban Development, Regional Planning, and Transportation. Current special projects include a task force on Chicago Housing Authority rehabilitation and reinvestment, and a task force on health care for the medically indigent.

In previous years the council has undertaken major projects on regional topics. One of the most significant was their 1982 study, MAP 2000, which evaluated public infrastructure and public capital budgeting in the region. That study found that the region lacked "a comprehensive approach to making public capital investment decisions for the region as a whole" and that plans to finance needed capital improvements were inadequate (Metropolitan Housing and Planning Council 1982c).

The Regional Partnership is a consortium of governmental, civic and business organizations that addresses key issues facing the six-county northeastern Illinois region. The partnership was established in 1983 to identify regional problems not being addressed, avoid duplication of efforts, and combine strengths and problem-solving abilities of existing organizations. Partnership members review and select projects that require regional private/public collaboration. Projects are carried out by the sponsoring organizations using their own staff and resources. Financial assistance is also sought from foundation and trust grants. The Metropolitan Planning Council has served as staff and secretariat for the partnership.

The partnership counts as its greatest accomplishment the Regional Agenda Project, which culminated in a State of the Region Conference held in Chicago in 1987 and in the publication of a State of the Region Report. Key public policy issues facing the Chicago metropolitan region in 13 topical areas were reviewed. Other achievements influenced by the partnership include a solid waste management plan developed by NIPC, an Infrastructure Action Plan by MPC, the Regional Marketing Project by MPC, and the Economic Source Book published by the Commercial Club, MPC, and other organizations.

THE 2010 PLAN: AN EXAMPLE OF REGIONAL PLANNING

Transportation planning is the most developed example of a regional planning and decision-making process in the Chicago metropolitan area. It is not much of an exaggeration to call it the only regional planning game in town. As such, the experience with it may be a useful guide to the possibility of other forms of regional planning. Work on a new regional transportation plan began on February 26, 1987 when the CATS Work Program Committee approved a committee structure for plan development. The process ended on April 12, 1989 with the CATS Policy Committee's endorsement of the plan. The aims of this brief case study are to describe the process, the roles played by each of the major actors, the mechanisms for agreement, and to assess the process.

The transportation planning process in the Chicago region is structured by an interagency agreement, as revised in 1981, which was strongly influenced by the existing federal regulations (CFR 450.108). CATS had been designated as the official metropolitan planning agency (MPO) by the governor. NIPC was the A-95 review agency for federal grants. Usually the MPO and the A-95 designations go to the same agency. The federal regulations stipulated that when they were different agencies "there shall be an agreement between the two organizations which prescribes the means by which their activities will be coordinated." The main substantive concern was that the agreement show how transportation planning would be part of the comprehensive development plan for the area.

Although the A95 review process was rescinded, NIPC is still given responsibility for assuring the consistency of the transportation plan with the comprehensive development plan. This gives NIPC the lead role in identifying goals, development policies, and growth strategies, responsibility for providing the land-use framework for transportation planning, and responsibility for assessing the impacts of alternate transportation investments on regional development. CATS is given the lead role in preparing and testing alternate transportation networks. This includes system performance, user benefits, costs and revenues, and air quality impacts. There are two additional parties to the agreement. The RTA is responsible for evaluating the public transportation proposals, and the Illinois Department of Transportation (IDOT) is responsible for assuring that the regional plan is consistent with statewide plans.

Care is taken in the agreement to assure that CATS and NIPC are equal partners in the planning process. The agreement requires that CATS staff provide full information so that NIPC "can act as co-equal with the (CATS) Policy Committee in providing guidance to CATS staff in preparing transportation plans and in endorsing these plans." The plan adoption process is similarly even handed. The draft plan is approved by the CATS Work Program Committee and forwarded to NIPC for adoption. If adopted, the plan is then sent to the CATS Policy Committee for endorsement. If NIPC does not adopt, it returns the plan to the Work Program Committee with recommended changes. If CATS does not agree with the plan as adopted by NIPC, the plan is referred to the standing Joint Subcommittee for the Resolution of Differences to work out an agreement. CATS may not endorse the plan until it has been adopted by NIPC.

The 2010 TSD Plan Development Process

In practice the supervision of plan development is done by integrated committees that represent all the interested actors, but the lines of responsibility laid out in the agreement are respected in the designation of technical staff responsibility, committee chairmanships, and committee membership. The CATS Work Program Committee oversees the plan development process and establishes the subcommittee structure for carrying out the process. The Work Program Committee has representatives from all interested parties: IDOT and other relevant state agencies;

CATS; NIPC; RTA; CTA; Metra; PACE; Chicago; each county; the Council of Mayors; and private transportation providers.

The Work Program Committee established five subcommittees for plan development. The Socioeconomic/Scenario Development Committee was chaired by NIPC and assigned responsibility for employment and population estimates and preparation and evaluation of alternate economic, energy, and socio-economic development scenarios. They also identified and evaluated specific issues for inclusion in the basic planning assumptions, such as proposals for a third regional airport and forecasts of energy costs. The Alternatives Generation Committee was chaired by CATS and assigned responsibility for compiling a list of transportation proposals, developing alternative schemes and testing them.

The Financial Considerations Committee was chaired by IDOT and given responsibility for identifying traditional and nontraditional sources of funding for transportation improvements. The Plan Evaluation Committee was chaired by Lake County and given responsibility for analysis of the tested alternative plans and preparation of the draft plan. They also reviewed public hearing comments and the financial analysis in developing the plan. The Public Involvement Committee was chaired by the Council of Mayors and given responsibility for designing and implementing the public review process.

The committees contained representatives from relevant agencies. For example, the RTA was represented on the alternatives, financial and evaluation committees. In line with the interagency agreement CATS was not represented on the public involvement and plan evaluation committees, and NIPC was not represented on the alternatives generation and financial considerations committees.

Developing the Plan

NIPC prepared the population, employment, and income estimates in consultation with the local governments of the region. The results of forecasting models at the regional level were compared with local forecasts and growth assumptions. By a process of analysis and negotiation the local and distributed regional estimates were brought into agreement. The forecasts project a regional population growth of 15 percent by 2010, a significant drop in average household size and a 29 percent increase in the number of households, and a 23 percent increase in employment. Three-fourths of the population growth is expected to occur in the five "collar" counties.

A list of 200 transportation projects was compiled from suggestions of public agencies, local governments, and public hearings. These were analyzed by CATS and reviewed by the evaluation committee. The committee approved some of the projects for further study, modified or combined others, and eliminated some. Fifty-three projects were given detailed study, and six alternative transportation system scenarios were considered. Twenty of the proposals made it into the final plan.

The highway portion of the plan proposes five new expressways, an expressway connection and two tollway improvements in addition to current committed projects from previous plans. Recognizing that it was financially infeasible to build all the expressways that could be justified by the projections, the plan also proposes designating some arterials as "strategic arterials" to be improved as locally required to supplement the expressway system. Finally, the highway plan proposes several future expressway corridors that should be preserved for meeting travel needs beyond 2010.

The transit system plan stresses the need for maintenance and improvement of the present system and proposes six major projects, including a new Chicago Central Business District distributor. Capacity constraints are expected to be most acute on the commuter rail system. Eight future transit corridors are designated.

Financial analysis estimates that the proposed highway improvements will cost $13.1 billion and the transit improvements $12.3 billion. The most optimistic revenue forecast estimates a shortfall of $2.5 billion, and the pessimistic forecast estimates a $14.2 billion shortfall.

The public involvement program included three separate rounds of meetings. The first round was to inform the public agencies and public officials of the planning process and their opportunities to participate. The second round presented planning goals and the plan evaluation criteria for discussion and issued a call for proposals for new transportation improvements. In the third round the 53 facility projects under final consideration were presented with computer simulation results of their 2010 performance, and the proposed Strategic Regional Arterial System was presented. A Public Hearing Draft Plan was released in December 1988, and a series of public hearings on the plan were held by NIPC in late January 1989.

In general, the planning process went very smoothly. Most major elements of the plan received broad endorsement, as did the Strategic Regional Arterial System and the Corridor of the Future proposals. What criticisms and controversy emerged, and there was only one major controversy, were mainly tied to particular subregional concerns or special interests. The public hearing record shows only one general or regional concern and that was a substantial amount of public testimony that urged a higher priority for traffic management over new construction.

The South Suburban Mayors and Managers Association and representatives of southern suburbs testified that the plan underestimated growth in their part of the region because it did not include the impact of a third regional airport, which they expect will be located in their area. The draft plan was amended to include a brief discussion of the airport issue and identification of four possible sites, but no changes were made in growth or travel demand estimates. The Northwest Municipal Conference objected to the proposed five-mile spacing of the Strategic Arterials on the grounds that this criteria was arbitrary and failed to recognize local conditions. CATS had developed the criteria on technical, system-oriented grounds. Subsequent committee review also included nontechnical and political considerations, and some proposed arterials were dedesignated and some additional roads were designated for the system.

The only major controversy involved the proposal for a major highway project in Lake County, in the northern part of the region, that would complete part of the regional expressway system. This proposal was not new. It has existed in some form for about 25 years. This is an area of rapid growth. The issue was framed in the classical terms of quality of life and environmental concerns versus accommodating growth and increased traffic. And, in fact, the issue pitted neighbor against neighbor. The Lake County Board testified in opposition to the project and the Lake County Regional Planning Commission and the Development Commission testified for it. Ten area municipalities endorsed it and two opposed.

The controversy placed NIPC in a difficult position. Opposition to the project was based on issues of stream, wetland, and groundwater protection that NIPC strongly advocates, but NIPC's own staff analysis supported the need for the project. NIPC resolved the process by recommending that the required Environmental Impact Statement be completed and followed by a second review of the project conducted by both CATS and NIPC. Failure of either to grant approval at that time would eliminate the project from the plan. NIPC also recommended that, in the meantime, affected local governments seek changes in state enabling law to allow municipalities and counties to enter into binding agreements on future land uses and land regulation, adopt ordinances to protect water resources based on a model ordinance presented, and form a corridor planning council, which should seek a moratorium on development until legal and planning issues were resolved.

The compromise gave something to each of the contestants and essentially left the issue open. It was approved by CATS and incorporated in the plan. NIPC was highly praised by the *Chicago Tribune* for its leadership in resolving the issue. However, critics of the project pointed out that the recommendations are not enforceable. It is not clear whether an EIS will be conducted; the responsible officials have stated that funding is not available. Further, the Illinois Toll Highway Authority could build the project without NIPC's approval.

Assessment of the 2010 Plan Process

From an outsider's perspective the planning process went very smoothly and resulted in a plan that easily won wide consensus. For an insider's look at the process we interviewed persons from the major agencies involved. One of the issues we presented to them is the typical outsider's view of the qualities and character of the principal actors—CATS and NIPC. That view is that CATS is technically oriented, analytically sophisticated, and somewhat narrowly focused on transportation issues with a bias toward highway transportation. NIPC, on the other hand is seen as a land-use and environmental agency with a very broad agenda and a preference for general policy planning where broad agreements can be negotiated and political compromise constructed within a rational planning framework. CATS, since it is a division of IDOT, is seen as a state agency with ultimate loyalty to Springfield. NIPC, as a membership governed agency, is seen as locally based but politically weak. The days when NIPC was seen as a federal intrusion seem to be long past.

As might be expected, CATS' staff take strong exception to this characterization and argue the opposite. The response of Peter Elliot, Director of Work Program Development, is typical. He feels that NIPC has its own biases, oriented to "bicycles and public transportation," while CATS "tries to look at the whole picture," although he admits CATS does have a leaning to highway transportation. He also took exception to the inference that NIPC has a stronger policy orientation, pointing to the many high-level policymakers on CATS' Policy Committee and the importance they attach to their role.

Phillip Peters, NIPC's Director of Planning and Chair of the Socioeconomic/Scenario Development Committee, feels that because CATS is primarily a transportation provider it is an uphill battle to introduce other issues such as land use and environment into the process. Reflecting on whether the situation would be different if the plan were prepared by a single agency, he suspects that there might be different divisions, but that the split between analysts and planners would still exist. Aristide Biciunas, Executive Director of CATS, likened the process to a relay race where one runner starts and runs for a while, then passes on the stick to another who runs for a while and then passes it on again. The difficult issue to judge is whether in this case where there are only two runners and many passes—CATS to NIPC to CATS to NIPC to CATS—one has a controlling advantage.

Those most directly involved with the process seemed pleased and proud of the resulting document. They pointed to the checks and balances provided by having two major agencies and committees with diversified membership involved as one of the virtues of the process, while acknowledging that the current structure can at times be unwieldy. Aristide Biciunas summed up the common view, "It doesn't look pretty on the outside, but it works."

Outsiders generally shared this positive assessment. In commenting on the smoothness of the process, many cited positive personality and leadership factors, particularly the role of Larry Christmas, Executive Director, in setting the tone for NIPC. The assessment of NIPC's role was generally very positive. However, many commented that NIPC's lack of secure funding severely impacts its operating ability. It is hampered in taking policy positions, making decisions, and even in performing staff work because of the need to constantly consider the ramifications of its activities and decisions on its funding.

RTA officials were most critical of the plan-making process, feeling that it fails to give sufficient attention to nonhighway solutions to growth. John Gaudette, an Assistant Executive Director of RTA, focused on the relevance of the transportation planning process to the contemporary situation. He feels that the process has not worked to integrate highway and transit planning and is too divorced from fiscal reality. He finds the plan making to be a "process for the sake of process" rather than a process for decision making. As he sees it, the key activity of the process is allocation of funds for highway improvement among cities and counties through a bargaining and rationing process rather than through a rational planning process. Like many others Ted Weigle, Executive

Director of RTA, feels that CATS is not directed by the local Policy Committee, but takes direction from the state. The balance of power among agencies and the different governments is a subject of considerable disagreement among the participants. Phillip Peters of NIPC agrees with Weigle noting, "In Illinois controversies find their way to Springfield because what happens in Chicago is so important to the State." Aristide Biciunas of CATS offers a different interpretation. He suggests that decisions are made at the state level because the decision making in the region is "checkmated"; there are so many different agendas that everything is nullified. The disagreements among local governments are reflected in the comment of Donald Kline, Executive Director of BACOG, which represents outlying communities, that CATS listens to powerful groups like the Northwest Municipal Conference, but not to less powerful groups or individuals. He thinks the "little guys" feel like everything is done before they become involved.

It is clear that the region has developed a very successful process for transportation planning that draws the relevant actors together, works smoothly, and is able to achieve consensus. The critics would argue that this is partly because the issues are not new or critical (most of the proposals have been around for years, and those battles are settled, and there will be no money available for controversial expensive projects anyway), and because the process is only that and is recognized as such by the participants. Final decisions are made in another arena. However, all would agree that the experience significantly enhances the regions representatives' ability to work together.

THE STATUS OF REGIONAL PLANNING

To develop a more general picture of the current status of planning for regional development and decision making and to inquire into the future of such planning we interviewed 16 knowledgeable persons from state government and the major regional organizations. They were very cooperative and responsive in the interviews, although there were some requests for anonymity on sensitive issues such as assessing the efficacy of competing agencies, and these requests have been honored. The results of these interviews are not presented as representative of the regional decision-making community or of the organizations where our respondents are employed. The results are the opinions of our respondents.

Current Issues

If we simply tally up the mentions of current major policy issues, two stand out: transportation and solid waste disposal. The transportation issue is in the forefront of awareness because of the recently completed 2010 Plan and because of the near crisis conditions of central city transit and suburban road congestion. Solid waste disposal by contrast is not being addressed on a regional basis but is being addressed everywhere in the region.

Only a small part of the concern for transportation is with the traditional issue of major new projects. Most of the concern among transportation providers is over securing adequate funds to both maintain the existing system and to accomplish already agreed upon extensions. Managing the balance between maintenance and expansion needs appears especially crucial in transit service. The second most common concern is with managing suburban traffic congestion due to increased development and the changing job and residence location patterns resulting in much more intersuburban and city to suburb work commuting.

Solid waste disposal is a major current issue because existing landfills are approaching capacity and because of the difficulty of locating new facilities for landfill or incineration. Waste disposal has been made a planning issue by the state legislature's requiring counties to prepare comprehensive solid waste management plans in 1991 and implement them by 1992. The law requires that all disposal methods be considered and that the county recycle 25 percent of its waste within five years. NIPC is credited with playing an important communication and coordination role on this issue, but all respondents agree that there are no regional approaches being developed. The planning will require county-municipal cooperation, and our respondents think this may be difficult. In Cook County the three municipal associations are developing plans for their constituents with little interaction or countywide coordination. In DuPage County the Solid Waste Committee composed of only county board members was changed by the state (Public Act 85-14) in 1987 to require equal county and municipal representation. A resulting draft plan has encountered stiff opposition to siting of proposed landfill and incineration facilities and has spawned an active oppositional citizen's group.

Two basic characteristics of development decision making in the region are demonstrated in these issues. One is that the major agencies and local governments have a strong tendency to "go it alone" on issues. For example, John Gaudette of the RTA stressed that whatever decision is reached on transit funding priorities, it will be made by the RTA Board and no one else. The other decision-making characteristic is that the state legislature is the place where local governments go to settle regional and subregional issues. Closely related to these characteristics of decision making are two characteristics of implementation. The multi-issue regional agencies are given very little influence, and there is heavy reliance on special districts to solve problems as they arise. The waste disposal requirements appear likely to generate a new set of such special-purpose organizations.

There are two further issues that get frequent mention, about half as often as transportation and solid waste disposal. These are water quality and distribution and affordable housing in the suburbs.

What is the Future Regional Agenda?

We explored the possible future agenda of regional development issues indirectly by asking what issues are currently left out of the regional planning and decision-making process and, directly, by asking what issues our respondents thought would require cooperative planning over the next 10 years. One issue stands out on the list of those currently left out. That issue is affordable housing in the suburbs. It was raised and discussed in a variety of ways and almost always linked with the changing distribution of job opportunities. The issue might be best called the housing/jobs imbalance problem. Employment opportunities have been growing rapidly in the suburbs, as discussed in the introduction to this chapter, and housing that could be afforded by people holding those jobs is not available and not being produced in the suburbs.

The only other issue to get much mention as a current problem not being actively considered is regional economic development. Our respondents mentioned the lack of any regional agency with a clear mandate and authority to address economic development and were critical of the state government, particularly the Department of Commerce and Community Development, for failure to perform adequately on this issue.

Turning to the discussion of a future regional planning agenda, two issues stand out clearly: solid waste disposal and the housing/jobs balance. State legislation has placed solid waste planning and implementation responsibility with the counties. Our respondents see this as an issue that will remain at the top of the regional agenda because of the cost of exporting waste and the difficulty of resolving conflicts over siting of facilities within the region.

The housing/jobs balance issue is also seen as centered in the conflict between local and regional perspectives. This is supported by NIPC's experience some years ago when they attempted to address fair and affordable housing policies with their member organizations. The results were clearly negative and cost NIPC much goodwill. Most of our respondents thought affordable housing should be addressed as a regional issue, but most also said they thought it would not be addressed regionally because it involves so many difficult issues, including racial and social discrimination, adequacy of property revenues to support development, local land-use regulation, and self-determination of the character of communities.

Three issues shared the second rank of projections for the next decade's agenda: water quality and quantity, air quality, and the balance between the maintenance of existing regional infrastructure and investment in new infrastructure. NIPC has been active in the past decade providing leadership in groundwater, stream, and wetlands protection. Lake and DuPage Counties have also been active and take credit for joint action resulting in state legislation for county storm water management planning. Because increased development will force more reliance on Lake Michigan water in the suburbs, access to lake water and control of its distribution have become major political issues. Lake County has joined with several suburban municipalities to create a water commission that would distribute lake water directly to the suburbs, freeing them from reliance on purchases from lakeside municipalities. In DuPage County access to lake water is crucial for further land development because local communities have been forced to rely on deep wells with limited and declining quantity and quality of water. In 1984 a multimunicipality commission in DuPage was contracting with Chicago for delivery of lake water. DuPage County went to the state legislature to try to get county control over all distribution of lake water in the county. In a counter move the municipalities succeeded in getting an amended bill in 1985 that created the independent DuPage Water Commission with half the members appointed by the county board and half by municipalities. The commission is now involved in a $379 million pipeline project to distribute lake water in the county.

Air quality has become a pressing issue because the USEPA has rejected the state's plan and is preparing its own for the Chicago region. This has caused considerable uncertainty and apprehension. The balance between funding maintenance and new infrastructure investments is seen as critical by both the service providing agencies and local governments and reflects concern about adequacy of state and local tax revenues to maintain the quality of public facilities and services. None of these top issues on the future agenda involve major new regional facilities. The most frequently mentioned facility issue is the possibility of a third regional airport. After that there is some mention of adding to the region's transit system.

So our respondents expect environmental issues (waste disposal, water, and air quality), financing existing infrastructure dependent services, and the politically difficult issue of affordable suburban housing to head the regional agenda in the next decade. Except for housing, the future agenda is much like the current agenda. And regional economic development has again been left off the list.

What Works?

The two agencies most admired by our respondents are the RTA and NIPC. The RTA is seen as very successful, following its reorganization, in bringing some coherence to regional transit services and providing a responsible financial and decision-making environment for transit. NIPC is valued as an information source and as a regional forum where issues are raised and views are exchanged. There is, however, considerable ambivalence about NIPC. For some it seems like a love/hate relationship. They like what NIPC does, but they don't want it to do much. Donald Kline, Executive Director of the Barrington Area COG, captured the dilemma. He admires NIPC, but says, as do others, that it is "a toothless tiger." He wishes NIPC had more power, but acknowledges that his constituent municipalities are not in agreement. Although commended, NIPC was mentioned as often on the list of things that don't work as it was on the list of things that do. Both those that judged NIPC positively and negatively agree that NIPC is too weak, and each group is split on whether it should be stronger.

Municipal associations were also mentioned several times as an example of what works. They were credited especially with representing the interests of their constituents before the state legislature and for developing cooperative and sharing programs (on purchasing, services, etc.) among their members. The state legislature received almost as many mentions on the list of which organizations are effective in resolving regional issues.

The pattern that emerges from our respondents is that regional agencies are most accepted if they have single issue, operational responsibilities; local autonomy is maintained through voluntary cooperation in multi-issue agencies whose mandate is clearly to represent the interests of the constituents; and the state legislature is a comfortable arena for settling issues.

Needed Organizational Change

Our respondents were nearly unanimous in agreeing that the present organizational base for resolving regional issues is inadequate for dealing with the issues that will have to be resolved in the next decade. The suggestion most often made for change was the creation of a strong comprehensive regional agency. Specific suggestions ranged from some form of regional government to a strengthened NIPC. However, the second most common suggestion was to seek greater voluntary cooperation among regional actors with emphasis on an issue by issue approach to determining participants and roles. And the third most common suggestion was to increase the state's leadership in regional decision making. The final suggestion, receiving limited support, was to strengthen local autonomy. Since the totals tallied for the first three suggestions were very close, it appears that our respondents are quite divided about how to effect the change in regional decision making they agree is needed.

CONCLUSION

The current practice of decision making on regional issues in the Chicago metropolitan area could be described as chaotic, where there is no consistency in how issues are raised and resolved. But such a description is too vague and fails to give the credit due to NIPC and others for their efforts to shape a regional agenda. Alternatively, current practice might be described as an ideal pluralist democracy, where all parties are heard at their discretion and their needs heeded. This political science textbook description is also inaccurate because political jurisdictions have very unequal influence in planning. Some groups, notably racial minorities, needs are not met; and general needs that are in the interest of the whole region, but engender competition, are not effectively addressed. Current decision-making practice does not even approach the rational planning ideal of open, comprehensive, and binding discussions and decisions on goals and alternatives.

The most mature regional decision-making process, transportation planning, somewhat resembles the political scientist's conception of "partisan mutual adjustment" to the extent that there is clear negotiation and compromise among the major participants. But even that process is faulted for not adequately treating the fundamental questions of the balance between highway and transit service, between maintenance and new investment, and between environmental protection and growth. And not all the affected groups think the process is representative.

The present pattern of initiative and action can be likened to a tug of war played with a spider web instead of a rope, with many players pulling and hauling the several strands, some in concert, some in opposition, depending on the issue. But almost never enough of them together for long enough to move in any direction. As things are presently organized, effective leadership is impossible. Some might liken this to the political scientist's concept of incrementalism were movement is in small, cautious steps. But this is more nearly a stalemate where even small steps are seldom achieved.

Now leadership is divided both by role and by issue. On the subject of role, Tom Berkshire of the governor's office stated the role division with which most of our respondents seem to agree: the state legislature is good for resolving issues but not for raising them; NIPC is good at bringing up issues. NIPC has been placed in the difficult role of being the region's conscience. It raises the problematic issues. If NIPC were in a strong position to follow through on its initiative with independent fact finding and analysis, it could offer some incentive to other actors for their participation in finding solutions and could legitimately advocate the region's interests before federal, state, and local lawmakers and regulators. Then NIPC could exercise the needed leadership. However, it has none of these attributes.

Its financial dependence on voluntary contributions is the clearest symptom of NIPC's dilemma. According to Larry Christmas, Executive Director, NIPC is one of only seven regional councils serving the nation's 25 largest metropolitan areas that do not receive regular funding through state appropriation, a direct tax levy or rebate, or state mandated local government contributions. To its credit NIPC currently raises a very substantial 38 percent of its revenue from voluntary contributions and from selling services locally. This shows the positive regard of local actors for the agency, but also indicates its vulnerability. NIPC has neither the level nor certainty of funding required to carry out a strong leadership role.

Probably the major change in issue leadership during the past decade has been the increase in municipal associations and county activity on subregional issues. Unfortunately the associations and county interests are often at odds, and there is considerable struggle between them. As in the DuPage water commission example, the state legislature is the arena where these conflicts are resolved. The state does not play a leadership role on regional issues, however. It simply reacts to local pressures. There is no effective state planning for the Chicago region, even across state provided services (Hemmens 1988).

A skeptic might ask whether the weakness of the region in settling internal issues is important. Are there significant regional issues that are not met? In its attempt to develop a truly regional rather than Chicago-based agenda, the Metropolitan Planning Council surveyed the region about regional issues. They found that transportation is considered the only problem that can't be solved by the localities (Metropolitan Planning Commission 1987). MPC has essentially given up on developing a regional program. Mary Decker, MPC Executive Director, summarized the difficulties: the region is too large; it is hard to fund suburban studies; and it is hard to find problems you can do something about. Larry Christmas, NIPC Executive Director, agrees that the large size and diversity of the region supports fragmented decision making.

But Larry Christmas, Mary Decker, and almost all of our respondents point to the existing unresolved problems and the unaddressed issues relevant to the regions's future as evidence of the need for better planning and decision making. Regional economic development is perhaps the most important of the unaddressed issues. There is general agreement that the state and its Department of Commerce and Community Affairs have failed to provide leadership on these issues, or even adequate marketing of the region. As discussed in the introductory section, the continued strength and competitive position of the Chicago area economy is an open issue, and not simply a central city or suburban issue, but a joint one.

Options

Given the present situation and the political history of the region, three scenarios of future organization for planning and decision making seem possible.

The first scenario is development of a strong regional agency. This could be accomplished by combining NIPC and CATS and possibly some parts of other existing regional agencies. Such an agency would have the benefit of building on past experience, custody of acknowledged regional issues, and, perhaps most important, the incentive for cooperation created by access to federal grant funds. It would need mandated funding to be effective. It would also require that the state yield to the region some of the power it now holds. The transportation planning process is successful in part because the cost of failure in loss of federal dollars is high. Similar sticks and carrots are not available on other issues. By granting increased regional autonomy but requiring regional agreement, the state could create similar sticks and carrots with state and federal pass-through funds. However, the tradition of local home rule, diversity of issues, and established issue constituencies would be major obstacles to the success of such an agency.

The second scenario features strengthened subregional planning, focused on county government. This would require county home rule and an increased role for counties in service provision and development regulation. Regional issues would still require a council of counties to resolve disputes and reduce conflict in the state legislature. This scenario runs counter to the established practice of municipal home rule and would run head-on into the growing power of municipal associations. It would also produce very unevenly matched regional partners. DuPage and Lake would emerge as very strong counties. The non-Chicago portion of Cook, which is physically divided into north and south sections by Chicago, would be difficult to govern integrally. The alternative of combining the city of Chicago and the remainder of Cook County into a single unit would increase the unevenness among regional partners, and would be politically improbable at best.

The third scenario is for the state to increase its role as regional policy leader. From a bureaucratic perspective this looks like a sensible proposition. State services are regionalized now, but these regions do not conform with the Chicago metropolitan region or with each other. State operations could be improved by more sensible regionalization. And regionalization of the state executive's policy process would promote a more consistent approach to Chicago region issues and to those of other parts of the state. A regional policy structure, however, goes against the entrenched rural/urban, suburb/big city divisions in the state. Also, while the Chicago suburbs look to the legislature as a participatory setting for resolving their issues, they are not likely to turn more of their interests over to the state executive. Nor is Chicago likely to agree to such a change.

Each of these scenarios has obvious strengths and weaknesses. None is clearly feasible because there are strong forces or traditions opposed.

In summing up the situation, it seems to us that three important actors are failing to meet their responsibilities. The state executive branch's shortcomings have already been discussed. Second, the city of Chicago is a quiet giant on regional issues. Recent city policy has understandably emphasized internal economic development, but the evolution of a new regional balance of jobs and housing can't be forestalled, and it might be guided to everyone's betterment. Chicago, with a large cadre of traditionally loyal legislators, has preferred to battle and bargain in the state legislature, forming varied alliances with other groups. A recent analysis of intergovernmental activity in the region found that "Chicago's involvement with suburban governments is minimal to nonexistent" (Banovetz 1988, 28). Third, the private sector, through the activities of the nonprofits, has been ineffective in addressing regional issues, except within the United Way/Crusade of Mercy arena, and even there regional efforts are limited primarily to fund raising. The Regional Partnership is the most recent effort to form a private/public agenda for the region. It is inadequately funded and staffed, but it continues to try. Its newest approach, started in July 1989, is to hold Briefing Councils for the directors of regional organizations, covering state legislation among other issues.   But it lacks the broad base and political legitimacy to be an effective leadership organization.

Each of these three has the opportunity to break the existing stalemate on regional development. A prerequisite for effective, practical change is the election of a Chicago mayor and an Illinois governor who share common interests and see that they have common problems. This has not been the case for more than a decade. No substantial, permanent changes are possible, however, until a regional perspective is developed and widely shared.

INTERVIEWS

Rita Athis, Assistant Director, Northwest Municipal Conference
David Baker, Executive Director, Illinois State Chamber of Commerce
David Bennet, Executive Director, West Central Municipal Conference
Thomas Berkshire, Governor's Office, Springfield
Aristide Biciunas, Executive Director, CATS
Robert Chave, Director, Lake County Planning Commission
Lawrence Christmas, Executive Director, NIPC
Mary Decker, Executive Director, MPC
Robert Duboe, Assistant Planning Analyst, CATS
William Dugan, Transportation Planner, Northwest Municipal Conference
Peter Elliot, Director of Work Program Development, CATS
James Ford, Director of Intergovernmental Relations, NIPC
John Gaudette, Assistant Executive Director for Program and Capital
   Development, RTA
Elizabeth Hollander, Commissioner of Planning, City of Chicago
Donald Kline, Executive Director, Barrington Area Council of
   Governments
Phillip Peters, Director of Planning, NIPC
Beth Ruyle, Executive Director, South Suburban Mayors and Managers
   Association
Theodore Weigle, Executive Director, RTA
Kermit Wies, Associate Program Planner, CATS
Paula Wolff, Director of Programs and Policy, Governor's Office

REFERENCES

Austrian, Ziona, and Thomas J. Zlatoper. 1988. The Role of Export Services. *The REI Review*. Cleveland: The Center for Regional Economic Issues, Fall.

Bania, Neil, and Lindsay N. Calkins. 1988. Local Government Expenditures in Large Metropolitan Areas. *The REI Review*. Cleveland: The Center for Regional Economic Issues, Fall.

Banovetz, James N. 1988. Taxation, Service Delivery and Government Capacity. *The State of the Region*. Chicago: The Regional Partnership.

Bouge, Donald J., and Albert Woolbright. 1983. *Population Projection: Chicago SMSA, Chicago City, and Metropolitan Ring 1980-2000*. Chicago: Metropolitan Planning Council.

Chicago Area Transportation Study (CATS). 1981. *25 Years of Transportation Planning*.

_____. 1982. *Year 2000 Planning Process and Appendix*. July.

_____. 1988a. *Transportation Improvement Program FY 89-93-FY 1989 Annual Element*. October 13.

_____. 1988b. *2010 Transportation System Development Plan—Public Hearing Draft*. December.

_____. 1989. *2010 Transportation System Development Plan—Technical Process Report*. January.

Chicago Transit Authority (CTA). 1987. *Transit in Transition—Year End Report*.

DuPage County Development Department. 1988a. Intergovernmental Issues Related to Updating the Comprehensive Plan for DuPage County.

_____. 1988b. *Annual Report of Development Department Activities*. December 7.

_____. 1988c. *Impacts of Land Development and the Role of the DuPage County Regional Planning Commission Within the Land Use Plan Update Process*. February 15.

_____. 1989. *1989 Draft Countywide Plan—Background, Analysis and Remaining Issues*. Planning Division, February 21.

Fiske, Barbara Page, editor. 1989. *KEY to Government in Chicago and Suburban Cook County*. League of Women Voters. Chicago: University of Chicago Press, 1989.

Gerut, John D. 1989. Lake Michigan Water for DuPage County: A Political Struggle. Mimeo, March.

Hemmens, George C. 1988. Social Services. *The State of the Region.* Chicago: The Regional Partnership, December.

Lake County Department of Planning Zoning and Environmental Quality. 1987. *Annual Report.* Waukegan, Ill.

Metra. 1987. *The Formation and Historical Development of Metra.* Office of the Executive Director. November.

Metropolitan Housing and Planning Council (MHPC). 1980. *Regional Transportation Authority: Future Financing, Structure and Operations.* Chicago, December.

_____. 1982a. *Strategies and Options for Development of the Chicago Regional Passenger Transport Network to the Year 2000.* Report No. 15, Map 2000 Project. James A. Bunch and Joseph L. Stopher. Chicago, July.

_____. 1982b. *An Assessment of the Condition and Reinvestment Needs of Chicago's Mass Transit System.* Report no. 12, MAP 2000 Project. Werner Paul Zorn. Chicago, September.

_____. 1982c. *Map 2000. Chicago Area Public Capital Investments: Toward the Year 2000.* Second Committee on Urban Progress. Chicago, December.

_____. 1984. *Final Report Infrastructure '84. Condition and Financing Needs of Northeastern Illinois' Public Capital Plant, and an Outline of Policy Options.* Chicago, May.

Metropolitan Planning Council (MPC). 1987. *Annual Report.*

Metropolitan Water Reclamation District of Greater Chicago (MWRD). 1982. *1982 Annual Report.*

_____. 1987a. *1987 Chief Engineer's Report.*

_____. 1987b. *1987 Annual Report of the Maintenance and Operations Department.*

_____. 1987c. *Comprehensive Annual Financial Report of the Metropolitan Sanitary District of Greater Chicago.*

_____. n.d. Tunnel and Reservoir Plan—Mainstream Pumping Station.

Norman, Andrew. 1989. Solid Waste Management in DuPage County. Mimeo, March.

Northeastern Illinois Planning Commission (NIPC). 1977. *Comprehensive General Plan for the Development of the Northeastern Illinois Counties Area.* August 18.

_____. 1981. *Annual Report—25th Anniversary.*

_____. 1986. *Annual Report.*

_____. 1987. *Annual Report.*

_____. 1988a. *Population, Households and Employment in Northeastern Illinois 1980 to 2010.* Data Bulletin 88-1. Chicago, May.

_____. 1988b. *1987—1988 Water Quality Report.*

_____. 1988c. *Planning in Northeastern Illinois.* Vol. 29, No. 3, Winter.

_____. 1989a. Minutes. Planning and Policy Development Committee. January 4.

_____. 1989b. Minutes and Annotated Agenda. Planning and Policy Development Committee. February 5.

_____. 1989c. Annotated Agenda. Planning and Policy Development Committee. March 8.

_____. 1989d. Letter from Lawrence Christmas to the Planning and Development Policy Committee, Recommendations Concerning the Inclusion of the Lake-Will Expressway North in the 2010 Transportation System Development Plan. March 2.

_____. 1989e. Letter from Phillip Peters to the Planning and Policy Development Committee, Recommended Changes to the Public Hearing Draft of the 2010 Transportation System Development Plan. March 3.

Northwest Municipal Conference. n.d. Fact Sheet and Issue Paper.

Pace. 1988. *Proposed 1989 Operating and Capital Program and 1989-91 Financial Plan and Strategic Plan Summary.* October.

The Regional Partnership. 1987. *The Leadership Agenda Regional Survey Report.* Chicago, January.

Regional Transportation Authority. 1987. *Annual Report—1987.*

_____. 1988. *Preliminary Regional Transportation Authority Annual Program and Budget for Fiscal Year 1989.* November.

_____. 1989. *Strategic Plan.* January.

Siemon. Larsen and Purdy. 1988. *Lake County Framework Plan Implementation White Paper.* (mimeo) Chicago, June 27.

South Suburban Mayors and Managers Association. 1988. *Annual Report.*

United Way of Chicago. 1988. Environmental Analysis Committee. *The Changing Face of Chicago's Human Need Environment.* Chicago.

West Central Municipal Conference. 1988. *Bylaws.*

_____. 1989. *1989 Legislative Position Statement*

Chapter 4

Planning and Servicing the Greater Toronto Area: The Interplay of Provincial and Municipal Interests

Frances Frisken

York University

INTRODUCTION

The name Metropolitan Toronto is virtually synonymous in North America with effective metropolitan administration. The creation of a federated form of metropolitan government for the city of Toronto and its 12 suburbs in 1953 and the rapidity with which it was able to overcome serious public service deficiencies made the Toronto model an object of admiration for students of metropolitan affairs throughout the continent. To some observers, the area seemed to have achieved the ideal administrative arrangement for the large, multimunicipal urban complex: a system of government that preserved the existence and integrity of local units while allowing for the coordinated and effective treatment of areawide servicing needs (Committee for Economic Development 1970, 70-81).

One of the few certainties about the nature and pace of metropolitan development in market-driven economies, however, is that metropolitan growth soon spills over political boundaries created to contain it. The city of New York expanded from 44 to 299 square miles in 1898 through

The author thanks the Donner Foundation and the Canadian Studies Program, University of California, Berkeley, for sponsoring the work of the Metropolitan Regions Research Group of the North American Federalism Project; the Canadian Social Science and Humanities Research Council for research support; and Judith Bates and Marc McAree for research assistance.

a consolidation with Brooklyn and four suburban counties (Adams 1974, 250). It has remained the same size ever since. The city of Chicago grew more slowly, by successive annexations, from 36 square miles in 1870 to its present 224 square miles, a size it had achieved by 1950 (Jackson 1972, 445). In 1986, both cities were the cores of metropolitan areas of nearly 4,000 square miles. Similar processes have been at work in the Toronto metropolis. Metropolitan Toronto, with 240 square miles, is now the central city of a provincially defined Greater Toronto Area (GTA) more than 10 times that size. Thus its government is no longer in a position to undertake regional planning or provide major urban services to the whole of the Toronto-centered metropolis. The only government able to perform those functions is the provincial (Ontario) government, which under the Canadian constitution has full responsibility for municipal affairs.

This paper focuses on the way the Ontario government is exercising its responsibility for managing the development of the Toronto metropolis. Such a focus not only accords with current reality but also permits examination of an issue that often arises in comparisons of governmental responses to metropolitan expansion in Canada and the United States: that of the relative autonomy of local governments in the two countries. Some writers have cited the creation of metropolitan or regional governments in several Canadian provinces as evidence that provincial governments are more willing and better able than state governments to act on urban problems as they arise, thereby avoiding the more severe problems associated with metropolitan area growth in the United States (Goldberg and Mercer 1986, 197-98; Robinson 1986, 247-48). There are others who argue, however, that provincial hegemony in local affairs has had the negative effect of preventing Canadian local governments from acting in the best interests of their own communities (Fish 1976; Bird and Slack 1983). The more directly involved provincial governments become in matters formerly delegated to local units, the more such criticisms are heard.

This paper deals with these issues in two ways. First, it shows that the powers the Ontario government has kept in its own hands have given it impressive legal and institutional *potential* to influence the way the Toronto area develops. Second, the paper uses case study evidence to show that local politics and the activities of local governments are not irrelevant to an understanding of the way the Toronto area has developed in the past and is likely to develop in the future. Local actions and priorities can in fact be as much a constraint on the way a provincial government responds to areawide issues as provincial laws and regulations can act as constraints on local self-determination.

THE GREATER TORONTO AREA

The term Metropolitan Toronto signifies the jurisdictional entity established in 1953 to take in the city of Toronto and the 12 (now five) suburban municipalities surrounding it. It does not signify the current extent of Toronto-related development. Even the Toronto Census Metropolitan Area (CMA), as defined by Statistics Canada, fails to serve that purpose. Instead, both the provincial and Metropolitan Toronto governments have drawn the boundaries of the Toronto metropolis to encompass most of the Oshawa CMA on the east and part of the Hamilton CMA on the west. This larger area takes in Metropolitan Toronto and four two-tier regional municipalities (Durham on the east, York on the north, Peel and Halton on the west) established by the province between 1971 and 1974 as part of a large-scale reorganization of the area's local governments (Map 4.1).[1] Metropolitan Toronto planners refer to this entity as the Toronto Region; provincial officials as the Greater Toronto Area. Because the regional municipalities are often referred to as "regions," a source of possible confusion, the name Greater Toronto Area (or GTA) is used in this paper.

With just over 2,700 square miles the GTA occupies only 0.3 percent of Ontario's total land area but in 1991 contained 41.6 percent of the province's population, up from 33.8 percent in 1961. From 1961-91 the GTA's share of the population of Canada rose from 11.5 percent to 15.4 percent. Projections based on current trends suggest that the area will have about 5.3 million people in 2011, at which time it will account for about 45 percent of the Ontario population (Ontario Ministry of Treasury and Economics, Office of Economic Policy 1989, 15).

---

[1]While most provincial ministries have accepted the five-region definition as the basis for analysis of GTA trends and the development of policy instruments to manage them, the provincial Ministry of Transportation has sponsored at least two studies that include a sixth region, Hamilton-Wentworth, which encircles the western end of Lake Ontario, (Frisken with McAree 1989; Transit Advisory Group, 1987).

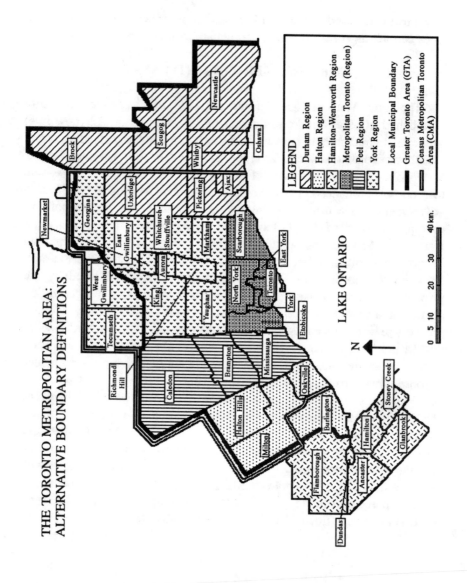

THE TORONTO METROPOLITAN AREA:
ALTERNATIVE BOUNDARY DEFINITIONS

Nearly 92 percent of the GTA's 1991 population of 4.2 million lived in Metro Toronto and 11 nearby municipalities comprising less than 40 percent of the GTA's land area. Thus, there is still considerable room for new settlement within currently recognized boundaries of the Toronto metropolis. Nonetheless, the area's population is becoming increasingly decentralized. Until 1971 Metropolitan Toronto absorbed the bulk of the area's new population growth, at the rate of about 50,000 persons per year, but after that date its growth dropped off sharply. While the GTA has continued to absorb more than 50,000 persons per year since 1971, most of that growth has occurred outside Metro Toronto.[2] Consequently Metro's share of the area's population fell from 77.0 percent in 1961 to 54 percent in 1991.

Projections based on current trends indicate that Metro's population (which currently stands at about 2.3 million) will grow little and may even decline by the year 2011 while the GTA continues to grow by slightly less than its current rate (Metropolitan Toronto Planning Department, Research and Policy Division 1989, 13). The provincial government has nonetheless accepted a Metro Planning Department population target for the year 2011 of 2.5 million, a figure that assumes that Metro will be able to encourage a substantial increase in in-migration and the production of new housing. Even if Metro succeeds in doing so, it is expected to account for less than half the area's population by 2011.

The change occurring in Metro Toronto's relative position in the Greater Toronto Area is parallel to the change that occurred in the relationship of the city of Toronto to the rest of Metro at an earlier time. In 1951, just before the creation of Metropolitan Toronto, the city had about 676,000 people, or 60 percent of the population of the 13 municipalities. In 1991 the city had 635,000 people, or 28 percent of the population of Metropolitan Toronto and only 15 percent of the population of the GTA.

Declines in Metro's and the city's relative positions in terms of population size have not been accompanied by signs of the economic decline that has afflicted other North American cities whose populations have been overtaken or surpassed by their suburbs (Gluck and Meister 1979, Teaford 1979). Rather, patterns and trends in the location of GTA employment indicate that both Metro and its core city are leading

---

[2]Between 1986 and 1991, the average population increase rose to just over 100,000 persons per year.

participants in the development of the GTA economy and are likely to remain so for the foreseeable future.

Economic Activity

In the words of the Metropolitan Toronto Planning Department, "The Toronto Region is the economic heartland of the country, accounting for nearly two out of every 10 jobs in Canada and more than four of every 10 jobs in Ontario" (Metropolitan Toronto Planning Department, Policy Development Division 1986a, 39). The importance of the GTA to both Ontario's and Canada's economy is clearly illustrated by figures compiled from 1985 Statistics Canada data (Table 4.1) showing the Toronto CMA's share of employment exceeding its share of population for most employment categories. They also attest to a high degree of diversification, a characteristic that has made the area less vulnerable, though by no means immune, to the effects of recession than other parts of the country.

Like metropolitan areas throughout the continent, the Greater Toronto Area is participating in two important trends having far-reaching implications for government policy. One is a gradual shift of employment, particularly manufacturing employment, from central to peripheral locations. The second is a decline in manufacturing sector and an increase in office and service sector jobs. While industrial decline seems to represent a generalized decline affecting the country as a whole, rather than a shift of industry away from the GTA to other parts of the country (Gertler 1985), a shift of industry out of the city of Toronto and, more recently, out of Metropolitan Toronto has given rise to concern in planning and academic circles (City of Toronto Planning Board 1974; Norcliffe and Goldrick 1986; Muszynski 1985). Metropolitan Toronto's share of total manufacturing employment in the Toronto CMA fell from 78 percent to 71 percent between 1971 and 1981. During the same period employment in manufacturing industries grew by 26.8 percent in the CMA as a whole but by only 15.5 percent in Metro Toronto (Metropolitan Toronto Planning Department, Policy Development Division 1986b, 55). Within Metropolitan Toronto, manufacturing and warehouse employment declined by 10.8 percent between 1981 and 1985 and is expected to decline by a further 9 percent by 2011. On the other hand, Metro is expected to gain jobs in all other categories (office, retail, service, institutional, and "footloose"), with the largest gain (78 percent) occurring in the office sector.

Table 4.1. *Toronto CMA Employment and Population, 1985, as Percentage of Ontario's and Canada's*

Employment	Ontario	Canada
Manufacturing	41.8	21.5
Construction	42.8	18.0
Transportation, Communication, and Utilities	40.6	13.8
Trade	46.4	19.0
Finance, Insurance, and Real Estate	61.0	27.0
Community, Business, and Personal Services	42.8	16.6
Goods Producing	40.8	19.2
Service Producing	42.9	16.6
Total	42.3	17.3
Population	35.1	12.5

Source: Metropolitan Toronto Planning Department, Policy Development Division, 1986a: 40. (Based on Statistics Canada Catalogues 72-002, 91-210, 91-211, 1985.)

Current trends in the area's economic development mean that the GTA's core municipalities have become increasingly reliant on their ability to attract office-based activities. By the beginning of 1988, Metropolitan Toronto's 112.5 million square feet of office space accounted for 89.3 percent of all office space in the GTA. Two-thirds of Metro's and over half of GTA office supply was located in the city of Toronto (Metropolitan Toronto Planning Department Research Division 1989, 22). And while both Metro and the city have experienced a decline in their share of GTA office space, they have nonetheless been absorbing a substantial share of GTA growth in this sector. Steady growth in office space and office jobs within Metropolitan Toronto has meant that Metro's 69.8 percent share of the area's employment in 1981 was higher than its share of the area's population (62.5 percent) and is expected to remain so at least until 2011.

The impacts of rapid growth, the location of an increasing share of the area's population and employment outside Metropolitan Toronto, and the growing importance of the office and service sectors to the area's economy are trends fueling the planning and policy deliberations of all governments operating in the GTA. The issues that have thus far attracted the greatest attention include problems of solid waste management, transportation, and an emerging need for increased sewer and water capacity in Metro Toronto and the regions of York and Halton.

The only social issue to attract much attention so far is an areawide shortage of "affordable" housing for low- and moderate-income residents. Social issues attract less attention in the Toronto area than they do in United States cities at least partly because the central city does not have badly deteriorated districts characterized by high concentrations of impoverished families and the problems associated with them. Instead, high demand for housing in Metropolitan Toronto, including the core city, has meant the conversion of many older districts to middle-class use. Public housing is scattered widely throughout Metro, not confined exclusively to the core city. In addition, the provincial grant structure and the allocation of local responsibility for education, policing, and social services to the metropolitan or regional levels of government have helped reduce intermunicipal fiscal and service disparities not only within Metro but in the GTA as a whole. For all these reasons the social problems associated with urban growth and decline have been less evident and therefore less likely to attract media attention or generate public demands for government action. Nonetheless a sharp rise in unemployment and welfare caseloads in the early 1990s, cutbacks in federal transfer payments to the provinces, and the 1990 electoral victory of the moderately socialist New Democratic party (for the first time in the province's history) have given social issues greater prominence in debates about the area's future. Those debates involve numerous representatives of a provincial-local governmental system that is steadily becoming more complex.

THE GOVERNMENTAL SYSTEM

The Provincial Government and Its Agencies

The unit of government with greatest potential to influence development patterns and the provision of services in the Greater Toronto Area is the provincial cabinet, a body composed of the provincial premier (the leader of the majority party) and ministers chosen from among elected members of his or her party (Bell and Pascoe 1988). While cabinet decisions have to be ratified by the legislature before becoming law, party discipline makes ratification a foregone conclusion as long as one party holds a majority of seats in the legislature. Elected members of the provincial parliament (MPPs) are able to influence provincial policymaking only within the confines of the party caucus and through their membership on parliamentary committees.

Two powerful committees, the Policy and Priorities Board and the Management Board of Cabinet, are respectively responsible for providing the cabinet with advice about policy and for overseeing the allocation of provincial resources. These two committees are expected to review and coordinate policy proposals and funding requests coming from the various ministries, as well as make recommendations as to their order of priority. Of approximately 30 provincial ministries, 10 have been closely involved in GTA planning and servicing issues. The most prominent of these are the Ministries of Transportation, Municipal Affairs, Environment, Housing, and Treasury and Economics. The others include the Ministries of Education, Community and Social Services, Agriculture and Food, Health, and Natural Resources.

A newcomer among provincial agencies concerned with Toronto area development is the Office of the Greater Toronto Area, headed by a Deputy Minister. The OGTA was established in 1988 within the Ministry of Treasury and Economics and then shifted in 1989 into the Ministry of Municipal Affairs. After taking office in 1990 the New Democratic government shifted it into the Ministry of the Environment, a move attesting to the importance that the new government was assigning to environmental issues, particularly those having to do with solid waste management. The OGTA has no legislative mandate but rather defines its role as one of (a) fostering communication among units and levels of government with an interest in the area's future development, (b) seeking solutions to immediate problems that no single government can solve on its own, and (c) helping governments in the area "develop a consensus on what the Greater Toronto Area should look like 20 years from now" (Office of the Greater Toronto Area 1989).

Another unit of provincial government with a decisive voice in GTA development is the Ontario Municipal Board, an appointed tribunal with broad powers to decide issues of municipal administration. Among the most important of its powers are the authority to hear appeals of municipal planning decisions and to approve municipal capital expenditures. Because most planning decisions of any substance are appealed, the OMB's power to decide the pace and pattern of development in the GTA is formidable. An OMB decision is final unless the government has already declared that it has an interest in the matter at issue, in which case it can be overturned by the cabinet.

The Environmental Assessment Board and the Environmental Appeal Board provide two additional avenues for public appeal of planning and development decisions and may thus have substantial influence on the way governments respond to growth. The job of the first is to facilitate public input regarding projects having "significant environmental impact," and to conduct public hearings on matters related to such projects (Bell and Pascoe 1988, 92). The Environmental Appeal Board hears appeals of Ministry of Environment or local health board decisions having implications for air, soil, or water quality.

In addition to the work being done by these and other provincial agencies, discussions and debates about planning and public services in the GTA are taking place within a number of hybrid organizations that allow for varying degrees of municipal involvement. Principal among these organizations are:

1. The Interim Waste Authority Limited (IWA), a crown agency established by the provincial government in April 1991 to identify new solid waste disposal sites for Metro, York, Peel, and Durham regions. The new agency replaced a Solid Waste Interim Steering Committee composed of provincial, regional, and local officials. Its management board consists of four senior civil servants who report to the Deputy Minister for the Greater Toronto Area. Opportunities for local involvement have been limited to (1) requests that municipal officials comment on documents prepared by IWA staff and (2) a series of open houses and workshops for the general public. The Minister of the Environment has said, however, that the authority is a one-time response to a serious deficiency of waste disposal capacity in the GTA, and that the government intends to make regional governments responsible for waste management and reduction as soon as that problem is solved.

2. The Toronto Area Transit Operating Authority, composed of the chairs of Metropolitan Toronto and the regions of Durham, York, Peel, Halton, and Hamilton Wentworth, and chaired by a provincial appointee. It operates the GO-Transit commuter system, a network of rail and bus lines radiating from Metropolitan Toronto to cities and towns in all parts of the GTA. The provincial government pays the system's operating deficit and must approve all extensions to it.

3. A Greater Toronto Coordinating Committee (GTCC) established in 1987 after the Deputy Minister of Municipal Affairs urged the government to improve its capacity to deal comprehensively with pressures

created by rapid growth outside Metropolitan Toronto. While the chair of this body is appointed by the provincial government, its members consist of the Chief Executive Officers of Metropolitan Toronto, the four regions, the city of Toronto, and seven local municipalities bordering on Metro. It was this committee that persuaded the government to set up the Office of the Greater Toronto Area (OGTA).

4. The Greater Toronto Area Transportation Planning Forum, assembled in 1986 by the Ministry of Transportation and Communications (now Ministry of Transportation) to involve local officials in discussions about the allocation of provincial funds for major transportation improvements. The forum holds regular meetings of provincial planning and transportation officials and their consultant advisers.

5. The Metropolitan Toronto and Region Conservation Authority and several other conservation authorities that manage watersheds within different sections of the GTA. The MTRCA has 53 members, 25 from Metro and 25 appointed by three regional governments (Peel, York, and Durham) and two rural townships lying north of the Peel boundary. The provincial government appoints three members to this and other conservation authorities and pays up to 55 percent of their costs. The MTRCA is not only the largest but also the best funded of Ontario's 38 authorities because it can draw on Metropolitan Toronto's healthy tax base for much of its local funding. Consequently it has been able to acquire 26,000 acres (about 40.6 square miles) of land in the south-central portion of the GTA, some of which it has turned over to member municipalities to manage for recreational purposes. Its authority to regulate the use of both publicly and privately owned lands in watershed areas allows it to influence the land-use plans of municipalities and private developers.

6. The Niagara Escarpment Commission (NEC). The province created this special purpose body in 1973 to prepare a plan governing the use of lands on and bordering the Niagara Escarpment, a distinctive height of land that once formed the outer rim of a shallow sea covering parts of what are now the states of New York, Michigan, and Wisconsin, and the Province of Ontario. The escarpment stretches over 450 miles of southwestern Ontario, with part of it cutting a diagonal path through the Regional Municipalities of Halton and Peel. The NEC's authority to administer the Niagara Escarpment Plan, completed in 1983, allows it to require local municipalities to make their official plans and zoning bylaws conform to it. Recommendations on proposed amendments to the Niagara Escarpment Plan must go to the Minister of Municipal Affairs for final decision.

The NEC has 17 members, all appointed by the provincial government. Nine are chosen to represent "the public at large," eight are selected from a list of names drawn up by the councils of the regional municipalities and counties through which the escarpment passes. This power of appointment essentially makes the NEC an agent of the Minister of Municipal Affairs, despite its "arms-length" status, its land-use control powers, and its municipal representation.

While municipal officials participate directly in some agencies concerned with immediate and long-term development and servicing issues in the GTA and are able to offer advice to others, there is nothing to compel provincial officials to take their preferences into account in deciding which policies to adopt or which programs to fund. Thus, it would seem that the provincial government has all the authority and the administrative capability it needs to decide how the region will develop. Nonetheless the Office of the Greater Toronto Area claims

> The history of planning initiatives has demonstrated that any
> plan—no matter how well thought out—will succeed only if it
> has the support and commitment of the Regional and Local
> Councils, as well as the Provincial Government (OGTA 1989).

It would be premature, therefore, to conclude that the province is in complete control of planning and servicing decisions in the Greater Toronto Area without looking more closely at the process by which those decisions are made. To do this it is first necessary to describe the other governments that may become involved in that process.

Local Governments

While still a long way from possessing the vast number of local governments that exist in larger metropolitan areas in the United States, the GTA has not entirely escaped local political fragmentation and administrative complexity. To begin with, the area is partitioned into the five "regional municipalities," in which local government responsibilities are divided between upper-tier councils and the councils of 30 lower-tier units. Six of these lower-tier "area municipalities" are in Metropolitan Toronto, the others are distributed among the four suburban regions as follows: Durham, eight; York, nine; Peel, three; and Halton, four. Nonetheless, the number of local municipalities in the area is less than half the number that existed in 1966, when the provincial government began a process of municipal consolidation that reduced the number of municipalities in Metropolitan Toronto from 13 to six. Consolidation of small units into larger units was also a feature of regional government formation in 1971 and 1974.

The mode of selecting members for upper-tier councils varies from region to region. The most common method is "double direct election," whereby municipal voters elect some persons to serve on both local and regional councils at the same time. Other regional councillors hold their position by virtue of their local office. Until 1985, most Metro councillors were chosen by a system of indirect election, meaning that persons elected to local councils were either selected to serve on the upper-tier body or automatically become upper-tier councillors by virtue of winning the larger majority in a two-member ward. The city of Toronto began to elect Metro Council members directly in 1985. In 1988 the provincial government legislated a system of direct election for the whole of Metro. Only the six local mayors continue to sit on Metro Council *ex officio*.

The change to direct election of metropolitan councillors was the third major change in the government of this inner region since World War II. The first was the creation of Metropolitan Toronto itself, which began with a 25-member council made up of 12 members from the city, one member from each of its 12 suburbs, and a chair appointed in the first instance by the provincial government and subsequently chosen by Metro Council. The second major change, a substantial reorganization of the Metro system in 1967, not only saw the consolidation of Metro's 13 municipalities into six but also instituted a system of representation based on population. The change immediately put the city of Toronto in a minority position on Metro Council, with 12 members to the suburbs' 20.

The province has made successive adjustments in Metro's system of representation to reflect suburban growth, with the result that the city's share of Metro representation has continued to decline. The newly instituted, directly elected Metropolitan Council has 34 wards, nine of them within the city of Toronto. Nonetheless city of Toronto representatives have retained a strong and usually influential voice in the metropolitan federation because of the strength of the city's economy and the city's healthy assessment base, which gives it the highest per capita assessment in Metro. Because each municipality contributes to Metro Council and Metro School Board budgets on the basis of assessment rather than population, the city, with 30 percent of the Metro population in 1986, contributed 40.4 percent of upper-tier revenues (Municipality of Metropolitan Toronto 1986, 56, 84). This method of allocating regional costs among local municipalities has been extended to the suburban regional municipalities.

The other five municipalities in Metro (East York, Etobicoke, North York, Scarborough, and York) vary substantially in population size and per capita assessment. While metropolitan government has reduced disparities among them by assigning a larger share of the costs of areawide services to the wealthier municipalities, it has not eliminated competition among them for new development nor allowed the area to escape conflicts over growth-related activities (highway building, urban renewal and redevelopment, location of publicly assisted housing). Over time, however, the six municipalities have become more like each other as the suburbs have become more fully developed and their populations more heterogeneous (Social Planning Council of Metropolitan Toronto 1979, 1980). What has become increasingly apparent is that Metro as a whole is in competition with its regional neighbors (and their member municipalities) for population, economic investment, and provincial funds for infrastructure.

Within the two-tier municipalities, most responsibilities are shared to varying degrees between the two levels of government, with only a few assigned exclusively to one level or the other. In general, upper-level councils are responsible for major capital infrastructure (trunk water and sewer lines, arterial roads, waste disposal), while local councils provide similar services (water distribution, local sewage collection, local streets, garbage collection) to their own residents. Planning is also a shared responsibility, a characteristic of two-level local government that has probably been the source of more confusion and dissension than any other feature, as will be discussed in more detail later. Regional governments administer most social services, although the city of Toronto operates the most extensive social housing program in the GTA. Policing is nominally a regional responsibility but is in fact administered by regional boards of police commissioners consisting of three members appointed by the provincial government and two members appointed by regional councils.

An important difference between Metropolitan Toronto and its regional neighbors is that within Metro public transit has always been an upper-level responsibility, administered by a five-member Toronto Transit Commission to which Metro appoints members and provides the local share of operating subsidy. (The local share is roughly equal to the subsidy given by the province). In the regions public transit has remained a responsibility of the local municipalities, an arrangement that has added greatly to the difficulties of developing a coordinated areawide transit system.

All the regions have systems of educational governance that function independently of their municipal councils. Metro Toronto has both a Metropolitan Board of Education, which finances the schools out of an assessment-based levy on local municipalities (which collect the taxes) and provincial grants, and local school boards, which operate the schools. In the regions public education is administered by regional boards of education with members elected in the lower-tier municipalities on the basis of population.

The only other elected bodies that operate in the area, and then only in some municipalities, are hydro-electric or public utility commissions. There is a large number of appointed special-purpose bodies, however, at both the regional and local levels. By far the most prominent of these is Metro's Toronto Transit Commission, which manages an extensive network of subway, bus, streetcar, and light rail rapid transit lines. Under its founding legislation the TTC was composed entirely of appointees who held no elected office. Throughout its existence it has been subject to periodic attempts to make it more directly accountable to Metro Council, and these have gradually eroded its independent status. In 1970 the provincial government passed a legislative amendment allowing Metro Council to appoint all five members of the transit commission from among its own members. Council continued to appoint citizen members (some of them former politicians) until 1989, when it opted for a board made up entirely of sitting council members.

The recent change in the composition of the TTC is symptomatic of a more general tendency in local government in Ontario—a gradual rejection of institutional arrangements that conform to the "apolitical ideal" of progressive reformers (who advocated the protection of politically sensitive or costly public services from interference by elected councils) in favor of arrangements that increase the powers of persons elected at the ward or district level. Nonetheless local and regional special purpose bodies still administer such services as policing, libraries, public health, Children's Aid, assisted housing of various types, public arenas, and so forth. Some of them have members appointed by municipalities; some operate with boards made up of provincial and local appointees in various combinations. The provincial government has also created special authorities to administer GO Transit and waste management for the entire GTA and has proposed the creation of a Crown corporation to administer provincial grants and loans for the construction of new sewer and water facilities in rapid growth areas. All these agencies both add to the complexity of the local government system and increase the difficulty of coherent policy formulation and coordination.

The Federal Government in the Background

A frequently noted difference between the situation of municipalities in Canada and the United States is the much less obtrusive role played by the federal government in urban affairs in Canada. The federal government tried to develop a capacity for broadly based urban research and coordination by creating a Ministry of State for Urban Affairs in 1971, but the agency survived only eight years. Otherwise, the federal government has refrained from becoming directly involved in urban policymaking. Its insistence that the provinces have constitutionally assigned responsibility for municipal affairs accords with the position vigorously promoted by some provincial governments, especially those of Ontario and Quebec. The only federal agency with an acknowledged interest in the way cities develop is the Canada Mortgage and Housing Corporation (CMHC), a crown corporation that administers nationally financed housing programs. Formerly it administered those programs in partnership with provincial governments (while paying the larger share of the costs). In recent years it has tended to turn over full administrative and greater financial responsibility to the provinces, which decide which municipal and privately sponsored programs to support. The federal government's principal means of influencing this process is by deciding how funds are allocated among programs and provinces.

Despite its noninterventionist stance, there are many ways in which the federal government influences urban development. It makes large transfers to provincial governments, which absorb them into budgets from which they make grants to municipalities. Any change in federal funding levels or funding formulae is likely to induce changes in the amount or type of provincial transfers to municipalities. Federal responsibility for interprovincial transportation allows it to make decisions (like those relating to airport location or expansion) with enormous potential for influencing the way metropolitan areas develop. Extensive land holdings in urban areas are another source of influence. Ownership of harbor-related land on the Toronto lakeshore, for example, has made the federal government a somewhat reluctant partner in a large-scale appraisal of the future of lands along the Metropolitan Toronto waterfront. Events leading to that appraisal illustrate the way all levels of government may become entangled in land-use planning decisions with major implications for the future development and character of a large urban region like the GTA.

Federal involvement in waterfront planning stems from a 1972 decision by the Liberal government in Ottawa to make available to the city of Toronto more than 100 acres of federally owned waterfront land for recreational use. Soon afterward it announced that it would fund activities on the site for only five years, after which time the district would have to be self-supporting. It then tried to distance itself from the site by turning over its management to the appointed board of a newly created crown agency, Harbourfront Corporation. The corporation adopted a development plan to which the city gave little attention, asking only that it provide the city with additional housing and maintain its recreational programs without imposing new costs on the city tax base. When the results of the Harbourfront plan began to materialize in the form of high rise apartment towers cutting off the city from the lake, critics therefore attacked both the city government for its failure to exercise sufficient planning control and the federal government for failing to pay enough attention to the agency it had created.

The federal government responded to the Harbourfront dispute by setting up a one-man Royal Commission to review not only the way Harbourfront lands had been managed but also matters related to the development of the entire Metropolitan Toronto waterfront. Not only its ownership of waterfront lands but also its responsibility for monitoring the environmental impacts of development along inland waterways justified a study of this scope. Its action immediately prompted the provincial, metropolitan, and city governments to develop or enhance their capacities for waterfront planning and regulation. This activity has added another dimension to the complex intergovernmental arrangements with which the Office of the Greater Toronto Area must deal in trying to develop "a consensus on what the Greater Toronto Area should look like 20 years from now."

A STRATEGIC APPROACH TO REGIONAL MANAGEMENT

A key element of the OGTA's consensus-building strategy is a consultant's study of the relative advantages and disadvantages of three conceptual models for the area's future development. The study assessed these models using a number of criteria, including costs of public services and implications for environmental quality, energy consumption, opportunities for economic growth, the ability to achieve sustainable development, conservation of the regional and global environment, and "quality of life for those living and working in the GTA and areas surrounding it" (IBI Group 1990, S-1). The models have become important foci of discussions and debates both among and within local and provincial agencies with an interest in the way the area evolves. They are:

1. *Spread.* This option, "representing a continuation of existing trends," implies substantial population growth in the suburbs, dispersed at a relatively low density, but with continuing concentration of office development in downtown Toronto and in subcenters both inside and outside Metro;

2. *Central.* This concept calls for substantial intensification of both population and commercial growth in the presently built-up parts of the GTA and a significant reduction in the rate of growth outside existing urban boundaries;

3. *Nodal.* This is an intermediate concept allowing growth to occur around existing communities but in a more compact form than in the past, in the interest of reducing the rate of consumption of undeveloped land.

The consultant's analysis suggests that the "central" option is the one that best meets the evaluation criteria. There are few who believe, however, that the government would be willing to exercise the amount of regulatory control needed to bring it about. On the other hand, there is widespread agreement within the GTA that the "spread" alternative is the least desirable future for the area, even if it is the one that public and private interests have been pursuing up to the present time. The compromise alternative is thus the "nodal" option, which would allow suburban municipalities outside Metro to continue to expand but in a more controlled and concentrated way than in the past. Government officials have been careful to emphasize, however, that they have neither the intention nor the desire to impose a "plan" on the area. What they are doing, they insist, is promoting an areawide "strategy" that will allow for continuing growth while maintaining a satisfactory "quality of life" for area residents. The emphasis is on "coordination" of the plans of local governments and provincial ministries to achieve a mutually agreed-on result; on "consultation" and "cooperation"; it is not on "planning."

Provincial officials insist that they are not in the business of producing a GTA plan because past experience has told them that provincial efforts to plan *for* the area imply high political and financial costs. That perception has nothing to do with political party fortunes or ideology. Rather it was passed on to the Liberal government that undertook the GTA initiatives and to the NDP government that is pursuing them by officials who worked for the Progressive Conservative government that left office in 1985. During its 42 consecutive years in office, that government intervened radically in the area's governmental system on a number of occasions. Not only did it create Metropolitan Toronto in 1953 but it also initiated, in the late 1960s and early 1970s, the most comprehensive program of local government reform ever attempted in Ontario. One element of that program was a conceptual proposal for the way the Toronto-Centered Region should develop (Ontario Department of Treasury and Economics 1970). The fate of that proposal and other elements of local government reform helps to account for the cautious approach that the Liberal and then the NDP governments have adopted in devising policies for the GTA.

The Brief Life of the Toronto-Centered Region

The Toronto-Centered Region (TCR) proposal (which provincial officials always insisted was a concept and not a plan) was adopted as government policy in 1971 and has never been formally repudiated. It served as a basis for provincial decision making in only a few instances, however, and was more typically honored in the breach than in the observance. Nonetheless it has contributed to a few decisions that help form the context in which provincial and municipal decision makers operate and for that reason remains relevant to an understanding of land use and public servicing options being discussed by governments in the GTA.

The TCR concept evolved out of two earlier provincial initiatives. The first was a 1966 regional economic development program for which the government divided the province into 10 economic regions for the purposes of regional planning and the design of programs aimed at reducing large intraprovincial disparities in wealth and rate of economic growth. The second was the provincially sponsored Metropolitan Toronto and Region Transportation Study (MTARTS) launched early in 1963 for an area slightly larger than the GTA as presently defined. That study's principal conclusion was that it was not possible to plan a transportation system for the area without some knowledge of how the area was going to develop. Consequently it devoted most of its final report to a discussion of alternative land-use scenarios for the Toronto Region, beginning with a discussion of a Trends Plan based on an extrapolation of existing municipal plans and policies (Ontario, Department of Municipal Affairs 1967). The Trends Plan, the study pointed out, implied the loss of good agricultural land; the absorption of natural landmarks (like the Niagara Escarpment) by urban expansion; the merging of existing towns and the steady outward spread of low-density residential development that would become increasingly costly to serve. As alternatives it outlined four "Goals" plans for the region, each having features to circumvent future problems implied by existing trends. Provincial planners incorporated elements of all these plans into the TCR concept.

The Toronto-Centered Region proposal took in a section of southern Ontario almost three times the size of the GTA. It was a Development Concept aimed at relieving a number of problems identified with the pattern and rapid rate of growth in and around Metropolitan Toronto. These problems included:

1.   A tendency for growth in the region to gravitate to the metropolitan core and to the south and southwest of that core, but not to the north and east.

2.   A tendency for new development in the province to gravitate to Metropolitan Toronto and areas to its west and southwest, bypassing other parts of the province.

3.   A loss of agricultural and recreational areas as the result of the rapid suburbanization of territory within commuting distance of Metropolitan Toronto.

4.   Pressures on existing urban services and the high costs of providing new trunk services to a scattered population.
The TCR concept sought to counter these problems by

1.   dividing the Region into three zones: an urbanized southern zone (Zone 1) along the lakeshore; an intermediate zone (Zone 2) just outside this urbanized zone but within easy commuting distance of it; and a peripheral zone (Zone 3) beyond Zone 2 but still within Metropolitan Toronto's sphere of influence. According to the concept, growth would be accommodated within Zones 1 and 3 but discouraged in Zone 2 (except in selected communities along the main north-south corridor leading out of Toronto) in the interest of preserving land for agricultural and recreational use.

2.   recommending that growth in the southern, urbanized zone be channelled into two tiers of well-defined municipalities: one tier close to the lake, the other further north and separated from the lakeshore "by a

parkway belt of open space with mainly nonurban uses, but containing high performance interurban transportation and other trunk services."

3. emphasizing the need to stimulate development to the east and northeast of Metropolitan Toronto to help balance growth occurring on the west and to improve Metropolitan Toronto's connections with less prosperous parts of the province.

The government indicated an intention to incorporate TCR principles and objectives into a more detailed land-use planning strategy for southern Ontario, which in turn would be a component of a comprehensive planning policy for the entire province. In 1973 it passed an *Ontario Planning and Development Act* outlining a step-by-step process for preparing a regional plan (Perry 1974, 39). Two other pieces of legislation passed that same year seemed to be additional steps toward an ongoing provincial planning program. *The Parkway Belt Planning and Development Act* allowed the government to implement a system of parkway belts and multiple-use corridors around Metropolitan Toronto, as had been proposed in the TCR concept. *The Niagara Escarpment Planning and Development Act* created the Niagara Escarpment Commission and empowered it to produce a plan for the escarpment and adjoining lands (2,000 square miles in total) with a view to their preservation as a continuous natural environment.

No provincial plan for the southern Ontario region, nor indeed for any other part of Ontario, ever appeared. Even before passing its regional planning legislation the government had displayed ambivalence about the concept. On the one hand it had persuaded the federal government to choose a site to the east of Metro for a proposed new airport and had purchased land immediately to the south of that site for a self-contained residential community. On the other hand it had agreed to land-use proposals to the north and west of Metro that violated TCR principles. These violations were noted in the 1974 report of a task force made up of provincial, Metropolitan Toronto, and regional government officials set up to review and refine the concept. It was the task force's conclusion that "The Government of Ontario is in fact now faced with a major decision: To reaffirm the TCR policy, or to abandon it" (Ontario, Central Ontario Lakeshore Urban Complex Task Force 1974, 48).

The government instead allowed the plan to languish. In 1975 it announced that it would not finance roads or other services to the new airport site, forcing the federal government to shelve the project. It persisted until 1980 with the planning of the proposed new town on Metro's eastern boundary but then abandoned that as well, saying it would go ahead only if the province and the Region of Durham were able to attract industry to the area. In the meantime the rate of growth to the west and north of Metro (some of it in Zone 2 lands targeted for recreational or agricultural use) has exceeded the rate of growth to the east ever since TCR became government policy.

Explanations for the failure of the Toronto-Centered Region Concept to shape government policy highlight the constraints perceived by government officials who are currently trying to devise a workable "strategy" for GTA development (Bordessa and Cameron 1982; Macdonald 1982; Richardson 1981). Intense opposition from powerful private interests was one explanation for the government's loss of interest. By the time the TCR concept had become provincial policy, virtually all land within a 30-mile radius of the city of Toronto was in the hands of or under option to private land developers. Those outside the urban development boundary (Zone 1) became an immediate and persistent source of pressure on government to change that boundary to allow their lands to be developed. The first to succeed was a developer whose land holdings were situated in the provincial premier's riding.

Second, the concept was incompatible with the mandates and activities of some of the province's own agencies. One of these was the Ontario Water Resources Commission, established in the mid-1950s to manage water quality, water supply, and purification. In 1968 the OWRC signed an agreement to provide municipalities immediately west of Metropolitan Toronto with facilities having enough capacity to allow them to develop to an overall density of 20 persons per acre (Urban Development Institute Ontario 1989, 11). Because most of the land to be served was already owned by private land development companies, the servicing agreement resulted in a rash of proposals for new development, many of which had been approved or were being processed when TCR appeared in 1970.

In 1972, the provincial government absorbed the OWRC into a new Ministry of the Environment, which began negotiations with the Regions of York (created in 1971) and Durham (created in 1974) for a second major trunk sewer and sewage treatment scheme for the two regions. The completion of this scheme in the late 1970s led to an intensification of development activity to the north of Metro, in areas designated by TCR for agricultural or recreational purposes.

Another provincial action that conflicted with the goals of the TCR plan was the initiation of the GO Transit commuter system in 1967. Originally introduced in an east-west corridor along the shore of Lake

Ontario, the system has expanded to provide service between Metro Toronto and communities to the north-west, north, and north-east as well. Its primary function is to bring commuters from these suburban communities to downtown Toronto, a mandate that conflicts with the TCR goals of population and employment decentralization.

High housing costs and a shortage of housing for low- and moderate-income households also generated government activities that proved to be inconsistent with TCR objectives. An Advisory Task Force on Housing Policy appointed in 1972 identified a shortage of serviced land and high servicing and development standards as factors responsible for the situation (Ontario, Advisory Task Force on Housing Policy 1973). The government acted on its recommendations by setting up an Ontario Housing Action Program (OHAP) and a Ministry of Housing with mandates to speed up the production of moderately priced housing in high need areas—a goal that did not accord well with efforts to control new development or place restrictions on where it could go.

Third, municipal governments were often as resistant as private land developers and provincial officials to TCR objectives they perceived to conflict with their own growth aspirations or jurisdictional responsibilities. The newly created region of York, much of it targeted to remain in agricultural and recreational use, took immediate exception to the maximum urban population figure of 250,000 (for the year 2000) allocated to it by TCR planners. This allocation became a central issue in negotiations about the provision of trunk sewer facilities for the region, with York insisting that a population of that size would not return enough in taxes to cover the cost of the scheme. If the province wanted the region to retain its rural character, York politicians maintained, it would have to pay the extra costs. York wanted the urban population allocation raised to about 750,000. In the end the parties compromised on a figure of 500,000, and the sewage system was designed to handle a population of that size. The region's population had gone over the 500,000 limit by 1991.

Not all municipalities wanted to grow, and those that did not also found reasons to oppose the TCR concept. To the east of Metro, in Durham region, local interests opposed the province's "go east" policy, with its implications of accelerated urban development and alteration of the region's predominantly rural character. Opposition focused particularly on the federal government's plan to build a new airport to the northeast of Metro and provided a justification for the province's 1975 decision not to provide services to the airport site.

A decline in the government's political fortunes is a fourth explanation for its loss of enthusiasm for TCR. The 1975 provincial election saw the Progressive Conservatives fail to win an absolute majority for the first time since coming to office in 1943. The results of a second election, in 1977, were similar. Thus for six years the PCs could govern only with the support of one of the two opposition parties, the Liberals or the New Democrats. Various forms of government intervention in municipal affairs were among the explanations advanced for the party's fall from favor. One of these was the regional government program (11 such governments were in place by 1975), which had aroused intense local opposition in some districts, and which was confused in the public's mind with regional planning. The increase in provincial intervention at the municipal level had also generated a strong reaction from local politicians, who maintained that the province was meddling unnecessarily in matters better handled at the local level.

Finally, the government was having to re-examine its position from a financial as well as a political perspective. Rising government expenditure and the increasing cost of servicing the provincial debt prompted the government in 1975 to create a special committee, chaired by the treasurer of Ontario, to consider ways to economize. Its recommendations, while not directly related to regional planning, did call for an end to the regional government program (because of its high costs) and for ways to control increases in provincial assistance to municipalities (Ontario, The Special Program Review 1975, 192-226). This report appeared just as the provincial economy entered a period of slower growth, giving rise to concerns about unemployment and a decline in provincial tax revenues. Increasing preoccupation with the state of the economy meant that any residual government interest in growth management quickly gave way to a willingness to accommodate new development in any locations it might choose to go.

The various reasons used to explain the Ontario government's failure to adhere to the TCR policy can be summarized as an unwillingness to follow a course of action that conflicted with the aspirations and activities of private sector interests and with the government agencies that were most responsive to private sector demands or heavily dependent on private sector investment. Those agencies existed within both the provincial and municipal governments and often worked closely together (especially with respect to sewage disposal and water facilities) to ensure that government activities maintained rather than counteracted prevailing development trends. As a result, the pattern of settlement in the GTA today is more like that described in the MTARTS Trends plan, which based its predicted land-use pattern on the plans of area municipalities in the 1960s, than it is like the patterns outlined in the TCR concept or its 1974 update.

There are only three remnants of the province's incursion into regional planning that remain relevant to current efforts to develop a strategy for future GTA development. One is the existence of segments of Parkway Belt in Peel and York regions. A good deal of land included in the Parkway Belt Plan, approved in 1978, has nonetheless been released for development. Government officials refer to what remains as a "Utility Corridor" in order to dispel residual expectations that it will serve open space uses.

A second remaining element of the TCR initiative is the Niagara Escarpment Plan, which partially protects lands for agricultural and recreational use in the GTA's rapidly growing western section (Halton and Peel regions). While the plan has managed to preserve the escarpment itself, it also has been subject to frequent amendments to allow residential development or other urban uses on contiguous lands originally designated as "natural" or "rural."

Finally, the provincial government still owns 9,000 acres of undeveloped land in Durham Region, south of land expropriated but not used for a new airport in the early 1970s. Growing concerns with a shortage of "affordable" housing in the GTA in the late 1980s prompted the government to revive its earlier intention to devote the site to the development of a model community (Seaton) featuring a mix of housing (both publicly and privately provided) for a range of income groups, densities high enough to support a good public transit system, an emphasis on conservation of land and natural resources, and the provision of employment opportunities for a substantial share of local residents. The economic slowdown and a sharp drop in housing prices in the early 1990s have once again made Seaton's future uncertain.

Apart from the lingering influence of the Parkway Belt, the Niagara Escarpment Plan and the Seaton site on provincial and municipal policy making in the GTA, the area's development pattern has been determined largely by the land-use policies of the local and, to a much lesser extent, regional municipalities. Thus, the declared intention of provincial agencies to produce a strategy that takes account of the plans and programs of the various governments at work in the area makes it important to examine the nature of those local planning activities.

Regional and Local Planning

The basis for all municipal planning in the province of Ontario is *The Planning Act*, legislation that dates back to the 1940s but has undergone substantial revisions since that time. Significant changes begun in the mid-1970s and consolidated in a major revision of *The Planning Act* in 1983 have removed the requirement that municipalities submit all planning decisions either to the Ministry of Municipal Affairs or to the OMB for approval. Instead, they allow the province to delegate most of its approval powers to regional councils that ask for such delegation, or to county or local councils in areas where regional governments do not exist. The only constraint on this power of delegation is a proviso that a municipality (including a regional municipality) cannot give final approval to its own official plan. The new procedures also require municipal councils to inform the public fully about planning matters under consideration: to hold public meetings to discuss official plans, official plan amendments, and zoning bylaws; and to inform all agencies that "council considers may have an interest" in planning matters under consideration. Persons or agencies that disagree with a local planning decision may appeal it to the Ontario Municipal Board.

The stated purpose of changes in the provincial planning system was to enhance local responsibility in planning. Countering this gesture toward heightened local autonomy, however, the revised *Planning Act* for the first time spelled out a number of "matters of provincial interest" that would justify government intervention in municipal planning. These matters include environmental protection; energy conservation; provision of major services; the health and safety of the population; the equitable distribution of educational, health, and other social facilities; and the financial viability of the government and its municipalities. The Minister of Municipal Affairs may use any of these matters as a basis for appealing local planning decisions to the Ontario Municipal Board. A board decision on such a matter does not come into effect until the provincial cabinet has confirmed it. This section of the act was a response to a frequently heard criticism that the province failed to make clear its interest in municipal planning or the basis for its objections or amendments to municipal plans.

The "matters of provincial interest" included in the act are worded so generally that they leave the province wide latitude for seeking changes in municipal planning decisions to which one or another provincial agency raises objections. When an OMB decision challenged the province's right to use that latitude in a matter for which it had not issued specific guidelines, the province simply amended its planning legislation to make it possible to "declare any matter to be of provincial interest, whether or not there is an approved provincial policy statement on that matter" (Farrow 1989, 5). The tendency, therefore, has been for Ontario's planning legislation to become increasingly explicit in specifying the government's right to override local planning decisions that it considers inconsistent with its own goals.

The Planning Act spells out the planning responsibilities of all municipalities (regional and local), beginning with the responsibility to produce an official plan. A municipal plan becomes official when it receives approval from the Minister of Municipal Affairs or his or her delegate. The act does not require municipalities to produce an official plan but it does require that municipal public works and municipal bylaws conform to municipal plans once they are in place. Lack of an official plan may weaken a municipality's ability to defend its position in planning disputes that go before the OMB.

Other matters covered by *The Planning Act* include "community improvement" (the successor to urban renewal); land-use controls, and plans of subdivision. In all cases the act describes procedures for preparing and securing approval of plans and for appealing planning decisions to the OMB. It does not specify what a plan should look like, however, nor does it require municipalities to adhere to uniform planning standards. It simply describes an official plan as "a document . . . containing objectives and policies established primarily to provide guidance for the physical development of a municipality or a part thereof . . . while having regard to relevant social, economic and environmental matters." Thus it allows municipalities substantial scope to decide the content and purpose of their own plans, but always in the knowledge that their decisions can be changed by the OMB or even by the provincial cabinet if they contravene a declared "matter of provincial interest."

This possibility makes it expedient for municipal planners and politicians to determine, through negotiations with provincial officials and a study of past OMB decisions, what is and what is not likely to be acceptable to provincial authorities. Thus the decisions that emerge from the planning process, whether or not they go to the province for review or to the OMB for adjudication, can be viewed as policy statements carrying the stamp of provincial approval. By extension, the accumulation of plans prepared by GTA municipalities constitute a government-sanctioned blueprint for the area's development. To be able to describe that blueprint, we must look at the state of planning in each of the five two-tier regions.

Planning in Metropolitan Toronto

The TCR concept was not the first attempt in the Greater Toronto Area to produce a cohesive, long-range strategy for the area's development. The first governmental body to undertake that task was the Metropolitan Toronto Planning Board (MTPB), an appointed unit established at the time of Metropolitan Toronto's creation and instructed to produce an official plan for Metropolitan Toronto (240 square miles) and an additional 480 square miles of predominantly rural territory outside its boundaries. The MTPB reported to Metropolitan Toronto Council, which was expected to adopt a plan and submit it to the provincial government for approval.

The decision to make a Metropolitan Toronto agency responsible for planning an area three times Metro's size was based on the advice of Lorne Cumming, the OMB chair who recommended Metropolitan Toronto's form of government. Cumming argued that metropolitan planning should encompass territory into which Metro was likely to expand (Ontario Municipal Board 1953, 70). The attempt failed, for Metropolitan Toronto did not manage to adopt a plan and send it forward to the provincial government until after it had lost its authority to plan for its hinterland to the four regional governments created in 1971 and 1974.

Although Metropolitan Toronto functioned without an official plan until 1980, planning has been an important activity throughout its history. Initial planning activity resulted in 1959 in a massive draft official plan that dealt in detail with those matters identified in the Metropolitan Toronto Act to fall within Metro Toronto's planning jurisdiction: land uses; sanitation; green belts and park areas; and roads and public transportation. Because the plan's detailed treatment of these matters provided many opportunities for criticism the document made little headway in the political arena. The next draft plan, issued in 1965, was a much briefer and more generally worded document. Neither this nor the earlier draft were attempts to plot a radical restructuring of the area's development pattern. Rather, both documents sought to accommodate and facilitate private sector decisions, which they depicted as the primary determinants of the area's development, by providing for orderly expansion and the provision of appropriate infrastructure. They also incorporated the planning objectives of other metropolitan agencies and local municipalities.

By 1965 Metro had adopted several elements of the proposed plan as statements of policy, including a sewage disposal plan, a water supply plan, a parks plan, a conservation plan, substantial portions of a proposed roads and transit plan, and the basic principles of a public housing plan (Comay 1964, 21). It decided not to seek "official" status for the plan itself, however, but instead adopted it as a "statement of policy," and continued to function on that basis for the next 15 years. Even though metropolitan planners had maintained close liaison with local planners and usually deferred to local planning objectives, local opposition to metropolitan planning was the principal reason for Metro Toronto's failure to adopt an official plan. For municipalities, the basic problem with metropolitan planning was a provincial requirement that local plans would have to be brought into conformity with the metropolitan plan once it had been approved. Municipalities outside Metro's boundaries objected to the idea that Metro Council, on which they had no representation, would be the agency that determined the areawide pattern to which they would have to conform. Members of Metro Council, all of them representing local councils, also had little enthusiasm for surrendering planning authority to another level of government.

Despite Metropolitan Toronto's failure to produce an "official plan" during its formative years, planning documents specified a number of planning principles or criteria that are consistent with the way Metropolitan Toronto has developed (Metropolitan Toronto Planning Board 1959, S3-S4; 1965, 3). These included an emphasis on preserving the central area (downtown Toronto) as the region's main commercial and cultural center; the promotion of secondary centers of commercial and high-density residential uses near focal points on the transportation system; the location of employment sites in all parts of the area so that people would have the opportunity to live close to their work; the provision of housing at different densities and for households of all income levels throughout the planning area (i.e., in the suburbs as well as the central city); and a transportation system that assigned a significant role to new transit facilities as well as to roads. In addition, planning proposals promoted an orderly pace and compact pattern of development by specifying an outer boundary for urban development and proposing that new areas should be opened up for development only when they were assured of a complete range of urban services.

The development of Metropolitan Toronto has been characterized by the maintenance of a strong central city; higher suburban densities than are found in most North American metropolitan areas; a diversity of land uses in all area municipalities; the dispersal of publicly assisted, low-income housing throughout the suburbs; and a transportation system in which public transit (subways, light rapid transit, and an extensive bus network) has played a prominent role.   While these characteristics conform to the principles and criteria outlined in early Metropolitan Toronto planning documents, it is impossible to distinguish the influence of metropolitan planning on the area's development from the influence of several other important factors. These include:

1. the incentive given Metro's suburban members to support measures of benefit to the central city by a financial arrangement that bases contributions to Metro on assessment rather than population;

2. the relatively large size of the area's five suburbs (particularly the outer suburbs of Etobicoke, North York, and Scarborough), which enhanced their ability to accommodate a large variety of residential and employment activities;

3. suburban enthusiasm in the 1960s for high-density residential buildings, which were perceived to yield more in revenues than they cost to serve;

4. provincial regulations enacted during the 1950s that subjected septic tank development to strict environmental controls. These not only helped to contain new growth within Metro but also meant that the outward spread of development would keep pace with the outward extension of lake-oriented sewer and water services;

5. a strong provincial role in the provision of publicly assisted family housing for a few years after 1964 (discussed later in this paper);

6. the success of Metro's first subway, opened the year Metro began, and built largely with funds accumulated by the Toronto Transit Commission during World War II. The subway's early success not only influenced transportation planning in Metro but also undoubtedly contributed to the continuing economic strength of the core city (Frisken 1991).

The official plan that Metro approved in 1980 restated most of the principles of earlier plans. It gave particular emphasis to the need to increase residential densities in order to provide new housing inside Metropolitan Toronto. It also emphasized the idea of multi-use subcenters to supplement the central area of the city, which it nonetheless expected to "remain the pre-eminent business, cultural, governmental, recreational and management center of the *Metropolitan Region*" (The Municipality of Metropolitan Toronto 1980, 15). Its stated aim was to achieve "a multi-centered urban structure" which could "be achieved through the development of *Metropolitan Centers* along *rapid transit* facilities" (italics in original).

Work on the 1980 plan began in the early 1970s with a comprehensive review of the metropolitan transportation plan, which was by then seriously at variance with the way the area's transportation system had actually evolved. In particular, city-based opposition to a major highway (the Spadina Expressway) linking downtown Toronto with suburban North York had persuaded the provincial cabinet to withhold support from the project and substantially increase its support to urban mass transit. The expressway revolt was part of a larger reaction to the perceived impacts on the city of the area's rapid development, impacts that included a proliferation of high rise office towers in the core, increasingly congested transportation facilities, and the threat posed by core expansion and residential redevelopment to downtown neighborhoods. In 1973 a recently elected "reform" city council initiated a Central Area Plan Review leading to a revised downtown plan that proposed limiting growth in the central area to the capacity of the existing transportation system (Frisken 1988, 20-52). It also explicitly favored the decentralization of some downtown functions to concentrated development nodes in the suburbs.

By the 1970s some of the suburbs as well as the central city were advocating a more decentralized urban structure. North York and Scarborough, the two largest suburbs, were particularly interested in developing "downtowns" of their own. This correspondence between local and metropolitan planning goals reflects a tendency, already apparent in metropolitan planning during Metro's first decade, for local planning goals and preferences to set the metropolitan planning agenda, in direct contradiction to the hierarchical planning relationship specified in the Metropolitan Toronto Act (Comay 1964, 14-15). Both the Metropolitan Toronto Planning Board and the Metropolitan Toronto Planning Department that replaced it in 1974 have tried to construct statements of areawide purpose that accommodate and reconcile the objectives already incorporated in local plans. Beyond that their principal roles have been to provide assistance to local planners when requested to do so (a function that has essentially disappeared as local planning staffs have grown in size and capability), identify emerging issues, and compile information that can be used for both metropolitan and local planning purposes.

The evolution of planning relationships between Metropolitan Toronto and its member municipalities was characterized in Metro's early years by disagreements between Metro and city of Toronto planners over housing and urban renewal issues, and between Metro Council and city neighborhood groups over transportation issues. (Kaplan 1982, 698-723). Such disagreements have lessened as Metro's suburbs have matured and become more like the city in their socio-economic characteristics. Nonetheless the local municipalities have become no more willing than formerly to surrender to Metro the power to decide in detail how the area is to develop. The 1980 plan is a "structure" rather than a land-use plan. That means, in the words of one metropolitan official, that it is limited to a consideration of "the broad distribution of population, households and employment activities" and the infrastructure of major physical services for which Metro is responsible (Rust D'Eye 1989, 25). It is concerned with "varying patterns of centralization and decentralization of population and employment," but leaves it up to local municipalities to determine how such a pattern is to be achieved. It is "intended to interact smoothly with area municipal official plans, rather than to mandate changes to them," sets out "principles and hoped-for or anticipated results, without the inclusion of . . . mandatory planning requirements," makes no attempt "to separate "Metropolitan interests" from local ones"; and leaves municipalities "directly responsible for the designation of land uses, zoning and development control."

Despite the high degree of generality of the 1980 plan, Metro Council adopted it only because the provincial government insisted it had to have a plan, and only after it had removed a number of contentious elements included in earlier drafts. One such element was a transportation network designed to support the plan's most fundamental principle: the multinodal urban structure. A proposal for a network of light-rail transit lines linking centers with each other and with downtown Toronto emerged several years later, after prolonged negotiations among Metro, the TTC, and local municipalities. This proposal was less a plan than a shopping list that linked together and assigned different levels of priority to the transit improvements favored by each of Metro's member municipalities (Metropolitan Toronto Planning Department and Toronto Transit Commission 1986).

While the acquisition of an official plan has not moved Metro Toronto perceptibly closer to the hierarchical planning relationship prescribed in the Metropolitan Toronto Act, it has given Metro a legal basis for appealing local planning decisions to the OMB on the grounds that they conflict with metropolitan interests. Not only has Metro been reluctant to use this power, but in two of three cases where it has done so the OMB has ruled against Metro and in favor of the local council (Rust d'Eye 1989, 50-55). Thus, Metro's role in shaping the development of the inner part of the GTA continues to depend on the ability of its planning staff to secure agreement on planning principles from the staff of local municipalities and the ability of local planners to persuade elected politicians to incorporate such principles into local plans.

The planning principle that has been most readily adopted by Metro's member municipalities is that of promoting the development of mixed-use commercial/residential nodes at or near rapid transit stations. The development of North York and Scarborough city centers is well-advanced; centers for York and Etobicoke are still in the planning stage. The city of Toronto continues to pay lip service to the idea of commercial decentralization while allowing intensive redevelopment of property in or near the downtown.

Continued development of Toronto's central area is one of the concerns being addressed by both city and metropolitan planners in recently undertaken reviews of their official plans. Not only new office/commercial development but also the construction of a major sports stadium in downtown Toronto are expected to put considerable stress on transportation facilities serving the core. Yet city officials are much more willing to approve sites for high density office and commercial use and for major entertainment facilities than they are to sanction additions or improvements to roads or rail transit lines.

A second concern is that decentralization of core area activities has not only contributed to the development of transit-oriented nodal centers but has also resulted in widespread dispersal of industrial and office employment to less accessible parts of Metropolitan Toronto. According to city of Toronto calculations, two-thirds of suburban office space in 1986 was auto-oriented (City of Toronto Planning and Development Department 1986, 50). An increasing use of automobiles for travel within Metropolitan Toronto and into downtown Toronto is not only a consequence of the decentralization and dispersal of activities within Metro itself but also results from the increasing amount of travel into Metro Toronto from the regions outside. Both Metro and city of Toronto officials are trying to come to terms with Metro's recently recognized "central city" status and to convey what that status means to local politicians. Complicating their task at the metropolitan level is the fact that members of Metro Council, the beneficiaries of the new system of direct election introduced in 1989, are still trying to develop a sense of identity and purpose that distinguishes them from members of local councils, on which many of them served in the past.

The change in Metro Council convinced Metro planning staff of the need for a completely new Metropolitan Toronto plan that would more clearly specify the nature of metropolitan interests and distinguish them from those of local municipalities. In working toward this objective, they prepared a number of reports aimed at making stronger and more specific some of the objectives contained in the 1980 plan or documents that preceded it. This work culminated in a new Draft Official Plan proposing a "reurbanization strategy" to bring about an increase of 300,000 in Metropolitan Toronto's population by the year 2011 in the interest of making better use of available service infrastructure, slowing down the rate of suburban expansion and allowing more people to live closer to their jobs (The Municipality of Metropolitan Toronto 1992).

A shortage of vacant land is a serious constraint on Metropolitan Toronto's ability to increase its population by increasing the size of its housing supply. Metropolitan Toronto is almost completely developed, which means that new housing will have to be secured through redevelopment at higher densities, residential infilling (construction of new dwellings on vacant or underused sites), and the conversion of large units into smaller units (Metropolitan Toronto Planning Department, Policy Development Division 1987). Any proposal to redevelop or increase densities on property in or near existing residential neighborhoods tends to be a source of intense political conflict in Metropolitan Toronto and thus commands little support from local councils and local politicians.

As has frequently been the case in Metro's planning history, the city of Toronto has taken the lead in seeking solutions to these problems by converting underused industrial lands to residential use and by allowing developers of downtown office space to build to higher densities in exchange for land suitable for housing elsewhere in the city. The city has a strong interest in increasing its residential component because of its desire to limit the amount of commuter traffic coming into the city. Thus its planners are now looking favorably on a proposal that the city make its approval of new employment sites conditional on the rate of production of housing within the city (Nowlan 1989). Also attracting considerable attention from both city and Metro planners is a proposal, known as the "Main Streets" concept, calling for zoning changes that would allow lands bordering shopping streets and major arterials to be redeveloped with buildings of five or six stories (instead of the usual two) containing both commercial and residential units.

Metro Council decisions have indicated an increasing willingness on the part of councillors to accept the principle of intensification and approve policies that will support it. Only time will tell, however, how far the city of Toronto and other Metro Toronto municipalities are prepared to go to allow the substantial changes in residential structure that will enable Metro to accommodate a significant share of the GTA's future population growth.

Planning in The Regional Municipalities

An interest in encouraging better, more comprehensive land-use planning in the more urbanized parts of the province was one of the government's justifications for creating two-tier regional governments between 1969 and 1974. Legislation establishing those governments contained a requirement that each should produce a regional plan within its first three years of operation, after which all local plans would have to conform to it. Of the four regional municipalities surrounding Metropolitan Toronto, only Durham and Halton Regions have managed to produce official plans, both of them within the allotted time limit.

The difficulties preventing the adoption of official plans in the fast-growing regional municipalities of York and Peel have been similar to the difficulties that prevented Metro Toronto from acquiring an official plan for more than 35 years. Reluctance of local councils to surrender control over their development choices to a second tier of government has been paramount among the constraints on regional planning. A second constraint has been uncertainty among planners and politicians about the nature of and requirements for regional plans, and how they are to differ from local plans. Provincial planning legislation and planning guidelines have never tried to make a distinction. A third constraint was the loss of enthusiasm for regional government among provincial officials after 1974. Not only had some of the regional governments proved to be politically unpopular but they also helped increase local government costs and demands for financial support from the province. While cost increases in reorganized areas often resulted from a backlog of unmet servicing needs, they made regional government a target of those for whom reductions in provincial debt and provincial spending became the primary objectives of government policy in the late 1970s (Ontario, The Special Program Review 1975, 194-208). The government's disaffection with the regional government program made it less inclined to insist that regional governments fulfill their planning responsibilities.

The absence of provincial directives has left it up to each regional council to decide whether to adopt and seek provincial approval for an official plan and to specify what it will contain. Consequently the experience with regional planning, both in process and in planning outcome, has varied from region to region. The two regions (Durham and Halton) with official plans have been less subject to intense development pressures than the two that have failed to produce them; Durham because it comprises the eastern sector of an area in which development pressures have always tended toward the west, Halton because it is separated from Metropolitan Toronto by Peel region. Both Durham and Halton also have planning directors who made early decisions to produce official plans and then persuaded their own staff, local councils, and the public to accept their views of what such plans should consist of.

A common feature of the plans of both regions is an emphasis on general policies that point to a preferred regional structure. The Durham plan favors the development of "central areas" containing a mixture of land uses. The policy aims at the preservation and enhancement of the downtowns or main streets of local municipalities in preference to the development of shopping malls on their outskirts. In one case, however, the plan designates an existing shopping center as a "central area" for a municipality lacking a downtown and in another has made the "central area" large enough to encompass both the old downtown and a newer shopping center about a mile away. Apart from this "central area" focus, the Durham plan seeks to preserve the distinctive character of the region's member municipalities by designating lands between them for agriculture.

Official plan policies in Halton Region have taken account of the need to protect two major provincial initiatives: the Niagara Escarpment Plan and the Parkway Belt West. Nonetheless regional planners have recently completed an Urban Structure Review that favors an extension of the urban development boundary of the town of Milton, in the center of the region, to open up an additional 15,000 acres for development. The area recommended for development may include a section of land presently reserved for agriculture in the Escarpment Plan.

Of the three regional official plans that now exist in the GTA, that of Durham goes furthest in specifying details of density and land uses—specifications to which local municipalities are legally required to conform (Hollo 1989, 14). The tendency of regional plans—both those that have been adopted and those still in the draft stage—is to maintain a level of generality that leaves local municipalities free to decide the specifics of land development. Their principal concern is with matters defined in provincial legislation as "regional responsibilities," such as major public works and transportation facilities. Regional review of local subdivision plans—a responsibility that the province delegated to the regions when they were created—tends to concentrate on their implications for regional services rather than their implications for the regional land-use pattern. And even the preferences of local municipalities—either to grow or not to grow—can have major impacts on regional planning decisions. In Halton, for example, the decision to enlarge Milton's urban boundary took account both of Milton's desire to grow and the desire of the two lakeshore communities, Oakville and Burlington, to limit their rate of expansion. The decision means that both the region and the province will pay higher costs to bring lake-based services to areas opened up for residential development.

The strength of local municipalities and local planning priorities has been particularly evident in the regional municipalities of Peel and York, where the regional councils have not yet approved official plans. Regional politics in Peel have been dominated by the city of Mississauga which, with 63 percent of the region's population, is the most fully developed of the region's three municipalities. The mayor and several members of Mississauga Council have opposed regional government from the beginning and have kept up a determined campaign to prevent regional staff from playing a meaningful role in planning and development. Interpersonal conflicts between senior staff members at the regional and local levels have further weakened the effectiveness of regional planners.

The least cohesive of the five upper-tier regions, however, is the regional municipality of York, immediately to the north of Metropolitan Toronto. The irony of York's situation is that it was the only region to emerge from a locally initiated and conducted local government review leading to a request for regional government (Regional Municipality of York 1988, 19-21). Other regional governments were imposed by the province, sometimes on the basis of and sometimes in contravention of recommendations of provincially sponsored reviews of their local government systems (Feldman 1974, 14-17).

The creation of regional government for York, as for most other parts of the province where reorganization took place, involved giving new responsibilities and new sources of revenue to an existing county government as well as consolidating small municipalities into larger, more viable units. Local officials in York Region sought the change in reaction to the growing strength and territorial aspirations of Metro Toronto. Not only did they resent the inclusion of large portions of the county in the Metropolitan Toronto Planning Area but they also feared that growth pressures would generate irresistible pressure for Metro to absorb the urbanized municipalities in the southern part of York County, just to the north of Metro, leaving the rest of the county with a seriously diminished tax base. Once regional government was in place and the Metro threat removed, local interests reasserted themselves. Resistance to regional planning was so obstructive that in 1977 the entire regional planning staff resigned, and the department had to be reconstituted.

Even local planning in York Region has failed to keep up with the pace of development, which has already gone beyond the urban boundaries specified in the plans of the region's southern municipalities. The most important influence on land-use decisions in the region is the location and capacity of the York Durham servicing scheme, the "big pipe" that provides the region with sewage treatment and disposal facilities based on Lake Ontario. Municipalities with access to that facility have experienced rapid growth; others have not been able to develop so rapidly. Thus there is a clear distinction within the region between five rapidly urbanizing towns and four rural or semirural townships, a distinction that influences regional politics. Planning policies adopted by some of the local municipalities—particularly the southern municipalities of Vaughan and Markham—have further intensified the region's fragmentation by maintaining undeveloped open space between preconsolidation communities as a way of maintaining their character and spatial integrity. The town of Vaughan represents an extreme example of local refusal to adapt to reorganization. Rather than producing an official plan for the town as a whole, its council has approved separate plans for four districts comprising preconsolidation towns and villages.

Planning in the Five Regions: An Overview

The existence of regional government and mandated regional planning in the Greater Toronto Area has done little to reduce the influence of local governments on the area's physical development. In the words of one observer,

> in a dispute between the upper and lower tier, the lower tier municipality will generally win in the long run, and particularly in the political sense, because the lower tier has the luxury of being specific, and somewhat closer to the electorate. (Hollo 1989, 8).

The existence of a regional plan may strengthen the ability of regional officials to argue for the "regional interest" before provincial agencies, but it does not guarantee it.

The creation of regional governments has not been without consequence for planning in the Greater Toronto Area, however. Probably the most important function performed by regional planning staff is that of providing local planners with information that they would otherwise find difficult to get because of limited resources. Where regional planners enjoy a good relationship with their local counterparts, they can also inject greater awareness of regional interests into local planning and strengthen the case for planning ideas with both local and regional councils. Finally, all the GTA's regional governments except Metropolitan Toronto have assumed responsibility for reviewing plans of subdivision and condominiums, a responsibility that in principle gives them control over the rate and pattern of new development. In actual fact, however, regional councils have agreed to take over this responsibility from the province because their locally elected members believe that it means less, not more, outside intervention in local land-use decisions.

The subservience of regional planning to local priorities and aspirations has meant that few parts of the region offer a coherent vision of the way the Toronto metropolis is or should be developing. Metropolitan Toronto, with its structure plan based on transit-linked nodes, has gone furthest in providing its member municipalities with a planning framework. The idea of developing mixed-use centers has found its way into the plans of some other GTA municipalities, most notably Mississauga, but usually with little thought as to how these should be linked to or by the regional (GO) transit system. There is also a concern evident in many plans with preserving or enhancing the historic downtowns of local municipalities, though usually without precluding the development of peripheral shopping centers. Finally, local and regional plans outside Metro have exerted some control over "sprawl" by designating "urban development boundaries" to separate areas targeted for future development from their rural surroundings. These boundaries are not inviolate; they are moved outward as growth pressures build up, sometimes without waiting for an official plan amendment.

WHITHER THE GTA?

Thirty years of experience with regional planning in southern Ontario makes it possible to identify a number of obstacles that will have to be overcome by any serious provincial attempt to exercise control over this fast-growing metropolitan area. The first is a lack of agreement among the five regions and their member municipalities. Apart from a general interest in promoting nodal developments with a mixture of land uses (including residential), there is little in local plans to suggest the outlines of a coherent, long-range strategy for the area's future growth. What exists is a confusing amalgamation of the plans of separate and distinctive municipalities, most of which want to grow, a few of which do not. Those that want to grow are competing with each other for allocations of projected GTA population increases, for provincially funded infrastructure improvements, and for new or relocated industrial, commercial, and office development.

A second obstacle to the development of a workable provincial strategy is the vigor with which municipal councils claim the right to decide the nature and rate of development within their own boundaries, despite legislated requirements that their decisions conform to regional (where they exist) and provincial planning priorities. Municipal assertiveness has not only made regional planning an activity conducted largely in response or reaction to local planning, it has also made the provincial government reluctant to appear to be dictating how or where municipalities shall grow.

A third obstacle to the success of provincial initiatives is fragmentation and competition within the provincial bureaucracy. The government has identified 10 separate ministries as having a direct interest in the way the Greater Toronto Area develops. Each of these has its own mandate and a set of programs to carry it out; its own priorities for new investment; its own way of assessing and responding to pressures of urban growth and expansion; and its own set of external supporters and detractors. These ministries and their component departments have traditionally been more inclined to compete among themselves for budget allocations and cabinet approval for pet projects than to engage in the dialogue and make the compromises needed to arrive at a common strategy.

Fourth, government attempts to respond directly to growth pressures in the GTA have to overcome a generalized antipathy to the Toronto area and its rate of development in the rest of the province. Provincial politicians from outside the area are less likely to view GTA growth and expansion as challenges to be met than as threats to the long-term viability of their own districts. As the GTA absorbs an increasing share of the province's jobs and people, the "Hogtown" epithet once applied to the city of Toronto can be extended to take in the entire area. Thus provincial cabinet ministers who want to address GTA problems have to convince elected members of their own party to support proposals that seem to bring no benefits to outlying constituencies.

Finally, the government must deal with the inescapable problem of responding to infinite demands with a finite budget. Not only do proposals for new infrastructure and community services in the GTA have to compete with similar proposals from other parts of the province; they also compete with demands for increased expenditure on health care facilities, education (particularly postsecondary education), and other social services.

In light of these major obstacles to the development of a provincial strategy for the GTA's future development, it is not surprising that the government was slow to acknowledge pressures stemming from GTA growth or to set up organizations to deal with them. The obstacles also help explain why the organizations it has set up have adopted a low-key, deliberative approach to their assignment, emphasizing the need for cooperation and coordination rather than areawide management or direction. Even this approach has its pitfalls, however, for it leaves the government open to charges that it is attempting to create a new level of government that operates in secret and has no direct accountability to area voters (Mackie 1989).

A measure of the success of the government's strategy for dealing with GTA issues will be its ability to alleviate the area's major problems without alienating too many government supporters. The problem that has tended to dominate regional discussions and has absorbed most of the OGTA's attention since its formation is that of finding a way to dispose of the area's enormous output of solid waste. While this problem stimulates intense political activity in communities close to potential landfill sites, it has also generated substantial willingness among regional officials to cooperate in finding a solution. Whereas local opponents of potential sites in the suburban regions like to depict the problem as one that Metro is trying to foist on its hapless neighbors, regional officials acknowledge that they are also running out of waste disposal capacity (Gilbert 1989). In considering possible solutions to the problem, they must contend not only with local opponents but also with the terms of the province's Environmental Assessment Act, which allows opposition to be prolonged through numerous hearings and legal appeals. Indicative of the dilemma in which provincial and regional officials find themselves was the 1991 decision of the Minister of the Environment, an adamant supporter of the environmental assessment process when she was a member of the opposition, to approve as "an emergency measure" the expansion of two existing dumps without an environmental assessment (*The Globe and Mail,* June 27, 1991).

Most public officials in the GTA are also in general agreement that there is a need to improve the area's transportation system, although they are not always able to agree on priorities. The number of daily person trips throughout the GTA has been increasing at an even faster rate than the number of people living in the area, placing increasing demands on the area's transportation facilities, particularly its road system. The number of automobiles and trucks crossing the boundary between Metro and the surrounding regions has more than doubled since 1975 (from .58 to 1.2 million), generating intense suburban pressure on the province to provide new road and commuter rail facilities. The most serious source of disagreement concerns the relative priority to be given demands by Metropolitan Toronto for new capital subsidies to build transit lines to support its multicentered urban structure and demands from suburban regions for more spending on highways, commuter rail, and local bus services.

The NDP government has largely endorsed a program of transportation investments proposed by its Liberal forerunner as a way of achieving balance among competing demands for scarce transportation dollars. Those investments entail both the construction of a major east-west highway through York and into Durham Region to the north of Metro and a 10-year program to expand service on some GO transit routes serving the outer suburbs. In addition, the government has agreed to help finance extensions to several TTC subway and light rail transit lines. GTA residents and businesses will pay most of the costs of these transportation investments through a commercial concentration levy of

$1.00 per square foot on owners of large commercial structures, parking lots and parking garages in the area, and through a surcharge on motor vehicle registration fees. The government has also told Metro that its future eligibility for new transit investment will depend partly on a demonstrated willingness to accommodate higher residential densities and partly on Metro's ability to persuade the private sector to contribute to new rapid transit lines. Metro planners have taken at least the first of these strictures seriously and have stepped up their efforts to promote higher density residential development in transit-accessible locations throughout Metropolitan Toronto.

While the transportation issue does pose a threat to a cooperative strategy, therefore, it is one that allows the province to reduce the possibility of conflict by making concessions to all contenders. It is also one for which it is relatively easy to allocate costs to beneficiaries. An issue that is more intractable because it is less amenable to compromise is that of increasing the supply of "affordable" housing for families of low- and moderate-income in all parts of the GTA. This issue is not a new one for the area. One reason for the creation of Metropolitan Toronto in 1953 was a shortage of low and moderately priced housing to accommodate workers in the area's rapidly growing industrial sector, combined with suburban reluctance or inability to finance services that would make such housing possible.

The government of Metropolitan Toronto removed constraints on suburban development by constructing new sewers, water lines, roads, and schools in the suburbs. Its planners encouraged the provision of suburban housing for a range of income groups, a principle that most suburban governments recognized by zoning some areas for multiple-unit housing. Metro also helped achieve an areawide distribution of publicly assisted family housing, especially after 1964 when the provincial government made Metro Council the only local government in the metropolitan federation with authority to negotiate for such housing. At the same time the province set up its own agency, the Ontario Housing Corporation, to build housing, both for rent and sale, by drawing on loan funds made available in the 1964 National Housing Act. The outcome of this arrangement was impressive. By 1973 Metro, with 24 percent of the province's population, had about 60 percent of its total supply of family public housing (Rose 1980; 175).

Like public housing throughout the continent, OHC housing (much of it in the form of apartments and townhouses) encountered intense public criticism and resistance. By the early 1970s the federal government had virtually ceased supporting such housing, substituting for it programs, like assisted home ownership and co-operative and nonprofit rental housing, that distributed government housing benefits over a much wider spectrum of family incomes.

GTA municipalities responded to the new programs in a variety of ways. The city of Toronto set up its own nonprofit housing corporation, Cityhome, to draw on federal and provincial funds to produce housing for a variety of users, at least 25 percent of whom qualify for rent subsidies. Since its inception in 1974, Cityhome has produced more than 6,000 units of housing. Metropolitan Toronto has its own nonprofit housing corporation that builds housing in other parts of Metro but its production of family housing has been much less than the city's. Thus it has not been able to secure a "fair share" distribution of publicly assisted family housing units throughout Metropolitan Toronto, even though such a distribution is a stated goal of Metro's 1980 plan. The issue that has gained greater prominence, however, has been the limited production of low and moderately priced family housing in municipalities outside Metro Toronto. The regional municipality of Peel was the only suburban jurisdiction to join the city and Metro Toronto in setting up a nonprofit housing corporation in the 1970s. Other suburban regions have established nonprofit housing corporations only in the last few years. Most lower-tier suburban municipalities have not only resisted becoming involved in government-assisted housing programs but some of them have also refused to allow the construction of private housing that would be affordable to workers in the industries they are striving to attract.

High housing costs and a shortage of rental housing both inside and outside Metropolitan Toronto are seen not only as problems for individuals and households of low-to-moderate income but also as threats to the GTA economy, insofar as they may discourage new investment in the area. There is widespread agreement that this is a problem that only the province can solve. It is unlikely that this would be so if the city of Toronto or even Metro as a whole were performing the traditional central city function of providing low-cost accommodation in deteriorated residential districts. But high demand for housing in Metro Toronto has meant that housing in older districts has undergone continual renovation or been replaced by newer structures. Even the city of Toronto program has been hard-pressed to produce enough low and moderately priced rental units to replace those lost to private renovation.

High land and building costs, rising interest rates and provincial rent controls are among reasons commonly given for high housing costs in the

GTA. There has been a noticeable tendency, however, for builders to specialize in the production of high value units—large single family homes, luxury apartments and condominiums—at least partly because of the greater ease of getting plans for such housing approved by local councils. The town of Vaughan, just outside Metro's northern boundary, has been particularly aggressive in its use and defense of planning measures (like large lot zoning) to exclude all but expensive single family homes. It has thus helped focus attention on the impact of suburban planning practices on the area's housing crisis (Fine 1988).

The province's Liberal government responded in 1989 to the crisis in housing "affordability" in the GTA and other Ontario cities by declaring the provision of "affordable" housing in new municipal subdivisions to be "a matter of provincial interest." This move gave the cabinet the right to reject municipal plans of subdivision even if they have been approved by the Ontario Municipal Board. As with all policy initiatives, the government announced its new policy in the form of a statement circulated among provincial municipalities and ministries for comment prior to its incorporation (with revisions) into *The Planning Act* (Hosek and Eakins, n.d. and 1989). This process of municipal consultation resulted in a number of significant changes in the wording of the policy. The proposed policy specified, for example, that "at least 25 percent of total housing units from new residential development and residential intensification" in the GTA should be "affordable," half of it to households with incomes up to the 30th percentile and half to households "with incomes between the 30th and 60th percentiles."[3] The policy statement as finally adopted requires that 25 percent of all new housing built in GTA municipalities be "affordable" to "households within the lowest 60 percent of the income distribution," thereby relieving municipalities of responsibility for accommodating households at the bottom end of the income scale. It also says that this type of housing "is not necessarily [to be] included in every application for New Residential Development or Residential intensification."

The tendency in provincial policy development, then, has been to remove language that implies a direct assault on specific municipal planning practices and to leave it up to municipalities in the first instance to decide how provincial policy will be implemented. The province also

---

[3]"Affordability" was defined to signify "annual housing costs . . . which do not exceed 30 percent of gross annual household income."

looks to regional councils to take the lead in developing regional housing policy and then to seek compliance from local municipalities through the subdivision approval process, without acknowledging the limited ability of regional agencies to influence local planning decisions. Thus the success of both public and private initiatives will depend on the willingness of municipalities to give planning approval to proposals that include an "affordable housing" component or, failing that, on the willingness of the provincial government to use its authority to intervene in local planning or to use its infrastructure funding to persuade local governments to comply with provincial policy.

CONCLUSION

Government of Ontario responses to growth and development in the Toronto metropolis attest to the pre-eminent place occupied by provincial governments in the management of Canada's municipal affairs. The Ontario government has acknowledged its responsibility in the Greater Toronto Area not only by making its agencies responsible for locating and building major services but also by establishing a variety of forums and institutions to pay specific attention to GTA concerns. The institutions established to deal with growth-related problems at the present stage of development in the Toronto metropolis are very different, however, from the federated system of local government established for Metropolitan Toronto in 1953 and used as a model for regional governments set up in 1971 and 1974. They have no formal mandates to plan, provide areawide services, or allocate resources among competing functional requirements and local jurisdictions. Rather they have defined their role to be one of promoting discussion, coordination, and, if possible, cooperation among and between a large number of local and provincial agencies with an interest in the way the area develops.

The approach taken by the Ontario government to the management of growth in the Greater Toronto Area rests on a realistic assessment of the limitations of regional planning as a device for structuring and channelling metropolitan growth and development. While regional planning has been treated as an important, even essential, element of government activity in the Toronto area for nearly 50 years, it has worked most successfully as a means of formulating general planning principles that show how private interests and local governments can reconcile their development aspirations with other community objectives. It has had limited effectiveness as a device for formulating comprehensive land-use frameworks to which public and private interests are willing to conform.

As Robert Wood found for the New York metropolitan region 40 years ago, the government agencies with greatest potential for influencing the form of the Greater Toronto Area are those that provide the major public services (trunk sewer and water, highways and rail transit) that either facilitate suburban development or influence the use value of alternative locations within the area (Wood 1964, 125-88). These agencies usually act in response to the pressures of major private investors and growth-hungry municipal governments, not out of any intention to channel growth in a predetermined way. There is an important difference, however, between the Toronto situation and the one Wood described. It is the extent to which the provincial government has kept responsibility for areawide services in the hands of its own ministries or of agencies closely controlled by them, thereby enhancing its ability not only to coordinate servicing decisions but even to use them to promote its own objectives.

How extensively the province will use its control over regional services to promote provincially defined interests remains an open question. While the provincial government has virtually unlimited legal authority to require local compliance with government-stated priorities, it has seldom used that authority to override local planning preferences. In addition, it has always been ready to modify its policies to accommodate local objections and local priorities when it has seemed politically expedient to do so. Because such priorities tend to vary according to the location of municipalities within the area, their population characteristics and their rates of development, the government's role has been less one of managing the activities of local governments than one of trying to work out compromises among competing local interests. That failing, its choice among the competing claims of local governments and local interest groups is more likely to be based on considerations of their relative costs and benefits to the provincial economy or their political costs and benefits to the government than on any concept of what constitutes an ideal or even a preferable pattern of metropolitan growth from an environmental and social perspective.

REFERENCES

Adams, Thomas, Harold M. Lewis, and Theodore T. McCroskey. 1974. *Population, Land Values and Government.* Vol. 2 of *The Regional Survey of New York and its Environs.* First published 1929. New York: Arno Press Reprint.

Bell, George G., and Andrew D. Pascoe. 1988. *The Ontario Government: Structure and Functions.* Toronto: Wall & Thompson.

Bird, Richard M., and N. Enid Slack. 1983. *Urban Public Finance in Canada.* Toronto: Butterworths.

Bordessa, Ronald, and James Cameron. 1982. Growth Management Conflicts in the Toronto-Centered Region. In *Conflict, Politics and the Urban Scene,* ed. Kevin R. Cox and R. J. Johnston, London: Longman.

City of Toronto Planning and Development Department. 1986. *1986 Quinquennial Review.*

City of Toronto Planning Board. 1974. *A Place for Industry.*

Comay, E. 1964. A Brief to the Royal Commission on Metropolitan Toronto. Unpublished manuscript.

Committee for Economic Development. 1970. *Reshaping Government in Metropolitan Areas.* New York: The Committee.

Farrow, G. M. 1989. Notes for Remarks . . . at the "Insight Seminar, *The Planning Act: Is Council in Control?*" Toronto: Insight.

Feldman, Lionel D. 1974. *Ontario 1945-1973: The Municipal Dynamic.* Toronto: Ontario Economic Council.

Fine, Sean. 1988. Suburban housing policy defended by mayor. *The Globe and Mail.* January 1.

Fish, Susan A. 1976. Winning the Battle and Losing the War in the Fight to Improve Municipal Policy-Making. In *Politics and Government of Urban Canada: Selected Readings,* 3d edition, ed. L. D. Feldman and M. D. Goldrick, Toronto: Methuen, 175-86.

Frisken, Frances. 1988. *City Policy-Making in Theory and Practice: The Case of Toronto's Downtown Plan.* London, Ont.: Department of Political Science, the University of Western Ontario.

_____. 1991. The Contributions of Metropolitan Government to the Success of Toronto's Public Transit System: An Empirical Dissent from the Public-Choice Paradigm. *Urban Affairs Quarterly* 27 (December) 268-92.

_____, and Marc McAree. 1989. *Relating Municipal Land Use Practices to Public Transit Operations in the Greater Toronto Area:*

Constraints and Opportunities. A report prepared for the Municipal Transportation Policy Office, Ontario Ministry of Transporation December.

Gertler, Meric S. 1985. Industrialism, Deindustrialism and Regional Development in Central Canada. *The Canadian Journal of Regional Science* 8: 353-75.

Gilbert, Richard. 1989. A Metropolis Down in the Dumps. *The Globe and Mail,* September 22.

Goldberg, Michael A., and John Mercer. 1986. *The Myth of the North American City.* Vancouver: University of British Columbia Press.

Gluck, Peter R., and Richard J. Meister. 1979. *Cities in Transition.* New York: New Viewpoints.

Hollo, William S. 1989. Enforcing Regional Priorities Through Regional Official Plans. Paper given at a session entitled *Working with Regional Government: Development Issues,* February 13. Toronto: Insight.

Hosek, Chaviva, Minister of Housing, and John Eakins, Minister of Municipal Affairs. n.d. Policy Statement. Housing. A proposed policy statement of the Government of Ontario issued for public review.

_____. 1989. Policy Statement. Land Use Planning for Housing. A statement of Ontario Government policy issued under the authority of Section 3 of The Planning Act 1983. Approved by the Lieutenant Governor in Council . . . July 13, 1989.

IBI Group and Associates. 1990. *Greater Toronto Area Urban Structure Concepts Study, Summary Report.* Toronto: The Greater Toronto Coordinating Committee.

Jackson, Kenneth T. 1972. Metropolitan Government Versus Suburban Autonomy: Politics on the Crabgrass Frontier. In *Cities in American History,* ed. Kenneth T. Jackson and Stanley K. Schultz, New York: Knopf, 442-62.

Kaplan, Harold. 1982. *Reform, Planning, and City Politics: Montreal, Winnipeg, Toronto.* Toronto: University of Toronto Press.

Macdonald, H. Ian. 1982. The Toronto-Centered Region in Retrospect. In *Conflict or Cooperation? The Toronto-Centered Region in the 1980s,* ed. Frances Frisken, Toronto: York University Urban Studies Program, 62-68.

Mackie, Richard. 1989. Peterson scoffs at NDP fears over "special" office, *The Globe and Mail,* July 13.

Metropolitan Toronto Planning Board. 1959. *The Official Plan of the Metropolitan Toronto Planning Area (Draft)*.

_____. 1965. *Official Plan (Draft) of the Metropolitan Toronto Planning Area*.

Metropolitan Toronto Planning Department, Policy Development Division. 1986a. Report No. 2. Toronto: The Municipality of Metropolitan Toronto Metropolitan Plan Review.

_____. 1986b. *Industrial Areas*. Toronto: The Municipality of Metropolitan Toronto Metropolitan Plan Review.

_____. 1987. *Housing Intensification*. The Municipality of Metropolitan Toronto Metropolitan Plan Review.

Metropolitan Toronto Planning Department, Research and Policy Division. 1989. *Projections and their Policy Implications*.

_____, Research Division. 1989. *Office Space Characteristics, Metropolitan Region, 1988*.

Metropolitan Toronto Planning Department and Toronto Transit Commission. 1986. *Network 2011, Final Report*.

The Municipality of Metropolitan Toronto. 1980. *Official Plan for the Urban Structure: The Metropolitan Toronto Planning Area*.

_____. 1986. *Annual Report of the Commissioner of Finance*.

_____. 1992. *The Liveable Metropolis*. Draft Official Plan. September.

Muszynski, L. 1985. *The Deindustrialisation of Metropolitan Toronto: A Study of Plant Closures, Layoffs and Unemployment*. Toronto: Social Planning Council of Metropolitan Toronto.

Norcliffe, Glen, and Michael Goldrick. 1986. Cyclical Factors, Technological Change, Capital Mobility, and Deindustrialization in Metropolitan Toronto. *Urban Geography* 7: 413-36.

Nowlan, David. 1989. Commercial Growth and the New Toronto Plan. Paper presented to Cityplan '91 Forum, May 29.

Office of the Greater Toronto Area. 1989. What is the OGTA. July 31.

Ontario, Advisory Task Force on Housing Policy. 1973. *Report*. Toronto: The Queen's Printer.

Ontario, Central Ontario Lakeshore Urban Complex Task Force. 1974. *Report*.

Ontario, Department of Municipal Affairs. Metropolitan Toronto and Region Transportation Study. 1967. *Choices for a Growing Region*.

Ontario, Department of Treasury and Economics, Regional Development Branch. 1970. *Design for Development: The Toronto-Centered Region.*

Ontario, Ministry of Treasury and Economics, Office of Economic Policy. 1989. *Population Projections for Regional Municipalities, Counties and Districts of Ontario to 2011.*

Ontario, The Special Program Review. 1975. *Report.*

Ontario Municipal Board. 1953. *In the Matter of Sections 20 and 22 of the Municipal Act. Decisions and Recommendations of the Board.* Toronto: Queen's Printer.

Perry, John. 1974. *Inventory of Regional Planning Administration in Canada.* Staff Paper No. 1. Toronto: Intergovernmental Committee on Urban and Regional Research.

Regional Municipality of York. 1988. *Insights: Local and Regional Government in York Region.*

Richardson, N. H. 1981. Insubstantial Pageant: the Rise and Fall of Provincial Planning in Ontario. *Canadian Public Administration* 24 (Winter): 563-85.

Robinson, Ira M. 1986. Some major differences in the Canadian and American planning approaches to selected urban issues affecting central cities in their respective countries. *Planning Perspectives* 1: 231-56.

Rose, Albert. 1980. *Canadian Housing Policies (1935-1980).* Toronto: Butterworths.

Rust-D'Eye, George H. 1989. The Planning Act: Is Council in Control? Toronto: Insight.

Social Planning Council of Metropolitan Toronto. 1979. *Metro's Suburbs in Transition. Part One: Evolution and Overview.* Toronto.

_____. 1980. *The Planning Agenda for the Eighties. Part II: Metro's Suburbs in Transition.* Toronto.

Teaford, Jon C. 1979. *City and Suburb: The Political Fragmentation of Metropolitan America, 1850-1970.* Baltimore: Johns Hopkins.

Transit Advisory Group to the Minister of Transportation for Ontario. 1987. *Crossing the Boundaries—Coordinating Transit in the Greater Toronto Area.*

Urban Development Institute Ontario. 1989. *The Greater Toronto Area Outlook—Year 2011.* A report prepared for the Urban Development Institute Ontario Annual Conference. Toronto.

Wood, Robert C. 1964. *1400 Governments.* New York: Anchor.

PERSONS INTERVIEWED FOR THE STUDY

Katharine Bladen, Manager, Socio-Economic Analysis, Planning Department, Regional Municipality of Peel

Sylvia Davis, Director of Long Range Planning, Office of the Greater Toronto Area.

Steve Dynes, City of Toronto Planning Department

Eric Fleming, Chairperson, Greater Toronto Coordinating Committee

Ivy France, Department of Housing, Regional Municipality of Peel

John Gladky, City of Toronto Planning Department

Geoff Hare, Manager, Regional and Community Studies, Ontario Ministry of Treasury and Economics

Barbara Leonhardt, City of Toronto Planning Department

John Livey, Director of Policy, Metropolitan Toronto

David McCleary, Senior Planner, Regional Municipality of Halton

Mofeed Michael, Planning Commissioner, Regional Municipality of Durham

Richard Peddie, General Manager of Land Development, City of Toronto Housing Department.

Richard Puccini, Executive Director, Municipal Transportation Division, Ontario Ministry of Transportation

Andriz Roze, Director of Long Range Planning, Regional Municipality of York

Martin Silver, Assistant General Manager of Housing, Regional Municipality of York.

Greg Stewart, City of Toronto Planning Department

Chapter 5

In Fits and Starts: The Twin Cities Metropolitan Framework

Judith A. Martin

University of Minnesota

In 1977 the Metropolitan Council of the Twin Cities reached the 10-year mark, having supplanted an earlier regional planning effort that also lasted for 10 years. The council was, at that time, widely studied and frequently lauded for having successfully addressed such regional planning issues as long-range airport needs, regional sewer concerns, and control of "leapfrog" development (Baldinger 1971; Harrigan and Johnson 1978; Naftalin 1986). By the late 1980s, this situation had changed somewhat. The Metropolitan Council found itself being criticized for trying to do many different things, even by staunch long-time supporters (Citizen's League 1984). While attentive critics argued that the council had become ineffective, most people in the Twin Cities probably still could not describe what exactly the council did, even if pressed.

Part of this perceived transformation was no doubt due to the Metropolitan Council becoming a regular "player" in Twin Cities decision-making circuit—by 1985 (or earlier) it was no longer new or special. Another part was undoubtedly related to the physical expansion of the metropolitan area; newly developing (and fast-growing) suburbs saw the council not as an agent of assistance, but as an obstruction. Typical late 1980s conflicts surrounding downtown redevelopment, suburban gridlock, and competition between central cities and their suburbs arose in the Twin Cities, just as in metropolitan areas without any regional planning mechanism. Three decades of planning for the Twin Cities have not significantly slowed outer urban growth, nor stemmed the tide of problems that came with it. Such observations leave us in 1990 asking: what has been the impact of regional government in the Twin Cities? How has this area evolved differently because of the Metropolitan Council?

The Twin Cities shares with Winnepeg some of the worst weather experienced by major North American cities—cold winters and hot summers, with temperature differentials of 125 degrees Fahrenheit separating the two. And like Winnepeg, this is a relatively isolated metropolitan area; there are no nearby competitors, at least none closer than 400 miles. Whether either of these traits has contributed to regional instincts is debatable. Many have argued that the Twin Cities' isolation has in part forced this metro area to be creative and enterprising (Borchert 1988). Of such necessities are innovations like regional government born.

THE DEVELOPMENT OF THE TWIN CITIES

Why has a relatively successful metropolitan structure been able to function in an area with two central cities? The usual answer to this question is that it is because there are two cities, and because together they hold only about 30 percent of the region's total population, that such a structure works for the Twin Cities. Unlike most American metropolitan areas, there is no single focus for opposition in this region, and neither city has been able to consistently dominate regional discussions in recent generations. In contrast to years past, Minneapolis and St. Paul have been more likely to cooperate on many issues during the past decade than to compete. In some ways both cities now view the suburbs as the greatest competition that each has, and most of the suburbs view one another as competition as well. Not surprisingly, the lack of a single point of reference goes a long way toward diluting the long-standing hostility toward the city that exists in such metropolitan areas as Chicago or Boston.

Two compelling explanations together account for the existence of the Twin Cities and for the spirit that seems to have preceded the emergence of a metropolitan structure. One is geographic, the other is cultural. Close observers of this region have long argued that because of the Mississippi River and its topography, two cities had to exist here (Abler 1976). St. Paul was founded in the early 1830s as an outlier of a minimal U.S. government presence at Fort Snelling. This was the effective head of navigation on the Mississippi, the place where river traffic heading north had to stop if any goods were to be unloaded. Later in the 19th century it was the place where north- and west-bound trains along the Mississippi turned inland—the steep river bluffs and lack of flood plain upstream from St. Paul's core precluded any rail lines locating there. Minneapolis had a later and different history. Initial settlement took place in the early 1840s, but only on the east bank of the Mississippi; the other side was off-limits until an 1851 treaty with the Sioux tribe. From the beginning, Minneapolis presented a strong industrial potential. The water power of St. Anthony Falls, at over 50 feet the largest drop along the entire length of the Mississippi, sat right next to the site where the center of Minneapolis grew. This location, 10 miles upstream from St. Paul, was enormously attractive to investors looking for cheap power. In the early days the distance between the two places was enough to forestall serious thought of municipal convergence, so the two cities grew separately, differently, and eventually grew together spatially, though not politically.

The cultural explanation for the Twin Cities' cooperative spirit stems in part from the immigration patterns that obtained over a long period. In 1980 the Twin Cities was the most homogeneous of the largest 30 major American metropolitan areas, with a total minority population of about 12 percent (Borchert 1988). Throughout the nineteenth century and well into the late twentieth century, migrants to this area came primarily from Northern and Western Europe, from rural areas of the Northeast, and from Canada. St. Paul and Minneapolis were located well off the beaten path of most streams of American urban migration: migrants from the Eastern U.S. had to bypass Chicago, Detroit, and Cleveland to get here, and blacks from the rural South could more easily get to any of these other cities. Reaching this part of the country by rail from the South involved at least one change of train. Anyone bypassing Chicago or other Midwestern cities for Minneapolis or St. Paul had to know something about, or someone from, this area.

Consequently, most who came here hailed from a relatively fewer places and arguably had more in common to begin with. An example of this might be found in the cooperative movement that flourished in the Upper Midwest in the early 20th century (co-op creameries, co-op rural electrification efforts, etc.), and that to some degree remains strong today. In the Twin Cities proper this cooperative spirit was visible in the efforts of competing businessmen working together in the late 19th and early 20th centuries to endow arts museums, symphony orchestras, and other cultural institutions (Borchert, et al. 1983). It is also visible in more recent efforts to create low- and moderate-income housing alternatives: excepting New York City, Minneapolis has a larger per capita share of co-op and mutual housing efforts than any other American metro area. Whether because of common ethnic roots or because of shared acquired values, people in this area have long worked together to improve life for everyone here. And it seems that investment in these communities has paid off in many different ways. For example, there is good contemporary evidence that people from the Twin Cities (even relative newcomers) are reluctant to leave here for other places when corporate transfers are discussed.

Historically, the Twin Cities has prospered, but not evenly. Early industries that relied on the river—saw milling, flour milling, and goods transporting—were in decline within a few decades of starting up, despite efforts to support them through such things as the federal government making Minneapolis a port by constructing a lock and dam in the 1960s. In the decades of the 1920s and 1930s, neither city was regarded as much of a positive role model. St. Paul freely harbored gangsters from Chicago as long as they behaved while in town. Minneapolis was such a staunch enemy of union activity that a mid-1930s Teamsters strike led to physical battle on downtown streets between strikers and the scions of some of the city's "first families" (Fortune 1936).

After World War II, the fortunes of the Twin Cities began to change in a beneficial way. A sizeable investment base and a well-trained, hardworking population combined with local creativity and entrepreneurship to position the area for economic growth. Unlike the spurt of postwar development in most sunbelt cities, fed largely by federal defense spending in amenity locations, most of the Twin Cities' economic growth was locally generated. Established old-line companies like Pillsbury, General Mills, and 3M successfully diversified into the conglomerates that they are today. A small 1950s company like Dayton's was able to ride the shopping center/discount retailing boom and to parlay an early friendly merger to become Dayton-Hudson, currently one of the nation's largest retailers. Meanwhile, technological advances provided opportunities for newer companies like Control Data, Medtronic, and scores of other high-tech offspring. The presence of the state's major research university in the center of Minneapolis had much to do with the high-tech explosion, and as we know about urban growth in other places, the university and the state government were also important job-generators here. Needless to say, all of this economic growth stimulated physical expansion well beyond the boundaries of both cities. (See Map 5.1.) Eventually the dimensions of physical expansion led to thinking about limits and finally led to intergovernmental cooperation.

Map 5.1.   *The Twin Cities Metropolitan Area (7 counties)*

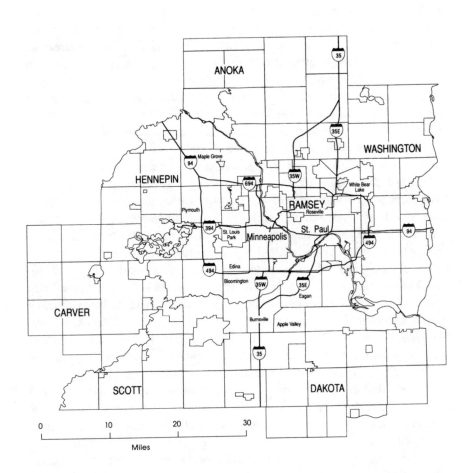

GOVERNANCE IN THE TWIN CITIES

Like most metropolitan areas in the United States, municipal governance in the Twin Cities is fragmented along many different lines. Governance and management are a tangle of co-existing and sometimes conflicting interests: separate city and individual suburban municipal governments, county governments, and the state government, in addition to dozens of locally controlled school, police, park, and other authorities. A recent count enumerated 272 separate local governmental units: 7 counties, 138 cities, 50 townships, 49 school districts, 6 metropolitan agencies, and 22 special purpose jurisdictions (Naftalin 1986).

The presence of the federal government in the Twin Cities is perceived to be limited, as in most other American cities. Yet, most citizens of this area interact with the federal government regularly, in such ways as visits to the post office, requests for passports or for social security information, dealings with the IRS, and boating on the Mississippi's federal "scenic" waterway. The U.S. Defense Department is locally represented by recruiting offices, by an army reserve post, and by the Corps of Engineers, which operates the locks and dams on the Mississippi. The Federal Eighth Circuit Court of Appeals is based in the Twin Cities. Not surprising for a metropolitan area serving a large farming region, the agriculture department is well represented in the Twin Cities. So is the Interior Department through its Bureau of Indian Affairs (Minneapolis has one of the largest per capita urban Indian populations in the U.S.). We drive on interstate freeways that were largely paid for by federal dollars, and fly into and out of an airport operating by FAA regulations, and every check we write is cleared through the Federal Reserve Bank. Still, most people would probably say that, apart from taxes, the federal government treads lightly on most of the citizenry.

A different perspective accrues to the state government, which is widely observed at close range, largely because St. Paul is the state capital. Most Twin Cities residents are keenly aware that the state is involved in their lives, if only at the level of licensing them to drive, registering their vehicles, and granting licenses for leisure-time activities such as fishing and hunting. The Department of Natural Resources, which maintains and oversees an extensive state park system, as well as thousands of lakes, is a well-known entity to most Twin Citians. Cultural institutions like the Minnesota Zoo and the Historical Society are overseen by the state. Most of those seeking higher education in the metro area attend the University of Minnesota or one of the state universities, and expenditures for higher education are one of the highest priorities in the bi-annual funding session of the state legislature. Parents of elementary and high school age students are increasingly knowledgeable about the state's important role in funding local school systems, though the state Department of Education does not involve itself in day-to-day school operations or decision making. In recent years Minnesota, like most of the other states, has gone looking for new economic development prospects, and such efforts have become a major focus of state government. This has led to state-funded initiatives of various kinds, though seldom are such efforts focused on the prosperous Twin Cities region.

Regulations formulated at the state level govern concerns in the social service arena, such as health (hospital oversight) and job training, while certification of professionals such as doctors and lawyers is also a state responsibility. We rely upon the state government to regulate the public utilities that we all use, through monitoring rate increases and establishing whether or not new power plants are needed; and monitoring pollution of all kinds—perhaps most important these days is the volatile issue of ground-water sources that are vulnerable to agricultural run-off (especially on the metropolitan area's perimeter, where extensive farming still occurs). These issues are often contentious, and they frequently lead into the state's judicial system, though most local residents are less likely to be aware of the separate responsibilities of the differing levels of courts. In contrast, Twin Citians are certainly aware of the state's role in relieving them of their tax money. In "high-tax" Minnesota, this is the issue that most provokes various local constituencies, from individual and corporate property owners to businesses that view the relatively high state-mandated worker's compensation levels as an unfair burden to their bottom lines. For the Twin Cities in recent years, tax disparities between the metropolitan region and the rest of the state have generated such an outcry that the governor has called a special session of the legislature this fall to address this concern. Whatever the outcome, we can be assured that local residents will continue to view many aspects of state government with suspicion. But it is important to recognize that, while the state looms as a large presence to Twin Cities residents, there is little need for most people to interact with the state or its representatives regularly—again, apart from paying taxes.

Setting aside the issue of metropolitan government for the moment, we next arrive at the level of local government in the Twin Cities. Here the situation becomes more complex, for not only are there two cities with separate mayors and city councils, but most of the surrounding suburbs also have their own individual mayors and many have councils. As in most U.S. metropolitan areas, there is enormous duplication of activities in managing the Twin Cities. Each municipality not only has an independent governance structure, but also independent planning and zoning regulations, school districts, and usually an independent police and fire protection system. The subunits of the metropolitan area are obviously brought together through infrastructure systems like roads, sewers and water lines, and through communications systems like newspapers, television and radio services, and telephone lines. But in the daily decisions that people make about their lives, there is more separation than cohesion at times.

Together the two central cities contain less than one-third of the region's population, yet they have the region's most complex administrative arrangements. Both cities have a mayor and city council, though predictably, their systems are quite different. St. Paul has a "strong mayor" government, with a part-time seven-member council, and all major departments report to the mayor. At times when the mayor is a strong personality (as during the past dozen years with George Latimer), it seems as if every decision emanates from that office. For years the city council had little to do but ratify the mayor's decisions, and until very recently the council members were all at-large representatives. Minneapolis has a 13-member "strong council/weak mayor" system that almost guarantees conflict because most department heads report to the full-time city council members, who also serve as commissioners of the city's development agency. Both cities have elected school boards with independent taxing authority, and Minneapolis' government is further complicated by two other independently elected boards (one for parks, one for the library) that also can raise taxes. Residents are made aware of the authority of each city in many ways, from parking tickets and towing regulations, to actions of the police, to housing inspections and restrictions on land use. Recently, as concerns about drugs and associated crime have escalated, city officials have broken down crack houses and set up a system to monitor vacant houses for drug-related activities. There are now programs in place in both cities to do such things as keeping tabs on housing vacancies, and working with community groups to get vacant houses recycled. This one example illustrates how closely local government is entwined in the lives of many of its citizens; many others could be added that would underscore the same point.

The suburban municipalities duplicate many functions of the governments of Minneapolis and St. Paul, usually in a much smaller and arguably more efficient fashion. Even the largest of the surrounding communities—for example, Bloomington, which is now considered a central city by the census bureau—have only part-time executives, and their full-time administrative staff spend most of their time on issues connected with planning and zoning. As in many other metropolitan areas in recent years, the long-assumed distinctions between city and suburb in the Twin Cities are becoming blurred. As several suburbs have struggled with problems like aging populations and declining school enrollments, problems all too familiar to Minneapolis and St. Paul in recent decades, perceptions of limited kinship (at least between the central cities and inner-ring suburbs) begin to surface. Such notions are limited of course by the reality of differing property tax situations and by nervousness about the unlikely prospect of cross-jurisdictional busing to achieve school desegregation.

Between the state government and the local level lie the least understood administrative layers in the Twin Cities: the county and metropolitan arenas. This region contains seven counties, and each has myriad responsibilities connected with overseeing state-mandated, and some federal, programs. Hospitals, jails, and courts operate under county auspices, as do most other providers of social services. County officials are the conduit through which welfare money is distributed, and through which programs for abused children and other vulnerable populations are authorized. County commissioners have recently had to become knowledgeable about infrastructure issues like waste incineration and light rail transit, as this region spends millions on planning and constructing new facilities. Despite the general public's lack of knowledge about the role that the counties play in this region, it is clear that their involvement in policy issues of all kinds is increasing.

A quick glance at specific counties illustrates the complexity and delicacy of local intergovernmental relations. Hennepin County, which contains Minneapolis, is the largest of the seven with nearly half of the region's total population (1 million out of 2.3 million). The seven extremely political Hennepin County commissioners, most of whom see themselves as eventual contenders for higher office, have recently stirred controversy with great abandon. Hennepin County started planning a light rail system to serve Minneapolis and its suburbs long before consulting with other counties about cooperation on building a system. Even now, with discussion of specific routes underway, Ramsey County (and St. Paul) have only belatedly been recognized as interested parties. Hennepin County also took on Minneapolis over the siting of a major new waste-to-energy plant. Suburban resistance combined with traffic data to suggest a site on the Minneapolis riverfront. Vocal city opposition derailed that site, but left as the only option some unused industrial land on the fringe of downtown, where the new facility now sits, despite city worries about toxic particulates swirling around in highrise downdrafts. Dakota County (south of St. Paul) is the fastest growing county in the region, and as such generates conflicts with the more built-up Ramsey County. One of the longest running disputes concerned a freeway link-up that would speed the travel of Dakota County commuters, and which Ramsey County resisted on behalf of St. Paul residents who lobbied against the increased noise and traffic. This freeway link is now nearing completion after a decade-long disagreement, including a court challenge.

Part of the responsibility for sorting out these and other conflicts rests with the Metropolitan Council, the final layer of administration/governance in the Twin Cities. That such major conflicts arise, despite the presence of a regional planning authority, underscores the difficulty of infusing a regional perspective into most local issues. The Metropolitan Council has now been around for over 20 years, having been created by the Minnesota state legislature in 1967. Its original charge was to coordinate long-range plans for the metro area and to recommend policies to local governments, specifically county boards and city councils. The Metro Council is also charged with reviewing proposed projects or activities that have "metropolitan significance," either at its own discretion or by request of citizens or other agencies.

The first metropolitan issues that the council had to face were physical planning ones—the acknowledged problems of sewage disposal and water pollution. It is important to underscore that the council was to work with other levels of government to adopt and implement regional policies; that is a large part of its success. Some observers and proponents of the council have acclaimed it over the years, calling it "unusually promising" and "somewhat extraordinary" for negotiating the treacherous shoals of metropolitan cooperation (Naftalin 1986; Harrigan and Johnson 1978). Others, including most ordinary citizens, still have difficulty trying to define exactly what the council is.

One should note that the Metropolitan Council did not arrive *sui generis* in 1967. It replaced the earlier Metropolitan Planning Commission (MPC), created by the legislature in 1957, which functioned much like the traditional "council of governments" voluntary association, without any enforcement powers. Prior to and contemporaneous with the MPC, there were several other efforts to deliver services on a regional basis, all established by the state legislature: the Twin Cities Sanitary District (1933) was to coordinate sewers for the two central cities; the Metropolitan Airports Commission (1943) was to dissuade each city from building its own airport, and focus on one site; the Metropolitan Area Sports Commission (1956) was to build and operate a suburban football/baseball stadium; and the Metropolitan Mosquito Control District (1958), whose function is fairly self-evident. Long-time observers have argued that a regional impulse, recognizing that there were limits to what each municipality could do, was alive and well long before the council was created (Naftalin and Brandl 1980).

There are a few salient facts that help in understanding the role of the Metropolitan Council in the Twin Cities: (1) It was created by, and reports to, the state legislature. The council may claim that local governments are its audience, but political realities argue differently. (2) None of the 17 council members (including its chair) is elected. All are appointed by the governor, usually in consultation with the state legislators whose districts a member will represent. (3) The council has, by design, very little operating authority. It oversees and approves the budgets of the operating commissions: the Metropolitan Transit Authority, the Metropolitan Waste Control Commission (MWCC), the Metropolitan Airports Commission (MAC), and others. But most of its charge is review and oversight, particularly of long-range capital expenditures. It was this oversight function that got the council up and running, that provided it a forum, and that helped achieve many of its early successes. These first two factors explain why the Metropolitan Council has no real leverage—being appointed, its members are virtually unknown (except to a few politicians), and they have no real constituency. Though a bill to have council members elected has been introduced in nearly every legislative session since its creation, it has always failed. The third factor goes to the heart of perceptions about the council's effectiveness—apart from planning, what is it supposed to do? In this question lies much potential conflict; the legislature wants the council to insulate it from the concerns of Twin Cities residents, but the council has no direct connection to residents, and little ability to get any.

Finally there is the fact that the council was created to deal with very real physical development issues. In the late 1960s the Twin Cities had a full plate of development problems: how and where to dispose of sewage and solid waste; whether and where to build a new airport; how to salvage the privately owned transit system; how to ensure that open space would be either reserved or provided for in rapidly developing areas; and how to balance growth at the edge with decline in the central cities.   In retrospect, the council's responses to these issues were predictable, and occasionally remarkable. But these issues were all ones that were amenable to study, consultation, and eventual solution, and their urgency gave the council a great deal to do very quickly. Most of them were resolved within 10 years. As the brunt of regional concerns shifted from physical development to social issues like education, child care, and the whole set of concerns that revolve around extremely disadvantaged populations, solutions became more difficult and the exact role of the council in responding to them became less clear.

CASE STUDIES

Quite a lot has already been written about the working out of "metropolitan issues" in the Twin Cities area, specifically with reference to the origin of the Metropolitan Council (Baldinger 1971; Harrigan and Johnson 1978). There is no need to replicate that here, nor is there space to detail everything the council has done in 20 years. Suffice it to say that many important concerns have been dealt with in a positive way through the existence of a metropolitanwide agency. But having a metropolitan authority in the Twin Cities area has certainly not resolved all of the region's problems. This section will attempt to shed some light on the workings of the Metropolitan Council by examining some of the issues that it has addressed, both more and less successfully. The intent is not to delve deeply into one or two issues, but to delineate broadly several areas that may lead to thoughtful comparisons.

Past Successes

Let's begin with what has worked well. Early on the Metropolitan Council took on the question of a new airport. In 1969 and 1970 the Airports Commission proposed a second large airport at Ham Lake, north of the Twin Cities. The council vetoed both proposals, contending that the evidence did not demonstrate a need for a second facility at the time. This decision effectively forced an upgrading of the existing airport immediately south of the cities instead and began the process of turning it into a true international facility. For almost 20 years, through several large expansions of the MSP airport, this decision has held. Only in the past year, and this time initiated in part by the council, has serious discussion of the need for a new airport surfaced once again. It is too early to say what the outcome will be—further upgrading and significant expansion of the existing airport, or a new one in an as-yet-undetermined site. It is typical of the council's operations that this issue has been framed as a task force study problem, with wide-ranging consultation and public hearings prior to any decision being reached by the council.

A similar situation obtained with respect to the late 1960s crisis surrounding sewer extensions and capacity limits. In 1969 the legislature authorized the council to develop a comprehensive system for sewage disposal, and it established a Metropolitan Sewer Board (now MWCC) to carry it out as an agent of the council. After some initial conflict and misunderstanding between these two groups, the council was charged in 1974 with developing a sewer policy for the metro region. This decision had a dual purpose: it gave the Metropolitan Council some needed authority to implement its planned regional development framework; and it would become the primary mechanism for bringing the quality of regional rivers and lakes up to those set in the 1972 Federal Pollution Control Act. For the past 15 years there has been steady progress in most aspects of sewage disposal—extensions have been limited to previously delineated areas, outdated sewer lines have been replaced, sewer separation is nearly complete even for the central cities, and the quality of even the Mississippi River water has been improved. The operation of a regional sewer/water system is now taken for granted. Conflicts arose during the 1988 drought about possible water provision for the Twin Cities, but it was limited to disagreements at the state level about draining the northern lakes for Twin Cities' residential use. Within the metropolitan region, there was near-unanimous foregoing of lawn watering and car washing, with little intraregional complaint.

Development Framework

At a macro level two policies of metropolitan significance have been developed, largely through the efforts of the Metropolitan Council and its supporters. The first was the "Metropolitan Development Guide," which began to be adopted in sections beginning in 1973. The guide was a major state-mandated planning tool, with chapters on recreation, health care, and virtually every other subject likely to have any impact on the metropolitan area. The focus here will be on the "development framework" portion of the guide (adopted in 1975), the section that would determine the path of future physical development surrounding the Twin Cities. The development framework was intended to rationalize and contain the costs of new construction by channeling growth into predetermined areas. It also had as subsidiary goals all of the following: to preserve the natural environment; to expand people's social choices and lower the concentration of minorities in central city neighborhoods; to diversify regional economic growth and equitably finance public services; and to get more citizens involved in regional governance (Harrigan and Johnson 1978).

The Development Framework outlined five distinct planning regions, three of which constituted the Metropolitan Urban Services Area (MUSA): the two central cities, the fully developed suburban areas, and the areas of planned urbanization. Outside the MUSA line were the two areas that were to be protected from urban sprawl—rural trade centers and freestanding growth centers (small towns on the region's periphery), and the rural service area (those portions of the metro area still in agricultural use). In essence the Development Guide dictated that the central cities and developed suburbs be completely filled in, or reused, before urban use of agricultural land would be permitted. The council had several tools available to enforce the dictates of the Development Guide: (1) a 1976 Land Planning Act that stated where, when, and under what conditions services such as sewers, transit, and parks would be extended to unserved portions of the metro area; (2) an upgraded septic-tank regulation by the state Pollution Control Agency; (3) its authority to review long-term plans and capital budgets of the metropolitan commissions, and to suspend action on any that do not conform to the guide; (4) its overall review authority for discretionary grants, certificates of need, and for a time, the federal A-95 review power as well.

Fifteen or so years after the appearance of the Development Guide, it seems reasonable to ask how well has it worked. The invariable answer is that it depends on who is asked the question. From the perspective of the two central cities, it has been reasonably successful in helping to promote the cities' own redevelopment ambitions. From the mid-1970s to the early 1980s there was at least $2-$3 billion of public and private investment in the inner areas of the two cities, much but not all of it in the two downtowns (Borchert 1988). John Borchert has estimated that perhaps one-third of the total new construction in the metropolitan area in these years was also in the two central cities—encompassing nearly half of the regional office space expansion in the 1970s and more than half of that estimated for the 1980s. This proportion is even more striking when we recognize that throughout this period both cities have continued to lose population (at about a 15 percent level of decline per decade).

Overall, the council's development policies have certainly not stemmed either suburban population growth or investment to any appreciable degree. The population growth rates of most suburban areas closest to the central cities slowed dramatically through the 1970s—Edina and St. Louis Park, two of the older western suburban communities, respectively gained 4 percent and lost 13 percent of their 1970 populations by 1980. At the same time, outer suburban areas were booming, with a developing area like Burnsville growing by 79 percent, while brand new communities like Maple Grove and Eagan grew from farmland at rates of 326 percent and over 2000 percent between 1970 and 1980. (See Table 5.1.) Most, if not all, of this growth occurred within the predetermined limits of "planned urbanization." The areas most obviously affected by the Metropolitan Council's development policies have perhaps been the older inner-ring suburbs. Many of these now have entire sections with much higher density development than anyone would have predicted 15 years ago, even including some highrise office and residential towers. One cannot of course say with certainty that this intensification of inner suburban land use is entirely owing to extant public land-use policies and is unrelated to land prices and cultural preferences. As freeway improvements and new connectors have appeared, the desirability of land that was once hopelessly far from either downtown has escalated enormously, not just in the Twin Cities. The Development Guide's policies, at the very least, have ratified some changing economic perceptions that emanated out of the early 1970s fuel crisis, and may be partially accountable for some of the more intense development patterns in some close-in suburbs with good freeway locations. (See Tables 5.2-4.)

What the Development Guide has done most successfully has been to prevent certain kinds of leapfrog development within the seven-county metropolitan area, largely by limiting sewer and water extensions onto working farmland. This achievement, though consistent with stated goals, has been something of a mixed blessing from a larger regional perspective—and it has also served to underscore the practical limits of the council's planning efforts. The council's authority extends only to the seven-county metropolitan area, but development pressures have expanded well beyond this point, particularly on the eastern and far northwestern

Table 5.1. *Population Change in Twin Cities Metro Counties 1940-1990 (By Percent)*

County	1940-50	1950-60	1960-70	1970-80	1980-90
Anoka	59	142	80	27	24
Carver	3	18	33	31	23
Dakota	24	60	79	39	42
Hennepin	19	25	14	-2	9
Ramsey	15	19	13	-4	6
Scott	6	33	48	35	32
Sherburne	2	21	43	63	40
Washington	31	52	58	37	28
Wright	1	8	30	51	17

Population Change in Selected Metro Suburbs and Central Cities

City	County	Pop. 1975	Pop. 1980	Pop. 1985	Pop. 1990	% Change 1975-1990
Apple Valley	Dakota	15,160	21,818	27,172	34,598	228
Burnsville	Dakota	27,807	35,674	40,115	51,288	84
Edina	Hennepin	45,059.5	46,073	44,940	47,070	4
Minneapolis	Hennepin	402,675.5	370,951	362,090	368,383	(9)
St. Paul	Ramsey	290,048	270,230	267,810	272,235	(7)
Robbinsdale	Hennepin	15,633.5	14,422	14,060	14,396	(8)
Anoka	Anoka	14,466	15,634	15,390	17,192	18
Blaine	Anoka	24,563	28,558	33,840	38,975	59

Source: Minnesota Department of Energy, Planning, and Development Office of Human Resources Planning, Population Notes, January 1982, SDU 82-2.
U.S. Dept. of Commerce, 1990 Census of Population and Housing, Minnesota

edges of the metro area. For example, the largely rural Wright and Sherburne counties that abut the northwest boundary of the metro area had small towns within them that grew by 50-60 percent between 1970 and 1980, *before* direct interstate freeway connections linked them to the core of the metro area. (See Map 5.2.) It is widely expected that the

Map 5.2.   *Seven County Metropolitan Area and Neighboring Counties*

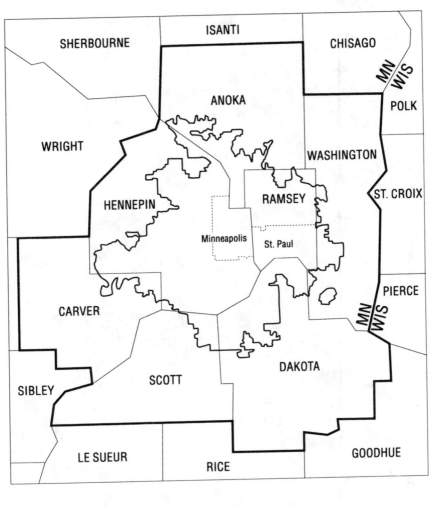

Table 5.2. *Employment Changes in Selected Twin Cities Communities*

Covered Employment City	1978	1980	1985	1988	% Change 1978-88
Apple Valley					
Manufacturing				210	
Retail	757	840	1,254	1,813	139
Contract Construction	143	142	199	263	84
Total for all categories	1,683	1,935	3,738	5,062	201
Burnsville					
Manufacturing	721	996	1,503	1,763	145
Retail	3,929	5,321	6,534	8,121	107
Contract Construction	743	966	845	909	22
Total for all categories	10,147	12,654	18,450	21,559	112
Edina					
Manufacturing	4,675	3,445	5,606	4,175	-11
Retail	6,831	9,204	8,937	10,227	50
Contract Construction	991	1,420	908	1,640	65
Total for all categories	33,689	39,185	45,616	47,337	41
Minneapolis					
Manufacturing	51,942	51,227	41,350	39,724	-24
Retail	42,362	40,424	39,917	41,296	-3
Contract Construction	6,259	7,300	6,395	5,794	-7
Total for all categories	268,543	272,733	270,946	281,036	5

					% Change 1980-88
St. Paul					
Manufacturing	54,357	49,481	51,664	47,575	-12
Retail	24,415	23,321	23,525	24,407	0
Contract Construction	4,904	5,916	5,312	5,449	11
Total for all categories	187,542	185,844	184,859	188,460	0
Robbinsdale					
Manufacturing	126	77	89	105	-17
Retail	1,081	1,064	1,089	1,062	-2
Contract Construction	122	124	84	193	58
Total for all categories	3,141	3,110	5,318	6,320	101
Anoka					
Manufacturing	1,435	4,382	1,946	1,924	34
Retail	630	1,564	658	671	7
Contract Construction		585			
Total for all categories	9,583	10,782	12,365	13,008	36
Blaine					
Manufacturing		263	2,698	2,739	941
Retail		2,458	3,347	3,823	56
Contract Construction		376	470	746	98
Total for all categories		4,857	9,351	10,637	119

Table 5.3. Selected Property Values in Twin Cities Communities

Value of Residential Property
(Adjusted to 1988 dollars)

City	1975	1980	1985	1988	% Change 1975-80
Apple Valley	$204,991,892	$404,710,460	$590,547,601	$875,704,840	327
Burnsville	$402,648,020	$709,167,877	$908,451,600	$1,269,643,413	153
Edina	$1,358,356,929	$1,817,693,689	$2,016,287,956	$2,370,888,924	75
Minneapolis	$4,709,339,391	$7,117,007,637	$7,613,825,954	$8,006,823,191	70
St. Paul	$2,841,982,783	$4,714,813,227	$4,932,086,992	$5,255,183,367	85
Robbinsdale	$249,783,160	$331,296,420	$330,370,611	$365,603,816	46
Anoka	$178,121,500	$274,875,484	$275,626,372	$325,672,461	83
Blaine	$250,335,577	$422,936,746	$526,409,709	$683,743,801	173

Value of Industrial and Commercial Property
(Adjusted to 1988 dollars)

City	1975	1980	1995	1988	% Change 1975-80
Apple Valley	$17,982,338	$23,595,731	$32,186,344	$66,783,760	327
Burnsville	$141,102,245	$199,266,274	$293,194,231	$392,662,611	153
Edina	$420,059,140	$386,861,420	$516,208,530	$666,001,009	75

City	1980	1985	1988	% Change 1975-88
Minneapolis	$2,175,786,269	$3,398,939,048	$4,219,057,979	70
St. Paul	$1,200,351,770	$1,561,670,368	$1,802,511,912	85
Robbinsdale	$25,558,314	$34,807,555	$43,638,332	46
Anoka	$52,514,309	$67,331,256	$74,246,101	83
Blaine	$52,852,620	$93,652,786	$161,974,152	173

Value of Agricultural, Timber, and Vacant Land
(Adjusted to 1988 dollars)

City	Area	1975	1980	1985	1988	% Change 1975-88
Apple Valley	17.5					
Agricultural, timber, & vacant		$11,597,128	$15,162,366	$25,110,620	$23,383,886	102
Residential		$204,991,892	$404,710,460	$590,547,601	$875,704,840	327
Industrial and commercial		$17,982,338	$23,595,731	$32,186,344	$66,783,760	271
Total		$236,138,402	$446,455,755	$650,457,188	$968,581,682	310
Burnsville	25.6					
Agricultural, timber, & vacant		$21,977,283	$61,479,753	$63,449,718	$66,134,481	201
Residential		$502,648,020	$709,167,877	$908,451,600	$1,269,643,413	153
Industrial and commercial		$141,102,245	$199,266,274	$293,194,231	$392,662,611	178
Total		$737,374,139	$1,039,495,090	$1,315,458,530	$1,821,487,505	147
Edina	15.8					
Agricultural, timber, & vacant		$23,607,953	$34,635,930	$23,418,353	$22,477,715	(5)
Residential		$1,358,356,929	$1,817,693,689	$2,016,287,956	$2,370,888,924	75
Industrial and commercial		$420,059,140	$386,861,420	$516,208,530	$666,001,009	59
Total		$1,804,730,530	$2,241,354,237	$2,557,724,228	$3,061,126,452	70

Minneapolis	52.6					
Agricultural, timber, & vacant		$20,316,666	$12,967,219	$40,834,696	$43,052,633	112
Residential		$4,709,339,391	$7,117,007,637	$7,613,825,954	$8,006,823,191	70
Industrial and commercial		$2,175,786,269	$2,013,727,408	$3,398,939,048	$4,219,057,979	94
Total		$7,001,398,739	$9,213,511,196	$11,113,757,963	$12,375,395,151	77
St. Paul	50.0					
Agricultural, timber, & vacant		$19,998,471	$11,039,065	$19,028,231	$25,956,351	30
Residential		$2,841,982,783	$4,714,813,227	$4,932,086,992	$5,255,183,367	85
Industrial and commercial		$1,200,351,770	$1,229,150,195	$1,561,670,368	$1,802,511,912	50
Total		$4,136,042,473	$6,012,879,420	$6,556,673,250	$7,128,043,565	72
Robbinsdale	2.7					
Agricultural, timber, & vacant		$1,425,124	$1,310,238	$805,445	$1,220,762	(14)
Residential		$249,783,160	$331,296,420	$330,370,611	$365,603,816	46
Industrial and commercial		$25,558,314	$22,915,905	$34,807,555	$43,636,332	71
Total		$276,970,746	$356,248,457	$366,469,027	$410,911,888	48
Anoka	6.8					
Agricultural, timber, & vacant		$2,605,888	$5,195,994	$4,583,051	$3,771,052	45
Residential		$178,121,500	$274,875,484	$275,626,372	$325,672,461	83
Industrial and commercial		$52,514,309	$66,582,503	$67,331,256	$74,246,101	41
Total		$233,273,628	$346,678,007	$348,830,224	$403,711,505	73
Blaine	33.5					
Agricultural, timber, & vacant		$8,868,314	$26,411,349	$25,641,251	$33,434,076	277
Residential		$250,335,577	$422,936,746	$526,409,709	$683,743,801	173
Industrial and commercial		$52,852,620	$80,078,091	$93,652,786	$161,974,152	206
Total		$312,494,730	$531,152,803	$647,093,559	$880,694,941	182

Table 5.4. *Selected Property Values in Twin Cities (All property)*

City	Area	1975	1980	1985	1988	% Change 1975-88
Apple Valley	17.5	$236,138,402	$445,455,755	$650,457,188	$968,581,682	310
Burnsville	25.6	$737,374,139	$1,039,495,090	$1,315,458,530	$1,821,487,505	147
Edina	15.8	$1,804,730,530	$2,241,354,237	$2,557,724,228	$3,061,126,452	70
Minneapolis	52.6	$7,001,398,739	$9,213,511,196	$11,113,757,963	$12,375,395,151	77
St. Paul	50.8	$4,136,042,473	$6,012,879,420	$6,556,573,250	$7,128,043,565	72
Robbinsdale	2.7	$276,970,746	$356,248,457	$366,469,027	$410,911,888	48
Anoka	6.8	$233,273,628	$346,678,007	$348,830,224	$403,711,505	73
Blaine	33.5	$312,494,730	$531,152,803	$647,093,559	$880,694,941	182

Total Value of all Real Property Per Square Mile
(Adjusted to 1988 dollars)

City	Area	1975	1980	1985	1988	% Change 1975-88
Apple Valley	17.5	$13,462,851	$25,396,565	$37,084,218	$55,221,305	310
Burnsville	25.6	$28,792,430	$40,589,422	$51,365,034	$71,124,073	147
Edina	15.8	$113,935,008	$141,499,636	$161,472,489	$193,252,933	70
Minneapolis	52.6	$133,157,070	$175,228,437	$211,368,542	$235,363,164	77
St. Paul	50.8	$81,370,106	$118,293,909	$128,990,227	$140,233,003	72
Robbinsdale	2.7	$101,084,214	$130,017,685	$133,747,820	$149,967,842	48
Anoka	6.8	$34,204,344	$50,832,552	$51,148,127	$59,195,235	73
Blaine	33.5	$9,336,562	$15,869,519	$19,333,539	$26,312,965	182

1990 census will underscore continued strong population growth in adjacent counties, including St. Croix and Pierce Counties in Wisconsin, which border the metropolitan area across the state boundary to the east. There is little or nothing that even the most sophisticated policy can do to control growth beyond the region's boundaries. So the Metropolitan Council has to live with the frustrating knowledge that the effective metropolitan area has outgrown its reaches, and that it is not at all likely that its own range of authority will be extended.

Fiscal Disparities Act

The second important tool for rationalizing the causes and effects of regional locational choices has been the Fiscal Disparities Act, passed by the legislature in 1974. This was not a Metropolitan Council policy *per se*; the council had no mandate to involve itself with overall fiscal operations or budgeting for the region. Still, the fiscal disparities law is quite consistent with the long-range planning goals set by the council, and in light of its operations, it has moved the council further and further toward overall regional fiscal planning.

The fiscal disparities legislation mandated tax-base sharing throughout the metropolitan area. It was intended to remove the impact that accidents of location have on local units of government. The law set 1971 as a base year and stipulated that 40 percent of the net gain in tax revenues generated by *new* commercial and industrial development would go into a pool. This money would then be shared by units of government that could not generate new development of their own, according to a formula based on population weighted by every jurisdiction's fiscal capacity. What this meant in practice was that some of the financial benefits accruing to fast-growing suburban areas would partially devolve on less advantaged areas, including, for a time, both central cities. In 1980, 13 percent of the region's tax base ($328 million) was being shared, and most officials expected that this percentage would continue to grow (Naftalin and Brandl 1980). In practice, the bulk of these funds has gone to built-up suburbs that are predominantly residential and to growing suburbs with little industry. Both Minneapolis and St. Paul were net gainers in the early years of fiscal disparities financing, but as new downtown developments have increased their property tax bases, they have become net contributors in recent years.

Subsidized Housing

Another arena in which the decisions of the Metropolitan Council have been influential is that of helping to disperse subsidized housing fairly widely throughout the metropolitan area. This policy was a step away from the traditional physical development concerns of the early Metropolitan Council, and it was one that, to some degree, raised local government concerns about the propriety of the actions taken by the *unelected* council members. Like most other metropolitan areas in the U.S., the bulk of low-income housing constructed with federal subsidies in the 1950s, 1960s, and early 1970s—outright public housing units as well as other sorts of subsidized housing units—was concentrated in the central cities of St. Paul and Minneapolis. Unlike many other U.S. metropolitan areas, however, most of the public housing and other subsidized units in the two central cities did not consist of the densely packed highrise towers made infamous when St. Louis imploded the Pruitt-Igoe project. Still, as in most other U.S. metropolitan areas, leaders in the two central cities had bemoaned what they identified as the unfair concentration of poor people for whom they then had to provide services. This concern meshed with observations made by advocates for the poor that the central cities were losing unskilled jobs, which were increasingly located in the suburbs, well away from the traditional areas that poor unskilled workers lived in or had access to.

Beginning in the late 1970s the Metro Council began a conscious policy of requiring that subsidized housing be scattered throughout the entire metropolitan area, rather than continuing to be concentrated in the two cities. There were many reasons for this new initiative: concerns about the regional supply of housing (amount, location, and cost), and the changing demographics of housing consumers; concerns about people's locational choices relative to constrained energy supplies (this has turned out to be a nonissue so far); specific concerns about the restricted choices of housing options, particularly for poor people; recognition that young people at many income levels could not afford to buy the kinds of houses that they'd grown up in. Given this wide range of concerns, the council chose to try to influence some portions of these equations where it could. As the review agency for federal sewer, water, and road-building dollars, the council had a "carrot" that it could use to encourage municipalities to accept some of its wisdom on this issue.

Many municipalities throughout the area were fairly sanguine about the disbursement issue, since many suburbs had already created some subsidized housing units for the elderly, and no one felt threatened by anyone's poor grandma. But real concerns and real objections emerged when it became obvious that the council meant that subsidized *family* housing had to be scattered along with the elderly units. (The formal requirement was that no more than 60 percent of all new family subsidized housing could be built in the two central cities.) Suddenly the specter of major social dislocation arose, for many believed that this requirement implied that large numbers of poor minority families would now move into the mostly white Twin Cities suburbs, threatening property values, perceptions about prestigious schools, and innate feelings of security. Many suburban municipalities felt that they were already doing enough in the subsidized housing arena and that an unelected group of officials had no right dictating to local governments. (Remember that one of the council's original charges was to recommend policies to local governments; no where did it say that the council should make local governments do what they were opposed to). Some suburban officials even got very defensive, going so far as to announce that they would do without federal funds rather than cave in to what they perceived as an intolerable intrusion in local affairs. Interestingly, there was even some opposition to the policy within the central city low-income community—here the concern was that the new policy would force people to move away from parts of the city where they felt comfortable, where they had a support network and nearby access to needed services.

Today far more suburban communities provide subsidized housing than did so in the early 1970s: 93 municipalities in 1986 versus 54 in 1971, despite steadily declining federal dollars to produce subsidized housing throughout the 1980s. Since 1983, over three times as many Section 8 new construction dollars have been spent in the suburbs than in St. Paul and Minneapolis combined, and this disproportionate allocation of resources has over time substantially altered the cumulative subsidized housing picture. In 1971 the two central cities held 90 percent of all subsidized units in the region, but by 1986 their combined allotment had decreased to 60 percent of the total; at the same time the suburban allocation had increased from 10 percent to 40 percent of the total (Vail and Zimbro 1986). And excepting only Scott and Carver counties, still the most rural parts of the metropolitan area, virtually all of the communities that had or have subsidized elderly projects have now built subsidized family projects as well.

In the years since the council's implementation of the subsidized housing dispersal policy, some but not all of the misperceptions have been laid to rest. Early opponents of the policy never considered the economic toll that divorce and nonpayment of child support might have on young people who grew up in their own communities. For example, studies have demonstrated that most who reside in subsidized suburban units come from the local community. In one suburb that boasts the state's third highest median income, only 22 percent of the residents of a 126-unit mixed project (family/elderly/handicapped) come from either Minneapolis or St. Paul (*Star and Tribune*, Sept. 4, 1989). In this and other projects there are sizeable nonhousing resources devoted to improving the lives of residents, including adult education classes and field trips for the children. Still, there are obvious problems. While suburban subsidized housing seldom resembles classic central city projects, neither does it look much like nearby single family houses. Children who live in these units, who likely lack the most current fashion statements are sometimes stigmatized by other children; many of the single mothers who head these households feel embarrassed about using food stamps in local grocery stores; and there are strong local perceptions that increases in crime rates accompany the existence of subsidized family housing (*Star and Tribune*, Sept. 4, 1989).

But the most intransigent current problem associated with both suburban and central city subsidized units is unrelated to location or to who lives there. Rather, a timebomb ticks away in the form of guidelines under which much of this housing was constructed. According to the regulations, the private developers of hundreds of thousands of subsidized units nationwide can prepay their federal mortgages beginning in 1990. When they do, the rents they charge will no longer be subject to any limits, and many households currently occupying subsidized units will be forced out. The units most threatened are precisely those in desirable locations, such as the fast-growing Twin Cities suburbs. There is little that the Metropolitan Council or any other agency can do to forestall the likely loss of much of this housing supply, short of intervening with mountains of cash to buy out developers—a tactic that one or two community development groups in Minneapolis are attempting for extremely endangered projects, with the city's assistance. The difficulties presented by this situation clearly underscore some of the limits of regional planning efforts (at least those accomplished with federal financial assistance). There are few guarantees in this business, and no local or regional agency can hope to replace or replicate large-scale resources lost at the federal level.

The Metropolitan Council has not succeeded in everything it has attempted, but these three issues reasonably represent the challenges and the choices that the council has made over the past 20 years. Seldom have the council's policies been successfully argued or overturned, and that may be one measure of its success. Still, there is a sense that as the physical limits of the region expand beyond the seven-county reach of the Development Guide, there will be more and more dilemmas that the council simply cannot resolve under its current legislative charter.

Present Challenges

Several concerns of recent years highlight the still evolving regionalization that the greater Twin Cities area is now experiencing. And these evolving regional concerns and issues portend difficulties for the Metropolitan Council, apart from its physically delimited mandate. To the great surprise of many, and despite over 20 years of highly regarded planning experience, the regional arrangements and understandings are still not settled in the Twin Cities. As one of the few large metropolitan areas outside the Sunbelt that is still growing (something that few might have predicted 20 years ago), the Twin Cities area finds itself still facing issues that were thought to have been resolved, as well as having to meet new challenges.

A sample of this new understanding of the Twin Cities began to appear in the early 1980s. On the heels of a serious economic downturn that seemed to affect the entire state of Minnesota *except* the Twin Cities, talk of a dual economy began. This new discussion clearly distinguished between the bullish economy of the metropolitan region and everything else. Declining prices for land and crops throughout southern and western Minnesota eroded confidence in the agricultural sector just as the industrial potential of the Iron Range faded away. More and more Minnesotans came to realize that their own hopes for jobs and better lives depended on the continued success of the metropolitan area, and this created bad feelings in the nonmetropolitan areas of Minnesota as well as a great deal of pressure for the Twin Cities area. It also led, in part, to the Twin Cities redefining its own idea of itself and created some jurisdictional problems for the Metropolitan Council.

Within a short space of time in the early 1980s, a widespread recognition arose that a regional reorientation was underway. The entire region was viewed as being in competition with other successful North American metropolitan areas, especially for new jobs and new investments. This was quite a leap from the reigning perceptions of earlier decades when St. Paul and Minneapolis were often locked in competition for just about everything. In a metropolitan region that had prospered for over a century relying largely on its own growth and that of its hinterland, this new understanding caused inevitable conflict. It came at a time when Minneapolis and St. Paul had reined in most of their directly competitive instincts, with each city instead now viewing many of the suburban municipalities suspiciously. It was no great surprise that the newly perceived need for all players in the metropolitan arena to cooperate was not immediately and warmly embraced.

The best indicator of the region's growing sense of importance and the internal conflicts generated by this came with the nearly simultaneous talk about the need for a world trade center, for a "state-of-the-art" convention center, and for the largest shopping center/entertainment complex in the world—only the latter of which had an identified location attached. It did not help that the vision of all of these new additions to the region's landscape and job base followed in the wake of an acrimonious battle between Minneapolis and Bloomington over the siting of a new football/baseball stadium. Supporters of a Minneapolis site won the right to build a domed stadium, but in the process antagonized local community groups as well as the city of Bloomington, which faced losing the existing football/baseball stadium built over 20 years earlier. The prospect of multiple large new facilities started the competitive juices flowing in Minneapolis, and in St. Paul and in Bloomington, each of which wanted at least one if not all of the new projects.

The Metropolitan Council was drawn in when it was asked to review in turn the "regional significance" of the world trade center, the convention center, and what came to be called the "mega-mall." The council did not have much prior experience in determining what regional significance a particular building or set of buildings might have; its major past participation in this kind of determination was largely limited to performing needs assessments for new hospitals. It was also quite clear that there was little the council could do to halt the locational conflict. If it found a negative regional effect, it still had no real power or authority to prevent the construction of whatever facility was being considered. The only real recourse was to appeal to the legislature to deny funding for these projects. In addition, it was not at all clear that any of the cities would accept a negative finding without challenge, given the investment and jobs base that was at stake.

The council conducted rather perfunctory reviews of the world trade center and of the convention center. The primary concern revolved around the pressure that each project would exert on the region's highways, and whether capacity needed to be increased to accommodate any of these projects. Essentially the council ended up declaring that there was no regional significance to these projects, at least none that would adversely affect the rest of the metropolitan area. Astute observers found some irony in this, since both projects had been touted as being crucially important to the future of the entire state.

To the casual observer it undoubtedly looked as if a trade-off of some sort had been made. St. Paul got the world trade center (opened for business in 1987) and Minneapolis got the convention center (now completed, but partially opened in summer 1989). Though each city submitted a fairly weak proposal for the other's project, each finally received the project that it most wanted. These two cities then turned around and worked together to try to prevent Bloomington from becoming the site of the mega-mall. There was perhaps more at stake for all of the players in the mega-mall project—the world trade center was really just another large office building, despite its international pretensions, and the convention center was really only intended to be a larger, more up-to-date version of the facility that Minneapolis already had. And while the convention center would eventually involve a hotel and other new facilities, and would likely draw some business away from St. Paul's Civic Center, the entire complex would not significantly rearrange the existing situation whereby most major conventions went to Minneapolis.

Bloomington's mega-mall was to be built on the site of the former Metropolitan Stadium, an irony that was not entirely lost on Minneapolis politicians. With its amusement park, office space, and projected 600-800 stores (including anchor tenants new to the Twin Cities), it posed a real threat to both downtowns, as well as to other shopping centers near and far. In addition to the mega-mall's potential negative impact on retailing throughout the metropolitan area, there was serious and reasonable concern about its effect on the already overcrowded beltline freeway separating its site from that of area's international airport. Promoters of the mega-mall (the Ghermazian brothers who had recently built a similar behemoth shopping center in Edmonton) maintained that the new mall would draw in so many new visitors (second only to the Disney centers) that existing retailers need not worry. They further contended that, because Minnesota was so fortunate to have this development, the state should gratefully supply any and all road improvements.

The Metropolitan Council's "significance" review of the Bloomington project was a good deal more thorough than the other projects, if only because this was clearly to be a major new addition to the Twin Cities. There was also added pressure from all of the public and private interests that were opposed to a development of this size and kind, as well as from its supporters, including the governor of Minnesota. For a time there was a frenzy of discussion about the likely impacts of the project, on the editorial pages and among the Twin Cities' numerous public policy interest groups.   Despite the clamor and widespread opposition—including some from Bloomington citizens wary of the bonding arrangements that city was about to make—the council's report finally found no reason to discourage the construction of the mega-mall. It noted the traffic problems that the new project would exacerbate, but even this was not seen as sufficient reason for a negative finding.

It is an interesting exercise to speculate about what the outcome might have been, had the council determined that the mega-mall's regional impact was too great. Most would probably agree that the effect would have been negligible and that the mega-mall would eventually have been built anyway. (Construction finally began in the summer of 1989, with commitments from four national retailers in hand, and after a major U.S. mall developer was brought in to assume a partnership role.) It is not clear that the council's opposition could have survived Bloomington's almost certain legal challenge, or that its influence might not have been diminished even more by opposing something that the governor enthusiastically supported. Moreover, it is still unclear what the ultimate effect of the mega-mall (now christened the "Mall of America") will be on the local retailing scene.   Despite consultants' glowing predictions that the mall will draw 40 million tourists, and despite one analyst's amazing description of the Twin Cities as "undermalled," local skeptics worry that if the mega-mall succeeds several local regional malls will be decimated, and both of the downtowns will also be adversely affected. Battle lines have already been drawn: Dayton's, the area's local retailing giant, refused to participate in the new mall, and has instead significantly expanded and upgraded two of its suburban stores (having revamped both of its downtown stores); the contest with Minneapolis continues unabated, with the downtown transforming itself into the Upper Midwest's "upscale" retail center (Saks Fifth Avenue and the country's second largest Polo store have opened, as has Nieman Marcus).   If anything, this situation highlights the Metropolitan Council's problematic stance when it tries to sort out locational decisions over which there are conflicts. The agency's all-too-apparent lack of enforcement power renders it almost useless at times like these; someone is bound to challenge whatever decision the council makes, and there is always the possibility of appeal to the legislature.

Another major issue that the Metropolitan Council has addressed in recent years is whether the Twin Cities International Airport will be able to meet the travel demands of the 21st century. For policymakers, the knowledge that between 1980 and 1985 passenger traffic at Twin Cities International had increased at more than twice the national average was a red flag (Airport Adequacy Task Force 1988). If this rate of expansion were to continue, then the current airport would soon be obsolete. If there were to be a new airport built, it would be far into the future and would have a major regional impact. It would also represent a major regional investment, so regionwide advance discussion and deliberation by the regional planning agency seemed entirely appropriate.

Unlike the projects discussed above, the question of airport adequacy, along with discussion of the potential need for a new airport, is quite consistent with the Metro Council's traditional long-range planning efforts. Another, perhaps crucial, difference is the fact that the legislature requested this study long in advance of the need for a final decision; the council was not having to respond to an immediate locational problem or choice.

In the years since airline deregulation the Twin Cities airport has become a touchstone for conflict, particularly surrounding the issue of significantly increased noise over nearby residential areas. The mid-1980s merger of Republic Airlines and Northwest Airlines turned the Twin Cities into a major hub for Northwest and also created a near-monopoly situation for air travelers. The Metro Council had not been a major arbiter of the noise issue, nor had it been much involved in the merger discussion and all the ancillary concerns that accompanied it. Because any discussion involving the airport was obviously going to become a highly politicized, it surprised many when the council took on the question of the airport's future. The council had come to be thought of as an administrative agency, so the reassertion of its planning function was a bit anomalous.

Being a planning agency, the Metropolitan Council approached the airport adequacy question in a very methodical way. A 35-member task force with wide-ranging representation from the community was created and charged with the task of studying the adequacy issue for eight months and reporting back to the council with its recommendations. The council would then hold public hearings and forward its own recommendations to the legislature. The council recognized that its work was really very preliminary and that the legislature rather than the council would be making the final decision; still, by shaping the study and shaping the questions that were asked, the council would stand to play a major role in whatever decision finally got made.

The task force began its work in February of 1988, with representatives from the airlines, from all levels of government, from business, from local communities, and from the general public. It reached far and wide for experts and consultants on everything from forecasting future travel trends to thinking about how the current airport site should be used if a new facility were built. Throughout the process the task force asked four key questions: Will air traffic outstrip the present system, and when might that happen? What level of service does the region want and expect? What are the consequences (economic, social, environmental) of failing to meet demand? Should the region start land-banking for a new airport or not (Apogee Research 1988)? Several realities were ever-present: (1) no one could say with certainty what 21st century travel patterns might be, particularly given possible technological changes and improvements; (2) the cost of doing nothing would be high, particularly if air travel needs could not be met; (3) the cost of making the wrong assumptions would be even higher, particularly for the region's long-range economic prospects. After much discussion, forecasting, and producing reams of reports, the Task Force emerged in late 1988 with its findings. Among them:

- the health of the metropolitan area, and of a large multi-state region, depends on good air service,
- it is highly likely that demand will exceed capacity at the current airport within 10 years,
- the metropolitan area will risk economic losses if airport capacity is not expanded within 30 years,
- significant physical constraints will prohibit sufficient expansion of the current facility, and
- it is likely that noise (and complaints about noise) will continue to increase, despite the introduction of quieter airplanes (Airport Adequacy Task Force 1988).

The task force recommended continuous monitoring of demand trends at the airport and also proposed a two-track planning strategy. It recognized the immediate need to improve the airport's current congestion by proposing that a new north-south runway be built by the mid-1990s. It looked toward future needs by recommending that the Metro Council and the Airports Commission initiate a search and site selection process for a new airport by 1995, with an eye toward building a new facility after the year 2005, should that become necessary. It also recommended that the Metro Council and the Airports Commission adopt an intergovernmental agreement by the end of 1989 that would specify what each agency's areas of responsibility would be.

The task force's thoughtful and sensible deliberations smoothed over many of the controversies surrounding any discussion of the airport, but its final report spurred both anger and debate. The idea of expanding the current airport is anathema to almost all who live nearby, in particular to residents of Richfield, some of whose homes would be taken to accommodate the expansion. The idea of relocating the airport, while appealing to residents affected by noise, poses problems for nearby businesses that depend on airport traffic, as well as for businesses in both downtowns that are well-served by the current facility. There is no doubt that any new airport will be much further away, making accessibility to it for much of the region more difficult, and even raising the question opens possibilities that alarm many residents. At the moment there are three sites being considered, two in the far southern portion of the metro area, and one to the north—all are being resisted by local forces. The proposal for selecting the site north of the far northeastern edge of the seven-county metro area is especially problematic. Discussion is being framed largely as an economic development tool for northern Minnesota (the dual economy discussion revisited).

The response from most in the metropolitan area has been disdain or disbelief—it seemed preposterous on the face of it to think of a new airport 25-75 miles away, and farthest away from the largest concentration of people in the region. Residents in the area near the proposed site, largely farmers and small town residents, were extremely negative, claiming it would destroy their way of life, and that they would resist the intrusion of noise and traffic that an airport would surely bring. The difficulty with this particular proposal, and one reason why it may not languish, is that the affected area is represented by a congressman who sits on the House transportation committee, and who apparently thinks this is a fine way to draw new resources into the northern part of the state. Should such considerations begin to affect future airport discussions, they will defeat the purpose of the task force's work, and raise even stronger questions about the efficacy of long-range planning in the Twin Cities region.

There are many other issues of regional magnitude that the Metro Council could take on, but likely will not. Probably the most important, the most difficult, and the issue least likely to be confronted on a regional scale, is public education and the perceived/real imbalances between the central city and suburban school districts. Despite a national reputation for strong public schools, Minnesota has lately come to face educational challenges akin to those in other parts of the country. This is perhaps best exemplified by the current Minneapolis situation: with a minority population of about 22 percent, the public schools have now reached a combined minority enrollment (black, Asian, American Indian) of over 50 percent, with all of the problems for continued segregation that such figures imply—and St. Paul's situation is not radically different. More of the children in public schools, white as well as minority, are from single-parent households, and many are economically as well as educationally disadvantaged. While the state government has leapt into the education fray with incentives for open enrollment, allowing parents (with some restrictions) to choose schools regardless of district of residence, there are few who believe that this will be enough to maintain a reasonable level of desegregation in the central cities or to promote more integration in the suburban districts.

Other social concerns, largely national in scope, affect certain parts of the region—the core areas of the two cities—more than others. Difficult issues abound: growing numbers of homeless people, increases in teenage pregnancies, decreasing educational attainments for low-income children, and the presence of "crack" and other drugs that torment and tear apart entire neighborhoods. It should not surprise us that the Metropolitan Council, or any other local unit of government, is reluctant to tackle problems that resist even federal intervention. Almost none of these are exclusively the problems of just Minneapolis and St. Paul, though most of the local discussion leaves an impression that the suburbs are largely untouched. Unfortunately, most of these issues are not amenable to local or regional solutions, particularly if the widespread perception is that the problem is limited to only a portion of the metropolitan area. But it is also obvious that energy for new social improvements will have to come from local initiatives, because local areas live with the consequences of these problems. What is unclear in all of this is the role there might be for the Metropolitan Council, or for any other regional institutional structure with no real enforcement powers. Should the council ever become elected, or have its persuasive powers restored to the level of the 1960s and 1970s, some creative discussion of these problems—along the lines of the subsidized housing initiatives—might become possible. No one locally expects this to happen anytime soon.

CONCLUSION

Many, perhaps competing, conclusions about the Twin Cities' metropolitan arrangements may be drawn from the foregoing discussion. One disheartening aspect for long-time observers of the local scene is the sheer amount of time that seems to go into maintaining what metropolitan consensus we have. Virtually every major policy issue in the Twin Cities has been given a life of its own through endless study and debate, and one wonders when concerned citizens will run out of energy to carry on the necessarily time-consuming process of achieving consensus.

The fragility of the regional relationships that have evolved in the Twin Cities is evident. A system that was created to respond to clear physical development concerns of the 1960s has had some difficulty responding to the more diversified concerns of the late 1980s. Despite many years of *de jure* metropolitan cooperation, there is a *de facto* lack of consensus on many issues that have metropolitan significance. Challenges to the current arrangements are abundant, among the strongest being the spatial growth of the Twin Cities area and the increasing role that the counties are being asked to play in programmatic and policy areas (especially Hennepin County with half of the entire metropolitan population).

Another possible view of the Metropolitan Council's experience over the past 20 years might hold that it has in some ways succeeded too well. The early and important successes of the council may have locked it and its constituents into predetermined ideas about what it does or should do. It will be an enormous challenge for the council to refocus or reshape the general understanding that most in the region have of it. Many issues now facing the region and the council are far beyond the purvue established by the council 20 years ago. These new issues threaten to overtake the traditional planning concerns overseen by the council, even as the planning issues themselves continue to expand. This places the council in the challenging position of having to grow in many directions at once, if it is to continue to have any regional influence.

Whether or not the early and eager metropolitanizing instincts of the Twin Cities can be maintained, duplicated, or revived, or whether the entire enterprise will wither away from disinterest, irrelevance, or open challenge, is a question that needs an answer in the near future. That answer, when it comes, will likely not emanate from the Metropolitan Council itself. The severity of this situation came into clear focus in early 1991 when the new Republican governor of Minnesota essentially gave the council a two-year deadline in which to figure out its purpose or he would propose its abolition. In response, the council and its staff are now increasing their visibility *vis-à-vis* local units of government and have once again embarked on a series of long-range planning discussions. Probably, the state legislature, local municipalities, the counties, and even areas beyond the current limits of Metropolitan Council authority, will provide whatever assessment of the council that is forthcoming, and will determine the future status of whatever metropolitan arrangements continue as the Twin Cities moves into the 21st century.

REFERENCES

Abler, Ronald, John S. Adams, and John R. Borchert. 1976. *The Twin Cities of St. Paul and Minneapolis.* Cambridge: Ballinger.

Airport Adequacy Task Force. 1988. Twin Cities Air Travel: A Strategy for Growth. Metropolitan Council.

Apogee Research. 1988. Is the Airport Adequate, Parts I & II. Metropolitan Council.

Baldinger, Stanley. 1988. *Planning and Governing the Metropolis: The Twin Cities Experience.* New York: Praeger Publishers.

Borchert, John. 1988. *America's Northern Heartland.* Minneapolis: University of Minnesota Press.

_____, David Gebhard, David Lanegran, and Judith Martin. 1983. *Legacy of Minneapolis.* Minneapolis: Voyageur Press.

Citizen's League. 1984. *The Metro Council: Narrowing the Agenda and Raising the Stakes.* Minneapolis.

_____. 1989. *Metro Council: Strengthening its Leadership Role.* Minneapolis.

Fortune. 1936. The Twin Cities, April.

Harrigan, John, and William Johnson. 1978. *Governing the Twin Cities Region.* Minneapolis: University of Minnesota Press.

Kasuba, Mike. 1989. Subsidized suburban housing dispersed poverty to fight it. *Minneapolis Star and Tribune,* September 4.

League of Women Voters. 1985. *Guide to Local Government: Minneapolis, Hennepin County, Metropolitan Council.* Minneapolis.

Metropolitan Council. 1982. *Metropolitan Council Act: Minnesota Statutes 1982 as amended by laws of 1983.*

_____. 1988. *Change, Challenge and Choice in the New Decade.*

_____. 1988. *Directory of Subsidized Rental Housing in the Twin Cities Metropolitan Area.* September.

_____. 1988. *Metropolitan Development and Investment Framework.* St. Paul.

_____. 1989. *Transportation Development Guide/Policy Plan.* February.

_____. 1989. Region's Identity at Stake in Airport Decision. *Metro Monitor,* March 8, 10.

Minneapolis Star and Tribune. 1989. Search for Possible New Site for Airport will Begin in July. May 13.

Minnesota State Planning Agency. 1984. *Metropolitan Agencies: Structure and Process Issues.* St. Paul.

Naftalin, Arthur. 1986. *Making One Community Out of Many.* Metropolitan Council, St. Paul.

_____, and John Brandl. 1980. *The Twin Cities Regional Strategy.* Metropolitan Council.

Office of the Legislative Auditor. 1985. *Metropolitan Council.*

Vail, Joanne, and Rosanne Zimbro. 1986. 1986 Subsidized Housing in the Twin Cities Metropolitan Area. Metropolitan Council, November.

Chapter 6

Edmonton: Planning in the Metropolitan Region

Ted E. Thomas
Mills College

Edmonton, the capital of Alberta, is located on the North Saskatchewan River almost at the geographical center of the province. It is the most northerly city of its size in Canada. The topography of the surrounding region is characterized by river valleys and creek ravines with high escarpments, rolling and hilly terrain to the west of the city, gently rolling terrain to the southeast, and level to undulating land in the remainder of the area.

The city is surrounded by rich agricultural lands that are found in a crescent-shaped area beginning southwest of the city, proceeding to the north and around to the east. The level, undulating lands—some of the best of the province's Chernozemic soils (grades A and B) found throughout 65 percent of the region are especially suited for crop production and dairy farming. In addition, there are valuable natural resources consisting of coal, sand, gravel, and most importantly, large quantities of conventional oil and natural gas that were discovered in the late 1940s throughout the region. These discoveries were major factors in the transformation of Alberta's economy and provided the impetus for the rapid urbanization of the region (Edmonton Metropolitan Regional Planning Commission 1984, 1).

The economy of the area has always been dependent on key staples, beginning with furs, then grain and animal products, and most recently petroleum, natural gas, and wood pulp. Significant development of secondary industry did not occur until after World War II. Presently, the region has one of the largest concentrations of manufacturing in western Canada, comprised of "basic goods" such as petroleum, coal, and chemical products that are marketed in the United States and eastern Canada. "Nonbasic" manufacturing serving the western Canadian market consists of food and beverage industries, metal fabricating, printing, textiles, clothing, wood products, and furniture. The rapidly expanding tertiary sector of the economy consisting of transportation, communications, utilities, as well as the retail and service trades such as finance, insurance, real estate, business services, public administration, and defense has experienced dramatic growth since 1970. With the urbanization of the region and the diversification of the economy, employment in the primary sector declined from approximately 8 percent in 1961 to 3.7 percent in 1981. Today, less than 2 percent of the area's labor force is in agriculture, which remains the most land intensive component of the economy (Edmonton Metropolitan Regional Planning Commission 1984, 62).

COMMUNITIES OF THE EDMONTON SUBREGION

The development of the metropolitan region is distinctly unicentric. The city of Edmonton by virtue of its size, diverse functions, power, and influence, dominates the region. Several smaller cities, towns, villages, and hamlets, many of which functioned initially as service centers for an agricultural economy, are arranged in a concentric pattern around the city. The development and growth of some of the newer urban and suburban centers occurred after the discovery of oil.

The "inner metropolitan area" consists of Edmonton, the historic city of Saint Albert just beyond its northwest border, and the "hamlet" of Sherwood Park, a comparatively new community approximately five miles beyond the city's eastern boundary. Saint Albert's history goes back to 1861, when a Roman Catholic Mission settlement was established there. It has functioned as an important center for church administration in western Canada ever since. It became a village in 1899, a town in 1904, a "New Town" in 1957, reverted to town status in 1962, and became a city in 1977. Its population increased seven-fold between 1957 and 1966, from 1,350 to 9,700 persons. By 1990 its population had quadrupled and stood at 40,707 persons (Edmonton Metropolitan Regional Planning Commission, winter 90/91, 5). It functions today essentially as a "dormitory residential suburb" for the region, with most of its labor force employed in the city of Edmonton. The hamlet of Sherwood Park, an unincorporated "urban center" of almost 35,000 persons, owes its existence to a controversial 1955 agreement signed between several developers and the Municipal District of Strathcona. Despite strong objections voiced by the city of Edmonton to the creation of a new town on 15 quarter sections of farm land just beyond "Refinery

Row" on its eastern boundary, the Department of Municipal Affairs approved its development. Today, the hamlet remains as an unincorporated "dormitory suburb" governed by the rural county of Strathcona.

The "outer metropolitan area," which grew significantly in the late sixties and early seventies, consists of several communities within 30 miles of the city center. Most of the growth can be attributed to the availability of low-priced, serviceable land for housing during a time when there were shortages of reasonably priced residential lots in the city of Edmonton. The growth of Leduc, Fort Saskatchewan, Spruce Grove, Stony Plain, and Morinville in this period was mainly in the residential sector with very little in the industrial/commercial sector (Alberta, Dept. of Municipal Affairs 1969).

The town of Devon, about 20 miles southwest of Edmonton, in the heart of the Leduc oil field, had its beginnings in the late forties as a company town established by Imperial Oil to house the sudden influx of workers to the area. To the south and west of the town are the communities of Calmer and Thorsby. Further southwest, well beyond Edmonton's commuter shed, lies the oil town of Drayton Valley, which was included within the Edmonton Regional Planning District until the early '80s. North of Saint Albert are the towns of Morinville and Legal. East of them are the communities of Bon Accord, Gibbons, and Redwater. The latter, located close to a major oil field, is somewhat beyond commuting distance of Edmonton. To the south and east of the hamlet of Sherwood Park is the rapidly expanding dormitory suburb of Beaumont, while several miles beyond lies the tiny village of New Sarepta. Three rural counties, Leduc, Parkland, and Strathcona, and the Municipal District of Sturgeon form a part of the outer metropolitan area. Within the region there are also two Indian reserves, one on Edmonton's western boundary and the other immediately west of Morinville; an international airport between Edmonton and Leduc;and a Canadian Air Forces Base in Namao, along Edmonton's northern periphery. Local autonomy, long fostered by the provincial government, is one of the overriding features of the political architecture of the region. Edmonton's dominance as a commercial and governmental centre with overwhelming influence is feared and resisted by many of the region's smaller communities. Local officials admit that although the communities are interdependent in many ways, their residents continue to be parochial and lack a "sense of region." This reality poses significant problems for planning at the metropolitan level. It is not only asymmetrical relationships between Edmonton and the smaller communities that pose obstacles to regional

Map 6.1. *Edmonton Region Planning Area*

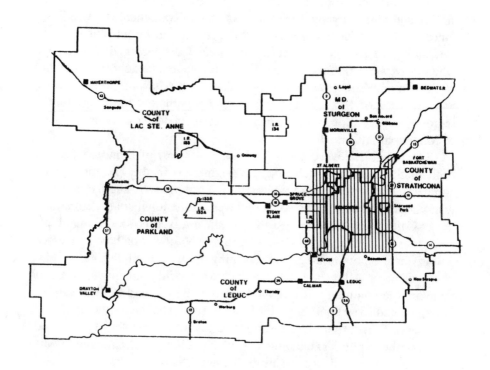

☐ Edmonton Regional Planning Commission

▥ Preliminary Regional Plan Metropolitan Part

cooperation, but also disagreements among the smaller municipalities. Recent land annexation conflicts between the county of Strathcona and the city of Fort Saskatchewan have strained otherwise, long-standing, collaborative relationships. The city proposed to annex additional land for industrial zoning south and east of the city. The county of Strathcona objected to the annexation as an intrusion on property that it wanted for its own industrial development. In the spring of 1991 the provincial cabinet ruled that the city could annex the land but would have to share the tax revenue derived from it with the county (City of Fort Saskatchewan, Minutes of Regular Council Meeting, March 25, 1989; EMRPC, *Metro Planning Review*, Spring 1991). A short distance away, the city of Leduc has had an ongoing disagreement with the county of Leduc and several smaller communities over the use of its city-financed services by noncity residents. Some of the latter are settled in areas zoned "country residential" where, apart from roads and electricity, there is a complete absence of urban services (interview with Leduc Mayor Oscar Klack, July 24, 1989). Throughout the region as a whole the conversion of prime agricultural land to "country residential," under provisions of a provincial act that had as its initial purpose assisting veterans in acquiring small land holdings to supplement wages, has caused both concern and controversy. As of 1984, "country residential" land use, with parcels averaging 5.2 acres, absorbed about 60,800 acres of land in the metropolitan region within commuting range of Edmonton. Approximately one third of this land is rated as Class 1, 2, and 3 land for agricultural capability. Many officials in Edmonton and other established communities view country residential as one of the most inefficient and reckless land uses permitted in the area. Comparatively, country residential land use equals in territory all the land used currently by urban municipalities in the region (EMRPC 1984, 96-97). The most controversial issues pitting Edmonton against its neighboring communities in the last quarter century has involved boundaries and governance of the region as a whole (Hanson 1956; McNally Royal Commission 1956).

POPULATION GROWTH AND CHARACTERISTICS

Population growth in Edmonton and surrounding regions reflects the city's changing role over the years as a staples service center for furs, agriculture, and mining (petroleum and natural gas). Wide fluctuations in the economy of the region are reflected in population growth during the past 90 years. Throughout the region responses of local governments to buoyant economic conditions and rapid population growth varied, but in the main they sought to make land available and committed themselves to the provision of the basic infrastructure and the usual range of essential services. In early times investments in these areas were based largely on sheer speculation whereas in more recent years computer-generated growth scenarios provide their justification. Because the economy of the province is largely staples-dependent, changes in levels of economic activity can occur suddenly and with little warning.

As the economy of such a region enters a "bust" phase, local governments frequently are faced with financial commitments far in excess of projected revenues, leaving them with two undesirable options, either increasing taxes or reducing the levels of service. The three pivotal periods in the history of Edmonton and the region were the years between 1910-1913, the era from the beginning of World War II to 1957, and the decade of the "oil price revolutions" from 1971 to 1981.

Edmonton's population of 2,626 in 1901 grew to 27,000 in 1909 and almost tripled by 1914 when it reached 72,516. The peak years of the land and railway induced boom were 1911 and 1912, when the increase amounted to 98 percent! This included the population of the town of Strathcona, which had amalgamated with Edmonton in 1912. With the collapse of the boom, the city's population plunged 27.5 percent by 1916, not to surpass its peak again until 1929. With the onset of the Great Depression, Edmonton experienced virtually no growth as an estimated 250,000 persons outmigrated from Alberta to other areas of Canada. A sudden increase in growth occurred during World War II when the city in 1942 became a strategic center for northern military operations that included the building of the Alaska Highway. Following the war and its "mini-boom" Alberta faced a bleak economic future with a very real likelihood of outmigration of its citizens.

The discovery of oil in the Leduc field in 1947 provided the pivotal event that led to an uninterrupted, if sometimes uneven, period of growth in the province. From 1925 to 1947 the average rate of population increase was 2.8 percent, with variations in the rate ranging from a -0.8 percent decrease in 1932 to a 9.1 percent increase in 1943. Growth after 1947 continued its upward trend, subject to variations in the rate of economic activity. It was during the "oil price revolution" of the 1970s that growth peaked with about 24,000 persons added to the metropolitan population each year. The end of the oil and real estate mega-boom years in 1981 brought an economic recession to the area. As the flow of immigrants diminished radically and outmigration increased, population

Figure 6.1. *Edmonton Population 1899-1990*

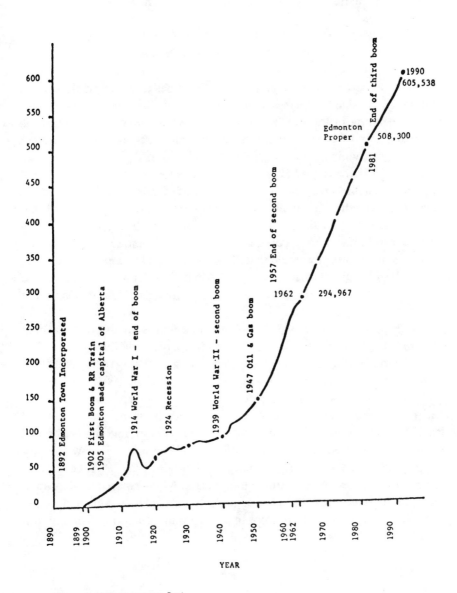

Source: City Assessors Dept

growth through the eighties was limited largely to natural increase. It was not until 1990 that Alberta experienced once again at least three consecutive quarters of growth due to immigration.

DISTRIBUTION OF POPULATION GROWTH
IN THE METROPOLITAN AREA

Over 90 percent of the region's growth resides in urban municipalities that range in size from less than 500 in New Sarepta to over a half million persons in the city of Edmonton. Although fluctuations in the urban segment of the population have been minor, there has been a shift in the way in which it has been distributed within the region. Between 1961 and 1971 the city of Edmonton housed about 85 percent of the total population of the area, but by 1981 this had declined to 74 percent as nearby surrounding municipalities captured about 17 percent of the region's growth. In the early eighties, following debate over a highly controversial annexation proposal submitted by Edmonton, the minister of municipal affairs suggested that 75 percent of future population growth should be concentrated in the city. (Alberta Order in Council issued upon the recommendation of the Minister of Municipal Affairs, December 31, 1981.)

In 1961 there were 98,000 private households in the metropolitan region. By 1981 there was a 150 percent increase in this sector. The major change during the period was the decline in average household size from 3.9 persons in 1961 to 3.4 in 1976 and to 2.8 in 1981. In Edmonton the average household size declined to 2.7 whereas smaller centers and rural municipalities tended to have larger households. The trend toward lower average household size coupled with an ongoing preference for owner-occupied, single, detached, family homes in low density developments had a significant impact on land use. By 1981, because of lowering of household size the region needed 65,000 more housing units than would have been the case if household size had remained at the 1961 levels (Edmonton Metropolitan Regional Planning Commission 1986).

EDMONTON'S EARLY YEARS

**Physical Economic and Social Forces
that Shaped City and Region**

Recent discoveries reveal that Edmonton's river valley setting attracted settlement about five thousand years ago when it served as a gathering place for roving bands of hunters. Edmonton's modern history may be traced to 1754 when it is believed that the explorer Anthony Henday wintered at the site. By the 1790s a series of fortified fur trading posts of the North West Company and the Hudson Bay Company were established in the region. When the two companies amalgamated in 1821, Edmonton House became the leading fur trading center for all the western prairies (MacGregor 1981, 49).

It was not until the late 1800s that settlement began to take place beyond the river fort, albeit slowly. A survey done for the Department of the Interior of the Dominion Lands Office dated May 25, 1883, shows that the original core settlement consisted of 45 property owners, each with a pie-sliced portion of the river frontage. In addition, the Hudson Bay Company had a very sizeable reserve of land beyond its fort to the north (City of Edmonton 1967, 13). By 1910 the city had "adopted the standard Grid Dominion Land Survey pattern for streets and parks and extended this form beyond the river lots, which themselves projected about a mile from each bank of the river. Superimposed on this pattern is a system of diagonal arterial streets that trace the routes of the original paths and trails into the City" (City of Edmonton 1967, 13).

The pace of settlement remained slow until the coming of the railways. Although the North Saskatchewan River provided Edmonton with steamboat passage to Winnipeg, the waterway, "with its shallows, current and shifting sand bars, made overland trails necessary in the pre-railway era" (Careless 1977, 127). The historian Careless notes that Edmonton like other prairie cities as well as Vancouver, the coastal city, "were to a critical degree creations of the railway, a fact that marks them off in a significant way from the older communities of eastern Canada" (Careless 1977, 129). Edmontonians who had hoped that theirs would be the first city in Alberta to be served by a transcontinental railway were deeply disappointed when the federal government, after some wavering, decided to build the Canadian Pacific Railway along a southern route to Calgary and then across the mountains to Vancouver. The first trains arrived in Calgary in 1883. It was nine years later that the Calgary and

Edmonton Railway was completed as far as Strathcona on the south side of the North Saskatchewan River. By 1902 the Edmonton, Yukon, and Pacific Railway crossed the Low Level Bridge and connected the city with the Calgary and Edmonton Railway. In 1905 Edmontonians were triply blessed—the transcontinental Canadian Northern Railway arrived, Alberta was granted provincial status, and Edmonton was chosen after much political jockeying to be its capital. In 1913 the Canadian Pacific Railway extended the C & E R line across the North Saskatchewan River to a terminal at Jasper Avenue and 109th street and the Grand Trunk Pacific Railway, with a route from Winnipeg to Prince Rupert gave the city a second transcontinental railway in 1914. Unfortunately this also marked the first year of the collapse of the economic boom that had been fueled by the arrival of the railways.

Edmonton's dramatic growth from a fur-trading post to a sizeable urban community sparked a wave of boosterism typical of early city development on the prairie west. As the railways brought a flood of settlers to the area to farm the rich black soils of the region or to labor within the city the growing dominance of Edmonton as an agricultural service and railway hub was well established. If Canada was the "land of opportunity," Edmonton was certainly the heart of the "Last Best West" where newcomers could secure 160 acres of land free and undertake any style of farming they wished (Scott 1910). As early as 1910, Edmonton was heralded as "The coming Metropolis of the Canadian Northwest. The Gateway to the Mystic Northland . . . and the market place of one of the richest areas in the world" (*Edmonton Journal*). Although it still had the "greatest traffic in raw furs on the continent," now "the keynote is struck when the magic word LAND is mentioned" (*Edmonton Journal*). As the boom reached its full bloom in 1912 the city's mayor declared in the anniversary issue of the *Edmonton Bulletin* that given its location in the midst of a fertile land, role as a staging center for the settlement of the great Peace River country, potential for industrial development, and the special advantage of municipally owned services such as water, electric light, and power, it was destined that there be a greater Edmonton (*Edmonton Bulletin* 1912). The city's regional advantage, combined with the business acumen of "Land Men eager to exert all legitimate and trustworthy efforts to build up their business, and "wide awake and progressive men and capitalists (who) recognized the opportunities . . . " would assure Edmonton's future greatness as the "metropolis of the North Country, the Winnipeg of the far North-West" (*Edmonton Bulletin* 1912). By 1914 the boom, with all the dreams of urban greatness it had spawned had run its course, leaving in its wake a legacy of unused lots and a huge civic debt.

Weaver, in an essay on Edmonton's "perilous course" between 1904-1929 writes, "In the golden year of the prairie boom, 1912, Edmonton consisted of as much fancy as fact. The city maps, bait for real estate speculators, sketched in streets that did not even exist—some never would" (Weaver, n.d.). In his classic study of urban government in Alberta, Hanson referring to the effect of the boom on city boundaries wrote, "The question of boundaries and area caused difficulties then as now. One of the members of the first Alberta legislature once said that all a place needed to qualify as a town was an optimist to draw an imaginary line and to call it Crystal City . . . some promoters even advertised lots outside boundaries of cities and towns as parts of such centers. . . . In Edmonton in 1913 even lots in the North Saskatchewan River were sold to unsuspecting buyers in Eastern Canada and the United States" (Hanson 1956).

In addition to the outmigration of residents after the boom, Edmonton experienced a dramatic devaluation of its real estate sector. In anticipation of unlimited city growth, owners of land in the region subdivided their properties and requested the city to extend services to them. When real estate values collapsed they had but two options, either to hold on to these properties in expectation of a revival in the market at some future date or simply abandon them. Most chose the latter course with the result that the city ended up as a major landholder through tax forfeitures. The city tried repeatedly to sell off the land but found virtually no buyers for the 44,348 lots or parcels repossessed between 1918 and 1927. In 1937, during the depth of the depression, the author of a brief prepared by several cities of Alberta for the Royal Commission on Dominion-Provincial Relations reported that as of December 31, 1936, "the total number of parcels of land forfeited to the City of Edmonton stood at 56,743, the assessed value being $10,279,032. The total lots contained within the City limits amount to 110,000 and from this it will be seen that the physical basis of taxation available to the City has now shrunk to 53,257 lots" (Duggan 1938). In 1914, the assessment of land based on the Single Property Tax (i.e., only on land, with buildings and improvements exempt), amounted to $191,283,970. By 1937, as a result of progressive reductions, Edmonton land assessment had shrunk to $24,018, 515, *even when* buildings and improvements were included. Such was the effect of the depression's deflation (Duggan 1938)! Apart from the annexation of a .3 square mile of land in 1917, the city had acquired enough land after the boom years to last it until 1947 when it again began annexing land along its periphery (City of Edmonton Planning Department 1972).

In appraising the nature and functions of early governance in western cities, Careless found that even in the smallest communities where face-to-face interaction was a daily occurrence "municipal elites" emerged with links to prominent merchants, lawyers, and "lesser entrepreneurs" (Careless 1977). Edmonton incorporated as a town in 1892 when its area encompassed 2,168 acres of land along the north side of the North Saskatchewan River, and its population numbered 700 persons. In 1904 the town applied to the Northwest Legislature for incorporation as a city, and a new charter was given it along with an additional 2,400 acres. The civic leaders, drawn predominantly from the city's merchant class, were committed to ideas put forth by the municipal reform movement in the United States and chose a Council-Commission Board of government. It featured an elected "nonpartisan" council that delegated administrative powers to several commissioners.

A major feature of the city's early government was the municipal ownership of utilities. Civic leaders, claiming that such ownership would assure a high moral tone in city politics, as well as provide superior, efficient service to the citizens, decided that the city should own all utilities except natural gas. The city took over a privately held electric utility, the forerunner of today's Edmonton Power Company, began operating a publicly owned telephone service, appropriately named, Edmonton Telephone, and requested permission from the provincial government to establish a city-owned streetcar system. In 1908, the senior government passed the Edmonton Tramway Act, which authorized the city to establish a tramway system and extend its lines to any point "not more than 80 miles from existing boundaries" (Province of Alberta 1908). The system, operated as a public service utility, had an immediate and significant impact on consolidating patterns of residential settlement within the city. It was greeted with much enthusiasm by land owners and real estate speculators who viewed the system's expansion as a prime means for enhancing their property values. By 1910, Edmonton had built 2.25 miles of street railways, purchased 13 streetcars, and transported 2,299,762 riders. By the end of the boom in mid-1913 the system had expanded to 40 miles of track with 66 streetcars and an annual ridership of 17,000,000. It is of interest to note that by 1939, the year in which the trackage of the system peaked, Edmonton had built only an additional 16 miles of track in the intervening years. During the boom years growth in other parts of the urban infrastructure proceeded at breath-taking pace. Street paving, installation of water mains and sewers, and extension of sidewalks all reflected boom-time growth (*Edmonton Journal* 1913).

Edmonton's civic boosters did have some very tangible evidence to support their dreams of the city's future greatness. Property assessment grew from $6,620,985 in 1905 to $180,000,000 in 1913 (*Edmonton Journal* 1913). According to Hanson, by the end of the boom years Alberta was left with "highly developed local government services. The cities, especially, had constructed facilities which were to prove adequate for decades" (Hanson 1956). For Edmonton, the facilities did not come without a very heavy price. By mid-1913 the city had piled up a debt of $22,313,968!

The excesses of speculative activity in Edmonton and Calgary during the boom years did not go unnoticed by the provincial government, which took several initiatives aimed at monitoring and regulating growth in the cities. In order to reign in the speculators and would-be developers the government took steps to standardize practices related to land use and development throughout the entire province. It passed a series of acts aimed at rationalizing the process of town and city building and asserted its legislative responsibility for the spatial ordering of villages, towns, and cities.

Planning Legislation and Urban Growth: 1912-1945

In 1912, Alberta's government enacted legislation that distinguished between town and municipal organization, established a Department of Municipal Affairs to implement the Town Act, a Rural Municipal Districts Act, a Village Act, and an Improvement District Act. The Department of Municipal Affairs undertook the responsibility for regulating municipal records and auditing local governments thus establishing uniform expectations of local officials throughout the province. By passing the first Town Planning Act in 1913 the government provided the legislation that when implemented at the local level, would limit unbridled land speculation (Province of Alberta 1913).

By passing legislation related to town and rural development the provincial government was carrying out the responsibilities decreed by the BNA Act of 1867. Urban and rural municipalities are creatures of the province with delegated responsibilities. Local government constitutes a subordinate "third order" of governance in the Canadian federal system. A "fourth order" may exist in the form of school and library boards, utility districts, planning commissions, etc., but these also, like municipal governments, are subject to the authority of the provincial government.

In Alberta, all provincial administrations, although possessing ultimate authority over local urban and rural municipalities, gave the latter wide latitude with respect to local development. According to Masson, this philosophical commitment to local autonomy prevented the province from evolving a provincewide plan for coping with problems created by rapid urbanization, especially in recent years. At the same time, the commitment to local autonomy served the province well. "The provincial government realized that a strong network of local governments would relieve pressure on the province to provide public goods and services" (Masson 1985).

The Town Planning Act of 1913 gave the minister of municipal affairs wide-ranging powers. Its intent was clearly to centralize authority for planning in the provincial government. Prior to the creation of the department there had been some controls governing the spatial ordering of cities. For example, at the time of Edmonton's incorporation in 1904 a grid system of street alignment was already in place. In 1906, the province enacted regulations with respect to water mains, sewers, fire access, and telephone post location. Streets and back lanes were to be included in all subdivision plans, and city engineers had to approve the entire plan. The Land Titles Act of 1906 required that streets be at least 60 feet wide and with a back lane width of 20 feet. Lanes were to provide rear access to every lot in a subdivision (Bettison et al. 1975, 17).

The Town Planning Act passed in 1913 reflected ideas that emerged from a growing body of planning theory that had developed in England and the United States up to that year. Town Planning Schemes had as their goal the rational ordering of urban space. The schemes would secure "suitable provision for traffic, proper sanitary conditions, amenity and convenience in connection with layout of streets and use of the land and of any neighboring lands for building or other purposes" (Province of Alberta 1913). Further, land likely to be used for building purposes" could be designated for "open spaces, roads, streets, parks, pleasure or recreation grounds," with the minister of municipal affairs exercising final authority as to use. Town Planning Schemes were to be implemented by a designated "responsible authority," and approved by the minister. The "responsible authority" could be a local town or city council or "a body constituted specially for the purpose of the scheme." This body or commission was to have no fewer than five and not more than 10 members approved by the minister.

One section of the act addressed the issue of financial enhancement or loss suffered by parties when a town planning scheme was implemented. In order to limit speculative profiteering by property owners whose land would be enhanced through such a scheme, one-half of the financial gain could be appropriated by the "responsible authority." Property owners who were injuriously affected by the implementation of the scheme could apply for compensation that was limited to the actual value of the property. Double compensation or damages were not permitted.

The overriding thrust of Alberta's town planning schemes was to effect the ordering of urban social space in the interests of economic efficiency. The "ineconomic features" of the act were the provisions for parks and open spaces as a part of the aesthetic ordering designed to mitigate the boredom of much established grid development. Thomas Adams, the English utilitarian planner, whose ideas had a profound influence on Canadian planning in the early twentieth century, conceded that complementary to planning for efficiency of the "business side of a city is the provision of satisfactory and healthy living conditions for the people" (Masson 1985, 255).

The Town Planning Act vested in the minister of municipal affairs broad-ranging powers over municipal planning and entrusted his office with the resolution of conflicts arising in implementing town planning schemes. The act, designed, among other things to stop rampant real estate speculation of the boom years, gave considerable leeway for planning to local authorities while retaining ultimate control in the hands of the provincial government. What the act failed to do was to provide specific guidelines for its implementation. The issue became moot when the economic boom ended. It would be a long time before Edmonton would be faced with problems of growth and expansion.

Minor revisions to the act were made in 1922 that clarified the role of the minister of municipal affairs in local planning and expanded the role of the office in the planning process. Reflecting pressures for what may be called the "aesthetic ordering" of town and country development the government passed in 1928 "An Act to Facilitate Town Planning and the Preservation of the Natural Beauties of the Province" (Province of Alberta 1928, 149). The United Farmers Women of Alberta was the interest group that was concerned about the countryside "being desecrated by billboards and hoardings and the increasing commercialization" of the province's highways. The act established a "Town and Rural Planning

Advisory Board" whose role was to cooperate with local authorities in formulating town planning schemes, advising the minister as to regulations and plans for subdivisions, assisting and advising rural authorities "in devising ways and means of preserving the natural beauty of the locality and ensuring the new buildings and erections shall be so designed and located that the same shall not bar the amenities of the locality" and "to promote in any community a pride in the amenities of the neighborhood" (Province of Alberta 1928, 149-50). Other purposes of the act involved regulating gasoline filling stations, garages, and rest stops along highways, the siting of tourist camps, prohibition of regulations of signs or notices along highways, fixing fees for sign boards, and general oversight of any land acquired for parks. The board could, with the approval of the lieutenant-governor in council acquire land for the purpose of preserving places of natural beauty or historic interest (Province of Alberta 1928, 152). Many of the provisions of this act were included in the "Town Planning and Preservation of Natural Beauty Act" passed a year later. The 1929 act gave local authorities power to appoint a Town Planning Commission of three, six, or nine members, which in addition to preparing town planning schemes would also administer zoning bylaws. Section 30 of the act made provision for local authorities to enact zoning legislation. The laws were to designate differing land uses of an area, govern building bulk, height, and square footage, define the size of yards, courts, and open spaces, establish maximum densities for each area, regulate classes of industries, housing type, public and semipublic buildings, control architectural design, character, and appearance of buildings in each district, and assure the local authority that adequate light, water, sewerage, street, transit, and other facilities were provided for proposed developments (Province of Alberta 1929, 395-96). The cities of Edmonton and Calgary as well as 30-odd smaller municipalities adopted zoning bylaws shortly after the act was passed (Dant c. 1963-64).

Most significantly, the act enabled two or more adjoining municipalities to appoint a Regional Planning Commission consisting of not more than three representatives from each member jurisdiction. This commission could be authorized to assume responsibility for carrying out official town plans or schemes where development crossed jurisdictional lines (Province of Alberta 1929, 391). It was not until 1950 that the first such commission was established in the Edmonton region. With the onset of the Great Depression, as urban growth remained stagnant, the provincial planning office was closed as an austerity measure.

In 1933, Edmonton issued its first Zoning Bylaw Map, which designated for the first time specific land uses within the city. At the time the city possessed much land that it had obtained through tax forfeitures. The full consequence of the acquisition of these surplus lots was not to be realized until the late forties and early fifties when their availability enabled the city to direct growth towards a tight, unicentric urban form in the postwar period.

With the outbreak of the Second World War the region benefited from the wartime economy in several ways. The surge in agricultural prices and the evolution of Edmonton as a major operations center for the Alcan Highway, the Alaska-Siberian Airlift, and the Canol Oil Pipeline project led to a mini-boom in the area. The shortage of housing became apparent immediately. The passage of the National Housing Act of 1944 by the federal government and the creation of the Central Mortgage and Housing Corporation, which guaranteed privately financed mortgages made for the purposes of residential urban construction set the stage for a strong housing market in the city during the postwar period. A regional CMHC office was established in Alberta in 1946.

Although in Canada the provincial authority over municipal affairs is paramount, policies of the federal government relating to railways and freight rates, housing, monetary and fiscal matters, airports, defense installations and army bases, regional development, and environmental concerns all have major implications for local and regional development. Additionally, the federal government's land holdings and buildings constitute a formidable presence in most major urban centers. The influence of the CMHC, however, is by far one of most significant for local development.

Revisions of the Town Planning Act in 1942 incorporated amendments made during the late thirties such as the 1937 provision requiring provincial authorization before a subdivision plan of more than 10 lots could be sold. The Provincial Planning Board had to be assured that the subdivision was registered for the purpose of residential construction to be undertaken within a "reasonable time." As wartime housing shortages became apparent the provincial government sought to limit the amount of land that might be obtained and held for speculative purposes. The action had the effect of controlling the direction of urban development within the major cities of the province. At the end of the war, anticipating the growing housing needs of veterans and their families, an amendment to the act increased subdivision size to 50 lots before requiring Planning Board approval.

Planning legislation in Alberta from 1913 to the end of the Second World War reflected the desire to order urban space efficiently. Wildly speculative activity during Edmonton's first boom prompted the government to control by legislation the "ineconomical" uses of urban land. Through planning the government tried to restore some semblance of credibility to the development process and thus reassure would-be investors. According to Noel Dant, who came to Edmonton from England in 1949 to become the city's first director of planning, both rural-based governments of the United Farmers and Social Credit parties had enacted over the years "perhaps the most progressive social planning legislation in this western hemisphere" (Dant c. 1963-64, 1).

Evolution of Regional Planning in Alberta, 1945-1990

The discovery of oil in 1947 in the Leduc field, 15 miles southwest of Edmonton, was the singular event that transformed Alberta's economy and hastened significantly the pace of urbanization within the province. The impact of frenetic, oil-related activity was felt immediately in Edmonton and the surrounding region. Virtually every sector of the urban infrastructure—housing, schools, roadways, transportation, and public administration—was woefully inadequate to meet the demand created by rapid economic growth.

In a series of *ad hoc* responses to growth pressures for example, Edmonton's city council found it necessary to amend the 1933 zoning bylaws six times in 1946, three times in 1947, seven times in 1948 and 19 times in 1949. Private developers scurried to buy and subdivide land along the city's boundaries and either requested annexation to the city or proposed land uses that were inappropriate for the area. In 1948, the provincial government amended the planning act to include "Interim Zoning Regulations in New Subdivisions," which was intended to assist cities in gaining some control over areas not covered by zoning bylaws.

In 1949, because of widespread citizen dissatisfaction with the city's antiquated planning processes, Edmonton moved to establish a city planning department and appointed Noel Dant as its first, full-time city planner. When Dant arrived he found an out-of-date master plan for major streets for the city, an ineffective zoning bylaw, and an advisory Town Planning Commission made up of unpaid lay citizens whose advice was seldom taken seriously by key city departments. Dant, together with McGill University Professors Spence-Sales and John Bland as well as the provincial planning director, after reviewing the wide-ranging problems confronting urban and rural development in the province authored a new Town and Rural Planning Act. By adding the word "rural" in the 1950 act they acknowledged the interdependence of rural and urban development in a region. The act called for a District Planning Commission to be established to help plan and give advice at the regional level with the ultimate objective of producing a regional plan or areawide scheme. In order to respond to pressures for immediate development in a region the act enabled local authorities to issue "interim development orders" and thus impose some control over land uses.

The District Planning Commission consisted of members appointed by contiguous municipalities as well as three members representing the province appointed by the Provincial Planning Advisory Board. The commissions were to act in an advisory capacity on planning matters of common concern to at least two member municipalities. Cities were permitted to create Technical Planning Boards and Planning Advisory Commissions, the latter made up of representatives of the public. Master plans were now to be designated as "General Plans" rather than "official schemes." In 1953, the District Planning Commissions were given powers to become the approving authorities of land subdivision where no local planning board had been formed.

The 1957 Town and Rural Planning Act described in some detail the major characteristics of district general plans, the key one being to "secure the orderly and economical development of the district planning area as a whole." In formulating a district general plan the commission was to "divide the district planning area or any part thereof into zones of permitted land-use categories, including low-density agricultural, high-density agricultural, small-holding, country residence, highway commercial, district recreational, general urban, new general urban, and major industrial zones, or any of these and such other zones as the commission may deem necessary and essential for the purpose of the plan." In addition, commissions were empowered to "establish stages, sequence, or order of priority of development for and within each zone" (Province of Alberta 1957, 495).

By 1963, due to the enormous increase in development proposals and the perception that the 1957 act was unduly cumbersome in its regulatory requirements, the minister of municipal affairs ordered the preparation of a new act. The Planning Act of 1963 had as its general aim, guiding and regulating "the public and private use of land so that public projects, such as the provision of roads, streets, utilities, schools and other necessary services, may be properly coordinated and carried out in an economical and orderly manner and so that private owners may utilize or develop their land to their best advantage provided that in doing so they do not injuriously affect their neighbors or the interests of the public generally (Dant c. 1963-64, 7). Simplification of the development process mollified the concerns of would-be developers. By vesting primary decision-making powers over planning in elected, not appointed representatives or administrators, the public interest would be protected.

Three provisions of the act dealt explicity with the issue of the "rights of individuals": (a euphemism for developer interests) and "the public interest." First, relevant authorities were required "to consider how specific projects or proposals may affect the general development of an area and the welfare of the community at large." Second, it gave owners the right "to contest planning decisions that may unjustly or unnecessarily restrict or deny them the most convenient or profitable use of their land." Third, it made explicit "the right of other persons to object against proposed developments that may injuriously affect their interest" (Dant c. 1963-64, 7).

The act also clarified the role of regional planning commissions. They were entrusted with studying "the resources and development of the regional planning area, with a view to preparing a regional plan." In order to exercise control over development while a full regional plan was under study, the commission could prepare a "preliminary regional plan" (Dant c. 1963-64, 7).

The Provincial Planning Board, which advised the minister of municipal affairs on planning matters and appeals, could "conduct studies with respect to the physical, economic, and social aspects of development and prepare reports on metropolitan growth, the planning of new towns, and any other matters related to the development of any part of the Province" (Province of Alberta 1963).

The 1963 act proved no less cumbersome in terms of administration than its predecessor. In order to facilitate development within the city of Edmonton its Planning Department began to prepare "outline plans" that provided a detailed, diagrammatic document specifying conditions for development of a specific area. City planners and developers had frequent conflicts, but the city retained tight control over the development process because it had large areas of developable land within its boundaries. Because much of this land that had been acquired years earlier through tax forfeitures was scattered throughout the Edmonton, the city assumed responsibility for servicing it.

Amendments to the act over the years were incorporated in the new Planning Act of 1977. This act sought to address the issues of explosive growth that were affecting Alberta's two major cities as well as the fast growing communities just beyond the cities' boundaries and those near major energy or transportation corridors in the province. The broad purpose of the act and its regulations was "to provide means whereby plans and related measures may be prepared and adopted to (1) achieve the orderly, economical, and beneficial development and use of land and patterns of land settlement, and (2) maintain and improve the quality of the physical environment within which patterns of human settlement are situated in Alberta, without infringing on the rights of individuals except to the extent that it is necessary for the greater public interest" (Masson 1985, 264). The act explicitly recognizes for the first time concerns expressed by environmentalists while at the same time being deliberately vague about the meaning of "the greater public interest." The latter seems to have been aimed at reassuring the province's major resource industries that when a conflict arose the government would accommodate their needs.

In 1980, the Planning Act called for each Regional Planning Commission to prepare a regional plan by December 31, 1982. In order to give coherence to all planning in a region, the government declared that the regional plan would be the primary planning document in a hierarchy of plans authorized by the act. Section 54 of the act declares, "(1) When a regional plan has been ratified by the Minister, no local authority shall enact any by-law, take any action or authorize any development that is inconsistent with the regional plan. (2) Every statutory plan, replotting scheme and land use by-law, every action taken or thing done by a local authority, regional planning commission or council, and every decision of a municipal planning commission, development appeal board or development officer *shall conform to the regional plan*" (Province of Alberta 1980, 29).

The first Edmonton Metropolitan Regional Plan as required by the act was issued in 1984. It marked the culmination of three and a half decades of effort to assure the "orderly and economic development of the region." The plan encompasses a range of laudable objectives for spatial ordering, urban settlement and land use, balanced economic growth, fringe area planning, rural settlement and land use, economic and industrial development, agriculture, extractive resource utilization, environmental protection, recreation land use, and transportation and utilities corridors. Overriding objectives of the regional plan involve reducing redundancy in the metropolitan infrastructure, sharing the costs as well as the benefits of economic development of the region, providing equitable levels of services, and service delivery systems. The 1984 Regional Plan was conceived in a period of explosive growth so it is not surprising that an overriding concern is with efficient accommodation of anticipated rapid development. It identified the central planning issue as "the management of growth and changes. All levels of government have become aware of the need to manage growth in order to ensure that the economic, social, and cultural benefits, which accrue from such growth, are fully realized and equitably distributed" (EMRPC 1984, 1).

In a general way the plan attempts to reconcile a multiplicity of diverse interests of rural and urban municipalities, addresses the reservations of major land owners and developers, and attempts to balance an ongoing commitment to local autonomy with the need for the most efficient possible development at the regional level. From the perspective of the provincial government the regional plan provides a mechanism for resolving at the local level many of the day-to-day controversies over regional growth. When the Alberta government appointed the Edmonton District Commission (since renamed twice as the Edmonton Regional Planning Commission and the Edmonton Metropolitan Regional Planning Commission), it did so with the belief that the commission would be the primary vehicle for resolving land-use disputes in the region. It took 34 years for the commission to produce a regional plan that was acceptable to the city of Edmonton, the other urban and rural municipalities, the Alberta Planning Board, and the minister of municipal affairs. During those years the inaction of a weak commission that could propose but not implement recommendations had mixed results in effecting the nature and direction of metropolitan development. In general, urban and rural municipalities surrounding Edmonton evaluate the overall performance of the commission favorably, while many of the city's officials view commission policies and actions as ineffectual and even detrimental to Edmonton's interests (Alberta Assn. of Municipal Districts . . . 1980). The provincial government's commitment to regional planning tempered moves towards the creation of a unicity or a two-tiered system of government for the metropolitan area. The reluctance of every provincial government to opt for either alternative may be due to fears of the political power a regional government in its own backyard might wield. Whatever efficiencies in urban services and infrastructural development may have been gained through a regional administration were outweighed by the province's ongoing strong commitment to local autonomy.

Planning the Region: Planner's Dreams or City Nightmares

"There is no doubt that the rather sudden emergence of regional planning in Alberta in 1949 was in response to the urban flood released by the rapid and large-scale development of oil and gas resources. Edmonton newspaper reports of the period bristle with comments about "mushroom growth," the city "bursting at its seams," the "disgrace of fringe area development" and with many expressions of civic helplessness. The establishment of advisory regional planning authorities, in this period, in broadly defined city centered regions was an attempt to deal, in an orderly and economic way, with all those uses that are generated in the city but invade the open country," wrote Leonard Gertler, one of the first professional planners of Edmonton's District Planning Commission (Gertler 1968). This DPC, the first regional one to be established by the province, consisted of representatives from the city of Edmonton, eight additional urban municipalities, and five municipal districts. Over the next 30 years the commission would grow to include 48 urban and rural municipalities, composed of two cities, one municipal district, four counties, 11 towns, 10 villages, and 20 summer villages.

From its inception the provincial government structured the membership to favor rural over city representation. Because proportionate representation would have given the city up to four-fifths of the voting power on the commission the government concluded that such an overwhelming representation of city interest would work to the disadvantage of the many smaller urban and rural areas. Over the years the credibility of the Commission's policies was called into question frequently by Edmonton's representatives, city officials, and the press. A review of some of the key regional growth issues between 1950 and 1990 reveals that from its beginnings many of the policies favored by the commission could be viewed as seeking Edmonton's containment while favoring growth in the surrounding communities.

Disorderly Fringe Growth or Satellite Cities

The most urgent issue confronting the first District Commission in 1950 was the unplanned, disorderly development occurring just beyond the city's boundaries. Inadequately serviced, low quality, unplanned development was especially common in two communities on Edmonton's periphery, Jasper Place to the west and Beverly to the northeast. The city attempted to accommodate growth through a long-standing policy of annexing land along its boundaries. City officials, committed to maintaining a strong and vital city center, feared random growth that might leapfrog beyond its boundaries.

One of the first tasks of the District Commission was preparing plans for the mushrooming developments along Edmonton's borders. Because these were beginning to strain the existing street and roadway system the commission sketched out the location of an Outer Ring Road as well as Orbital Roads in relation to the city of Edmonton. The road lay-out was essential in order to obtain rights of way as well as give guidance to municipal officials, land owners, and developers as to the direction of possible future development. It was in the debate over the location of roadways that some commission members suggested the creation of satellite or "new towns" as a possible solution to problems created by random growth along Edmonton's borders. Satellite towns, some distance from the city, could be established as well-balanced communities. The idea, derived from and reflecting a very different experience in England, was endorsed by the commission, "as being a reasonable and logical solution to those complex urban and regional problems stemming from over-population and over-development of an urban agglomeration such as is being built up around Edmonton City now" (Edmonton Dist. Planning Commission 1951). Edmonton, with a population at the time of a little more than 150,000, hardly fit the mold of the kind of city that should be decentralized. Nevertheless, the commitment to decentralization in satellite towns was adopted as a goal by some commission members who viewed them as a solution to fringe development. Edmonton's commission members and officials on the other hand, intent on accommodating most new residential and commercial growth within the expanded borders of the city, viewed the satellite city idea with disdain and fear.

The first major test for the city and the District Commission occurred in 1950 when a landowner, developers, and the Municipal District of Strathcona submitted a proposal for the development of Campbelltown on 15 quarter sections of land in an area approximately five miles beyond Edmonton's eastern boundary. The project was vigorously opposed by the city and the towns of Beverly and Jasper Place. Campbelltown, later to be called Sherwood Park, had all the characteristics of a dormitory suburb and virtually none of those of a well-balanced satellite city. During the ensuing controversy the Municipal District of Strathcona withdrew as a member of the DPC and effectively removed the issue from the planning commission's agenda. The Provincial Planning Advisory Board and the minister of municipal affairs, who held ultimate authority over the development gave Strathcona approval to proceed with the project. In the commission debates, Leonard Gertler, now its executive director, opposed the project and pointed out that sufficient land existed in the southeast quadrant of Edmonton for residential development, growth would be preferred in older existing towns of the regions that were more distant from the city and already had made substantial investments in their urban infrastructure, the proposed area had neither a water supply nor a railroad connection which would make for the development of a balanced (residential and commercial) tax-base possible, and the establishment of Campbelltown could lead to development pressures in contiguous areas, creating undesirable urban sprawl (Edmonton Dist. Planning Commission 1953-54). The hamlet was built and, as predicted by Gertler, has become an upscale, single-family, residential dormitory on Edmonton's outskirts with virtually no industrial development, no significant employment base for its residents, and governed by the rural county of Strathcona. At the time the hamlet was approved, the county was the primary beneficiary of industrial taxes from the region's major oil refining complex known as Refinery Row, a revenue source very much sought after by the city of Edmonton.

Tax Inequities and "Metropolitan Tragedies"

The provincial government, recognizing that patterns of urban development in the Edmonton and Calgary regions had led to great financial disparities among communities, established in 1954 a Royal Commission to examine the "administration and financing of school and municipal services in the City of Edmonton and surrounding areas, and the City of Calgary and surrounding areas." It suggested the commission recommend "the boundaries and the form of local government which will most adequately and equitably provide for the orderly development of school and municipal services," and "to recommend any practical measures which may be taken in the interest of the ratepayers and citizens . . . " (Royal Commission on Metropolitan Development of Calgary and Edmonton 1956, 1V).

The McNally Commission Report represents one of the most thorough studies ever done of Alberta's two metropolitan regions. It has had a lasting influence on debates over urban growth, municipal governance, and finance in the Edmonton region. Population growth, rising city indebtedness, lack of new sources of city revenue, the physical condition and fiscal stress of fringe communities, tax-base inequalities within the metropolitan area, and forms of urban governance were the key issues discussed by the McNally Commission.

Analyzing the Edmonton area, the commission found that the city had on its borders two communities, Jasper Place and Beverly, which were peopled by low-income families, living in poor housing, provided with inadequate municipal services, and had very limited fire and police protection. The property tax-base of these fiscally-stressed communities was insufficient to fund existing, below standard services, let alone make improvements in them. Neither community had any industrial or commercial tax revenue. The contrast between the *assessment poverty* of these two communities and the county of Strathcona was striking. The latter, largely because of Refinery Row taxes, had a per capita assessment of $4,570. That of Jasper Place was $540 and Beverly's was $650. These were truly communities of the working poor who the commission found chose to live in lower-priced, substandard housing that they could call their own rather than rent better accommodation in the city.

After a thorough review of inequities in municipal services, school tax bases, transportation, and other services in the Edmonton and Calgary regions, the commission concluded that,

(1) It is unjust and inequitable that wide variations in the tax base should exist among the local governing bodies that comprise a metropolitan area where that area is one economic unit.

(2) A metropolitan area that is in fact one economic and social unit can ordinarily be more efficiently and effectively governed by one central municipal authority than by a multiplicity of governing bodies (Royal Commission on Metropolitan Development 1956, 5).

In the Edmonton region "It is the disparity in the tax base that emphasizes that tax wealth of one municipal unit in the metropolitan area as against the tax poverty of another. Again, it is this disparity that accounts for the total absence of or inadequacy of normal municipal services on the fringes, resulting in marked inequalities" (Royal Commission on Metropolitan Development 1956, 13). The commission's solution to the disparities and inefficiencies in the inner metropolitan area was the amalgamation by Edmonton of the towns of Jasper Place and Beverly, the annexation of the Refinery Row area within the municipality of Strathcona, and the new community of Cambelltown thereby creating a single city. It was unequivocal in its conviction that allowing another new city to develop on Edmonton's eastern boundary, "independent of, and duplicating the existing city . . . would constitute nothing short of a *metropolitan tragedy*. . . . The spectre of a second city being actively promoted just beyond Edmonton's eastern outskirts at present is a negation of careful metropolitan planning" (Royal Commission on Metropolitan Development 1956, 35).

The report included specific recommendations for the planning of the metropolitan area and its fringe communities that dealt with regional representation on the District Planning Commission, preparation of a district general plan, the continued use of the "interim development control" mechanism pending the completion of the plan, and the designation of the Provincial Planning Advisory Board as the final appeal body.

The provincial government accepted the recommendation to amalgamate the towns of Jasper Place and Beverly within the city of Edmonton but disagreed with the McNally proposal to annex the industrial areas of Strathcona County and Campbelltown to Edmonton. For the city the "metropolitan tragedy" was compounded when it assumed the problems of two tax-poor communities without the new revenue sources it had hoped to derive from the industrial areas of Strathcona County.

The commission's analysis of city revenues pointed out that although the province received all the royalties and leasing fees from the oil and natural gas development, it was the cities, towns, and villages of the province that bore the cost of rapid, resource-induced growth. The provincial government responded to this criticism by establishing a grant program to help impacted communities pay for some of the costs of such growth.

In 1957, the status of the District Planning Commission changed from an advisory to a zoning body. Its expanded role included providing technical advice to numerous municipalities (except to Edmonton, which had its own Planning Department), preparation of bylaws and general plans. As the outer metropolitan area gained an increasing percentage of regional growth the commission began to articulate a policy of "decentralized concentration." Increasing development in the municipalities of the outer ring required far more intermunicipal agreement regarding such matters as zoning, utilities, roads and intersections. By 1960, almost all development outside Edmonton's boundaries was highly land-intensive, single-family residential. The new developments were perceived by everyone as "better" in terms of housing structural strength and design, although houses were excessively standardized and presented a tract appearance. Aesthetic ordering of space in village, town, and city was swept away by the exigencies of rapid expansion.

Dreams of Megacity and the Annexation Battles

The emerging pattern of regional growth in the sixties and seventies prompted the city of Edmonton to undertake a series of initiatives that would resolve issues related both to boundaries and governance in the area. In 1967 Eric Hanson, one of Alberta's foremost authorities on local government, prepared a report for the city of Edmonton that came to conclusions very similar to those of the Royal Commission headed by McNally. He recommended the annexation of Sherwood Park and the industrial area east of the city, the amalgamation of the town of Saint Albert, and the acquisition of enough additional land "to permit the planning and provision of a continuous supply of residential housing to provide room for industrial expansion, and to create a pleasant physical environment" (Council of City of Edmonton 1973, 6-8). The enlarged city of Edmonton would have a unitary government.

The shortage of low-priced, serviced land for housing in Edmonton in the late sixties increased pressures on city officials to annex more land along its borders. Through a unique arrangement between the city and the Alberta Housing Corporation a public land bank was created in the south-eastern quadrant of the city to be used for new housing. Enough land was set aside for a residential community of 100,000 people housed in a mix of single- and multi-family dwellings. The concept of a "suburb within the city" planned around several "neighborhood units" accommodating a range of socio-economic groups was a novel one. Mill Woods, as the development was named, relieved some of the immediate pressures within the city for affordable housing.

The seventies proved to be one of the most turbulent and unsettling periods of urban growth in the region. The impact of the oil price revolutions was felt almost immediately in the area. Explosive population growth contributed to drastic shortages of housing. The city needed land for expansion, and its leaders hoped that the Lougheed's Progressive Conservative government, far more representative of the new "urban elites," would respond favorably to their plans for metropolitan government. In 1972, Edmonton's mayor declared, "I hope the provincial government will see that the best solution for this city to progress is under a single government. It is unlikely the nearby self-governing municipalities will agree to voluntarily let themselves be merged into an expanded City of Edmonton. Only the province can force the issue" (*Financial Post* May 20, 1972).

In a brief submitted to the minister of municipal affairs in 1973, the city made a formal case for boundary adjustments, noting that the new government did not need to be bound by the policies of previous administrations. "The incipient confusion and frustration of proliferating authorities in the Edmonton area require provincial attention. Examples abound in other jurisdictions of the destructive force of a fragmented jurisdiction run wild, which renders local government impotent" (Council of the City of Edmonton 1973, ii-iii). The city recommended that the province accept the adjustments of municipal boundaries essentially along the same lines proposed in the Hanson report and argued that " . . . the best form of the future of the City is a single municipality, encompassing the whole urban unit, with a single local government which includes in its organization localized focii of citizen interest" (Council of the City of Edmonton 1973).

Support for a unitary system of government came also from the Alberta Land Forum, which had been established by the province to make a thorough study of land-use issues in urban areas. The forum noted that Edmonton was bearing the major impact of development in the surrounding dormitory suburbs while deriving virtually no benefits. "It is the opinion of the Forum that the City of Edmonton should be accorded adequate influence over development in its region. The most desirable way to achieve the necessary influence . . . is within a unitary system of local government for the metropolitan region" (Alberta Land Use Forum 1974, 68). The forum suggested that in the absence of unitary government a newly constituted Metropolitan Regional Planning Commission with Edmonton having a majority of the votes could help direct area growth in ways less detrimental to the city.

The conflict between Edmonton and the Regional Planning Commission came to a head during a major Growth Alternatives Study funded by the Provincial Planning Board and conducted by the commission. The studies focused on major issues of regional growth ranging from investments in utilities and services, housing, transportation, education, health and recreation, public safety, and human welfare. The study recommendations reflected the commission's bias for "decentralized concentration." Proponents for decentralization argued that such a policy maximized diversity of quality of life choices, which meant living in diverse communities, i.e., suburbs outside the city. The city claimed that efficiency benefits in the region should be paramount and could be obtained only through greater centralization. The commission suggested that future area planning policies should weigh carefully the need for local autonomy, balanced growth, and quality of public services. It favored the development of a city-centered region surrounded by several self-sufficient communities, with the commission as the main forum for intermunicipal cooperation (Alberta Land Use Forum 1974, 69). The city, which favored an immediate move to a unitary government, opposed the Growth Study conclusions and subsequently, on the advice of the minister of municipal affairs, applied to the Local Authorities Board in 1979 to annex and place under single governance most of the growth areas of the region, creating in the process a megacity especially in terms of total area.

After a long and costly hearing where 12,000 pages of transcript were recorded, over 300 exhibits filed, and over seven million dollars spent, the Local Authorities Board recommended the expansion of Edmonton's boundaries in all directions to include Sherwood Park and Saint Albert. However, when the government received the report it decided to have it debated in the legislative assembly. Members representing areas to be annexed such as Sherwood Park and Saint Albert, while agreeing that Edmonton needed more land for residential and industrial development, also argued that their communities remain autonomous. In June 1981, the provincial cabinet rendered its decision that gave the city much of what it wanted in territory without disturbing the local autonomy of neighboring communities. A total of 86,000 acres of land were added to the city's area, enough for 30 to 40 years of development at 1980s rapid pace of growth. Additionally, a 30,000 acre public land bank was created northeast of Edmonton for future expansion.

The government rejected both a two-tier government as well as Edmonton's request for unitary governance of a megacity. The minister of municipal affairs pointed out that the annexation decision gave Edmonton about 19 percent of Strathcona's assessment, 17 percent of the tax-base of the Municipal District of Sturgeon, and 12 percent of that of the county of Parkland.

The cabinet also directed the newly named Edmonton Metropolitan Regional Planning Commission to incorporate policies that would achieve five broad objectives: (1) growth was to be city-centered with Edmonton to continue as the dominant center of the region containing 75 percent of the population; (2) remaining population growth was to be focused in the inner metropolitan area and other existing urban municipalities; no new towns that had been proposed in the 1970s would be permitted; (3) an unduly dispersed pattern of residential, industrial, and other types of human settlement was to be avoided; (4) better agricultural land was to be conserved along with wise use of other natural resources; and (5) the land-use pattern in the region was to provide transportation and utility services so as to reinforce the city-centered region.

The government's new policy tempered the Regional Commission's long-standing preference for "decentralized concentration." Especially contentious was the government's proposal that Edmonton should capture 75 percent of the future population growth in the area. One of the city's commission representatives declared that the government's action assured that "This . . . will be a city-centered region, not city dominated but city-centered metropolitan in nature. As such the issues will be of a more consistent urban nature and we will be required to develop new skills to deal with them" (Edmonton Metropolitan Regional Planning Commission 1982). The annexation decision giving Edmonton responsibility over a much larger territory reduced significantly the workload of the Regional Commission. Statements of provincial officials at the time made clear that the government would act independently and far more forcefully in resolving future regional land-use controversies.

Further, the government declared that it would receive no annexation decisions unless they covered at least 15 years of future growth. Many local authorities had received numerous development applications from landowners in fringe areas who hoped to enhance land values. If all requests for annexations between 1976 and 1980 had been honored the city would have grown by 360,000 acres, enough for about 1 million homes housing over 2 million persons! Ironically, about the time that the government made its annexation decision, the provincial economy nose-dived, and the eighties' recession set in eliminating many of the issues posed by boom-time growth.

Noting the need for the coordination of certain services throughout the region the provincial government passed a Regional Municipal Services Act, which provided for a Regional Services Commission. This commission would assume responsibility for the provision of water, sewer, storm drainage, and solid waste disposal in municipalities outside Edmonton. The commission was empowered to "acquire, finance, construct, operate, and dispose of water lines, sanitary or storm sewer lines, and water, waste, and sanitary or storm sewerage plants and facilities" (Province of Alberta 1981, 3-4). The city of Edmonton, the major provider of several utilities within the region, opted not to be a member of the Regional Services Commission. This government action represented a significant step in rationalizing the service delivery systems of the region.

Roadways, Highways, Freeways, and Light Rail Transit

One of the most urgent problems of rapidly growing urban municipalities is the movement of goods and people throughout a region. In 1961, the District Planning Commission undertook the Metropolitan Edmonton Transportation Study, a project that had significant implications for the nature and direction of regional growth. Representatives of the province, the city of Edmonton, towns, and rural municipalities attempted to forecast the roadway, highway, and freeway needs of the region for the next 20 years. Deconcentration and decentralization of population in the region were furthered by widespread automobile usage that made dispersal easy. The commission's stated policy was to encourage a concentrated central area complemented by strong subcenters in the suburban areas and district towns. Because freeways on the continent had become increasingly popular it is not surprising that they were proposed for the region. Among the most controversial suggestions was the routing of major freeways through the scenic McKinnon and Mill Creek ravines as well as creating a downtown freeway loop around the city center (not unlike the San Francisco Embarcadero), which would be linked to five radial freeways. Edmonton's council accepted the study recommendations for what may be described as the "Los Angelization" of the city and the surrounding region. However, as the full political, economic, aesthetic, and environmental implications of the elevated freeway loop and its connector freeways became known, enthusiasm for the projects receded leading to a search for other alternatives. One of these was some form of mass rail transit.

Although the city of Edmonton had a well-developed electric trolley and diesel bus system there was a steady decline in ridership and increasing use of automobiles by the center city work force. City-commissioned studies in the sixties showed that mass rail transit as an alternative form of travel would become highly popular with persons travelling to the city center area. A study done by Bechtel proposed a grade-separated, heavy rail transit system for the city. Its high cost was enough to dissuade city officials about its feasibility.

The city's plans for a "balanced transit strategy" incorporating some form of light rail transit were given a boost when the Canadian National

Railway decided to relocate its central city terminal to the city's outskirts thereby eliminating the need for its railway right of way. The right of way following a northeast/southwest alignment seemed ideal for light rail corridor purposes because it had the potential of connecting the city with several major "activity centers" along its route.

The evolving "balanced transportation strategy" integrating light rail, buses, and automobiles was attractive on several counts. It would reduce fuel consumption, eliminate the need for new parking garages in the city center, reduce street and roadway congestion, and could lead to new commercial as well as residential development along Light Rail Transit routes. During the time Edmonton was considering the development of mass rail transit the federal government put forth proposals for tri-level approaches to addressing urban problems in Canada and established a Ministry of State for Urban Affairs. Some advocates of rail transit at the local level believed that there might even be the possibility of federal capital assistance for the development of new modes of urban transit.

The boom time growth of the seventies convinced local officials in Edmonton that their plans to create a strong viable city center where commercial, governmental, and cultural activities would be concentrated would be aided significantly by a light rail transit system. An "automobile oriented" transit strategy could lead to the strangulation of the downtown area thereby decreasing its attractiveness.

In 1970 the provincial government passed a City Transportation Act that was aimed at helping Calgary and Edmonton develop an integrated transportation system, which would meet each city's needs. Although the act made provision for sharing costs of capital investments, the minister of highways stated that "rapid transit is too rich for the blood of the provincial government right now" (Bettison et al. 1975, 405). Some time later he suggested that it would be foolhardy to let the center of the city strangle to the point that real estate values would decline.

By August of 1973, Edmonton's city council, after reviewing the conclusions of numerous studies, moved to establish a rapid transit system and allocated money for engineering studies. Despite warnings that the capital costs of such a system would be higher than projected and operating revenues lower than anticipated, the city proceeded with the construction of a light rail transit system in 1974 (Thomas 1985).

Once begun, the city found a friend and benefactor in the provincial government, which embarked on an extensive program of upgrading the province's transportation needs and allocated a $7.50 per capita grant to cities that were designated for public transit. Edmonton committed all funds received to its light rail project. By the time the city completed the first five miles of the LRT system the province had provided a total of 45 million in grants or approximately two-thirds of the system's cost. The city justified its need for this assistance by noting that Alberta's boom economy had created the traffic problems in the first place. By 1978, 50 percent of all the municipal debt Edmonton had amassed was attributable to the cost of LRT construction.

The enthusiasm that greeted the opening of the light rail transit system in Edmonton, the first of its kind on the continent built in the postwar period, was dampened by the realization that the city's transit system was burdened with huge construction debts and future operating deficits. The provincial government, troubled by the city's transit expenditures, imposed new conditions on the city before it could expand the system, which involved a thorough review of capital and operating revenue. Studies conducted in 1979 revealed that the system was operating well below capacity. Although three years later ridership on the system had increased, it was obvious that transit revenues would be insufficient to meet either capital or operating costs. Once again the provincial government, awash with oil revenues, came to the city's rescue.

As the recession of the eighties spread throughout the provincial economy the future of Edmonton's light rail transit system was in doubt. Cabinet ministers grumbled about excessive costs involved in extending the system and its high operating budget. However, after investing $250 million dollars in the system by 1984 the province had invested so much that abandoning it was politically unpalatable. It has since allocated funds annually for the gradual extension of the system to the government center and beyond to the university.

Edmonton's light rail transit system is a prime example of the proactive role the provincial government played in accommodating growth within the city of Edmonton. It represents one of the most visible legacies of the oil boom years. Additionally the system helps the city preserve its unicentric form and contributes significantly to the maintenance of a vital city center. Edmontonians continue to point with pride to their light rail transit system, which has become a prototype for other similar systems on the continent.

CONCLUSION

In Alberta, the origins of metropolitan planning can be found in early town planning legislation intended to curb speculative development during a period of boom-time growth in Edmonton and Calgary. In the 1950s as the provincial economy was being transformed from an agricultural one to a resource-based one the government responded by establishing District Planning Commissions to help resolve conflicts over land use and attempt to rationalize urban and rural development. In the opinion of many planners, Alberta's governments, although having as their political base in the rural areas of the province, responded to the needs of urban communities with diverse planning initiatives. In many instances Alberta's planning for its neighborhoods was progressive and forward-looking.

Although the province retained the ultimate control in planning matters, all governments were committed to the belief in strong local autonomy, a commitment that often stood in the way of effective regional planning. When crises of an unresolvable kind came to the fore, the government would take the initiative to resolve them. Regional planning in the Edmonton metropolitan area was affected significantly and frequently adversely by the asymmetrical relationship between Edmonton, a large dominant urban center and several small towns, villages, hamlets, and rural municipalities. The relationships between the regional planning commissions with heavy representation from the smaller centers and the city were often strained as were the relations between the city and the provincial government. From its inception the District Planning Commission favored a regional growth policy of "decentralized concentration" while Edmonton desired to expand its own population and territory with the objective eventually of establishing a unicity for the area. Provincial policies and commission actions tended to work towards Edmonton's containment. The provincial government resisted all proposals for regional government, likely out of fear of the influence such a unified government in its own backyard might have on provincial politics. By emphasizing repeatedly its commitment to local autonomy of the communities within the region, the government was quite willing to accept the inefficiencies and redundancies that followed from the policy.

REFERENCES

Alberta Association of Municipal Districts and Counties and the Alberta Urban Municipalities Association. 1980. Municipal Affairs Towards Regional Planning in Alberta. Joint Report, October 7.

Alberta Land Use Forum. 1974. *Urban Residential Land Development.* Technical Report, no. 4.

Bettison, David, John K. Kenward, and Larrie Taylor. 1975. *Urban Affairs in Alberta.* Edmonton: University of Alberta Press.

Careless, J. M. S. 1977. Aspects of Urban Life in the West, 1870-1914. In *The Canadian City: Essays in Urban History,* ed. Gilbert Stelter and Alan F. J. Artibise. Carleton Library, no. 109. Toronto: McLelland-Stewart Limited.

City of Edmonton. 1967. *Proposed General Plan.*

City of Edmonton Planning Department. 1972. Map of History of Annexations in the City of Edmonton, April.

City of Fort Saskatchewan, Minutes of Regular Council Meeting. March 25, 1989.

Council of the City of Edmonton. 1973. The Future of this City or Does this City Have a Future? (mimeo). October 1. Submission to the Minister of Municipal Affairs of the Government of Alberta.

Dant, Noel. c. 1963-64. A Brief History of the Planning Statutes of Alberta, (mimeo). Alberta Archives, Edmonton #70393.

Duggan, J. J. 1938. Cities of Alberta (mimeo). Submission to the Royal Commission on Dominion-Provincial Relations. Edmonton, January.

Edmonton Bulletin. 1912. Anniversary Issue, July.

Edmonton District Planning Commission. 1951. Minutes of December 12.

_____. 1954. *Annual Report, 1953-1954.*

The Edmonton Journal. 1910. Edmonton, Alberta: The Capitol City, 1910. Edmonton City Archives.

_____. 1913. Statistics of Edmonton's Growth. July.

Edmonton Metropolitan Regional Planning Commission. 1982. *Minutes.* January 13.

_____. 1984. *Edmonton Metropolitan Regional Planning.*

_____. 1984. *Technical Appendix to the Edmonton Metropolitan Regional Plan.*

_____. 1984. *Technical Report.*

_____. 1986. *Population Growth and Change: The Edmonton Metropolitan Region.*

_____. 1990-91. *Metro Planning Review.* vol. 5, no. 3, Winter.

_____. 1991. *Metro Planning Review.* vol. 6, no. 1, Spring, 10.

The Financial Post. 1972. May 20.

Gertler, Leonard. 1968. *Planning the Canadian Environment.* Montreal: Harvest House Ltd.

Hanson, Eric. 1956. *Local Government in Alberta.* Toronto: McLelland Stewart Ltd.

MacGregor, James G. 1981. *A History of Alberta.* Edmonton: Hurtig Publishers, rev. ed.

Masson, Jack. 1985. *Alberta's Local Government and their Politics.* Edmonton: Pica Pica Press.

Province of Alberta, Department of Municipal Affairs. 1969. *Metropolitan Edmonton: Background Information.* July.

_____. 1908. *Statutes of Alberta, Edmonton Railway Tramway Act.*

_____. 1913. *Statutes.* Chapter 18, An Act Relating to Town Planning.

_____. 1928. *Statutes.* Ch. 48.

_____. 1929. *Statutes.* Ch. 49.

_____. 1957. *Statutes.* Ch. 98.

_____. 1980. *Statutes.* Ch. P-9, Section 54, with amendments in force as of July 6, 1988.

_____. 1981. *Statutes.* Regional Municipal Services Act.

Royal Commission on Metropolitan Development of Calgary and Edmonton. 1956. Report. January.

Scott, W. D. c. 1910. Superintendent of Immigration, Ottawa, advertisement.

Thomas, T. E. 1985. "Light Rail Transit in Edmonton: What Are We Learning?" Unpublished paper delivered to the biennial meeting of the Association for Canadian Studies in the United States, Philadelphia, September.

Weaver, John C. 1978. "Edmonton's Perilous Course, 1904-1929." (mimeo).

Chapter 7

Urban Growth Decision Making in the Houston Area

Robert D. Thomas
University of Houston

INTRODUCTION

Houston has the popular reputation of being a uniquely governed city, and evidence abounds to support that perception. Planning and zoning are standard fare for all U.S. central cities, yet Houston eschewed zoning until the 1990s. The typical picture of metropolitan America is an atomized pattern of municipal governments where a central city is surrounded by a number of suburban cities, but Houston dominates other area cities territorially and politically. After World War II, U.S. cities became more "bureaucratic" as demands for public services increased (Salamon 1977, 424-25), but Houston continued to support a free market, *laissez-faire* doctrine that allowed private developers to shape urban growth. Many central cities experienced precipitous economic decline in the 1970s. Houston didn't.

Popular images are sometimes misguided. Houston is really an enigma. It is a city where certain unique characteristics blend with features found in all U.S. central cities and metropolitan areas. From one perspective, therefore, Houston's growth is characterized by many of the same conditions operating in other cities. Consider how economic cycles, demographic trends, territorial concerns, and governmental issues of cities across the U.S. apply in Houston.

This essay is largely based on Robert D. Thomas and Richard W. Murray's recent book *Progrowth Politics—Change and Governance in Houston* (Berkeley, California: Institute of Governmental Studies Press, 1991).

Economic Cycles

Economic cycles are usually part of a city's economy as evidenced by prosperity and severe decline in Seattle; sustained prosperity from 1800 to 1950 in New York; and, sharp decline over the last 25 years in Buffalo. Houston experienced each of these patterns in the twentieth century. As measured by private-sector employment, through the 1960s Houston had a steady, although not spectacular, pattern of economic growth. In the 1970s, Houston's economy—bolstered by sharp increases in oil prices—sky-rocketed (e.g., an average of 75,000 jobs a year were added to the metropolitan area's labor force from 1979 to 1982). After reaching a pinnacle in the early 1980s, the economy took a roller coaster ride after oil prices plummeted. For example, between 1983 and 1987, 200,000 net jobs were lost, then 35,000 jobs were added in 1988.

Demographic Trends

Demographic shifts accompany economic changes. In Houston and in other areas, a variety of problems result from people constantly redistributing themselves across the urban landscape. During Houston's economic boom in the 1970s, for example, immigration of numerous white and blue collar workers from other parts of the U.S. contributed to traffic and mobility problems, pollution, and overused infrastructures. These problems lingered into the 1980s and were further intensified when an economic downturn brought revenue shortfalls caused by the outmigration of "richer" workers attracted to the earlier boom. Immigration did not cease, however. Since 1978, more than 100,000 southeastern Asians and ever-increasing numbers of Central Americans have moved into Houston creating an entirely different set of public needs.

Territorial Concerns

Territorial issues are an ever-present part of urban growth decision making. Public officials must constantly grapple with political boundary problems because economic and demographic growth broach territorially established political boundaries with impunity. On the other hand, since these boundaries encapsulate certain economic activities and demographic patterns, urban growth (and decline) issues almost always have territorial components such as city-suburban authorities; representational divisions;

new incorporations; occasional consolidations; and the creation of new special-purpose governments.

Government's Role in Urban Growth

As local officials face more severe problems, they have turned to the state and/or the national government for assistance. Hence, over time localities not only rely on more and more intergovernmental funding but also must subject their decisions to scrutiny by state and national officials. Government's role in urban growth decision making in all arenas thus changes over time as different needs arise, yet government is more than just an instrument serving the community's economic and social needs. The relationship between government and urban growth is symbiotic. Government establishes the general "rules of the game" for urban growth by direct intervention and regulation, by facilitating certain interests, or by benign neglect. These rules usually vary depending on temporal circumstances. At one point in time, they may facilitate private-sector investments and capital improvements; while, at another point in time, they may stimulate economic growth through public financing of infrastructure developments or regulate growth through land-use planning requirements. As the urban area develops, these patterns become more complex and more intergovernmental. That is to say, while local decision makers still have the ability to determine their area's growth priorities, their decisions become more vulnerable to "rules" established outside their own governing institutions. This means urban growth decision making is increasingly characterized by a paradox: *ability in the context of vulnerability.*

This paradox of urban growth decision making is examined in Houston by describing the general role of the public sector in urban growth decision making since World War II; and by analyzing how that role has changed and why.

THE HOUSTON METROPOLITAN AREA

The city of Houston is located within the U.S. census-defined Houston-Galveston-Brazonia, TX, Consolidated Metropolitan Statistical Area (CMSA). This CMSA includes seven counties (Brazonia, Fort Bend, Galveston, Harris, Liberty, Montgomery, and Waller), covers 7,151 square miles of the upper Gulf Coast of Texas, and has a population of 3,711,043 with a civilian labor force in 1986 of 1,800,697. The bulk of the CMSA's population and economic activity is in Harris County. Its 1,734 square miles covers 24.2 percent of the CMSA, and within its boundaries are 76 percent of the CMSA's population and 78.9 percent of the area's civilian labor force. At the core of Harris County, as shown in Map 7.1, is the city of Houston, which has 61.2 percent of the county's population and 58 percent of its labor force.

These characteristics of the CMSA indicate that most social, economic, and political activities are centered generally in Harris County and specifically in Houston; therefore, the central focus of this analysis is necessarily on the county and the central city. What factors then shape urban growth decision making in the metropolitan area?

CENTRAL CITY DOMINANCE

Houston is the dominant political jurisdiction in Harris County. As used here, dominance means more than legal and administrative control. Even though Houston does not enjoy a superior legal and administrative position in many intermetropolitan relationships concerning urban growth, a number of factors provide Houston with circumstantial opportunities to be more effective than other jurisdictions. Some of these opportunities have diminished in the 1980s, but Houston is still the dominant governmental entity in the area.

Territorial Size

The most distinguishing territorial feature of American metropolitan areas is a central city encircled by numerous suburban cities; a characteristic that has been identified as one of the root causes of central city decline (Jackson 1972). When a city can no longer capture fringe area growth, it increasingly becomes socio-economically and racially segregated. Wealthier and better educated citizens, who are also mostly white, settle in the suburbs to escape a multitude of inner-city problems affecting the quality of life (e.g., crime, congestion, and pollution). Central cities then confront an eroding tax base and a heavier concentration of racial minorities who cannot flee the decay and deterioration that are inevitable when service demands increase, while the resources to meet such needs shrink.

Most central cities resemble St. Louis, locked-in by more than 100 municipalities, where one city's limits blur into the next. Houston, on the other hand, is less territorially closed-in at the present time. It enjoys

Map 7.1.   *The Houston Metropolitan Area*

Houston's City Limits

Houston's Extraterritorial Jurisdiction (ETJ)

territorial dominance over other governments, even though governmental fragmentation is still prevalent. For example, Houston is largely in Harris County, and overlaying its borders are countywide hospital and flood control districts and an areawide metropolitan transit authority (MTA). Jutting in-and-out of the city's limits are four junior college districts and 19 independent school districts. Outside Houston's corporate limits are about 400 special-purpose municipal utility districts (MUDs) providing services to residential, commercial, and industrial developments in unincorporated areas. As shown in Map 7.1, Houston is the municipal giant (e.g., Houston is 2.6 times larger than the combined land areas of the other 32 Harris County cities).

Several economic and political realities are enhanced by Houston's territorial size. Most corporate and commercial developments are located either inside Houston or in its extraterritorial jurisdiction (defined below). Even the Houston Ship Channel in eastern Harris County, which contains the bulk of the metropolitan area's heavy industry, is subject to annexation by Houston. Politically, Houston voters elect a majority of local state legislators and other officials. Three of Harris County's four commissioner districts, for example, are mostly inside Houston. The county pattern is also true of state legislative seats: city voters comprise a majority of the electors in four of six state senate districts—all largely in Harris County—and in 20 of 26 house districts—all in Harris County.

Home-Rule Authority for Cities

The Texas Constitution authorizes the incorporation of two classes of cities: general law and home-rule. Before a home-rule amendment was ratified in 1912, cities had to attain their charters from the legislature. After 1912, home-rule charters could be adopted by a majority vote in cities over 5,000 in population. Home-rule cities have some distinctive advantages over general law cities. For one, they have more extensive authorities to tax and incur debt, define internal structures, offer services, and expand their borders. This means Houston and the other 11 home-rule cities in Harris County are considerably more autonomous than the 21 general law cities. Second, the 1912 amendment gave home-rule city mayors, with their councils' approval, the legal foundation to annex land by simple ordinance-action—one of the most liberal processes for city expansion in the U.S. Prior to 1963, home-rule cities could expand their boundaries whenever their officials wished without interference or supervision from the state legislature or bureaucracy, without seeking voter approval, and without assuming the burden of service delivery to citizens. "First-in-time, first-in-right" was the legal tenet guiding annexations. That is to say, if a city passed an annexation ordinance on a first-reading, it had a superior legal claim to the designated territory even if it did not complete the ordinance process. State courts upheld this tenet by ruling that within an area claimed by a city's annexation ordinance on first reading, no new incorporations or annexations by other cities could occur (McCorkle 1963, 13, 14). Under these legal conditions, the state legislature and bureaucracy remained out-of-the fray if and when territorial disputes arose, leaving their settlement to city negotiations or court decisions.

The Municipal Annexation Act (MAA) of 1963 finally gave some state direction to city annexations. First, it merely formalized annexation procedures that had informally evolved under the broad guidelines of the 1912 home-rule amendment (e.g., authority to annex without voter approval; to settle territorial disputes locally or, failing that, go to court). Second, it required annexing cities to meet procedural and servicing responsibilities (e.g., public hearings; completion of annexations within 90 days; equivalent services to annexed areas within three years) (The State of Texas 1963, 447-545). Third, in a given calendar year, a city can annex no more than 10 percent of its corporate limits; however, unused territory may be accumulated from year-to-year, so long as it never exceeds 30 percent of a city's size.

These new requirements were seen as concessions to suburban interests, and they did slow large-scale annexations by home-rule cities. On the other hand, the MAA solidified Houston's territorial dominance by creating extraterritorial jurisdiction (ETJ) authority for home-rule cities. A city's ETJ extends from one-half to five-miles beyond its corporate boundaries depending on its population. Cities with 100,000 or more residents are given a five-mile reach. Since the ETJ is measured from a city's corporate limits, each time a city annexes its ETJ expands proportionately. In its ETJ, a city can impose subdivision regulations, approve the creation of MUDs, designate tax-exempt "industrial districts," and prohibit new incorporations (The State of Texas 1963, 447-545).

Houston's ETJ presently blankets almost all the unincorporated land in Harris County, plus portions of six other counties, including rapidly urbanizing parts of south Montgomery County and eastern Fort Bend County. As shown in Table 7.1, only Pasadena and Baytown have populations (119,363 and 63,850, respectively) that afford them a substantive ETJ, but the geography of these cities constricts that legal

Table 7.1. Selected Characteristics of Cities in Harris County and Their Territorial Relationship to the City of Houston

City	Population[a]			Legal Authority	Form of Government	ETJ Authority[b] (miles)	Land Area[c] (sq. miles)
	1980	1986	% Changes				
Houston	1,594,086	1,728,910	8.46	HR	MC	5	556.4
Surrounded by Houston							
Bellaire	14,950	14,500	-3.01	HR	CM	1	3.6
Bunker Hill Village	3,750	3,610	-3.73	GL	MC	n/a	1.5
Galena Park	9,879	10,040	1.63	HR	MC	1	4.9
Hedwig Village	2,506	2,900	15.72	GL	MC	n/a	0.9
Hilshire Village	621	—[d]	—	GL	MC	n/a	0.1
Humble	6,729	12,220	81.60	HR	MC	1	9.5
Hunter's Creek Village	4,215	4,570	8.42	GL	MC	n/a	0.5
Jacinto City	8,953	11,130	24.32	GL	MC	n/a	1.8
Piney Point	2,958	3,290	11.22	GL	MC	n/a	3.2
South Houston	13,293	14,450	8.70	GL	MC	n/a	2.9
Southside Place	1,366	—	—	GL	MC	n/a	0.3
Spring Valley Village	3,353	2,970	-11.42	GL	MC	n/a	1.4
West University Place	12,010	13,340	11.07	HR	CM	1	2.0
Encircled by Houston							
Jersy Village	4,084	5,230	28.06	GL	MC	n/a	2.1
Katy*	4,475	10,610	137.09	GL	MC	n/a	3.6
Pearland*	13,996	17,020	21.61	HR	CM	1	15.8

Tomball	3,996	6,450	61.41	GL	MC	n/a	0.8
Waller	1,241	—	—	GL	MC	n/a	0.9
Abutted by Houston							
Deer Park	22,648	25,380	12.06	HR	CM	1	15.4
El Largo	3,129	3,260	4.19	GL	MC	n/a	0.3
La Porte	14,062	25,030	78.00	HR	MC	1	15.4
Lomax	2,964	—	—	GL	MC	n/a	0.3
Morgan Point	428	—	—	GL	MC	n/a	2.2
Nassau Bay	4,526	4,730	4.51	GL	CM	n/a	1.7
Pasadena	112,560	118,050	4.88	HR	MC	5	42.5
Seabrook	4,670	5,070	8.57	GL	MC	n/a	6.3
Shoreacres	1,260	—	—	GL	MC	n/a	1.9
Taylor Lake	3,669	3,840	4.66	GL	MC	n/a	0.5
Webster	2,168	—	—	GL	MC	n/a	3.1
Can Grow Outside ETJ							
Baytown	56,923	62,770	10.27	HR	CM	3.5	25.4
Missouri City*	24,533	32,020	30.52	HR	MC	2	27.5
Stafford*	4,755	5,920	24.50	GL	MC	n/a	9.2

*City is only partly in Harris County, but the population and land area is for the entire municipality.

[a]1980 population figures based on U.S. Bureau of the Census, 1980 Census of Population and Housing (Washington, D.C.: Government Printing Office, 1981). 1986 estimates based on U.S. Bureau of Census, City-County District Data Book (Washington, D.C.: Government Printing Office, 1988).

[b]Cities surrounded by Houston do not have ETJs; those encircled by Houston's ETJ must negotiate with Houston if they wish to expand; those abutted by Houston have only limited places to grow.

[c]Houston and Harris County Atlas (Houston: Key Maps, 1980).

[d]Data for these cities are not available.

authority. Cities to the east and southeast of Houston, including Pasadena and Baytown, are almost entirely hemmed in between Houston and Galveston Bay. Elsewhere in Harris County, 13 cities are enclaves within Houston and do not have ETJs. Five other cities are forced to negotiate with Houston (or go to court) if they want to expand because they are encircled by Houston's ETJ. Three cities (Stafford, Missouri City, and Baytown) can grow into other counties but not into Houston's ETJ.

Population changes, in both incorporated and unincorporated areas, between 1970 and 1980 illustrate the consequences of Houston's territorial control over other Harris County cities. Most of the county's population growth took place either in the city of Houston or in its ETJ. During the 1970s, for example, Houston had 51.7 percent (or 345,057) of Harris County's population growth of 667,632. The unincorporated portions of the county—almost all of which is in Houston's ETJ—gained 37.9 percent (or 252,901) of the total. Thus, 89.6 percent of the county's growth took place inside Houston and its ETJ. The county's other 32 cities attained only 10.4 percent of the total (69,674).

Since Houston restricts the territorial growth of the county's other cities, their populations must expand within fixed boundaries. Houston, on the other hand, has enormous potential for growth, not only within its corporate limits, but also in its vast ETJ. Houston's dominant territorial place in the region is vividly illustrated when we consider its population potential. While Houston's 1980 population of 1,594,086 represents 55 percent of the population of the CMSA, Houston's ETJ gives it the potential of expanding to 75 percent of the total CMSA population.

Suburban Authorities

To support growth in unincorporated areas, an infrastructure of roads, drainage, water, and sewer must be developed. Generally, an array of service deliverers responds to these needs. Among the service deliverers in the Houston metropolitan area are Harris County, independent school districts, and municipal utility districts. These governmental authorities do not impede Houston's dominance over growth decision making in the area.

Harris County

Harris County would seem to be the appropriate government to deal with metropolitanwide problems, since it is such a large territorial unit.

However, county officials have limited legal authority, which restricts them from competing with their Houston counterparts in urban growth decision making. The Texas Constitution provides for a traditional county structure. All Texas counties are administrative arms of the state government. Since county officials do not have ordinance-making authority, their activities are largely determined by the mixture of state tasks they are obligated to perform such as operating the courts, supervising the jails, administering elections, building and maintaining roads, establishing libraries and parks, and tending to a bevy of house-keeping functions. These tasks generally supplement and support, not supplant, city functions. Indeed, county commissioners see their service role as one that is in addition to, not in place of, city services.[1]

County officials are also limited in taking an active political role in areawide growth decisions by the internal organizational arrangement of county government. Harris County operates with a fragmented, multiple-executive structure. Each commissioner has a special service responsibility and a voting constituency. Each is only loosely tied to the commissioners court, the central governing body. While the commissioners court has administrative authority over a number of service areas, its control is very diffused. As county services have expanded in Harris County because of urbanization, each commissioner has taken primary responsibility for certain departments (e.g., welfare or mental health) and oversees that specific function without interference from other commissioners. Furthermore, county business is parceled out to a number of boards and commissions whose citizen-members—although appointed either by the court wholly or jointly by the court and other local governments—are farther removed from commissioner court supervision.

Commissioners thus operate more as independent ward politicians than as a collective decision-making body. Ward politics and particularism characterize their precinct activities. This is reinforced in commissioners' relations with land developers because the primary tool a commissioner has to develop a constituency is a road maintenance fund. How and where a commissioner uses these funds is, of course, important to developers.

What has emerged are close ties between commissioners and developers. County government has generally been a reactive force in responding to growth. The political welfare of both commissioners and

---

[1]Based on interviews with selected county officials.

private economic interests depends on maintaining existing structures and organizations. As one commissioner put it: "Commissioners are very cooperative with developers. They initiate, we respond." Another observer summarized the consensus of opinion on the relationship between developers and Harris County's government this way: "When developers speak, commissioners listen. If they don't [listen], commissioners are usually in a precarious political position."

Independent School Districts

Frederick M. Wirt (1975, 129) argues that school districts "have traditionally represented diminished responsibility for suburban government," a phenomenon he refers to as "the lateral axis of suburban autonomy." Wirt says that special districts, of which school districts are "prototypical," diminish suburban governments' responsibilities, thus making it easier for incorporated suburbs to develop and thrive.

The structure of independent school districts in the Houston area also diminishes responsibilities, not of the suburban governments but of the city of Houston. Houston is the main beneficiary of independent school districts, principally because its boundaries are not linked to school district boundaries.

There are 23 independent school districts in Harris County. These districts lie either wholly or partially within the city of Houston. As unincorporated areas have been engulfed by Houston's annexations, independent school districts continue to provide educational services in neighborhood or near-neighborhood schools. Houston's annexations are thus more palatable to suburbanites, because their schools are not disrupted when they become Houstonians.

Independent school districts also shield Houston from certain fiscal burdens. In other states, a major roadblock to annexation is when "the city government has responsibility for school financing without substantial equalization from the state" (U.S. ACIR 1973, 21). Being able to move freely across school district boundaries, Houston does not have to assume the fiscal burdens of educational services; thus it avoids not only the political problems associated with the upheaval of existing schools but also the fiscal problems of financing public education.

Municipal Utility Districts

Diverse approaches to suburban service needs are taken in metropolitan areas. For example, in four major Texas areas—Houston, Dallas-Ft. Worth, San Antonio, and Austin—municipal services, water districts, private water companies, and regional agencies are used (Texas Legislature 1975). Each of these service approaches has a differential impact on the central city's control over suburban developments. Extending municipal services to suburban residents—the principal method used in Austin and Dallas-Ft. Worth—allows the city to impose its standards on suburban developments, but the city faces the thorny issue of financing capital construction outside its boundaries (e.g., as the project manager of suburban utility construction, the city is obligated to bureaucratic and service costs). If MUDs prevail, as they do in Houston, the city forgoes direct control, but does not have to provide upfront capital-construction funding for infrastructure developments. The type of service delivery system in operation directly impacts decisions about suburban growth and where city decision makers fit into the process. If the central city is the service provider, groundwork is laid for future annexation. If another device is used, central city officials must cooperate with the service provider, or allow the seeds of suburban incorporations to be planted. Since Texas central cities enjoy extensive ETJ authority, there is usually a close alliance between the city and suburban entities.

THE USE OF MUDs IN HARRIS COUNTY

State Authority for MUDs

The legal antecedents for MUDs are two amendments to the Texas Constitution ratified in 1904 and in 1917. Each was designed to give ranchers and farmers the financial means to deal with flooding, drainage, and conservation problems. The 1904 amendment allowed landowners to establish taxing districts to finance water conservation and reclamation projects, but prohibited bonded indebtedness from exceeding 25 percent of a district's real property value. The 1917 amendment deleted that limitation and allowed land owners to have unlimited and unrestricted debt financing for flood control, drainage, irrigation, and power projects (Texas Constitution). Not even cities and counties have this much financial latitude! On a simple majority vote of resident taxpayers, the

1917 amendment extended exclusive authority to landowners to create a taxing district to make improvements.[2]

The principle is certainly sound—those who benefit, pay—and works on a proportionate basis for rural areas. However, the benefits are skewed when applied to urban developments, particularly in their early stages, because the developer as the initial landowner can use publicly generated revenues through district debt financing to make land improvements. Developers' investment risks are minimized in relationship to benefits simply because those risks are transferred to a public entity, the district.

Over the years, the legislature has expanded the constitutional authority for districts to urban land developments. Fresh Water Supply Districts (FWSDs)—authorized to conserve, transport, and distribute fresh water supplies—were the first districts used to provide urban-type services. Water Control and Improvement Districts (WCIDs)—authorized to provide for "domestic and commercial water supply, sewage disposal, drainage, irrigation, reclamation and conservation"—became an ideal development tool (Schroer 1971). Developers found that the WCID legislation allowed them to sell bonds before the construction of facilities, thus providing public capital funding to build these facilities (Mitchell 1972, 20). The process came full-circle with the enactment of the Municipal Utilities Act of 1971, which updated the WCID statute by directly applying the district concept to urban development.

Land developers received the most direct support in two specific ways. First, the MUD Act linked district creation to "project feasibility" and "land benefits." By tying a project's feasibility to its land benefits, the legislature "recognized that water districts used by developers have no people at [the] time of [their] creation" (Texas Legislature). Second, the MUD Act allowed districts to carry out a broader array of urban development functions than WCIDs, which include: (1) water supply for all beneficial uses; (2) waste disposal services; (3) all forms of drainage; (4) irrigation; (5) alteration of land elevations; (6) navigate coastal and

---

[2]The 1904 amendment required a two-thirds vote of taxpayers, while the 1917 amendment modified the voting requirement to a simple majority. Also, the political status of districts was enhanced when the Texas Court of Appeals ruled in *Baker v. Jefferson County WCID #1*, 277, S.W. 2d 130 (1955) that a Water Control and Improvement District, legislated under the 1917 amendment, was a political subdivision of the state, like a city or county.

inland waters; and (7) parks and recreational facilities (Texas Water Code, 297).

The Developers' Role in Creating Districts

The state of Texas allows water districts to be created by special acts of the legislature, by the Texas Water Commission (TWC), or by the county.[3] Before the MUD Act of 1971, developers used the legislative process extensively because they found the TWC route too cumbersome.[4] After the MUD Act broadened the scope of district authority for urban purposes and eliminated many of the previous difficulties associated with bureaucratic creation, developers used the TWC process almost exclusively. For example, Table 7.2 shows that before the MUD Act went into effect in 1972, the TWC authorized 93 districts in Harris County compared with 149 originated by the legislature. Since 1972, these numbers were reversed with the TWC establishing 285 districts during this period and the legislature creating only 8.

Changes enacted in the 1971 MUD Act and in 1973 in the 63d session of the legislature (e.g., more uniform administrative standards in the TWC's review of developers' applications for district creations) have significantly affected the state approval process for creating water districts. However, these did not alter the developer's role in district creation nor his control over district operations in their formative years. As indicated above, the MUD Act solidified the developer's "right" to use district bonds to improve undeveloped land; and the developer still determines a district's location, its size, initial board of directors, and bonded indebtedness.

A *Governor's Report* (1975) gives a succinct account of the developer's control.

Developers control their districts from inception until subdivision lot owners take over two or three years later. They draw the district boundaries, put the first voters on the property, tell them

---

[3]Presently, the Commissioners Court seldom is involved in district creation because its process is too complicated and time consuming for developers.

[4]The Texas Water Rights Commission (TWRC) was the predecessor to the TWC. Prior to 1977, the TWRC was a separate agency. In 1977, the TWRC was consolidated with the Texas Water Development Board and the Texas Water Quality Board to form the Texas Department of Water Resources.

Table 7.2. MUD Creations and Bond Approvals in Harris County by Year and Agency (In Thousands)

Year	Texas Water Commission			Harris County Commissions Court			Legislature			Total		
	Number Created	Bonds ($000)	No. Issued	Number Created	Bonds ($000)	No. Issued	Number Created	Bonds ($000)	No. Issued	Number Created	Bonds ($000)	No. Issued
1949	1	—	—	1	215	1	—	—	—	2	215	1
1950	4	1,425	3	—	325	1	—	—	—	4	1,750	4
1951	10	2,150	4	—	—	—	—	—	—	10	2,150	4
1952	1	1,550	4	—	—	—	—	—	—	1	1,550	4
1953	1	750	1	1	—	—	2	—	—	4	750	1
1954	6	3,692	5	—	—	—	—	—	—	6	3,692	5
1955	12	8,835	8	2	—	—	2	—	—	16	8,835	8
1956	7	18,698	19	2	—	—	1	—	—	10	18,698	19
1957	1	475	1	3	52	1	1	—	—	5	527	2
1958	2	1,697	3	—	—	—	—	430	1	2	2,127	4
1959	1	1,440	4	3	—	—	—	—	—	4	1,440	4
1960	1	850	3	1	—	—	—	—	—	2	850	3
1961	1	1,350	2	2	—	—	1	—	—	4	1,350	2
1962	5	3,375	7	1	—	—	—	700	1	6	4,075	8
1963	3	3,375	4	1	—	—	3	6,160	2	7	9,535	6
1964	4	1,450	2	1	—	—	—	1,100	2	5	2,550	4

Year												
1965	4	1,718	2	1	—	—	15	3,770	5	20	5,488	7
1966	4	4,650	4	—	—	—	—	5,320	7	4	9,970	11
1967	—	8,755	9	1	—	—	15	12,435	10	16	21,190	19
1968	13	3,210	5	1	—	—	—	26,975	9	—	30,185	14
1969	4	13,275	16	—	—	—	41	17,505	18	45	30,780	34
1970	5	20,547	23	—	355	1	—	72,260	25	5	93,162	49
1971	4	28,415	26	—	6,625	2	68	93,540	25	72	128,580	53
1972	35	16,240	17	—	1,800	1	—	30,510	19	35	48,550	37
1973	34	43,700	22	—	6,474	4	1	43,191	26	35	93,365	52
1974	28	54,015	28	—	1,400	2	—	96,675	21	28	152,090	51
1975	9	32,675	18	—	—	—	—	19,195	13	1	51,870	31
1976	13	40,495	21	—	4,100	1	—	28,975	20	13	73,570	42
1977	21	87,595	45	—	1,620	2	—	43,915	24	21	133,130	71
1978	33	83,935	42	—	—	—	—	93,055	34	33	176,990	76
1979	23	131,755	56	—	11,275	4	—	46,710	21	13	189,740	81
1980	25	168,610	62	—	5,500	1	—	42,170	15	25	216,280	78
1981	12	106,885	33	—	—	—	1	24,075	10	13	130,960	43
1982	16	119,935	34	—	2,380	1	—	21,710	8	16	144,025	43
1983	18	213,625	53	—	247	1	5	19,065	8	23	232,937	62
1984*	18	141,485	42	—	8,725	3	—	47,620	10	18	197,830	55
Total	399	1,372,632	628	21	51,093	26	157	797,061	334	557	2,220,786	988

Source: Data compiled from Texas Water Commission records, 1949 to Nov. 1984.
*Through Nov. 8, 1984 only.

how to vote, specify the bond amounts, and identify who will serve as district directors. Everyone in the act—voters, directors, and the district itself—is the captive of the developer, doing his bidding to provide sewer and water services for a private developer. Under such circumstances, governmental procedures tend to be secret and even farcical, e.g., approval of several millions of dollars of district bonds in a district-wide election by a vote of 3 to 0.

This report was published in 1975, but remains descriptive of how districts are used to aid and abet the economic aims of land developers. This does not mean the TWC, the city of Houston, or other public entities assume a passive role in the creation and operation of districts. To the contrary, there has been an ever-evolving governmental role in the past decade, although it still facilitates land developers' economic aims.

Developers used the legislative method extensively prior to the enactment of the MUD Act, because the legislature could form any type of district it desired so long as it conformed to the requirements of the 1917 amendment. A special water district bill had to include only those provisions from the Texas Water Code that its sponsors felt were necessary for passage. District legislation could be designed to fit a developer's particular circumstances rather than adhere to uniform standards. Consequently, special act districts were established without adequate financial information, virtually no consideration of district location, and no planning requirements (Schroer 1971; Lawson 1977).

In the early 1970s, a number of developers' abuses of water districts for their own gain came to a boiling point. After Houston's 1956 around-the-city annexation took in 26 water districts, an audit of the operations of the newly annexed districts found a number of questionable financial activities (e.g., excessive developer profits, misuse of funds, and incomplete financial reporting) (*Houston Post*, Oct. 8, 1958). During the 1960s, districts continued to be scrutinized, especially the way in which legislatively created districts circumvented a number of legal requirements that normally faced water districts (Katz 1972, 160-73). As the district creation process became more controversial, state representatives from Harris County became reluctant to sponsor water district legislation. Then, in 1973, the creation of special act legislation was virtually halted with the enactment of 13 reform bills by the 63d session of the legislature. The most important of these reforms that operated as a disincentive to the creation of special act districts was the power given the TWC to regulate water districts established by the legislature.

These reforms extended TWC's regulatory authority to various phases of district organization and administration. Among other things, they allowed TWC to increase penalties for districts that failed to file required reports, to conduct audits of their financial statements, and to standardize procedures for organizing districts. The latter authority reduced the developer's control over key administrative positions of the district. For example, TWC prohibited persons related to or employed by the developer from serving as a district's tax assessor and collector or board member within two years of district creation.

Figure 7.1 illustrates how developers—along with bankers, financial advisors/brokers, engineers, and lawyers are at the center of the process in the creation and formative years of a district. Developers decide to prepare land in the unincorporated suburbs for subdivision or commercial or industrial projects. Armed with a plan designed by a consulting engineer, the land is prepared for construction development by platting lots, paving streets, and installing minimal water, sewer, and drainage facilities.

How to finance these facilities is the most immediate problem for the developer. Prior to 1974, the developer could time a project so that an interest-only loan would suffice until a district was created to issue bonds. At that point, the developer would repay the loan and rapidly build the needed infrastructures; an extremely advantageous method to fund 100 percent of needed improvements with district bonds.

After the 1974 recession, the TWC diminished some of the leverage features of district bonds. Many developers faced financial difficulties, putting a number of districts on the verge of bankruptcy. If a district were to default on its bonds, residents would lose their homes and be saddled with the district's indebtedness. To ease this situation, the TWC established a rule requiring developers to finance 30 percent of the "construction costs for all water, sewer, and drainage facilities including attendant engineering expenses and fees."

However, the impact of the ruling was softened by two qualifications. First, the TWC could use its discretion in applying the rule, "if [it] determines [project] feasibility is not dependent upon developer contributions." Second, some costly infrastructures (e.g., wastewater treatment plants, main and trunk lines linking a district's facilities with another system, and water lines used on a regional basis) are exempted from the rule (Texas Water Development Board).

A public process of district approval occurs coincidental with or immediately following the developer's initial start of a project. The first

Figure 7.1.   *The Private and Public Process of MUD Creation*

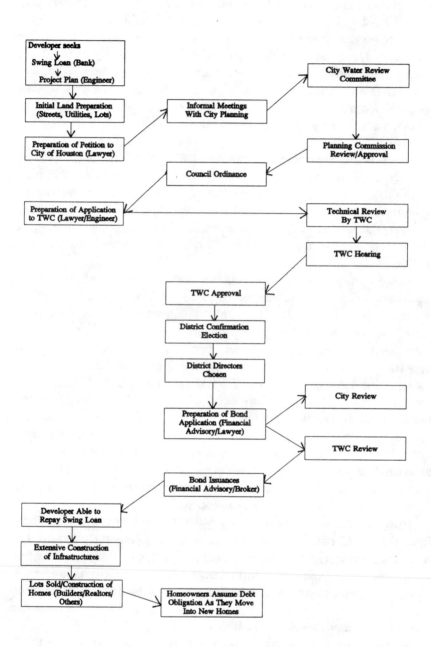

contact the developer has with a governmental agency comes in informal discussions with Houston bureaucrats in the Departments of Public Works and Planning. These cooperative meetings involve city officials advising developers about potential problems that may arise in the city's district approval process. The criteria applied are whether or not the developer's planned project meets Houston's standards for districts such as guidelines for building and operating facilities, plat recording, and various certifications. The developer and city officials are usually mutually supportive of one another's needs in these face-to-face meetings.

The most extensive city review of a developer's plans occurs in the Water District Review Committee (WDRC). This is a bureaucratic committee with representatives from the Departments of Public Works, Health, Planning, Solid Waste, Aviation, and Legal. A sanitation engineer from the Harris County Health Department is also a member. Neither the developer nor his representatives participates in the WDRC's discussions.

Before explaining the current city process, it is necessary to step back momentarily to see what the city did before the creation of the WDRC.[5] During the "boom" years of the 1970s and early 1980s, *growth overwhelmed the city's review process.* In the words of a WDRC member, "we had more than we could say grace over!" City departments did not—perhaps because they could not—closely examine crucial aspects of developers' applications. For example, city officials glossed over whether or not the wastewater treatment plant of a proposed district could adequately handle long-term needs; consequently, as subdivisions grew, many "package plants" were used far in excess of their maximum loads. Also, city officials did not pay attention to the siting of district facilities, which later meant the city could not integrate these facilities into a regional wastewater or water supply system.

The review process was cumbersome and time consuming for developers, even though city officials were supportive of district starts. The Texas Water Code required Houston to complete its district review in 120-days, and a wait of the full 120 days for developers was not uncommon. Compliance with this requirement was (and still is) of major concern to Houston officials; because, if a response is not given in the allotted time, a majority of electors in a district can petition Houston's

---

[5]The following analysis of Houston's review process before and after the creation of the WDRC is based on interviews with members of the WDRC.

council to make services available. The WDRC was created to streamline the city's review process and assure compliance with the 120-day rule. The timing problem has taken on added significance lately because the requirement for completion was lowered to 90 days in 1987 and to 60 days in 1988.

Houston's policy to encourage MUD development in its ETJ as a means of financing the construction of an urban infrastructure is as strong today as it was in the past. Yet, a slowdown in economic growth has allowed the city to "catch up" and more closely examine developers' plans. Since the city can now better manage the flow of district applications, the WDRC focuses on districts meeting technical requirements as follows: public works (engineering specifications), planning (plats), aviation (noise and "airport" zones), health (discharge permits and inspections), and legal (water code compliance).

Underlying the more specific technical review is a broader concern that proposed developments do not get out of hand in accommodating present and future wastewater treatment demands, water supplies, and debt obligations. Of utmost concern to the WDRC is future integration of a district's wastewater treatment system and water supply facilities with the city's system. Therefore, the WDRC focuses on whether or not a proposed district's facilities duplicate or otherwise impede existing facilities. If so, city officials may encourage the developer to cooperate with neighboring districts. The guiding norm for city bureaucrats is to coordinate the development of district water supplies and treatment facilities with the aim of integrating them with a regional city system, if and when annexation occurs. The watchwords are coordination, integration, and regionalization.

Once a developer's petition goes through the WDRC, Houston's council must enact an ordinance legitimizing the district. Occasionally, early in the review process, an individual council member may discuss a district proposal with selected WDRC members. The WDRC is very receptive to council concerns and tries to deal with them in its review. Hence, rarely do council members' reservations linger beyond the early discussion stages of the review.

Overall, the TWC's approval process—just as the city's—is geared to accommodate the developer's interests. MUDs are originated by a petition to the TWC from a majority of the property owners—or 50 persons, whichever is less—within the boundaries of the proposed district. Since "majority" is defined as value of land, one property owner (usually the developer) can initiate the application if his land is valued at more than that of all others combined. During the economic "boom" of the 1970s and early 1980s, developers sometimes "created" land owners by deeding lots to personal friends or employees allowing these "owners," rather than the developer, to initiate the district: a ploy that enabled the developer to hand-pick the same individuals as temporary district board members.[6] In the approval process, the TWC names five temporary district directors, who are almost always nominated by the developer. In most cases, the few property owners placed on the land by the developer are the only property owners (rather, in this example, property "holders," because the developer holds a lien on their lots), they have no competition in becoming district directors.

A final step in district creation is a confirmation election for the district's board of directors. Before that election can occur, the developer must get residents into the subdivision, which requires the platting of lots, the construction of streets and utilities, and the construction of a few houses. The first houses in a subdivision are called "water district houses." The buyer takes a substantial risk in purchasing one of these houses. If the developer's project fails (which means the district would also fail), the first homeowners risk their entire investment. On the other hand, with successful projects, which most have been, these homeowners make a large profit because "water district houses" are bought at near cost. Buyers of these homes, typically, understand the risks; and in the past, they were often directly associated with the developer.

District confirmation elections are usually *pro forma*, with homeowners favoring district creation. Since there are usually only a few homeowners in a subdivision when confirmation elections are held, district boards are constituted by a vote of fewer than 10 residents. Nonetheless, the confirmation vote is very important to the developer, because it involves the formal approval of the district's five directors and establishes an upper ceiling of bonded indebtedness. No bonds are sold at this time, but the approval allows the process to proceed rapidly to bond financing, which, in turn, means the developer can proceed rapidly to construction.

Once the legal structure of the district is in place, the developer starts the application process for a bond sale. Residents of the district are responsible for bond indebtedness, yet the financing of district facilities

---

[6]The following analysis of the TWC's review process is based on interviews with selected officials in the Texas Department of Water Resources.

continues to remain with the developer outside resident's control. To receive reimbursement for out-of-pocket construction costs, the developer wants to start the bond application process as soon as possible. A bond application to the TWC is required. It is reviewed by engineers in the TWC's District Permits section. The developer is asked to provide technical data such as the purpose of the bond issue, the extent of proposed developments, connections and improvements, the total authorization amount of the bonds, any usual features of the development, and any financial history of the district that might affect repayment of the bonds.[7] The application does not require any input from resident homeowners, who are the ones responsible for repaying the bonds.

After district creation, the bond application process is the most important and critical step to ensure the developer's success. An unsuccessful application would force the developer to finance utility construction—an unlikely occurrence—or abandon the project. The developer usually does not have to make the choice, because most applications are approved.[8]

Bond applications normally go through the process more quickly and with less scrutiny from TWC engineers if substantial preconstruction of water and sewer facilities has occurred. Having a portion of these facilities completed when the application is submitted indicates to the TWC that the developer is financially stable and capable of following through with the planned project. It also indicates to the TWC that the developer can comply with the 30 percent rule.[9]

Second, using water district bonds to finance facilities, the developer passes on much of the risk of development to others by deferring to them initial and long-term obligations. Just as in all business enterprises, the

---

[7]Water district bonds are tax exempt. These bonds sell at higher rates than municipal bonds (e.g., they are seldom backed by the full faith and credit of a district). However, they are marketed at lower interests rates than private bonds, which the developer would have to sell in the general market without their availability.

[8]A cursory examination of the TWC records indicates bond applications are rarely disapproved. For example, in fiscal year 1977, of the 103 applications submitted to the TWC not one was rejected. The 1977 record is not an unusual one (Texas Water Rights Commission, *Thirty-third Annual Report for the Fiscal Year 1977*, A-48, A-54.

[9]Interview with water district attorney of Fullbright and Jaworski, Houston, TX.

developer invests his assets, time, and reputation in a project. However, soon after he does so, the water district assists him in passing the burden to others. Some of the water district's upfront costs can be transferred to builders to whom the developer sells lots. The faster houses are constructed and sold, the faster the developer's initial costs can be recouped. Moreover, as houses are sold the bond obligation is spread over a larger number of residents. While district bonds support the costs of development, the developer is absolved of assuming the obligation for this debt even during the start-up phases of a project. The developer is at the center of all initial district activities and functions by (1) hiring the engineer to design district facilities; (2) selecting the attorney to establish the legal structure of the district and to make it a public entity; (3) determining who the first directors will be; (4) controlling when and by whom the bonds will be marketed; and (5) supervising construction. But homeowners assume the obligation for paying back the bonds as developments pass into their "public" control.

Summary

MUDs are empowered by the state to provide public services, to raise revenues, and to have a governing board. They surround Houston on all sides of its borders. As Table 7.2 shows, the number of districts has steadily increased in the postwar years; and starting in the mid-1960s, they proliferated rapidly each year thereafter.

Districts are territorially and fiscally important to developers and public entities, especially Houston. Individual districts are usually very small, but collectively they blanket a sizable part of Harris County's unincorporated territory and provide basic service to much of the population living in those areas. As shown in Table 7.2, districts are also financially significant (e.g., over a 35-year period over $2.2 billion in district bonds was authorized to provide capital for suburban developments).

Since MUDs are the principal service system used in Houston's ETJ, they take on added significance in the area's growth, especially in contributing to Houston's enormous territorial growth since World War II. Districts provide land developers with a substantial amount of capital to build service facilities to support residential, commercial, and industrial projects, effectively allowing them to use districts as extensions of their own businesses to finance this construction. As a result, suburban development is essentially shaped by the happenstance of economic conditions, land ownership, and developers' plans.

MUD use does not intrude on Houston's authority, so city officials have encouraged and supported their use by private developers. Districts lessen political and fiscal responsibilities for the public, generally, and city and county governments, specifically. The boundaries of districts may be tailor-fitted to the developer's land, thus neither the city nor the county is obligated to finance capital construction costs of facilities to serve general areas of development. Basic service structures are built and financed neighborhood-by-neighborhood without increasing city or county debt; without diminishing city or county authorities (MUDs are service units, not regulatory ones); and without obligating the public at-large to pay for fringe area developments. Once suburban developments have reached a favorable debt-to-tax ratio, Houston has annexed.

THE TERRITORIAL IMPERATIVE IN METROPOLITAN DEVELOPMENT

Houston grew steadily over the first 100 years of its existence, reaching a size of 72.8 square miles by 1940. After World War II, circumstances abruptly changed. As shown in Table 7.3, from 1949 to 1956, Houston's size quadrupled to 349.4 square miles. Through the 1960s and 1970s, Houston continued to expand its borders, although at a decelerated pace. Today, Houston sprawls across 579.6 square miles, an area roughly equivalent to the combined sizes of New York, Chicago, and Philadelphia.

Annexations through the postwar era have had a profound impact on Houston's population size. As shown in Table 7.4, if Houston's 1940 boundaries were in place today, its 1980 population would have been 76 percent smaller (385,000 compared with 1,593,000). Furthermore, Houston's 1940 population of 384,514 would have decreased to 375,467 by 1980. In effect, without the opportunity to annex over the last four decades, Houston's population growth would have resembled other locked-in central cities.

Since World War II, Houston's annexations have evolved through three stages. First, through the 1950s, massive, around-the-city annexations were undertaken to gain control of surrounding territory. Second, in the 1960s through the mid-1970s, protective annexations occurred to surround important resources (e.g., Lake Houston) and to control an existing and future tax base (e.g., the evolving developments of southeast

Table 7.3. *Territorial Growth of the City of Houston: 1949-1986*

Year	Major Annexation	Mayor	Area Annexed (Square Miles)	City Total (Square Miles)
1949	Around City	Oscar F. Holcombe	83.7	159.7
1950			.2	159.9
1951			2.1	162.0
1952			1.1	163.1
1953		Roy M. Hofheinz	.3	163.4
1954			.8	164.2
1956	Around City	Oscar F. Holcombe	184.8	349.0
1958		Lewis W. Cutrer	.4	349.4
1959			.1	349.5
1960			1.5	351.0
1961			.4	351.4
1962	Jetero Airport	Lewis W. Cutrer	10.0	359.2 [a]
1963	Southeast Strip		.1	359.9
	(Brock Park);		.4	
	Radial Strips		.2	
1965	Southeast Harris	Louie Welch		446.8
	Co. Bayport		19.8	
	Lake Houston-			
	Intercont.			
	Airport		50.8	
	Other Areas		16.3	
1966			.1	446.9
1967			5.7 [b]	452.6
1968			-2.7	449.9
1969			3.6	453.5
1970	Pasadena-Houston			
	Exchange		-8.1 [b]	446.7
			1.3	
1971			5.7	452.4
1972	Addicks-Baker		48.7	506.2
	Res.			
1973			-5.5 [b]	500.7
1974		Fred Hofheinz	2.3	503.0
1975			5.7	508.7
1977	Clear Lake	Fred Hofheinz	14.7	542.4 [a]
1978		Jim McConn	14.0	557.8 [b]
1982		Kathy Whitmire		566.6

1984	574.5
1986	579.4

*Takes into account areas deannexed in this year.
ᵇTotal for annexations and deannexations.

Table 7.4. **Population Comparisons for Houston's City Limits By Decade**

Area Considered	Population by Decade (in 100,000)				
	1940	1950	1960	1970	1980
1940 Limits	385	457	423	402	375
1940-49 Annexations		139	268	358	336
1950-59 Annexations			247	405	563
1960-69 Annexations				68	88
1970-79 Annexations					231
Totals	385	596	938	1,233	1,593

Source: U.S. Bureau of Census as disaggregated by city of Houston Department of Planning and Development, Research Section. (This is a slight revision of data presented by Margaret K. Purser and Mary P. Beeman, "Implementing Equality: The Voting Rights Act and Its Impact on Municipal Government," paper presented at the Southwestern Political Science Association Annual Meeting, Dallas, Texas, March 18-21, 1987.)

Harris County). Third, in the 1970s and 1980s, annexations became more selective and piecemeal. During each stage, political compromises determined the territorial patterns of cities in the area; however, such compromises became more difficult to attain locally. In the initial stage, territorial disputes were settled almost entirely in the local arena or in the courts. In the second and third stages, other governments became involved. Today, the territorial development of cities in Harris County is a complex intergovernmental process.

Stage I: Massive, Around-the-City, Annexations

Since the late 1940s, annexation plans have been designed and led through the political process by Houston's mayors.   Mayor Oscar Holcombe's aggressive use of the city's annexation authority in the massive 1949 and 1956 annexations became the prototype for future mayors.   Holcombe leadership in reshaping city government was also important. After his election in 1947, Holcombe obtained voter approval of a charter change that abolished the city manager position and established the mayor as chief executive with extensive appointment and budgeting powers.   Since that change, the key public decisions about annexations have been made in the mayor's office.[10]

Using his newly acquired authority, Holcombe moved swiftly to curb suburb city development in 1949 and 1956.   In each of these years, he presented plans to the council that proposed doubling the city's size. The council immediately adopted the 1949 and 1956 proposals on a first reading.   As shown in Map 7.2, these two annexations doubled and redoubled the city's territorial size in less than 10 years.

For Holcombe and other city leaders, suburban city development had to be prevented.   The prevailing attitude was a "bigger Houston is a better, more economically prosperous Houston."   The appeal for public support in both 1949 and 1956 was based on civic pride and competiveness to make Houston the growth capital of Texas and the South.   For example, in 1956, Holcombe argued that the massive annexation was needed to reflect the "true growth situation" of Houston. He argued that

---

[10]Houston received its charter from the legislature in 1905.   A commission-style of government was established with four aldermen to fill designated administrative positions (e.g., tax and land; streets and bridges; water; and fire).   Severe polio and diphtheria epidemics struck Houston in the early 1940s.   A laggard governmental response was blamed on a patronage-laden commission government.   Voters then approved an amendment to the charter to create a council-manager form of government in 1942.   The eight-member, at-large council appointed the manager and acted like a board of directors.   The mayor was little more than a ceremonial figure.   After only four years, the manager-system was replaced by a strong-mayor government by simply taking the manager's charter powers and giving them to the mayor.   A strong-mayor, eight- member council arrangement remained until 1979, when the council was enlarged to 14 members (nine elected from districts and five elected at-large).

Map 7.2. *Houston Annexations*

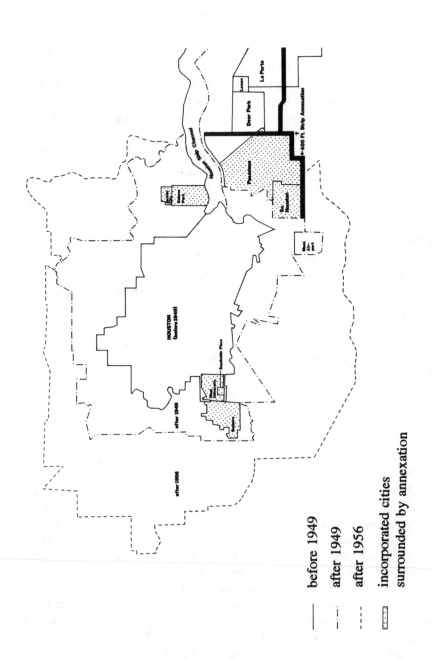

unincorporated areas were growing faster than the city, which was discouraging corporate growth in Houston. Holcombe reasoned, since corporations base their location decisions on indices such as building permits and since building permits are required only inside the city, rapid suburban growth diminished Houston's chance of capturing the amount of corporate growth that it should. The public, along with its leadership, felt that Houston should be the growth capital. Annexation was the most optimal method to continue Houston's growth rate.

During Houston's 1949 annexation, suburbanites in a number of communities formed committees to support being annexed by Houston, reasoning that "better" services were available in the central city. Additional annexations by Houston seemed to portend a more integrated service structure for the metropolitan area, but ironically it had an opposite affect. Twelve suburban cities immediately began capital improvement programs to quiet citizen complaints. The most extensive programs were initiated by cities most directly affected by Houston's annexations.

Houston also felt pressured to provide new services. Industrial, commercial, and residential developments outside Houston had to be supported by basic water, sewer, and drainage facilities not provided by Harris County. As explained above, MUDs are the principal public entity providing these services in the unincorporated environs.

With the 1956 annexation, water districts became an especially thorny problem for Houston officials. As noted, districts support suburban developments without obligating Houston to capital improvement costs. When Houston annexes and assumes the bonded indebtedness of districts along with their facilities, that can be either good or bad. In the mid-1950s, the consequences were mostly bad. Houston officials felt they could not profitably annex many of the new districts, but neither could they wait for suburbanization to encircle the city. The latter consideration prevailed, and districts were annexed.

Twenty-six districts with bond indebtedness totaling $36.5 million were taken in the 1956 annexation, but only nine districts with indebtedness of $4.25 million were annexed in 1949. Many Houstonians, generally supportive of the annexation, were outraged by the assumption of this debt. Mayor Holcombe tried to still their concerns by producing evidence to show that taxes from the new areas offset the city's costs in servicing district bonds. He did not indicate, however, that over the next several years, city services would have to be extended to the new subdivisions.

Problems of implementing the 1956 annexation (e.g., servicing the water districts and the land area acquired) influenced the annexation strategy of Mayor Lewis Cutrer, Holcombe's successor.

Doubling Houston's size twice in less than 10 years created a political dilemma for city officials. Rather than operate under city codes and restrictions, private developers hopscotched across large tracts of undeveloped land inside Houston to build homes, businesses, and industries in unincorporated areas. A rash of water districts was created to finance services for these developments. By the late 1950s, unincorporated areas were again growing more rapidly than Houston.

Changing economic and political conditions necessitated a new annexation approach. Mayor Cutrer was still committed to city growth, just like his predecessor. The consequences of enormous land acquisitions, however, forced him to arrive at this goal through different means. In response to the problems of implementing the 1956 annexation, Cutrer and the council adopted a new annexation policy. While the cornerstone of the new policy was a reaffirmation of earlier policy that annexations should be used to protect the city's territorial integrity, it departed from Holcombe's approach by advocating more deliberate, planned annexations. It held that land should be annexed before it is subdivided to ensure the enforcement of city building codes, the integration of suburban water and sewer systems with city facilities, and the prevention of new incorporations. Cutrer said the new policy was needed to stop the proliferation of water districts and to force developers to start projects inside the city or pay a share of the cost of capital improvements in the county. Otherwise, Houston would have to assume large debts when these areas were annexed or face new suburban incorporations if they did not annex.

Stage II: Protective Annexations

The new annexation policy was short-lived. The 1949 and 1956 annexations established Houston's geographic dominance over other Harris County cities and effectively stopped new incorporations; however, lucrative tax plums of existing and planned developments in unincorporated areas were still outside Houston's jurisdiction. The tax potential of these developments did not escape the watchful eyes of suburban leaders who wanted their communities to grow and reap the benefits of economic development just as Houston was doing.

In 1960, suburbanites demonstrated they too could use their annexation authority aggressively. On June 6, 1960, the councils of Pasadena, Lomax, LaPorte, and Deer Park passed annexation ordinances annexing 106 square miles of territory in southeast Harris County. Pasadena claimed 77 square miles; LaPorte, 20; Deer Park, 2; and Lomax, 7. Following the four cities' annexations, a number of small Gulf Coast cities in other counties passed ordinances expanding their limits by hundreds of square miles. The most extraordinary example was in Nederland, a 4.3 square mile city in Jefferson County, whose council planned to annex 655 square miles.

These annexations precipitated a state legislative investigation into the annexation authority of home-rule cities. That investigation had both short- and long-term consequences on Houston's annexations. It began the formulation of the MAA of 1963. Anticipating the MAA passage, Cutrer downplayed the significance of the annexations of neighboring cities. Cutrer felt any large-scale annexation by Houston in reaction to those annexations would hasten legislative controls, especially since suburban interests were finding sympathy from small town and rural legislators.

Cutrer thus fashioned a two-step strategy. He wanted to quell opposition to his annexation policy within the city, and he wanted to avoid an outright confrontation with suburban city leaders. To hold his own ranks together, he assured the council that Houston had a superior legal claim to the territories annexed by the suburban cities because one city—Pasadena—has illegally broached Houston's boundaries when it annexed land in southeast Harris County. Second, Cutrer sought a compromise with the four cities' mayors by offering to relinquish some of the territory Houston had acquired in 1949, if the mayors gave up part of their annexed land.

Cutrer's strategy received a cold reception from council members and prominent civic leaders. Some segments of Houston's leadership advocated a "Holcombe" response. Their solution was to annex the entire county! The council rejected Cutrer's argument that Houston could afford to negotiate because it enjoyed a superior legal position. "If we have such a strong legal position," they reasoned, "why should we give up anything?" Three council members, therefore, introduced a plan to annex 34 square miles of the same territory that Pasadena had claimed. Also introduced at the same session was an ordinance to annex all of Harris County. Although Cutrer argued vehemently that the 34 square mile annexation was unnecessary (i.e., if Houston's legal position was secure, then Pasadena's annexation was illegal; but if it was not, then Pasadena had a first-right claim to the land anyway), he finally agreed to this annexation when the council came close to adopting the countywide proposal.

With this, the four mayors broke off negotiations with Cutrer. To make matters worse, only hours after Houston's council rejected the countywide proposal, Tomball, a small community in northwest Harris County, annexed a sizable tract of land. The next morning the council of Baytown, a small industrial city to the east of Houston, passed a 110 square mile annexation plan. Forty of these square miles were in Harris County and included industrial areas along the Houston Ship Channel. Houston's council immediately reconvened and passed on first reading the countywide proposal over Cutrer's objections. The countywide annexation changed the scope of the controversy. It foreclosed hopes of a negotiated settlement. All sides prepared for a protracted battle, which would now shift to the courts.

After a series of court cases, Houston's superior legal claim to the land was upheld. These court cases and the 1963 legislative actions settled the legal and political issues surrounding the June 1960 annexations. Houston's claim to the developments of southeast Harris County was solidified in its court battles with Pasadena and the other Harris County cities. The ETJ provision of the MAA gave Houston the same control over the metropolitan area that was enjoyed with the countywide annexation. (Houston ensured its countywide control by annexing 10-foot strips along major highways to extend its ETJ control over the entire county.) Still, Houston had to be concerned with metropolitan growth. Subdivisions, industrial plants, and commercial enterprises were sprouting on all sides of the city.

These growth conditions necessitated protective annexations around the city. Mayor Lewis Welch proposed, first, annexing a narrow 21.4 mile-long strip extending eastward from the southeast corner of the city all the way to Galveston Bay. This strip would encircle the all-important southeast Harris County developments. Next, Welch's plan advocated annexing another 87 square miles including: 50.8 square miles to the north and northeast to encircle Lake Houston, the city of Humble, and fringe developments around the planned airport; and four tracts on the west and southwest sides totaling 36.1 square miles. (See Map 7.3.)

While the 1965 annexation was intended to accomplish what earlier ones had (expansion and protection of the tax base, prevention of new

Map 7.3. *Houston's 1965 Annexations to Protect Resources and Territory*

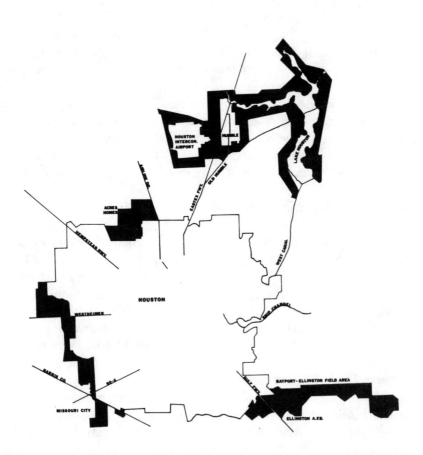

incorporations and continued growth), new and more complicated reasons motivated Welch's proposal. First, there was a need to protect Houston's surface water supply. City officials could not tolerate the deterioration of Lake Houston, which was a distinct possibility without the imposition of some pollution control standards. Second, there was a need to ensure the success of the city's new intercontinental airport.[11] Third, the MAA created overlapping ETJs for some Harris County cities, and unincorporated areas outside any city's jurisdiction. Aggressive annexation of selected areas would prevent encroachment by other home-rule cities. The annexation in southeast Harris County would solidify Houston's control over the southeast development around NASA—Johnson Space Center—by preventing future annexations by Pasadena, Deer Park, LaPorte, or other home-rule cities. It would also give Houston control over Bayport, a community that was attempting to incorporate, and the huge Humble Oil and Refining Company's Bayport project near NASA.

Stage III: Piecemeal Annexations

Many city officials still prefer to capture suburban growth in much the same fashion as it had been done during the first stage. As a top planning official put it: "Large-scale annexations are being planned for in the future, especially after the 1990 census." However, certain political realities now prevent that from happening. With large-scale annexations, Houston would face horrendous service delivery cost problems (indeed some areas taken in 1956 still do not have city water services). Next, a large and growing suburban population would undoubtedly unleash a strong legislative protest, thus adding to the stakes. Then, there would be strong opposition from innercity minorities who do not want their growing political strength diluted. Cumulatively, these factors have forced Houston to undertake smaller, piecemeal annexations over the last decade. Perhaps the single most important impediment to

---

[11]The annexation was necessary to acquire federal dollars for airport construction. To meet federal conditions, the city had to establish a protective zone around the airport to ensure safe air operations. Although Houston had a long history of rejecting all forms of zoning and city officials had foregone federal dollars for public housing because of zoning requirements, federal funds were considered crucial to the airport's immediate success. Mayor Welch and other city leaders were willing to set aside their aversion to federal strings in the case of capital construction funding.

Houston's continued use of annexation will come from the application of the U.S. Voting Rights Act.

APPLYING THE U.S. VOTING RIGHTS ACTS

Texas was not included under the provisions of the 1965 U.S. Voting Rights Act (VRA) or its 1970 extension. In 1975, the VRA was extended to Texas, and the state became an active source of VRA disputes. Of 7,470 electoral changes reviewed in 1975, 4,694 (62.8 percent) were from Texas (Cotrell 1980). Section 5 of the VRA says that changes in a local government's electoral system cannot be altered without prior approval of the U.S. attorney general or a declaratory judgment from the district court for the District of Columbia (Public Law No. 89-110, 1965). In practice, most localities have submitted proposed changes to the attorney general and have only gone to court if their plan was rejected (Zimmerman 1978, 621-60). The amendments in 1975 not only extended the act's provisions to Texas but also made a significant change in Section 5 by making it applicable to language minorities as well as blacks.

This change has become a stumbling block to large-scale annexations by Houston, because it prevents alterations in the city population that diminish minority voting strength or minority representation in the councils of government. When these circumstances are considered in light of Houston's 1980 population that was 46 percent minorities (28 percent blacks and 18 percent Mexican American), then the impact is apparent. Furthermore, when Asians reach five percent of the population, which will likely happen after the 1990 census, they must also be considered.

Houston's At-Large Council System

Since 1942, Houston's charter required the at-large election of all eight council members. (Five, however, had to live in and "represent" geographic areas.) Minorities, thus, had to compete against a citywide, white-dominated, electorate with a history of racial voting with regard to minority candidates. Like other cities with similar systems, Houston's at-large elections, citywide voting majorities, and traditions of racial voting severely disadvantaged minority candidates (Jones 1976, 345-56; Karnig 1976, 223-42). Houston's practice of annexing large suburban areas has also worked against minorities' efforts to gain electoral power.

Postwar annexations added white suburbs to Houston and moderated the proportionate growth of minorities inside the city, preventing minorities from gaining significant voting power. Houston's widespread use of annexations, thus, have placed minorities in a somewhat different situation from their counterparts in New Orleans, Atlanta, Chicago, and Birmingham where minorities (blacks) have been able to win citywide elections despite racial voting patterns.

Despite the council's weak role in city governance, critics made it the focal point for political reform. Blacks and Mexican Americans consistently emphasized the underrepresentation of minorities on the council. Other groups, convinced that a reformed council would make city government more responsive to their concerns, joined with minorities in attacking the representation of the council.

Initiative for council reform originated in several diverse ways. Starting in the late 1950s, proposals were made for single-member districts. These efforts intensified in the early 1970s when mayoral candidates began raising the single-member district issue and pledged to work for such a structure if elected. Finally, proponents of the district concept mounted petition drives in an effort to require a public vote. None of these efforts was successful.

Council members were understandably reluctant to change the election system under which they had won and held their seats. The council did allow a nonbinding straw vote on single-member districts to be placed on the 1975 city ballot. The proposal was approved by 54.8 percent of those voting. While blacks and Mexican Americans favored the change by almost 3 to 1, whites were slightly opposed. The council ignored the results. After all, the at-large system worked well for the incumbents, especially since each lacked a partisan or neighborhood political base from which to launch a winning campaign in smaller districts. The council's reluctance to act meant that reform advocates faced an arduous task locally. Thus, they sought assistance outside Houston to secure internal reforms.

The first step in the extracommunity process occurred in federal court. The impetus was the election of Mayor Fred Hofheinz in 1973. He campaigned for council reform, and he was elected with black support. Advocates for council reform thought the time was ripe; therefore, they challenged the city's at-large council system in federal court. The legal avenue was the principle of equal protection of the law as defined by the U.S. Supreme Court's decisions in *Westbury v. Sanders* and *Reynolds v. Sims* (376 U.S. 1, 1964 and 377 U.S. 533, 1964). Their efforts were immediately stymied when the judge delayed hearing the case—a delay that lasted three years. The 1975 changes in the VRA allowed the plaintiffs in the pending lawsuit—just 15 days after the VRA's provisions became effective in Texas—to file a second suit charging that the city of Houston had violated the VRA by not seeking approval by the U.S. Department of Justice (DOJ) for various annexations since 1972. The suit asked that (1) the city be enjoined from holding its 1975 general election; (2) the DOJ object to the annexations because they diluted minority voting strength; and (3) Houston be required to revise its charter to allow future councils to be elected from single-member districts.

Houston survived this challenge. The DOJ chose not to enter the suit. In 1976, DOJ officials informed the city that it would not object to its annexations and would require no change in its council election system. When the court case was finally heard in late 1976, Houston's attorneys countered charges that the at-large system was inherently discriminatory or that it placed insurmountable obstacles to the election of minority candidates. The city's position was that while few minorities were elected under the at-large system, that did not diminish city services to these groups because all members of the council had to be responsive to minority voters since they constituted a sizable part of the electorate. The trial judge sided with the city, concluding that the plaintiffs had "failed to prove that the city discriminates against minorities in providing city services or that minorities are denied access to processes of city government" (*Houston Chronicle*, March 8, 1977, 1).

Houston's 1977 and 1978 Annexations

Certain policy pursuits have a momentum of their own. That was certainly true of Houston's postwar annexation policy. Territorial growth was deemed to be a vital part of Houston's continued progress, especially since new developments were sprouting all around Houston. Houston officials were alarmed by this occurrence. The potential of suburban encirclement anywhere on Houston's borders, loss of the city's future tax base, and increased minority numbers in the inner city—all perceived to be avoidable through annexations of unincorporated areas—led to a series of annexation proposals at the end of 1977 by outgoing Mayor Fred Hofheinz. These proposals were then supported in 1978 by Hofheinz's successor, Jim McConn. The council approved an annexation plan to take in about 75 square miles of territory containing more than 150,000 people, most of whom where middle-income whites. This action was strongly supported by the Chamber of Commerce and established business interests.

Houston's desire for territory overrode some changed circumstances. Business and developer interests, traditionally in favor of annexations, strongly pressured council to act decisively. Furthermore, the mayor and council were not concerned about legal complications, because the legal department had assured them that Houston was not covered by the VRA and did not need DOJ approval for the annexation. Therefore, the city did not even submit its 1977 and 1978 annexation plans to the DOJ for review and clearance.

The opportunity was thus ripe for the proponents of single-member districts to seek a solution through the courts. In the summer of 1978, the plaintiffs in the earlier suit on appeal in the U.S. Fifth Circuit Court urged the DOJ to use the VRA to block Houston's annexations. The DOJ, accepting their premise, joined the plaintiffs by asking the appeals court to vacate the earlier decision that upheld Houston's at-large elections (*Houston Post*, September 14, 1978,: 1). One week later, the DOJ filed suit against the city for failing to secure approval for the 1977 and 1978 annexation plans and then blocked all municipal elections until the issue could be settled.

After six months of review, the DOJ formally objected to the annexations on the ground that they had reduced minority voting percentages. The head of the civil rights division of the DOJ, Drew Days III, informed Houston officials that the DOJ would consider withdrawing its objection if the city adopted a system "in which blacks and Mexican Americans are afforded representation reasonably equivalent to their political strength." Days indicated that such representation "would include the election of some (not all) city council members from single-member districts, if the districts are fairly drawn and if the number of districts is sufficient to enable both blacks and Mexican Americans to elect candidates of their choice" (letter of Attorney General Edward H. Levy, April 2, 1976).

Adoption of the Nine-Five Council Plan

The DOJ's decision started a process of local negotiations to change Houston's council. The solution emerged from the mayor and council and traditional power brokers in the city—not from the advocates of council reform. Understanding that change was inevitable, the mayor and council tried to devise what they regarded as the best solution. What they came up with was a plan for a mixed council of nine members elected from districts and five members elected at-large. But, while they understood that change had to come, they did not give up trying to hold onto the status quo. When the city council scheduled an August 11, 1979 vote on the 9-5 plan, it also attempted to put another proposition on the same ballot to retain the existing system. Acting as the referee, the DOJ refused to allow voting on anything except the 9-5 plan. Tacitly, the DOJ put its stamp of approval on the 9-5 plan.

In a strange twist of circumstances, almost all of the long-established opponents to the council change lined up to campaign for the proposed change. These champions of the 9-5 plan included such earlier stalwarts of no-change as business leaders, the Chamber of Commerce, and the mayor and council. However, most of the reform advocates who had worked long and hard to come to this point now found themselves opposed to the council change. Blacks and Mexican Americans—joined by labor leaders, neighborhood activists, and recently annexed suburbanites—wanted a 20-member council with at least 16 district seats.

In the campaign that ensued, local political clout was the decisive factor, not DOJ intervention. On the one hand, the 9-5 opponents were at a severe disadvantage, as they had been historically when they attempted to contest citywide elections. They hastily put together a "Citizens Coalition for Responsive Government," but could raise only $4,595. They could not even buy a 30-second, prime time TV commercial. On the other hand, a blue-ribbon group of Houston's most prominent business leaders was assembled. That group quickly raised almost $200,000 to put together a media campaign supporting the charter change. These efforts were supported by many large business firms that urged their employees to vote for the proposal.

The die was cast. On election day, with only an 11 percent turnout of eligible voters, the 9-5 plan passed almost 2-to-1. As shown in Table 7.5, the margin of victory was attributable to the far heavier turnout in affluent and middle-class white areas (22 and 13 percent) than elsewhere in the city. Moreover, despite the favorable vote, the electorate voted along racial lines. The plan was opposed by 91 percent of the blacks and 77 percent of the Mexican Americans who voted. On the other hand, whites strongly favored the plan, except those whites in newly annexed areas: Clear Lake, where 92 percent opposed and Alief, where 53 percent opposed.

Table 7.5. **Voting Patterns on the Nine-Five Council Plan**

Precinct groupings	Percent turnout	Percent for	Percent against	N precincts
Affluent white	22	94	6	5
Middle-class white	13	85	15	10
Working-class white	6	70	30	5
Homogeneous black	7	9	91	10
Predominantly Mexican American	6	23	77	4
City Totals	11	64	36	

The last remaining step was to draw district lines. Again, the DOJ largely left the decision to the city's traditional power brokers, although the DOJ retained its position as rules interpreter. With the aid of three outside consultants (recommended by DOJ staff), Houston drew various district plans. Each was based on population estimates for 1979, which had the effect of shifting more representation to fast-growing suburbs, rather than on official 1970 census counts, which would have favored minorities. Although strong objections came from blacks and Mexican Americans, the DOJ approved the city's district plan even though the plan did not maximize minority political influence.

CONCLUSIONS

The activities of government during the development of the Houston metropolitan area since World War II have generally facilitated the objectives of private economic interests. Government initiatives and responses were interrelated in most cases with the marketplace activities of private economic interests. Yet, government was not passive: it established the "rules of the game" to allow marketplace activities to be the driving force behind local decisions.

As the preceding analysis has shown, Texas constitutional and statutory authorities were extraordinarily beneficial in providing a setting for local governance to support the economic and territorial objectives of land developers and the city of Houston. In many ways through such constitutional authority as home-rule and MUD creations, opportunities were provided for economic interests to maximize their objectives. Legislative extension of these authorities in the MAA of 1963, various acts related to the creation of water districts, as well as others established a framework within which the courts and bureaucracy could legitimate and sustain economic initiatives.

Several consequences have resulted from these arrangements. First, various types of local governments respond to urban growth. As shown above, suburbanization in the Houston metropolitan area is serviced by activities of the state, county, city, and special districts. Furthermore, public authorities are in a cooperative relationship with private interests (e.g., land developers), thus an integration of public and private interests occurs out of this diverse response to urban growth. This is a relative rather than an absolute integration. Jacob and Teune (1964, 7) tell us "political integration [is not] a specific condition that exists or does not exist [rather it is] a set of relationships which are more or less integrated, or a progression of events leading to an increase or decrease of integration."

Second, through most of the postwar years, Houston has dominated urban growth decision making. Governing "rules"—derived mainly from the Texas Constitution and statutes and embellished locally—have created a context for the city of Houston to be the center of urban growth decision making. Several key factors contribute to Houston's dominance. For one, county governments in Texas are subordinate to home-rule cities in urban growth decision making mainly because they operate under nineteenth century structures and processes. Next, a system of independent school districts and special-purpose districts, on one hand, diminish the central city's suburban infrastructure responsibilities (e.g., the city does not participate in the cost of providing water, sewer, drainage, roads, as well as others); but, on the other hand, does not prevent the city from either annexing across suburban jurisdictions (e.g., when Houston annexes, independent school districts remain intact) or absorbing districts into its jurisdiction (e.g., when the city annexes, MUDs are abolished and Houston acquires their assets and liabilities).

Third, private economic interests (e.g., land developers) have been able to focus on Houston city government and politics (or city hall decision making) to advocate their causes, rather than on numerous incorporated suburban cities. The structure of suburban governments that has facilitated Houston's political dominance has also prevented suburbanites from gaining political control over growth and development policies in their own areas—a typical occurrence in many metropolitan areas. As urban populations across the U.S. dispersed rapidly in the 20th century, suburban areas incorporated and typically gained legal powers equal to those of central cities. Suburban communities often used their autonomy to practice a politics of exclusion, designed to preserve local privilege or segregation (Judd 1979, 365). A fragmentation of local governmental structure and dispersal of local authority made it difficult for business and other economic interests usually based in central cities to extend their influence throughout the entire metropolitan area.

Houston business leaders and other economic interests have not encountered this difficulty. Just as in other urban areas, the Houston metropolitan area population dispersed outside the central city. Although developers' use of MUDs contributed to suburban sprawl, Houston's aggressive annexations in the 1940s, 1950s, and 1960s stifled new incorporations and brought suburban growth into the city's borders. When annexations were slowed in the 1970s, Houston had extraterritorial jurisdiction to block new incorporations where developments were located or could occur. Thus, unlike what happened in many other metropolitan areas, suburban-central city conflicts were largely avoided because there were no serious challenges to city political dominance over the metropolitan area. Consequently, business and economic interests centered their attention on city politics. Urban growth decision making thus largely came down to what was decided within the city of Houston, greatly enhancing the political influence of those who could capture positions of power in the city, especially the mayor's office.

The structure of suburban authorities coupled with Houston's home-rule authority, the ability to annex, and extensive ETJ control creates the framework for urban growth decision making. However, as illustrated, this framework is changing. On one hand, some changes have been slow and subtle. In the use of MUDs, for example, initially developers had almost a free-rein to do as they wished. Then, more controls were imposed by both the state and the city. On the other hand, some changes have been abrupt, such as the application of the VRA. But, even when the VRA was applied, Houston officials still decided the details of the change (e.g., a nine-five plan), although their decision was subjected to "outside" rules monitored by national bureaucrats.

REFERENCES

Cotrell, Charles. 1980. *A Report on the Participation of Mexican Americans, Blacks and Females in the Political Institutions and Processes of Texas.* Austin: Texas Advisory Council.

Governor's Report. 1975. *Texas Land Use.* Austin, Texas.

Houston Chronicle, various dates.

Houston Post, various dates.

Jackson, Kenneth T. 1972. Metropolitan Government Versus Suburban Autonomy: Politics on the Crabgrass Frontier. In *Cities in American History,* ed. Kenneth T. Jackson and Stanley K. Schultz, New York: Knopf.

Jacob, Philip E., and Henry Teune. 1964. The Integrative Process: Guidelines for Analysis of the Bases of Political Community. In *The Integration of Political Communities,* ed. Phillip E. Jacob and James V. Toxcanco, New York: J. B. Lippincott.

Jones, Clinton. 1976. The Impact of Local Election Systems on Black Political Representation. *Urban Affairs Quarterly* 11: 345-56.

Judd, Dennis R. 1979. *The Politics of American Cities: Private Power and Public Policy.* Boston: Little, Brown.

Karnig, Albert. 1976. The Impact of Local Election Systems on Black Political Representation. *Urban Affairs Quarterly* 11: 223-42.

Katz, Harvey. 1972. *Shadow on the Alamo: New Heros Fight Old Corruption in Texas Politics.* Garden City, New York: Doubleday.

Lawson, Veva Dianne. 1977. Municipal Utility Districts. A working paper prepared for the Southwest Center for Urban Research, Bates College of Law, University of Houston, September.

McCorkle, Stuart. 1963. *Municipal Annexation in Texas.* Austin: University of Texas Press.

Mitchell, John T. 1972. The Use of Special Districts in Financing and Facilitating Urban Growth. Rice University: Unpublished Master's Thesis.

Public Law No. 89-110. 1965.

Salamon, Lester M. 1977. Urban Politics, Urban Policy, Case Studies. *Public Administration Review* 37 (July/August): 424-25.

Schroer, Lee Charles. 1971. The Water Control and Improvement District: Concept, Creation and Critique. *Houston Law Review* 8 (March).

The State of Texas. 1963. Municipal Annexation Act. *General and Special Laws.* 57th Legislature, Ch. 160, 447-54.

Texas. *Constitution.* Art. 16, Section 59.

Texas Legislature, House. 1975. *Water Supply and Waste Disposal in Texas Urban Areas.* A Report by the House Interim Committee on Water Supply and Waste Disposal in the Metropolitan Area (January).

Texas Water Code, Ch. 54.201.

Texas Water Development Board, Section 156.06.30.006 (a).

Texas Water Rights Commission. 1977. *Thirty-Third Annual Report for the Fiscal Year 1977.* Austin, Texas.

U.S. Advisory Commission on Intergovernmental Relations. 1973. *Regional Decision Making,* Report A-43. Washington, D.C.: Government Printing Office, October 1973.

Wirt, Frederick M. 1975. Suburbs and Politics in America. *Publius: The Journal of Federalism* 5 (Winter): 129.

Zimmerman, Joseph F. 1978. The Federal Voting Rights Act and Alternative Election Systems. *William and Mary Law Review* 19 (Summer): 621-60.

Chapter 8

Governing Metropolitan Vancouver:
Regional Intergovernmental Relations in British Columbia

H. Peter Oberlander
University of British Columbia
Patrick J. Smith
Simon Fraser University

INTRODUCTION

The dynamics of public policymaking and local intergovernmental relations offer important foci for the comparative analysis of governance in North America's metropolitan regions. This chapter examines several key issues of public policymaking and process confronting urban development in metropolitan Vancouver; it assesses obstacles to effective governance in the metropolitan region; and it places these public policy

---

The authors have received financial support from the Donner Foundation and the Canadian Studies Program, University of California, Berkeley. Two grants from the Social Sciences and Humanities Research Council of Canada, and two from Employment Canada are also gratefully acknowledged. The authors also thank Frances Christopherson, Librarian at the Greater Vancouver Regional District (GVRD), and Greg Hazel, Jacqui Kenney, Natalie Minunzie, and Lisa Spitalli for research assistance. Finally, the authors thank Ken Cameron and Rick Hankin of the GVRD and provincial-government staff for providing both materials and interviews. All illustrations were provided courtesy of Ken Cameron, Manager, Development Services for GVRD and are from the agency's publications: *Freedom to Move* and *Creating Our Future*. His personal cooperation is gratefully acknowledged.

developments in the context of local-senior governmental relations in British Columbia (B.C.) and Canada.

BACKGROUND

Jane Jacobs contends that "city regions are not defined by natural boundaries," rather they are "artifacts of the cities at their nuclei" (Jacobs 1984, 45). In the same way, "metropolitan Vancouver" is a social fact, with the city of Vancouver at its center. The region exists independently of its governance; and, indeed, the governing of the Vancouver metropolitan area has often been substantially at odds with its social reality, though increasingly there is recognition that this need not be—and might not appropriately be—the case. This was illustrated during the campaign for the October 17, 1991, B.C. General Election, in policy statements by candidates for all parties and by municipal politicians. These included consistent "pitches" for a return/expansion of regional powers to the Greater Vancouver Regional District (GVRD) (Lee 1991).

In Canada, regional and local authorities are constitutional "creatures" of the provinces (Jones 1988; Smith 1988). While most are created by provisions of general municipal legislation, in British Columbia there are separate legislative enactments such as the City of Vancouver Charter and amendments such as those to the Municipal Act creating Regional Districts after 1965.

British Columbia, on the Pacific Coast, is Canada's third most populous province—3,131,700 citizens—representing approximately 12 percent of the total Canadian population (British Columbia, Ministry of Finance 1991). It is also Canada's third largest province (948,600 square kms), slightly larger than the states of Washington, Oregon, and California combined. Yet despite this size, 83 percent (almost 2.6 million) of the provincial population resides in 149 incorporated municipalities encompassing less than one percent of provincial territory (Canada, Statistics 1991).

Over half (1,711,915, 54.7 percent) the citizens of the province reside in the "Lower Mainland"—comprising four regional districts along the Fraser River Valley adjacent to Vancouver. This Lower Mainland is bounded on the south by the U.S. border, on the north by mountains that extend virtually without interruption to Alaska, and on the east by similar mountain ranges; its western extremity, including the city of Vancouver, is the gulf waters of the Pacific Ocean. In Jacobs' terms, this Lower Mainland forms one coherent city region (Jacobs 1984, 45-58).

Most of the Vancouver metropolitan area is contained within the Greater Vancouver Regional District. Established in 1967, the GVRD is currently an amalgam of 18 municipalities and three unincorporated electoral areas, covering just under 3,000 sq. kms at the mouth of the Fraser River. The Greater Vancouver Region contains a little under half (1,477,760 million, 47.2 percent) of the provincial population and a majority (eight of 12) of the largest (over 50,000 population) local authorities in the province. As of the October 17, 1991 B.C. General Election, the Vancouver metropolitan region has 35 of the 75 legislative seats, 47 percent of the provincial total. The current GVRD has 33 seats, 44 percent of the provincial total.

The Vancouver Census Metropolitan Area (CMA) is slightly larger than the GVRD. It is projected that this Vancouver region will grow to 1.8 million by the end of the century—and 2.5 million by 2040. Apart from the 18 municipalities and three electoral areas in the GVRD, three additional municipalities (Pitt Meadows, Maple Ridge, and Matsqui) belong for specific (water/sewage and/or parks) service functions. Current discussions suggest that the first two of these will join the GVRD, making the GVRD and the Vancouver CMA essentially the same (GVRD 1989b).

The somewhat larger "Pacific Fraser" region, utilized by Seelig and Artibise, is currently 1.7 million, with anticipated population growth to 2.7 million by 2010 (Seelig and Artibise 1991). The region is larger than the current Vancouver CMA; it includes the rest of the Lower Mainland, B.C.'s adjacent Sunshine Coast, and the area north/northwest of Vancouver, including the destination resort of Whistler. Other local notables have projected much more substantial population growth over the next 60 years—up to 10 million in one extreme case (Lee and Kines 1989). Whatever its growth potential, the fastest growing areas in the Vancouver metropolis are in the Fraser Valley suburbs within and beyond the eastern boundaries of the GVRD. By 2010, for example, GVRD projections have the Greater Vancouver suburb of Surrey surpassing the central city Vancouver, 550,000 to 540,000. Adjacent non-GVRD outer suburbs, such as Maple Ridge, Mission, Abbotsford/Matsqui, and Chilliwack are among the fastest growing areas in the province. Such growth will still result in a population density of only 493 persons per sq. km, compared with 3,467 for Metro Toronto and 6,591 for Montreal (GVRD 1990d).

Since its initial settlement more than a hundred years ago—the city of Vancouver was incorporated in 1886—the Lower Mainland has

Map 8.1.   ***GVRD Plus the Central Fraser Valley District and the Dewdney-Allouette Regional District Form Three Regional Districts in the Lower Mainland Valley***

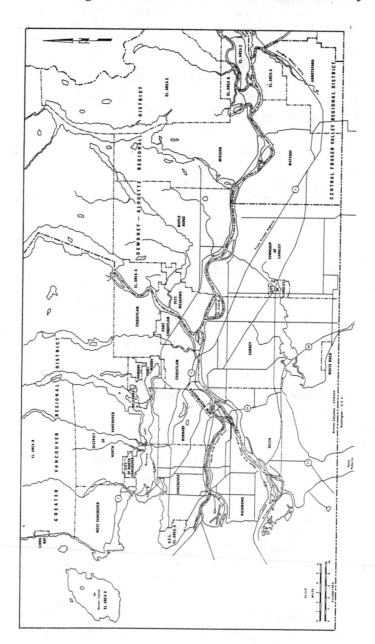

developed a distinctive cultural base—socially, economically, and politically. Metropolitan Vancouver residents are different from residents, for example, of the Peace River region in northern British Columbia (Dyck 1986, 511-12; Morley, et al. 1983). As elsewhere, this political culture is an important basis of the "local" political system. This is evident in such factors as the ethnic makeup of the region's population, which has become increasingly multicultural—almost half the public school population of Vancouver has English as a second language (Smith 1991). It is also demonstrated in the development of metropolitan Vancouver's economy. Much of the province's economy is resource extractive, with heavy reliance on logging, mining, and fishing. The economic base of the Lower Mainland, on the other hand, is increasingly service-oriented, with a strong reliance on personal and corporate services, including tourism, and provincewide distribution of goods and services. With its significant multicultural population, a more globally oriented regional economy, and its Pacific port location (the Port of Vancouver is the second busiest in North America), metropolitan Vancouver has become an international city (Cohn, Merrifield, and Smith 1989; Smith 1992).

Most of the best arable land in British Columbia is found in the Lower Mainland. Only one-quarter of the land in the province is suitable for *any* form of farming. Thus, the potential for policy conflicts and the necessity of devising regional solutions to resolve urban development problems—on such issues as land use, transportation, water, waste management, health, or parks and open space—become immediately apparent.

Three areas where policy dilemmas exist—on land-use planning, transportation, and parks/open space policy—form the case bases for this study of metropolitan Vancouver governance. The premise argued here is that metropolitan governance has emerged in place of metropolitan government in the Vancouver region: that is, metropolitanwide services and their spatial implications are managed regionally in the absence of metropolitan government. In certain instances, as the cases demonstrate, this involves local definitions of regional solutions to service challenges; in other cases, the provincial government has set regional policy solutions; and in still other situations, the regional district acts as the primary policy instigator. It is also the case that in metropolitan settings such as Vancouver, the federal government often has an important involvement (Oberlander and Symonds 1988).

REGIONAL GOVERNANCE IN GREATER VANCOUVER

In Vancouver, service challenges requiring regional solutions were apparent within 20 years of the city's 1886 incorporation. By 1911, the inability of the adjacent municipalities of Vancouver, Point Grey, South Vancouver, and Burnaby to respond individually to sewage treatment problems created the local impetus for a regional response. The municipalities established the Burrard Peninsula Joint Sewerage Committee; they funded a study that recommended "an ongoing cooperative response," and by 1914 had convinced the provincial government to create a Joint Sewerage and Drainage Board (GVRD 1979).

Other regional special-purpose agencies were established later: in 1926 the Greater Vancouver Water District and from 1936-1948 four area health/hospital boards (Higgins 1979, 124-62; Bish 1990, 35-62). In 1948, under provisions of the Municipal Act allowing for contiguous local authorities in a metropolitan area to develop a joint land-use planning capacity, the Lower Mainland Regional Planning Board (LMRPB) was established. Tennant and Zirnhelt have persuasively argued that the proliferation and success of these early joint boards and authorities led the way to provincial consideration of more regional solutions to urban development problems, particularly with regard to their application in metropolitan Vancouver (Tennant and Zirnhelt 1973, 124-38).

Perhaps the most successful of the special regional authorities was the LMRPB. The Social Credit provincial government led by W. A. C. Bennett (first elected in 1952) had the advantage of reviewing the early experience of metropolitan government in Ontario. In 1957, community and regional planning provisions were added to the Municipal Act that empowered the minister to direct adjacent municipalities in metropolitan areas to establish a joint committee "to study and report on such matters of an intermunicipal nature as shall be set out by the Minister. . . . " The LMRPB was able to produce an official regional plan for the Lower Mainland, but as the LMRPB was moving toward this success in the mid 1960s, the provincial government, perhaps feeling threatened, determined that administrative and political diffusion was a more appropriate response. Accordingly, a regional district system for the entire province was created in 1965-67. As stated by Municipal Affairs Minister Dan Campbell, the B.C. government's intention was clear: "Regional districts are not conceived as a fourth level of government, but as a functional rather than a political amalgamation" (British Columbia, Department of Municipal Affairs 1972).

As a result, the Lower Mainland was divided into four separate regions. Within the GVRD (originally incorporated as the Regional District of Fraser Burrard on June 29, 1967), as elsewhere in the system, there were two types of functions. First, there were *mandated functions*, including general planning for the region as well as governing the hospital district. In Greater Vancouver, mandated functions also included Water Board and Sewage and Drainage District responsibilities. Second, there were 78 *voluntary functions*. Each district could choose the ones it wished to perform (British Columbia 1989d).

In the context of these changing and evolving regional administrative responsibilities, this study will assess the interplay of local, regional, and senior (provincial and federal) authorities in dealing with urban development in the Lower Mainland and in governing metropolitan Vancouver. The reality that emerges is one of considerable governmental interplay, at times in conflict, at times cooperative, and in some instances benignly neglectful by local or senior authority: in Greater Vancouver, the *federal government* is the largest single employer and its largest single landowner; its activities range from responsibility for the Port of Vancouver, to acting as landlord for Granville Island Market, parts of the North Shore mountains, veterans' hospitals, military bases, and regional offices for federal departments and crown agencies. And while its constitutional authority on regional issues is limited, its market influence is considerable—for example, through the airport and sea port. The *provincial government* has chosen to locate an extensive array of its ministries and crown corporations in Greater Vancouver. It also has a long and continuing capacity and inclination to be an active policy player in the Vancouver region—on transportation, land-use planning, trade and investment, and strategic land ownership. *Local governments* have generally recognized the benefits of regional solutions to metropolitan policy challenges. All of this interplay across divergent policy fields has produced policies that operate at cross purposes, as well as demonstrations of intergovernmental cooperation and policy agreement. It has also shown the capacity of one level of government to constrain and frustrate another (Swainson 1983).

Map 8.2.   *Greater Vancouver Municipalities*

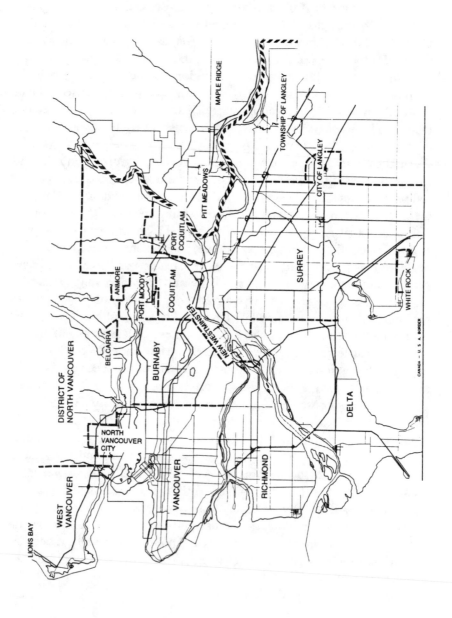

CASE ONE: TRANSPORTATION PLANNING
AND POLICYMAKING

Vancouver-area transportation planning can be divided into four eras. First, there was *an early mass transit* era, which began in 1890 with state of the art *streetcar* technology. Despite initial financial difficulties, by 1897 the private B.C. Electric Railway Company was providing profitable interurban public transportation from Vancouver, through Burnaby to New Westminster, 21 kilometres away. At its peak, 300 streetcars operated on over 1,800 miles of track (Metro Transit Operating Company 1980-81).

Second, there was the *trolley bus* era, which provided the link between streetcars and recent transportation policy choices. Although some streetcars continued until 1955, by World War II they were being replaced by trolley buses. In 1946, 146 million passengers used the system.

Third, there was the era of the *private automobile*. It had two antecedents: (a) the commitment of the Social Credit government (1952-72) to expand significantly the provincial highway network; and (b) the 1961 "provincialization" of B.C. Electric. Yet B.C. Hydro did not see its public bus system as having a high priority. Coupled with the general provincial emphasis on highways, the result was a transit system that declined substantially for a decade.

In Greater Vancouver, the policies of encouraging private automobile use and allowing public transit to decline culminated in 1966 with proposals to build a *freeway system*, mimicking urban transportation policy choices throughout North America. One of the proposed Vancouver-area freeways was to go through the long-established Chinatown, North America's second largest, adjacent to downtown Vancouver. The Chinese community, and other freeway opponents were quick to mobilize in opposition. The ensuing "Great Freeway Debate" created considerable public pressure against provincial and municipal officials supporting the freeway/automobile option. In retrospect, "the freeway debate was a turning point in the history of metropolitan Vancouver transportation" (Kopystynski and Powlowski 1980, 33-6). Certainly the debate, led by local communities in the region, about the implications of unrestrained automobile use, represented a fortuitous opportunity for those wishing a re-examination of transportation policy options in metropolitan Vancouver. Vancouver City Council, together with the Town Planning Commission, fully supported the freeway option.

However, the Town Planning Commission chair, H. P. Oberlander, resigned over this issue to lead the antifreeway forces. Shortly thereafter, they formed The Electors Action Movement (TEAM)—a local political party that controlled Vancouver City Council from 1968-74. An early TEAM member, Mike Harcourt, was elected to city council, subsequently became mayor, and is now B.C. premier.

The fourth era, the *re-emergence of public transit*, began with defeat of the freeway proponents. In Greater Vancouver this resulted in at least half a dozen transportation studies between the end of 1967 and the beginning of 1972. All recommended an *increased provincial role* in this transportation policy field and consideration of additional public transit options, such as rapid transit for Greater Vancouver (Lea 1967, 1968; Wooster 1968; Cather 1970; Kelly Report 1971; Parkinson Report 1971). With the election of the social democratic New Democratic Party (NDP) government (1972-1975), provincial involvement in metropolitan transportation planning did increase significantly. Under the NDP, the public transportation system was expanded and upgraded considerably; one result of this was a greatly increased transit system deficit (Metro Transit Operating Company 1980-81, 6). To oversee this broadened role, the NDP provincial government centralized planning and policymaking with the creation of the Bureau of Transit Services (BTS). The mandate of BTS was "to study transit needs, financing, purchasing and operations" of public transit in the province.

Regional transportation and transit were not functions assigned to the GVRD in 1967. However, as a service it was seen as an integral part of the GVRD's Livable Region Plan (LRP) developed in the early/mid 1970s. (See Case Three below.) The GVRD had requested the transportation planning function from the outgoing Socred government in 1972; the NDP response through BTS was to create a more obvious provincial role in both developing and operating transit systems throughout the province.

After the return of the Social Credit Government to power, the Municipal Affairs Minister Bill Vander Zalm introduced legislation in 1978 further consolidating and expanding the province's authority by creating the Urban Transit Authority (UTA), a crown agency, to oversee all transit planning and financing in the province. The legislation also gave the minister the power to designate local/regional operating authorities. While the UTA simply represented a shift in transit responsibility from one provincial agency to another, Vander Zalm did respond to further GVRD requests for authority in this policy field with an announcement that this would occur by April 1979. Before this date, however, the provincial government announced the creation of a second agency—the Metro Transit Operating Company (MTOC)—to operate the public transit systems in Greater Vancouver and the Capital Region of Victoria.

Over this 1978-79 period, the GVRD Board discussed and ultimately rejected the Provincial Transit Financing Formula as established under the UTA bill. However, in spring 1980, the UTA and Greater Vancouver signed a Transit Service Agreement, stating that responsibility was to be shared jointly among the GVRD, UTA, and MTOC. This became known as the three-headed monster because of the coordinating conflicts (Smith 1986, 11-2).

A GVRD Review Committee in 1982 indicated six specific areas of local concern about public transit:
1. A lack of clarity at political and staff levels as to the roles and responsibilities of each of the three parties to the agreement.
2. Virtually no public accountability.
3. A lack of flexibility on the part of the GVRD to improve transit quality and performance or to act independently regarding fiscal responsibility.
4. An unnecessarily complex procedure for modifying the transit service levels and costs.
5. A duplication of staff within the agencies.
6. A general lack of local autonomy in dealing with regional issues such as labor relations, financial accounting, and transit system identity.

As a result of this concern over "responsibility, accessibility, accountability, operational efficiency and coordination ability," the GVRD proposed a Regional Transit Authority, under direction of a board with three GVRD and three provincial government appointees, and a seventh director mutually agreeable to both (GVRD 1982). Within months, the province took up the issue, but not in ways anticipated or supported by the GVRD. In June 1982, the UTA was replaced by a new provincial agency, B.C. Transit. The change was justified on the grounds that "the province funds public transit systems that operate in rural areas as well as urban areas" (Vander Zalm 1982). The "new" B.C. Transit agency recommended removal of any transit service responsibility from the GVRD (and other regional districts). Despite ministerial denials (*Vancouver Sun* 12/11/82) and local/regional opposition to the proposal, this occurred between January and April 1983. The GVRD response, as expressed by its chair, was that the provincial "government's main interest in transit is to get as much credit as they can and reduce the cost of exposure" (*The Province* 1/10/83). From April 1, 1983, the provincial agency, B.C. Transit, had responsibility for transit planning in the Lower Mainland region.

The subsequent creation of a Regional Transit Commission by the province, consisting of provincially appointed local mayors or aldermen was an attempt to provide some opportunity for local involvement. Nevertheless, former GVRD Transit Commission Chairman Bob Bose called the shift in transit function to the province "arbitrary" and "highly undemocratic"; the result was nothing short of "a crisis" for local input and control (Bose 1983). The response of B.C. Transit was that a changed and smaller board would "bring transit more to the people" (from interview notes with B.C. Transit official, May 2, 1983).

Subsequent developments offered some support for the contention that the shift toward more centralized provincial control was, and would be, substantial. For example, in March 1985, the Greater Vancouver Regional Transit Commission responded bitterly to the *provincial* announcement of a rise in regional bus fares. The regional commission criticized the province for forcing it "to take the heat for a decision that was essentially made in Victoria." Richmond Mayor and Regional Commissioner Gil Blair argued that he found "it repugnant to sit here and have to make a decision after other bodies have made the decisions leaving us no other choice" (*Vancouver Sun* 3/13/85).

A final factor illustrating the province's dominance in this fourth era was its unilateral commitment in 1979 to build an Advanced/Automated Light Rapid Transit (ALRT) system. Its technology, timetable, and planning were centrally controlled and tied to the province's sponsorship of Vancouver's Expo '86, a world exposition with transportation as its central theme.

One rationale for the continued centralization of the transit planning function in metropolitan Vancouver was that it limited the capacity of local and regional authorities to "frustrate" the senior government's intention to complete its ALRT project in time for Expo '86. The route chosen—apart from providing access to two areas of the Expo site—connected Vancouver with Burnaby and New Westminster, a total of 21 kilometres through the core of the metropolitan region. This route provided an effective framework for the regional town center concept of the Livable Region Plan (LRP); in this sense, ALRT substantially implemented the LRP in a part of the GVRD, if not by explicit design, at least by benign default.

Recent Developments in Transportation Policy in Greater Vancouver

There have been four significant subsequent developments in transportation planning in metropolitan Vancouver. They highlight differing dimensions of the governing—and intergovernmental—framework of the urban region. Each will be treated in turn.

The Metropolitan Transportation of Hazardous Goods: Tri-Level Cooperation Promised

Between 1983 and 1986, the Canadian Transport Commission held a series of hearings—through its Railway Transport Committee—on the rail routing of hazardous materials to the Vancouver port area, and within the metropolitan region. These hearings led to the conclusion that broader questions about all forms of movement of dangerous goods went beyond the Rail Transport Committee's jurisdiction and to the recommendation that all levels of government and all interested publics develop a comprehensive plan regarding the transportation of hazardous goods throughout the Lower Mainland region.

The result was a Tri-Level Government Task Force to conduct the first such comprehensive study in the Vancouver metropolitan region. It was chaired by the Federal Department of Transport, with representation from the B.C. Ministry of Transportation and Highways. Local government representation on the task force was through the GVRD. Its objective was "to collect information necessary to understand and comment on the existing transportation of dangerous goods system and, using this information, to recommend ways of developing and maintaining a comprehensive plan for future movement of dangerous goods" (North Vancouver District 1989; British Columbia, Ministry of Regional Development 1989b, 6).

The Task Force established four working groups—on road, rail, marine, and emergency response. These working groups included representation from the three levels of government and others concerned about the issue of safe transportation of dangerous goods in the region. Throughout 1987-88 a series of public hearings were also held; and public polling and newsletter distribution in the region solicited further public comment (Canada, Transport Canada 1989b; Port of Vancouver 1989).

The result of this multilevel consultation was broad agreement on the task force report, *Vancouver Area Transportation of Dangerous Goods*

Study, published in July 1988. The tri-level governmental cooperation on this transportation policy problem has led to ongoing intergovernmental involvement through a tri-level council (of federal, provincial, and local [GVRD] governmental representatives). As a process, it represented not only cooperation promised, but cooperation delivered. It also contributed to provincial-municipal dialogue on other dimensions of transportation policy in the region (British Columbia, Legislative Assembly Debates 1989a).

Freedom to Move*: The Report of the Greater Vancouver Transportation Task Force—Provincial-Regional Cooperation Postponed*

In the autumn of 1986, with the election of the Vander Zalm/Socred Government, a number of policy studies were undertaken. Following this initial thrust, provincial ministries carried out major reviews of their responsibilities. Much of this was subsequently ignored in a provincial pattern of policy gambling and surprise. For example, the B.C. Ministry of Transportation and Highways carried out such a comprehensive review in 1988. The result was an 18-volume report: "A Transportation Planning Overview for the Province of British Columbia." It reviewed transit, rail, marine, air, and highway systems. Among its recommendations were proposals that *each* of the eight Economic Development Regions (EDRs) established by the Vander Zalm government undertake a more in-depth study to: (a) establish regional transportation strategies that will serve as the blueprint for future expansion of the existing transportation networks; and (b) identify the priority transportation infrastructure projects that should be undertaken in the short term and that are consistent with the strategy in the long term (Greater Vancouver Transportation Task Force 1989). The urgency for metropolitan Vancouver was reflected in the fact that the last comprehensive regional transportation study had taken place in 1954, during the early period of the LMRPB planning mandate.

The Economic Development Region for the Vancouver area includes the GVRD, and the three other regional districts of the Fraser Valley, as well as the Sunshine Coast, north of Vancouver. The transportation mandate, as defined by the minister, was:

> to prepare an integrated transportation strategy for the Greater Vancouver Region which will encourage orderly economic development at the lowest possible cost to taxpayers and system users in a manner consistent with the maintenance of liveability and environmental quality (Veitch 1989).

Map 8.3. *Existing Regional Road Network*

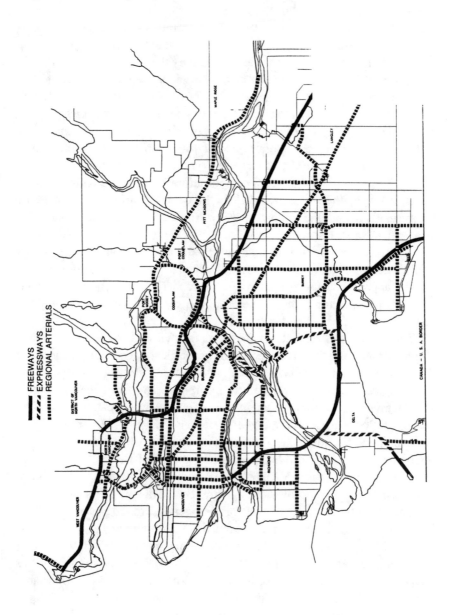

Phase I of the study was to report on (1) a transportation strategy, (2) a 2001 transportation plan, and (3) the setting of short-term priorities within three months (by July 1989) to feed into the provincial Ministry of Transportation and Highways budgeting cycle for fiscal 1990/91. The time frame for this initial phase established by the province, presented the first problem. While apparently consultative and representative, the task force report—entitled *Freedom to Move*—provoked considerable opposition from the local/regional governing units in the metropolitan area. The report noted this problem: "This time frame meant that a full metropolitan area . . . transportation study, which normally would take 12 to 18 months to undertake, had to be completed in approximately three months" (Greater Vancouver Transportation Task Force 1989). As a result, many of the tasks intended for Phase I were postponed to Phase II (originally scheduled to commence in August/September 1989). It also meant that the task force did not engage in any significant debates.

According to one task force member, the process was also flawed by a fundamental paradigm problem: "a campus pathway planning model" may be appropriate for Spuzzum (B.C.'s archetypical community of one hundred) but not for a major metropolitan centre"—certainly not when tied to an inadequate timetable.

These pressures resulted in a final report that was isolated from many of the communities it was to represent; it was also, according to one task force member, "unjustified by data" and too detailed for a process that lacked agreement. It was prepared and released without the agreement of a number of committee members. (interview, Greater Vancouver Transportation Task Force member, October 13, 1989.) Interestingly, it was completed under the direction of then GVRD Manager Mike O'Connor. O'Connor had been second in charge of B.C. Transit prior to his appointment to the GVRD. Within months of the task force report, he moved back to the provincial agency, B.C. Transit, as its president.

This provincial effort to control the agenda proved inadequate, and the report—with $2 billion in planned spending over 10 years—was opposed by a large number of local authorities in the Greater Vancouver region (Fraser and Turnbull 1989; Horn 1989). Many municipalities agreed with specific aspects of the final report; few found it supportable as a whole. Phase II did not begin in August-September 1989 as originally planned. Negative reactions to Phase I caused initial issues to be re-opened.

Phase II was to develop a longer term transportation strategy—including "Strategic plans (for) . . . air, rail and marine modes;

investigate the relationship between, and impacts of, alternative land use scenarios and transportation networks; and establish a regionwide road network to provide continuity between adjacent municipalities for all freeways, expressways, arterial roads or municipal roads." It also anticipated "an ongoing transportation planning process that will enable all three levels of government to work together cooperatively to continually plan . . . Greater Vancouver's transportation system" (Greater Vancouver Transportation Task Force 1989, 3). There was little indication of such cooperation in the provincially sponsored *Freedom to Move* policy initiative.

Recent Policy Development on Regional Rapid Transit: Policy Cooperation Lost

If the Vander Zalm government's actions concerning *Freedom to Move* meant consultation postponed, its response to regional rapid transit needs in Greater Vancouver represented consultation lost. The stated intention of various reviews of transportation in the metropolitan region was to be consistent with the *Livable Region Strategy for the 1990s*, a GVRD update of its Livable Region Strategy (LRS), originally stated in 1976. The overall goal of the LRS was "to maintain Greater Vancouver's livability as it grows and develops." The 1990s update of the LRS planning guide sought to maintain a "healthy and safe region," "a region of diversity and vitality," an "equitable," "efficient" and accessible region; its transportation strategy to do this placed considerable emphasis on "improvements to the public transit system and programs to encourage its increased use" (Greater Vancouver Transportation Task Force 1989).

Yet subsequent to the *Freedom to Move* report, the premier and minister of municipal affairs invited all the mayors and other local/regional government representatives to "a major transit announcement." Rather than confirm earlier discussions about conventional rail links to some northeastern metropolitan communities and an extension of the existing rapid transit lines to faster growing areas such as Coquitlam, (which had returned opposition members to the B.C. legislature), the premier announced $1 billion in provincial expenditure for a skytrain extension across the Fraser River into Surrey, the constituency of Municipal Affairs Minister Rita Johnston. The premier also announced up to $750 million for a new skytrain link into his own Richmond constituency (by 1995). The latter new link was to have preferred emphasis over the previously discussed link to Burnaby (1995, $210

Map 8.4.   *Existing Regional Transit Network*

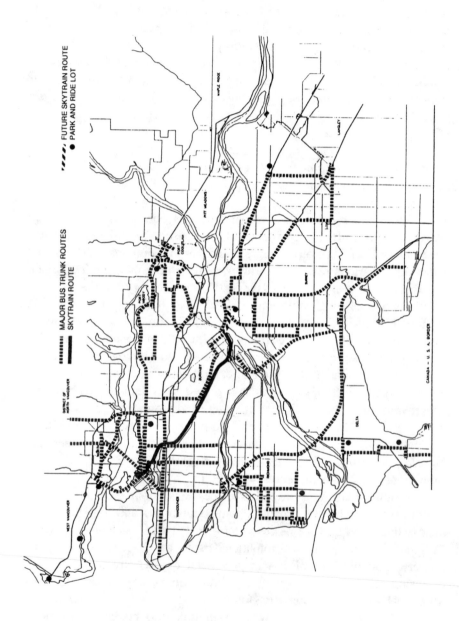

million) with no timetable for an extension to Coquitlam (British Columbia, *Provincial Report* 1989c).

This five-year timetable, geared to Socred ministerial ridings, did not reflect at all the GVRD priorities on rapid transit. In addition, the premier included a Burrard Inlet marine rapid transit service. This highlighted the lack of provincial governmental forethought in its transit planning for the region. As the mayor of Port Moody indicated, in 20 years of discussion, no proposals for such a sea-based link had been seriously considered. During the previous federal general election, a multimillion dollar support package had been offered by the federal government to develop a several-year test of commuter rail from that part of the region. The latter had been rejected by the province. The process and the result ran entirely counter to the spring 1989 "Partnership in Transportation Planning" signed by the GVRD and the provincial government. Rather than "working together"—the partnership's logo—to achieve "a comprehensive transportation plan (as) an urgent priority for Greater Vancouver if the region is to maintain the high quality of services, and living standards," (British Columbia, Ministry of Regional Development/GVRD 1989b) the province had reverted to a paternalistic approach. Between March and summer 1989, the policy process had shifted from "an open, consultative process . . . [with] cooperation between the municipalities, the GVRD, the Ministry of Transportation and Highways, B.C. Transit, port and airport authorities and other partici-pants," (*Ibid.*) to one where the "cooperative approach" had been abandoned by the senior authority, and the regionally determined needs had been ignored.

The Johnston Interlude, The Harcourt Start

On April 2, 1991, Premier Bill Vander Zalm resigned over conflicts of interest. His Minister of Transportation (and formerly of Municipal Affairs), Rita Johnston, succeeded him in the final months of the govern-ment's five-year term. Johnston made some efforts to distance herself from her former political mentor, but without success. She had an opportunity to respond to the extensive summer 1990 process of community consultation on metropolitan Vancouver that culminated in documents entitled *Choosing Our Future* (GVRD 1990a), and *Creating Our Future* (GVRD 1990b, 1990c), issued in the later summer of 1990. The consultations involved examinations of regional policy options on the quality of community life, affordable housing, regional town centers, the metropolitan land supply (including its agricultural uses), metropolitan transportation, and urban futures.

The Johnston government, however, continued the rapid transit priorities of the Vander Zalm era. Advisory committees on skytrain extensions were established; all ran into local opposition. For example, it was alleged that one route choice had been predetermined by the provincial government; a leaked document indicated the consultative process had been "cooked." (See *Burnaby Now*, various articles, summer 1991.) The early fall 1991 general election put on hold major decision making for most of these transportation initiatives. For Premier Johnston "the bottom line [was] that the provincial government must have a very strong voice considering the substantial amount it contributes to transit in the Lower Mainland." Rita Johnston lost the governmental majority and her own seat in the October 1991 provincial general election.

The newly elected provincial NDP government, led by former Vancouver Mayor Mike Harcourt, faces many of the same challenges. As a critic of the expensive ALRT system imposed on the city by the province, Harcourt may reflect a different view of local authority over such matters. If so, he will confront a metropolitan region with a clearer view of its developing future. The GVRD, now chaired by Vancouver Mayor Gordon Campbell, has initiated major policy plans in 1990-91: the *Creating Our Future* policy statement established 54 priorities for "A More Livable Region"—at least 19 of which had transportation components (GVRD 1990c).

Many of these regional transportation policy priorities relate to expansion of rapid and public transit, and developing a more "co-operative transportation process with the provincial government and its agencies" (GVRD 1990c). More importantly, "the region's municipal leaders want the management and operation of public transit in this area turned over to the Greater Vancouver Regional District so there is control and accountability at the local level" (Mills 1991). In unanimously endorsing the idea that transit should be a regional district function, the GVRD supported the conclusions of a consultant's report prepared by a former vice president (planning) of B.C. Transit. He concluded that "effective and responsible transit management in Greater Vancouver ha[d] been hampered by conflict between provincial and local representatives almost from the time the system was removed from B.C. Hydro in the late '70s" (*GVRD News* August-October 1991).

The report also argued that:

The residents of the region deserve a transit system that is responsive to their concerns and can be coordinated with an overall strategy to address the multitude of urban structure and metropolitan development issues facing the Lower Mainland over the next decade.

The regional district provides the best mechanism to achieve regional transportation coordination in concert with an overall regional strategy. . . . It can provide the autonomy that the regional transit system requires to make "appropriate transit decisions."

A transit system that functions within the framework of regional authority will be more accountable than a transit system that exists outside the regional district's jurisdiction (Mills 1991).

Whatever the outcome, there is some expectation that dealing with a premier who was a former Vancouver mayor and GVRD director will produce more local-regional-provincial cooperation than was previously the case with two Social Credit premiers who had served as ministers of municipal affairs as well as Surrey aldermen. Harcourt represents center city, regional core issues, whereas Vander Zalm and Johnston were rooted ideologically in suburbia.

CASE TWO: REGIONAL PARKS AND OPEN SPACE POLICYMAKING

In contrast to its role in transportation, the GVRD has considerable policymaking autonomy concerning regional parks and open space. By 1992, it had created 16 regional parks, with 10,000 hectares of open/green space, including mountain, river-valley, island, farmland, and ocean-front habitats, both within and beyond its boundaries. Providing parks and open space has been one of the most successful regional functions. It has also become the largest, with 23 municipalities and electoral areas participating, including a number from outside the GVRD itself (GVRD 1990c, 1990d).

The GVRD parks function has its origins in the provincial Regional Parks Act, 1965. The act provided regional districts with the authority to acquire public parkland on a regional basis. A goal established at that time was that by the year 2000 the Lower Mainland should have a developed and operating system of regional parks to complement local and provincial parks in meeting the needs of area residents. Throughout the years, the regional role of GVRD parks has changed: while GVRD has been a "retailer" of regional park services to the general public, and a "wholesaler" in land acquisition, planning, development, and maintenance of such parks, it has also become the primary developer of open/green space for the whole Lower Mainland. The designation of open space has shaped the metropolitan region and established its limits while providing a rational system of outdoor recreation.

The provision of regional parks has involved policy decisions in land use at the local, provincial—and occasionally, the federal—levels of government. Often, it has also reflected preferences of the public: at times, private property and native land claims also were central factors. All of this provided ample scope for conflicting interests, yet regional open/green space policymaking in metropolitan Vancouver has seldom been confrontational. Green is "good" and more is better.

Parks Governance

The acquisition of parkland, and its development, maintenance, and management, form an integral part of local and regional governance in metropolitan Vancouver. As the population of urban areas spilled over their historic boundaries, parkland had to be acquired beyond their boundaries leading to the need to create a regional or metropolitan scale park agency. Initially it stood alone as a means of park management, but increasingly the parks function was grouped with other areawide public activities such as water or sewage, constituting a means of metropolitan governance for selected functions. Governance for parkland and its integrated use encouraged cooperation with other related functions leading to increased efficiencies in service provision and growing responsiveness to public demands in terms of locational preferences and priorities. Parkland and its function-specific administration at the metropolitan/regional level became a desirable and readily accepted central element in the apparatus of governance without unduly threatening local government responsibilities for parkland and its increasing use, even when it began to supersede localities. The GVRD park system was built on the initial work of the LMRPB, with early cooperation by the provincial government. In 1966, the Regional Parks Plan for the Lower Mainland region set forth desired acquisition goals and a framework for their achievement (Lower Mainland Regional Planning Board 1966). New sections of the Municipal Act, passed with the Regional Parks Act in 1965, provided a 1/3 provincial—2/3 municipal cost-sharing regime for capital expenditures on regional parks acquisition and development. The GVRD inherited the regional park responsibility in 1967.

Many of the policies for regional parks and open space that have developed over the years reflect the basic outline for a park system described in the Regional Parks Plan of 1966. The plan proposed incorporating provincial and municipal parks into an integrated new system. Parks were to include *typical* Lower Mainland natural landscapes situated close to regional town centers, interconnected by trails wherever possible (GVRD 1980b). Some park land has been acquired from private owners. Other important parcels have been conveyed or leased to the GVRD by municipalities and by the federal and provincial governments. The GVRD does not pay for publicly owned land. Recently, community nonprofit groups have become increasingly important in assisting with the acquisition and development of new land (GVRD 1976, 1985).

The existing political structure of Greater Vancouver Regional Parks (GVRP) reflects the 1966 Parks Plan philosophy that regional parks should "have strong local representation to guide . . . park policies" (Lower Mainland Regional Planning Board 1966). Locally elected politicians are appointed by their councils to represent their constituencies at the regional level. There, the GVRD's governing body—the board of directors—appoints municipal representatives to the committees through which the board operates. The Parks Committee is part of this committee system. Its members meet monthly and make recommendations to the board regarding the acquisition and management of regional park property (interview, Rick Hankin, Manager, Greater Vancouver Regional Parks, April 1989).

Financing Regional Parks

The Regional Parks Act

Financing for operating and capital expenditures is governed by the Regional Parks Act, which provides a district with the authority to generate and expend funds to sustain the function (GVRD 1985). Operating funds are requisitioned from member municipalities through the property tax. Initially, funds for land acquisition were derived from an annual budget based on a levy of 0.25 mills plus one-third contribution from the provincial government. By 1970, rapidly increasing land values created a need to accelerate land acquisition, and the GVRD board (after repeated efforts on the part of the Parks Committee) voted to increase the levy to 0.35 mills. A further source of revenue became available in 1972 when the act was amended to authorize park districts to borrow money for acquisition or development. But provincial costsharing, the major incentive for the GVRD to take on the regional parks function, was being gradually reduced by 1979, and was discontinued completely by 1982 as economic conditions deteriorated (interview with Rick Hankin).

Though the cost per capita for regional parks has grown since 1970, it still remains far below municipal expenditures for parks and recreation. For example, per capita expenditures in 1970 were $1.50 per resident; by 1984 they had risen to $2.40, and in 1988, to $4.00. By comparison, municipalities in 1985 were spending, on average, about $60.00 per resident on local parks and recreation (GVRD 1985).

Intergovernmental Relations in Parks Governance

While the intention of regional parks was to *complement* local and senior policies and programs, Greater Vancouver Regional Parks has come to predominate. Where the shift began to emerge was on park development. Consequently, while local authorities continued to spend more on parks/recreational budgets, many began to assume that the acquisition of large parks was the role of the regional district.

This was the case in Langley (population 70,000). Here, in response to considerable local pressure to be more involved in parks and green-space, the municipality undertook in the summer of 1990 an extensive survey of its citizens. The survey determined that there was strong citizen support for maintenance of the rural quality and natural attributes of the area. To implement this, the municipality held a series of public meetings in autumn 1990. The local consultative process showed that there had been no area green-space inventory. With urban development pressures amongst the strongest in the province, Langley responded to criticism from local groups such as the Field Naturalists about lack of local green space concern by referring to the GVRD's Campbell Valley Regional Park located within the municipality. Here, the success of regional district park planning allowed for some *local* abrogation of its "complementary" park responsibilities. This was not always the case; nor was it true that the province was always a benign actor.

Burnaby, an inner suburb adjacent to Vancouver, has worked in concert with GVRP in the creation and operation of the Burnaby Lake regional park. Burnaby leased all of its Burnaby Lake lands to the GVRD; the GVRD agreed to purchase all privately owned lands within the designated park's boundaries, and Burnaby convinced the federal government to release .4 acres of adjacent land expropriated from the municipality during World War II for a veterans' hospital.

Adjacent to Burnaby Lake is Deer Lake, the single most important recreational body of water in the municipality. Part of this area also housed the Oakalla prison farm, which dated from the late 19th century. The municipality, and the GVRD, had designated this Oakalla land as part of the regional park system. After years of public lobbying by the municipality, and extensive local pressure to remove this Lower Mainland Regional Correctional Center, the province promised to close down the facility in 1978. It deeded 158 acres between Deer Lake and the Oakalla prison to Burnaby with the proviso that this land be kept as parkland in perpetuity; it also stipulated that the municipality dedicate all of *its* Deer Lake land for park purposes. The land was transferred to the municipality as a result of the provincial government accepting the recommendation of a committee it had formed to look into the disposition of the Oakalla lands. Having acquired all but 68 acres of the Oakalla lands, and a mandate from the Burnaby electorate to set aside the Deer Lake/Oakalla lands for park use only, Burnaby proceeded—in consultation with the public and the GVRD—to plan for an integrated regional town center/regional park system (District of Burnaby 1980).

In September 1982, the premier announced, to the astonishment of Burnaby officials and residents, the closure of Oakalla prison by 1986 to make way for a multimillion dollar 640-acre residential and parkland development. The area extended well beyond the municipal designated park boundaries, taking in both private and public lands. The provincial Deer Lake/Oakalla Lands Project called for 1,800 residential units, a golf course, and a network of trails throughout the valley farmland (Powers and Fralic 1988). In his announcement, the premier talked of the "handsome profit" the project would earn for the province. He estimated the development would generate $150 million of revenue providing a "substantial excess of revenue over expenditures"—a share of which would be allocated to Burnaby in return for which the municipality would be required to forego its own plans (District of Burnaby 1980, 1988).

The announcement was met with anger and disbelief. Over 80 percent of the total land contained within the provincial project area belonged to the municipality, yet there had been no discussion with Burnaby officials nor had there been any inkling that even the remaining Oakalla lands would be developed for anything other than a park. Few local officials shared the premier's view that the project represented a "partnership for progress between Victoria and Burnaby." Burnaby's mayor, a Social Credit supporter, did not oppose the project. From his perspective, the municipality could only afford to develop its plan incrementally. He viewed the housing development as the " . . . engine that created the money to develop the park" (Powers and Fralic 1988).

For most, the announcement resembled earlier encounters with the senior government when Burnaby had been coerced to give up substantial areas of parkland for provincial priorities and had gained little in return. As for the public, residents living in the vicinity of the correctional center stated that the prison's barbed wire fencing—along with wide open spaces and grass and trees, and a spectacular, unobstructed view of Burnaby Mountain and the mountains of the North Shore—were preferable to the high density housing proposed for the provincial project; others resented the provincial government bypassing officials they had elected and interfering in matters of local concern (Morton 1982).

Faced with such provincial-government attitudes, municipal staff decided that the partnership concept had some merit and concluded there might be a way of working with the province to relocate the Oakalla prison, protect park areas, provide additional housing, and share in the profit from the development of Deer Lake Park, provided the development was compatible with Burnaby's and the GVRD's regional town/park system. If the municipality could strike a bargain with the province, park development and improvements could begin more quickly than would be possible under the municipality's "pay as you go" approach (District of Burnaby 1982). Burnaby proposed an alternative plan with an equitable sharing of cost and revenue as well as a sharing of park development costs. In return for a scaled-down housing development on the Oakalla lands, the municipality would make available to the province 158 acres of undeveloped land that it had been banking for future residential development. It would be developed for housing on the same cost-revenue sharing basis.

The next four years were a period of ongoing discussion—and bargaining—between Burnaby municipal planners and the provincial government. By 1986, a substantially altered provincial proposal was presented to Burnaby Council for its consideration (District of Burnaby 1986). Housing development was reduced from 1,800 high-density units to 610 low-density units to be located on the remaining 68-acre site of the prison facility. Traversing the location was to be a major landscaped public walkway providing access from the regional town center/Metrotown to Deer Lake, all of which would complement the regional park function of Burnaby Lake. The 158 acres deeded to Burnaby were designated parkland to be developed to Burnaby's specifications, and ongoing negotiations were to address Burnaby's share of the revenue. Perhaps most important from Burnaby's (and the region's) perspective was that the whole proposal was contingent upon the construction of three new separate correctional facilities in the Lower Mainland region and the demolition of Oakalla in 1991 (District of Burnaby 1988). "Over the years the residents of Burnaby have been promised these institutions would be closed and the Oakalla Lands would be made available to the municipality. The promise has been made and broken, time and time again" (Robinson 1982). Oakalla prison was finally demolished in 1992.

Burnaby's ability to maintain the integrity of its long-range planning for the Central Valley Regional Park System seemed to rest on several factors. Unlike the remote provincial designers, Burnaby officials were well acquainted with local issues and public preferences. This knowledge proved to be a distinct advantage in the bargaining process for a new provincial plan. Faced with the *potential* of having the senior government's will imposed on them, Burnaby was determined to formulate an alternative proposal that would be compatible with municipal aspirations while retaining some of the elements of the provincially inspired plan—one which could provide the municipality with resources to develop its own plans. Burnaby planners also recognized that the development of an integrated local/regional park system providing public open spaces for citizens was dependent not only on senior government, but on citizen support as well. The public, which since the early 1970s had input in the planning process through public hearings, written submissions and open houses, rejected the imposition of the senior government plan that ignored their wishes (*Burnaby Today* 12/20/82). In this they were aided by the earlier deeding of some of the property as municipal parkland. This provided a stronger legal basis for Burnaby's plan. As a result of these conditions, the local government was able to outmaneuver the province on an important park issue. In other instances, senior governmental cooperation has been more complementary.

Regional Parks and the Livable Region Plan(s)

The regional park concept outlined in the 1966 parks plan became part of the GVRD's 1976 Livable Region Plan (LRP). The goal of the LRP was to ensure that rapid population growth of Greater Vancouver, the major urban center of the Lower Mainland, did not diminish its own and the region's "livability." The strategy was to create regional town centers to encourage residential development and job creation in outlying municipalities that would provide an alternative to downtown Vancouver concentration. A significant feature of the program was the protection and enhancement, wherever possible, of natural open spaces for public recreational use (GVRD 1980a).

When the GVRD undertook its major review of the LRP in late 1989-early 1990, these principles continued to guide its policy choices. Through its extensive *Choosing Our Future* consultative process, the region developed a regional agenda—with "made in Vancouver solutions"—for joint action.

These included a strong commitment to "protect wilderness, park and agricultural land" to ensure "a more livable and healthier region" (from a September 1990 letter from the GVRD chair to all member municipalities). To do so, the GVRD has spearheaded a policy of "urban containment to distinguish developed areas from permanently reserved wilderness, parks, wetlands, watersheds, wildlife habitat and farmland" through creation of a Green Zone (GVRD 1990c).

Protecting migratory flyways; establishing a Land Conservation Trust Fund; encouraging the inclusion of wetlands, wilderness, and rural planning for agriculture and urban forestry in official community plans; and developing wildlife sanctuaries were all park-related steps in the 54-point Strategy for Regional Livability. Many of the regional initiatives involved local governmental action. Local and regional work on the new LRP for the 1990s and beyond did not anticipate extensive involvement by the province. The reality was that, with few exceptions, the GVRD had come to dominate greenspace planning in the Lower Mainland. This may be all the more significant when other aspects of land-use planning are considered. Here the policy discourse has been more contentious.

CASE THREE: LAND-USE PLANNING AND POLICYMAKING

Regional land-use planning for the Lower Mainland began in 1937 when six metropolitan municipalities (Vancouver, Burnaby, Coquitlam, Port Moody, North and West Vancouver) created a voluntary planning association for the Lower Mainland. Although significantly preceding the creation of the GVRD, it underwent considerable changes in response to the challenge posed by major flooding in the Fraser River Valley in 1948. Yet despite these changes in legislation and locus of responsibility,

Map 8.5.   *Regional Parks and Green Zones*

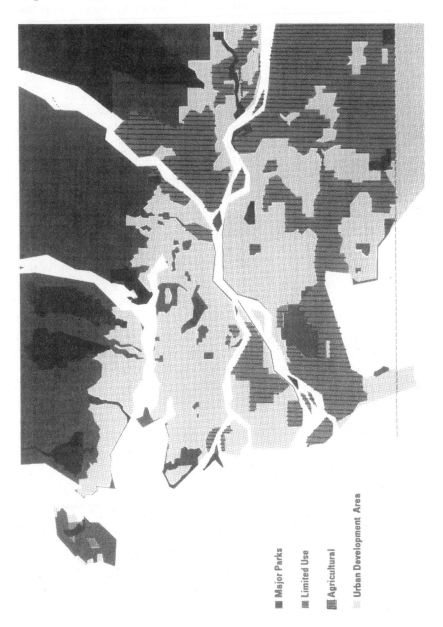

■ Major Parks

▨ Limited Use

▦ Agricultural

▤ Urban Development Area

regional planning has continued to the present. On the themes of regional governance and jurisdictional interplay, the local responses to senior governmental ambivalence and hostility to regional initiatives in the field of planning provide a significant index of local governing capacity.

The LMRPB and Regional Planning

Under the LMRPB, established in 1949, regional planning in the Lower Mainland focused on the preparation of a plan for the entire area and making it binding on the municipalities through its official status. An "Official Regional Plan" (ORP) was defined under the Municipal Act as "a general scheme without detail for the projected use of land within the regional district" that had been approved as such by the regional board. An ORP was seen as a preventive policy or enactment, so no development could be undertaken in opposition to it; it prevented changes in land use within and between designated areas; it did not require or authorize any positive steps, public or private, to implement the stated objectives of the plan. Prior to 1983, the Municipal Act stated "neither the Regional Board nor the Council . . . of a member municipality . . . shall enact any provision or initiate any works which would impede the ultimate objectives of the regional plan," but the plan "does not commit the Regional Board or a Council . . . or any other administrative body, to undertake any of the projects therein suggested or outlined."

Each municipality in the area—there were 28 in all—was required to nominate a member to the regional board. The board was empowered to hire staff, to prepare and publish reports, and for these purposes, to collect a per capita levy from the member municipalities to meet its annual budget. In 1963, the official response plan, "Change and Challenge," was initiated by the board. Early in 1965, the board and its staff consulted with the municipalities in the region on the maps, text, and schedule of the regional plan. During 1966, the board carried out a broadly based formal review of the plan in light of the reaction of the municipal councils and the general public. The plan was reconsidered, incorporating a number of amendments and subsequently formally considered by the member municipal councils. On August 8, 1966, the board received notice that the plan had received the necessary approval of two-thirds of the Lower Mainland municipalities and thereby became the official regional plan—a major achievement.

While the plan established a significant framework for regional and local land-use development and achieved the original purpose of the

LMRPB, its very success led to friction, jealousy in local bureaucracies, and conflict with the provincial government. In fact, it began to threaten provincial authority.

In the period 1965-68, some board and staff members of LMRPB became critics of the provincial government concerning a number of provincial land-use decisions at variance with the newly adopted official regional plan. Here the LMRPB was instrumental in changing some public policies but at a political price. In addition, the LMRPB was critical of the ministry of municipal affairs program of creating regional districts that had begun in 1965.

As a result of such intergovernmental friction, the demise of the LMRPB was sealed in the late 1960s. Without much warning or public debate, it was dissolved in 1968 by the minister of municipal affairs. Its territorial responsibilities were divided among the four regional districts created within the Lower Mainland. One outcome of the regional-provincial disputes was that the professional staff of the LMRPB were not taken on by the new regional districts. The LMRPB went so far as to offer its staff publicly to the GVRD; neither the minister nor local municipal officials responded favorably. Ironically, the only professionals fully familiar with planning in the area, long-term employees of the LMRPB, were not hired by the GVRD, although the original regional planning authority was transferred to it. Nevertheless, the success of the LMRPB in fulfilling its mandate—and the success of other regional single-purpose authorities such as hospital boards, water, sewage and drainage districts—had a distinct impact on provincial policymakers. More importantly, the legacy of the LMRPB experience was to ensure that regional land-use planning remained central to governance in metropolitan Vancouver and the rest of the Lower Mainland.

The GVRD and Regional Planning

After the creation of regional districts in the mid 1960s, the planning activities and responsibilities in the region fell into five major categories:
1. providing local planning services to electoral areas;
2. providing advisory opinions to the B.C. Land Commission concerning release of land from the agricultural land reserve (ALR) within the region after 1973;
3. maintaining the official regional plan inherited from the LMRPB;
4. developing a "Livable Region Program";

5. developing proposals concerning future public transport within the region.

Between 1967-69 and 1983, the GVRD operated visibly like a level of government despite provincial denials of such status. Its planning role was substantial and involved working with provincial agencies and local authorities. Two examples stand out as illustrations: (1) its interaction with the provincial Agricultural Land Commission, and (2) its development of a Livable Region Program in the 1970s. In the early 1980s, it was the confluence of these two aspects of regional planning, and an ongoing GVRD-provincial government land-use dispute that ended regional planning *authority* for the GVRD (and as a byproduct for the 28 other regional districts in B.C.).

The GVRD and the Agricultural Land Reserve

In 1973 the Agricultural Land Commission was created by the NDP government led by Premier Dave Barrett (1972-75) as a provincial agency to administer the use of all arable lands in the province. Since then, designated agricultural land is held in a provincewide reserve system, and its use is regulated jointly with respective municipal councils. In the Lower Mainland, originally the ORP designated the lands reserved for agricultural use. To jointly regulate the ALR, the Municipal Act had to be amended to link land-use zoning under ORP with the arable-land-reserve designation. If an amendment to the ORP was called for, the new land use was first approved by the municipal council concerned and then submitted to the GVRD and ALC for advice and final approval. The regional planning function, local zoning approval, and the agricultural land reserve system initially worked well together. One significant reason was that Mr. W. T. Lane, who had been chair of the Agricultural Land Commission since its inception, in 1975 became the director of development for the GVRD and personally initiated policy coordination and continuing consultation on development proposals affecting regional planning issues and arable land designation (interview, W. Lane, July 1988).

Agricultural Land Commission System

The Land Commission Act of 1973 was one of the most dramatic and comprehensive legislative attempts to control the use of arable land introduced anywhere in North America. The act authorized the creation of a commission of not less than five members with powers to designate agricultural land (with the ultimate approval of the provincial cabinet) and to restrict its use to farming). The Agricultural Land Commission had four major objectives:

1.　to preserve agricultural land for farm use;
2.　to preserve greenbelt land in and around urban areas;
3.　to preserve land banks for urban and industrial development; and
4.　to preserve parkland for recreational use (Land Commission Act, section 7[1]).

The creation of agricultural land reserves throughout B.C. involved all the regional districts. Each of the 28 regional districts was given the responsibility of identifying, reviewing, and designating agricultural land reserves within its boundaries and within the context of its own integrated land-use plan, with the advice and financial assistance of the commission. The latter could amend any proposed plan if deemed desirable, with the approval of cabinet, after holding public hearings. After approval of the plan by cabinet, the commission was empowered to designate the land therein as an agricultural land reserve. Appeals for exclusion of land parcels from an agricultural land reserve were to be divided into two basic categories: those from the municipalities, the regional districts, or the commission itself (the government-to-government appeals) and those from individuals (usually land owners). Under section 9(1) requests for exclusions by a municipality, regional district, or the commission itself would be decided by cabinet. With respect to appeals from individuals, section 9(2) of the act states that "an owner aggrieved by a designation of the commission could make an application to the commission to have the land excluded from the ALR." Here a public hearing was required. The provincial cabinet was seen as the final arbiter of agricultural land reserve designation; and as the final authority in appeals for exclusions requested by the municipalities, the regional districts, the commission, or individuals. Under the Social Credit Government elected in 1975, the use of appeals to cabinet became more frequent. This "political" dimension became more contentious over the next seven years. To ensure cabinet's role was clear, the Agricultural Land Commission Act was amended, for example in 1977, to narrow the scope of the ALC's powers and purview. This ALC role was seen as particularly important in the Lower Mainland. In 1972, the conversion of arable land for urban use had reached approximately 4,000 hectares per year, one quarter of it in the Vancouver region.

The province's solution was to propose a stronger role for itself. In September 1980, the Minister of Municipal Affairs Bill Vander Zalm addressed the annual convention of the Union of B.C. Municipalities (UBCM) and proposed a new Land Use Act. The act was to reform the regional planning process throughout the province. Under the act the minister was to exercise ultimate control over almost all local land-use planning and zoning. Regional planning functions were to be taken over by new "regional coordinating committees" formed by officials appointed by the provincial government's Environment and Land Use Committee. In the minister's view the Land Use Act would ameliorate many existing problems in the Land Use and Agricultural Land Reserve System of B.C.: "ever since I became involved in the development approval process . . . I recognized certain resolvable problems with the system . . . I became more and more convinced that the land development regulation system could better serve the needs of British Colombians if some necessary, but fundamental changes were initiated" (Ministerial Statement, *Land Use Act*, September 15, 1980). The new act was to rectify problems in two areas: "provincial land-use planning" and "local government planning." At the provincial land-use level, Vander Zalm sought to establish a system that would coordinate provincial land-use planning on an interministry basis. When Vander Zalm first proposed his legislation, it was this clause that municipal leaders supported. However, due to strong opposition by his cabinet ministers, it was eventually removed.

The second problem that the Land Use Act was to ameliorate was the local land-use planning process. In broad terms, regulations under the Land Use Act would supersede regional plans. The municipal and regional district response to the changes was understandably negative. Many municipal and regional representatives perceived them as a move by the province to centralize land-use planning. It can also be added that this governmental policy would circumvent the traditional legislative process; instead of policies based on legislation this act provided for cabinet governance by regulation. According to the solicitor for the UBCM "there is no limitation on the government or the Ministers or Cabinet as to the type or form of regulations they may make" (Pearce 1980). This particular Vander Zalm initiative did not come to fruition, since on July 29, 1982 the provincial legislative session ended without passage of the proposed Land Use Act. The cabinet rejection—allowing the bill to die on the order paper—resulted in Vander Zalm's resignation, who called his cabinet colleagues "gutless."

Continuing differences between the province and the GVRD came to a head over a particular ALR exclusion proposal in the metropolitan suburb of Delta. Over several years, George Spetifore, a Social Credit supporter and agricultural land owner, together with local developers including the area's legislative assembly member, had sought an exclusion for a substantial farm area to allow extensive housing development. Provincial cabinet support for the proposal confronted GVRD opposition. The province's response in October 1983 to this local/regional frustration of its policy wishes was to strip regional districts of their planning and zoning authority (Magnusson, et al. 1984; Allen and Rosenbluh 1986). All regional plans and official regional plans prepared or designated before passage of the legislation were canceled. The rationale of the new Minister of Municipal Affairs Bill Ritchie was that "In view of the number of comprehensive municipal plans now in place, and which are the most important means of defining a community's planning objectives, the official regional plans have become an unnecessary level of land-use control" (Ritchie 1980). For GVRD officials, the issue was different: the act was "a move of retribution over the Spetifore land issue" where the GVRD opposed a cabinet decision to have this agricultural land removed from the ALR (Kirstein 1980).

Interestingly, although there were subsequent changes in ownership, the Spetifore lands were not developed as planned despite the provincial declaration of regional plans as null and void. Throughout the rest of the 1980s, the issue continued. In the summer of 1989, Delta Municipality held the largest public hearing in B.C. history—25 nights, 400 presentations and over 2,000 written submissions. This followed a disagreement between then Premier Bill Vander Zalm and his cabinet colleague, the MLA for Vancouver South, who questioned the accuracy of previous information made available to cabinet. Even the relevant federal minister became involved, calling for a one-year moratorium on "Spetifore Land" development—because of its potential impact on the Pacific (migratory bird) Flyway. The development plan was defeated by Delta Council on August 8, 1989. Subsequently, most of the earlier prodevelopment council was defeated in municipal elections. The impact of earlier regional planning with its provisions for agricultural land had an ongoing impact despite loss of planning *authority* in the region.

The Livable Region Plan(s)

As the inheritor of major portions of the LMRPB's official regional plan for the Lower Mainland, the GVRD undertook its own process of developing a planning strategy in the late '60s-early '70s.

In 1975, the GVRD adopted the Livable Region Plan (LRP). The LRP sought to create guidelines—based on forecasts, citizen preferences, and economic conditions—for the future development of the Lower Mainland. The LRP was distinct from the ORP; the LRP was intended to be pro-active and dynamic enough to respond to changes. Harry Lash, the GVRD's first director of planning and initiator of the LRP, depicted the LRP as flowing from "a new process, a different kind of planning" in which the interaction of public, planners, and politicians resulted in a set of strategies for dealing with regional growth.

The LRP centered upon five strategies that would manage growth within the GVRD:
1. establishing "job targets" for the various core areas,
2. establishing "regional town centers" as growth poles,
3. allocating residential growth consistent with services and jobs,
4. preserving farmland, parkland, and significant views, and
5. establishing a system of light rapid transit as the key to achievement of the other four strategies.

The LRP had the widespread support of the metropolitan community based on an extensive citizen participation process. It had a lasting impact on regional development decisions between 1976-1983, particularly the "Regional Town Centers" concept and their strategic locations throughout the GVRD. This has had a lasting imprint on regional urban development in metropolitan Vancouver. This was demonstrated in continuing GVRD support for regional agricultural land. It was also shown in the continuing capacity to plan regionally, even after the 1983 loss of regional planning authority.

Over the rest of the 1980s, the consensus achieved throughout the LRP process in the 1970s "helped shape the region and focus action" (GVRD 1990b), with encouragement from the GVRD Development (formerly Planning) Services Department. Its successes included identifying the alignment of the regional rapid transit system, encouraging regional town centers as foci for higher density development and rapid transit in suburban communities, and acquiring regional parks. Improvements in air quality and waste disposal and treatment were also byproducts of the LRP strategy.

By spring 1989, the GVRD had concluded that a major update of the LRP was needed because of the changes to the region. In March, "The Livable Region: A Strategy for the 1990s" was published to initiate this discussion. In July, the board approved seven broad "Livability Goals" to start the formal consultative process:

1. A Region in Nature—a blending of urban development and the natural environment;
2. An Economy of Growth and Change—a blend of livability with economic growth and diversity in an interdependent world;
3. Accessibility for People and Goods—ease of communication, e.g., job-home links etc.;
4. A Healthy and Safe Region—such as air and water quality, good social services, functional space patterns, etc.;
5. A Region of Diversity and Vitality—to support and enhance physical and social diversity;
6. An Equitable Region—sharing the region's livability across all communities;
7. An Efficient Region—with effective spending and intergovernmental cooperation amongst municipal and with senior levels (GVRD 1989a).

This was followed by the *Choosing Our Future* consultative process in 1989-90. The process included a series of seven regional challenge seminars (on urban mobility, the environment, culture, health and aging, urban design and suburban development, changing values, and community life), a forum, six community meetings, and a number of research reports.

Late in 1990, the GVRD's *Creating Our Future* revision to the Livable Region Plan set out 54 steps to maintaining and ensuring a more livable region. These included limiting private automobile use; creating a better housing-jobs balance through the creation of "complete communities" that use land wisely; conserving land resources, including agriculture, with an appropriate and accessible "green" mix; all within a region of good air and water quality, with environmentally appropriate waste treatment, disposal, and recycling. That the GVRD achieved such policy consensus without formal planning authority attests to the thesis that planning regionally has been established as a staple of governance in the metropolitan Vancouver region.

Map 8.6. *Regional Centres*

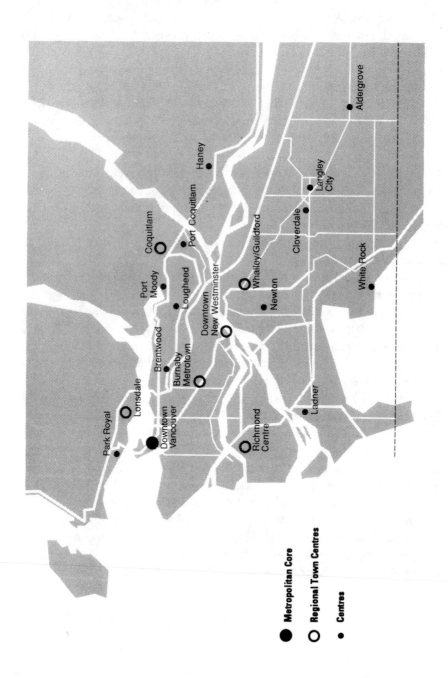

- ● Metropolitan Core
- ○ Regional Town Centres
- • Centres

CONCLUSION

Evidence from the case studies suggests that the tri-level process amongst local, provincial, and federal governments is the appropriate response to the conundrum of metropolitan governance. In this, the regional districts (in current or perhaps altered form), will have an important policy role. It is entirely possible to talk of regional *governance* in metropolitan Vancouver as a viable alternative to more traditional forms of regional government. A regional *government* would have the following five characteristics: (1) representation, (2) revenue-raising capacity, (3) autonomy, (4) authority, and (5) the capacity to coordinate. It is this coordination of multiple functions, enabling priority establishment and budgetary trade-offs, that characterizes government (Oberlander 1991).

Former Municipal Affairs Minister Don Campbell is right when he assigns a "B+ moving to an A" in his assessment of the GVRD. It is not a full-fledged regional government. It does, however, play an important—even central—role in the governance of the metropolitan Vancouver region. The case evidence demonstrates that transit and transportation, parks and green space, land-use planning and other vital public services are administered supramunicipally, on a regional area basis without a coordinated accountability to a single representative government (and in the absence of a metropolitan government).

In some instances, local governments are the essential (though not necessarily exclusive) decision makers. In many cases the federal government has a significant regional role. In other circumstances, the province is the key determiner. For example, at its first cabinet meeting on November 6, 1991, the new NDP provincial government dealt with the Agricultural Land Reserve as the first priority. The Minister of Agriculture announced the rescinding of golf course building permits on prime agricultural land, the strengthening of the ALR, and elimination of appeals to Cabinet—"to end abuses of the ALR." His cabinet colleague, the Minister of Finance and Crown Corporations, proposed a rethinking of skytrain extensions into Surrey and Richmond. One additional station is to be built to link skytrain to the Surrey regional town centre but the new priority has become its extension into the eastern NDP-represented suburbs such as Coquitlam. The Minister of Municipal Affairs has consideration of regional planning authority on his current agenda.

In a considerable number of policy areas, the regional district has performed the central function of establishing an idea or concept for an urban regional forum in metropolitan Vancouver. Its role has involved the public as a regional constituency in the formulation and reformulation of policy consensus on urban development for the Vancouver Lower Mainland—from the Burrard Peninsula Joint Sewage Committee of 1911 to recent tri-level governmental cooperation on air and water quality, waste treatment and disposal, transit, land use, and green space. In the case of governance in metropolitan Vancouver, that regional consensus was achieved early, maintained consistently, and has formed the basis of a system of regional governance where livability and its preservation is the watchword of regional policy formulation, whatever level of government is involved. With that policy consensus, regional governance has established itself as a formidable alternative to metropolitan government in the Vancouver region.

REFERENCES

Allen, Robert, and G. Rosenbluh. 1986. *Restraining the Economy: Social Credit Policies in B.C. in the '80s.* Vancouver: New Star.

Bish, Robert. 1990. *Local Government in British Columbia,* 2d ed. Vancouver: Union of B.C. Municipalities.

Bose, Bob. 1983. Recent Developments in Transit Management. At Action Now Conference, February 19.

British Columbia, Ministry of Finance and Corporate Relations. Department of Municipal Affairs. 1972. *Regional Districts in B.C., 1971.* Victoria: Department of Municipal Affairs, Queen's Printer, 6.

_____. 1989a. Legislative Assembly Debates, Province of British Columbia, 3d session, 34th Parliament, May 17, vol. 13, no. 7.

_____. 1989b. Ministry of Regional Development/GVRD. Cooperative Transportation Planning for Greater Vancouver, *Bulletin,* March.

_____. 1989c. *Provincial Report,* $1 Billion Expansion Near for Transit by Land, Sea, September, 2.

_____. 1989d. *Statistics Relating to Regional and Municipal Governments in B.C.* Victoria: British Columbia, June, 3.

_____. 1991. Population and Social Statistics Section, Planning and Statistics Division, January.

Burnaby Today. 1982. Council Plans to Call the Shots at Deer Lake. December 20.

Canada. 1989a. Port of Vancouver, October 18.

_____. 1989b. Transport Canada, Dangerous Goods Directorate, Pacific Region, October 13.

_____. 1991. Statistics Canada, 1991 Census. Vancouver Economic Development Office.

Cather, De Leuw. 1970. Rapid Transit in Vancouver. September.

Cohn, Ted, David Merrifield, and Patrick Smith. 1989. North American Cities in an Interdependent World: Vancouver and Seattle as International Cities. In *The New International Cities Era: The Global Activities of North American Municipal Governments,* ed. Earl Fry, Lee Radebaugh, and Panayotis Soldatos, Provo, Utah: Brigham Young University, 73-118.

District of Burnaby, Planning Department. 1975. *A Development Program for Burnaby Lake Regional Park.* December, 5, 31-33.

_____. 1980. *Manager's Report,* no. 23, Council Meeting, March 24.

_____. 1982. *Manager's Report*, no. 68, Council Meetings, December 13.

_____. 1986. *Manager's Report*, no. 1, December 24.

_____. 1988. *Manager's Report*, no. 30, April 7.

Dyck, Rand. 1986. *Provincial Politics in Canada*. Toronto: Prentice-Hall.

Fraser, Keith, and Malcolm Turnbull. 1989. Mayors Blast Transit, Scheme Upsets Three Mayors. *The Province*, Vancouver, July 13, 1-3.

Greater Vancouver Regional District. n.d. *Regional Parks . . . Yours to Discover*. GVRD.

_____. 1976. *Regional Parks Review, 1976*. June, 3.

_____. 1979. Planning Report, *Legislative Framework of the Greater Vancouver Regional District*. Vancouver.

_____, Planning Department. 1980a. The Livable Region from the '70s to the '80s. September.

_____. 1980b. *Policy Master Plan* (draft).

_____. 1982. A Review of Organizational Requirements for Transit in the Lower Mainland, February, 2-3.

_____. 1985. *System Plan and Policies*, 16-20.

_____. 1989a. Livability Goals for Greater Vancouver. GVRD board, policy adopted July.

_____. 1989b. Who Are We? What Do We Do? April.

_____. 1990a. *Choosing Our Future*. Burnaby: GVRD, March-May. A series of reports.

_____. 1990b. *Creating Our Future: Steps to a More Livable Region—Technical Report*. Choices Make a Difference. July.

_____. 1990c. *Creating Our Future: Steps to a More Livable Region*. Burnaby: GVRD, September, 15-17.

_____, Development Services. 1990d. *Greater Vancouver: Key Facts*. July, 19.

_____. 1990e. *Greater Vancouver . . . The Liveable Region*. GVRD, January, 14-18.

_____. 1991. Local Control of Transit Backed by Regional Board: Should be Handled by GVRD, Directors Say. *GVRD News*, August-October, 1.

Greater Vancouver Transportation Task Force. 1989. *Freedom to Move: Report of the Greater Vancouver Transportation Task Force*. vol. 1, July.

Higgins, Don. 1979. *Urban Canada: Its Government and Politics.* Toronto: Macmillan.

Horn, W. 1989. Mayor Prepares Transit Attack. *The Burnaby and New Westminster News,* July 26, 5.

Jacobs, Jane. 1984. *Cities and the Wealth of Nations: Principles of Economic Life.* New York: Random House.

Jones, Victor. 1988. Beavers and Cats: Federal-Local Relations in the United States and Canada. In *Meech Lake: From Centre to Periphery—The Impact of the 1987 Constitutional Accord on Canadian Settlements: A Speculation,* ed. H. Peter Oberlander and Hilda Symonds, Vancouver: University of British Columbia, Centre for Human Settlements, 80-126.

Kelly Report. 1971. Regional Transit as a GVRD Function. October.

Kirstein, Tom. 1980. GVRD Planning Committee Chair, Statement. *Vancouver Sun,* September 18.

Kopystynski, Adrian, and Syd Powlowski. 1980. The Genesis of LRT in Vancouver. In *Light Rail Transit in Vancouver,* ed. Michael C. Poulton, Vancouver: Center for Transportation Studies, University of British Columbia.

Lower Mainland Regional Planning Board. 1966. *A Regional Parks Plan for the Lower Mainland Region,* Report to the Regional Parks Committee, Lower Mainland Municipal Association, prepared by the Municipal Planning Service, May.

Lea. 1967. Automated Transit, December.

_____. 1968. Transportation System for the City of Vancouver. November.

Lee, Jeff. 1991. Candidates Pitch Policies to Woo Vancouver. *Vancouver Sun,* October 9, A16.

_____, and Lindsay Kines. 1989. Mayor Can't Conceive of 10 Million in City. *Vancouver Sun,* October 11, 1-2.

Magnusson, Warren, et al., eds. 1984. *The New Reality: The Politics of Restraint in B.C.* Vancouver: New Star.

Metro Transit Operating Company. 1980-81. *Annual Report,* 6.

Mills, John. 1991. *Vancouver Regional Transit System: A Proposal for Improving the Structure and Accountability of the Transit Service.* Consultants Report, GVRD, Summer.

Morley, J. Terrence, et al. 1983. *The Reins of Power: Governing British Columbia.* Vancouver: Douglas and McIntyre.

Morton, Brian. 1982. Prison Fencing Preferred to High-Density Housing. *Vancouver Sun,* September 16, A18.

North Vancouver District. 1989. Task Force Objectives: Office of the Mayor, North Vancouver District, October 10.

Oberlander, H. Peter. 1991. Urban Policy: One Canada or Ten? An Integrated Speculative Scenario Towards the 21st Century. In *Canada on the Threshold of the 21st Century: European Reflections Upon the Future of Canada*, ed. C. H. W. Remie and J. M. Lacroix, Amsterdam/Philadelphia: Johns Benjamin Publishing. Initially presented at the First All-European Canadian Studies Conference, The Hague, The Netherlands, October 24-27.

_____, and Hilda Symonds, eds. 1988. *Meech Lake: From Centre to Periphery—The Impact of the 1987 Constitutional Accord on Canadian Settlements: A Speculation.* Vancouver: University of British Columbia, Centre for Human Settlements.

Parkinson Report. 1971. A Preliminary Study of Light Rapid Transit in Vancouver. February.

Pearce, Ted. 1980. Union of British Columbia Municipalities Solicitor. *Vancouver Sun*, September 18.

Powers, Brian, and Shelley Fralic. 1988. Oakalla Housing Plan was a Shocker. *Vancouver Sun*, September 16, A1-2.

The Province. 1983. Vancouver, January 10.

Ritchie, Bill. 1980. Minister of Municipal Affairs, Statement. *Vancouver Sun*, July 8.

Robinson, Svend, M.P. 1982. Special: Oakalla Lands. Spring.

Seelig, Michael, and Alan Artibise. 1991. *From Desolation to Hope: The Pacific Fraser Region in 2010.* Vancouver: Board of Trade. Previously published as *Future Growth, FUTURE Shock, Vancouver Sun*, November 9-17.

Smith, Patrick. 1986. Regional Governance in British Columbia. *Planning and Administration*, vol. 13, no. 2 (Autumn): 11-12.

_____. 1988. Local-Federal Government Relations: Canadian Perspectives, American Comparisons—A View Through a Kaleidoscope. In *Meech Lake: From Centre to Periphery—The Impact of the 1987 Constitutional Accord on Canadian Settlements: A Speculation*, ed. H. Peter Oberlander and Hilda Symonds, Vancouver: University of British Columbia, Centre for Human Settlements, 127-40.

_____. 1991. British Columbia. *The Almanac of Canadian Politics*, ed. Munroe Eagles, James Bickerton, Alain Gagnon, and Patrick Smith. Petersborough: Broadview Press.

_____. 1992. The Making of a Global City: Fifty Years of Constituent Diplomacy—The Case of Vancouver. *Canadian Journal of Urban Research*, vol. 1, no. 1 (June): 90-112.

The Sun. 1985. March 13, A3.

Swainson, Neil. 1983. Provincial-Municipal Relations. *The Reins of Power: Governing British Columbia*, ed. T. Morley, N. Ruff, N. Swainson, J. Wilson, and W. Young. Vancouver: Douglas and McIntyre, 263.

Tennant, Paul, and David Zirnhelt. 1973. Metropolitan Government in Vancouver: The Politics of "Gentle Imposition." *Canadian Public Administration*, vol. 16 (Spring): 124-38.

Vancouver Sun. 1982. Minister Denies Change in Transit Administration, December 11, A1.

_____. 1985. March 13.

Vander Zalm, William. 1982. Minister of Municipal Affairs, News Release. June 15.

Veitch, Hon. Elwood. 1989. Ministerial Announcement, February.

Wooster, Swan. 1968. Vancouver Public Transportation Plan in the Future. May.

Chapter 9

Governance of the San Francisco Bay Area

Victor Jones
University of California, Berkeley
Donald N. Rothblatt
San Jose State University and
University of California, Berkeley

The San Francisco Bay Area is again undergoing a conscious, soul-searching but wrenching effort to reorganize its governance. For a decade and a half between 1959 and 1975, a succession of similar efforts failed to produce anything resembling a multipurpose regional government. The present activity is likely to persist for at least a decade. Regardless of any formal institutional outcome, the debate and accompanying adjustments among existing governmental agencies—national, state, regional, and local—will affect the governance of the Bay Area and, perhaps, set the stage for another round of structural and accommodative relationships among governments and with the private sector (ABAG 1966; Detling and Bacon 1977; V. Jones 1973, 1974).

WHAT IS THE BAY AREA?

The Bay Area by common usage consists of the nine counties touching San Francisco Bay, San Pablo Bay, and Suisun Bay: Alameda, Contra Costa, Marin, Napa, San Francisco, San Mateo, Santa Clara, Solano, and Sonoma (see Map 9.1). The 1990 population of the Bay Area is 6,023,577 (see Table 9.1). It is more populous than 80 percent of the American states, than all Canadian provinces except Ontario and Quebec, than many nations. The area contains approximately 7,000 square miles—almost as large as Massachusetts.

Map 9.1.   *San Francisco Bay Region*

Table 9.1. Population by County in the San Francisco Bay Area: 1980-90

County	Population		Difference		% Distribution of Absolute	% Distribution of Population	
	1980	1990	Numerical	1980-90 %	Increase	1980	1990
Alameda	1,105,379	1,279,182	173,803	15.7	20.6	21.3	21.2
Contra Costa	656,331	803,732	147,401	22.5	17.5	12.7	13.3
Marin	222,592	230,096	7,504	3.4	0.9	4.3	3.8
Napa	99,199	110,765	11,566	11.7	1.4	1.9	1.8
San Francisco	678,974	723,959	44,985	6.6	5.3	13.1	12.0
San Mateo	587,329	649,623	62,294	10.6	7.4	11.3	10.8
Santa Clara	1,295,071	1,497,577	202,506	15.6	23.9	25.1	25.0
Solano	235,203	340,421	105,218	44.7	12.5	4.5	5.7
Sonoma	299,681	388,222	88,541	29.6	10.5	5.8	6.4
Bay Area	5,179,759	6,023,577	843,818	16.3	100.0	100.0	100.0

Source: U.S. Department of Commerce, Bureau of the Census. 1991 *Preliminary 1990 Census.*

The Bay Area, then, is by no means a compact single-centered metropolis. It is rather a multinucleated regional community comprised of local and subregional communities extending approximately 150 miles from Cloverdale in the north to Gilroy in the south and 50 miles from Dixon in the east to the Pacific Ocean. There is no single dominating central city, although San Francisco remains the symbolic center and the actual center of financial and related service activities in Northern California and much of the West (James Vance 1964; Jean Vance 1976; ABAG 1989, 1991b, 1991c; Bay Area Council and McKinsey 1986; Brady 1987; Davis and Langlois 1963; Hoerter and Wiselman 1986; Kroll 1984; Kroll and Eurengil 1989; O'Connor and Blakely 1988; Rothblatt and Garr 1986). Since 1988, San Francisco is no longer the largest city in the Bay Area, relinquishing that position to San Jose. It is still, however, along with Silicon Valley in the San Jose area, a major job center for the region.

Do the nine counties constitute a single metropolitan region (Davis and Langlois 1963; James Vance 1964)? Some residents of counties on the fringe assert that they are distinctive metropolitan areas. Sometimes this claim is based on the size of the population—as in Santa Clara County (Elder 1989), in distance from the more highly urbanized portions of the region, or in differences in land uses and lifestyles of the North Bay counties (Napa, Solano, Sonoma). To say that Cloverdale has little in common with Gilroy, 150 miles to the south, does not mean that Sonoma and Santa Clara Counties, for instance, are not integral parts of the same metropolitan complex (Meltzer 1984). In a region of over six million people living in an area of 7,000 square miles, there are many subregions, few covering the entire region, but with many overlapping relationships. Thus, very few residents of Santa Clara County commute to Contra Costa, Marin, Napa, Solano, and Sonoma Counties, and vice versa. But there is a sizeable commutation between Santa Clara County and Alameda County and between Alameda County and Solano County. The West Bay (Marin, San Mateo, and especially San Francisco Counties) and the East Bay (Alameda and Contra Costa Counties) interact through commutation with all of the nine counties.

Furthermore, the local governments, including special districts of the nine counties, have developed many formal and informal relationships with each other. Some of the formal institutional relationships involve all nine counties, such as the Association of Bay Area Governments (ABAG), and the Metropolitan Transportation Commission (MTC). The Bay Area Air Quality Management District (BAAQMD) covers all but the northern portions of two counties, others involve two or three adjoining counties, and still other subregional institutions are within a single county. These are political relationships that Kingsley Davis and Eleanor Langlois did not consider when they asserted that "The nine-county area is not a meaningful unit in any economic and social sense and has no significance when used over time as if it were such a unit" (Davis and Langlois 1963).

The Bureau of the Census divides the Bay Area (which it calls the San Francisco-Oakland-San Jose Consolidated Metropolitan Statistical Area) into six primary metropolitan statistical areas: (1) San Francisco, Marin, and San Mateo counties; (2) Oakland (Alameda and Contra Cosa Counties); (3) San Jose-Palo Alto (Santa Clara County); (4) Santa Rosa-Petaluma (Sonoma County); (5) Vallejo-Fairfield-Napa (Napa and Solano Counties); and (6) Santa Cruz (Santa Cruz County). Santa Cruz is not traditionally considered to be part of the Bay Area—its local governments belong to the Association of Monterey Bay Area Governments. However, Santa Cruz, Monterey, and the nonmetropolitan county of San Benito are part of the Silicon Valley labor market area. The number of commuters will undoubtedly increase during the next decade.

There are four major subregions in the Bay Area: West Bay consists of San Francisco and San Mateo counties. (We include Marin County in the North Bay subregion). South Bay is Santa Clara County. East Bay contains Alameda and Contra Costa Counties and North Bay Marin, Sonoma, Napa, and Solano Counties.

It is certain that any legislation proposed by Bay Vision Action Coalition, and quite likely any other legislation originating outside the Bay Area, will provide for subregions as intermediaries between local governments and any proposed regional agency. Each of the nine counties for some purposes, is a politically active subregion. County officials in the Bay Area (but not in the California County Supervisors Association) no longer insist that county governments can serve as regional governments. Nevertheless, state legislation, for instance, on solid waste disposal, air quality, and transportation, increasingly uses the county as a unit for planning and implementation. The County Congestion Management Agencies (CMA), established in 1990 under Proposition 111, may well be recognized as the principal subregional planning agency. Thus each of the nine counties would be the principal territorial subplanning unit, involving all local governments within the county. However, other overlapping plates of subregional planning and action jurisdiction will be needed for special and multiple purposes. Two illustrations are the I-80 corridor in western Alameda and Contra Costa Counties and the 101 corridor in Marin and Sonoma Counties. There will be many needs and possibilities for *ad hoc* subregions, some larger, some smaller than the county.

West Bay

San Francisco has remained the symbolic center of the region, even though it is no longer "the City" to which seekers of culture, recreation, merchandise, professional services, and specialty restaurants must go to satisfy their needs and desires. As in other metropolitan areas, San Francisco's proportion of regional jobs, housing, population, educational and cultural institutions, retail, wholesale, manufacturing, transportation, and service firms has been declining. Nevertheless, there is a higher concentration of most of these activities in a smaller compact land area than anywhere else in the region. The dispersion of people and activities over so many other municipalities means that "what is left in San Francisco" constitutes the largest single shopping and recreation center in the region (even though San Francisco's taxable sales decreased from 22.3 percent in 1970 to 13.5 percent in 1989 of the Bay Area total) (ABAG 1989, 1991a, 1991b, 1991c). San Jose, with a land area of 173 square miles, as compared with the 49 square miles of San Francisco, and with a larger and more rapidly growing population as well as a larger concentration of jobs, does not yet fill this regional role. Yet the basic characteristic of the region is increasing dispersion in and around new and expanding older centers. The Bay Area is not a region made up of a central city and its suburban hinterland. It can best be understood as a region of overlapping subregions—larger overlapping plates for some characteristics, such as the San Francisco and Santa Clara County labor markets and smaller overlapping plates for such activities as retail shopping.

In 1990, there were approximately 590,000 jobs in San Francisco, but only 420,000 employed residents—an excess of 188,000 jobs to be filled by commuters (ABAG 1989). In fact, there are many more commuters since some of the employed residents work outside San Francisco. However, the Metropolitan Transportation Commission reports that residents of the city have the shortest average commute of any transportation subarea in the region. The city has the heaviest transit service both inside and from outside its boundaries.

Corporate job relocation was high during the 1980s—mostly into industrial and commercial parks in Alameda and Contra Costa Counties. In 1990, the Bank of America announced the relocation of over 2,000 of its employees into Solano County—a rapidly growing Bay Area county half-way between San Francisco and Sacramento. ABAG projects that:

> By the end of 1986, most of these shifts were substantially complete. Between 1987 and 1990, trends indicate that San Francisco's total employment will increase by about 18,000 new jobs or 6,000 new jobs annually. Most of this growth is occurring in four broad sectors: Business Services, Legal Services, Retail Trade and Hotels. Job losses continue in Finance and Communications and most of Manufacturing. Between 1990 and 2005, job demand in San Francisco County is expected to rise by 93,000 new jobs or about 6,200 new jobs annually. In terms of overall regional growth, San Francisco County will rank fourth in the Bay Area in job demand. Santa Clara will lead the region, followed by Alameda and Contra Costa counties (ABAG 1989, 180).

There is no indication that any other center will replace San Francisco as the site or the producer of major region-serving activities. Golden Gate Park is used by regional residents as well as tourists and San Franciscans. The U.S. Parks Service operates a park along the Marina and the western shore of the city and will take over the Presidio (to be closed as an Army post) in a few years. San Francisco sells water from the Sierras to 30 suburban municipalities and water districts in San Mateo and parts of Alameda and Santa Clara Counties. It also operates in San Mateo County the major international airport in northern California. In fact, it buries its dead and houses its prisoners and juvenile delinquents in San Mateo County—from which it was separated and established as a consolidated city and county in 1856.

San Mateo County to the south of San Francisco is oriented in two directions—north to San Francisco and south to Silicon Valley in Santa Clara County. The largest employment center is San Francisco's international airport—with no residents and 19,560 workers. There are six municipalities with 88,390 jobs and only 81,800 employed residents. The remaining 14 municipalities and their immediately surrounding spheres of influence are bedroom communities—276,200 employed residents and only 165,370 jobs. In the county as a whole, 54,400 of its employed residents work outside the county. Of course, the number of people who commute to work is much larger as people travel to jobs within their municipality, into other county municipalities, and to other counties. Net commutation data do not measure gross commuting (ABAG 1989).

According to an MTC survey of average distance to work, northern San Mateo County ranks tenth, southern county twelfth, and central county municipalities rank fifteenth among surveyed subareas of the region.

South Bay

Santa Clara County, south of San Mateo and Alameda Counties, has a strong labor market association with the northern part of San Benito and Monterey Counties and with Santa Cruz County to the west. In fact, since 1980 Santa Cruz County has been included by the Bureau of the Census-Office of Management and Budget along with the traditional nine counties as a Consolidated Metropolitan Statistical Area. Santa Clara County is more strongly tied, however, to the Bay Area. Still, one might have expected it to behave like San Diego County in asserting its political independence of the larger Los Angeles urban region. There has been some talk along these lines—witness the editorial in the *San Jose Mercury News* of March 11, 1990:

> By defining this region as the traditional nine-county Bay Area, [Assembly Speaker] Brown missed an important point: It's far more practical, given commute patterns and other realities, to think in terms of two regions, with San Jose as the hub of one which extends well into Monterey and San Benito counties.

A recent poll in the county shows that 37 percent of telephone respondents accept the nine counties as the Bay Area; 40 percent thought the region should be smaller—either Santa Clara only or Santa Clara and San Mateo Counties. Only 6 percent would define the region as Santa Clara, Santa Cruz, and San Benito Counties. If we combine those who look upon the nine counties and those who prefer a Santa Clara-San Mateo Counties region, we find that 56 percent or 70 percent of those who have an opinion have oriented toward the Bay (Elder 1989).

Furthermore, the strongest support for regionalism in the Bay Area has come from public officials in Santa Clara County, San Jose, and other county municipalities. County Supervisor Rod Diridon, not supported by all of his fellow local government officials, has provided local government leadership in sponsoring the creation and work of the Bay Vision 2020 Commission—a broad-based commission established in 1989 to develop a vision and plan of action for improving the quality of the Bay

Area in the year 2020. The city of San Jose, alone among the larger Bay Area cities, is very active in the Bay Vision Action Coalition. San Jose's mayor, city manager, and other officials personally participate in the work of the Coalition. Local officials have been supported and assisted by the Santa Clara County Manufacturers Group. Members of the group have been active in the Bay Vision 2020 Commission (Peter Lydon 1992).

The San Jose area is a world center of high technology covering over 1,300 square miles and possessing all the political, social, economic, and physical complexities of most major American metropolitan areas (Rothblatt 1990). During the 1950-80 period, the metropolitan population grew from 290,500 to 1,295,000 (346 percent), making it one of the fastest growing metropolitan areas in the nation. The city of San Jose itself grew even more spectacularly from a modestly sized agricultural processing center of 95,300 in 1950 to 628,300 in 1980—or an increase of 559 percent.

This expansion has transformed Santa Clara County from an agriculturally oriented valley to an international center of technological innovation called "Silicon Valley." The San Jose area became the most dynamic engine of economic development for the entire San Francisco Bay Region as it generated nearly one-half of the region's total employment growth between 1970 and 1980 (Schoop 1986).

As the economy of Silicon Valley matures and diversifies, substantial new employment opportunities are expected to be generated in such areas as services and retail and wholesale trade (Brady 1989). Indeed, the Association of Bay Area Governments (1989) projects that nearly 250,000 new jobs (about a 28 percent increase) will be created in the San Jose area during the 1990-2005 period. However, during the current recession, new jobs decreased by 1.92 percent in Santa Clara County while they increased by 3.36 percent in Sonoma County.

By 1989, the city of San Jose's population grew to 738,400, enabling it to overtake San Francisco as the most populous city in the Bay Area and to become the twelfth largest city in the United States. The San Jose area contains over 80 governmental units—15 cities, 37 school districts, and numerous park, sewer, water, and other overlapping entities. In actuality, the subregion is even more complex politically, since many private groups representing various business, environmental, cultural, and other interests are often involved in metropolitan issues, as are a growing number of governmental units outside the county that are providing housing for the expanding San Jose area. For example, in 1985, about 125,000 persons commuted daily to Santa Clara County from the five surrounding counties (Alameda, San Benito, Monterey, Santa Cruz, and San Mateo) (Santa Clara County Transportation Agency 1985). This process of metropolitan expansion is likely to continue not only because of global forces of economic dispersion (Castells 1985; Hall and Markusen 1985), but also because of the 1978 Proposition 13 tax change in California that encourages in-lying local governments to capture the more fiscally desirable commercial and industrial activity and push service demanding residential development to the periphery of metropolitan areas (Dowall 1984). In addition, this pressure for decentralization is being reinforced by the large numbers of baby boomers who are now entering the low-density single-family housing market.

During the past two decades, the expanding Bay Area economy has been generating employment opportunities at a substantially faster rate than new housing, and reasonably affordable housing has been located at increasing distances from centers of employment. This trend is especially pronounced in Santa Clara County. Most of the electronics-related employment opportunities in the Bay Area have developed in the northern portion of the county near the original centers of technological innovation of Stanford University and the National Aeronautics and Space Administration (NASA), while the bulk of the housing has been provided increasingly in the southern part of the county or in adjacent counties where land is most readily available and is relatively less expensive. This widening supply-spatial gap has been bidding up the cost of housing dramatically and has resulted in severe traffic congestion, air pollution, and fiscal inequities in the region (Saxenian 1985; Cervero 1986).

Silicon Valley is one of the highest cost-of-living areas in the nation, and it is under increasing pressure to relocate much of its low-wage manufacturing activities to less costly regions in the United States and abroad (Hall and Markusen 1985; Saxenian 1985). For example, in 1975, there were 501,600 jobs in Santa Clara County and 411,500 housing units (Rothblatt 1982). During the 1975-85 period, about 318,000 new jobs were created, while only 74,850 new homes were constructed in the county (ABAG 1987). This gap between the number of jobs generated and the number of housing units supplied has created an enormous shortage of housing in Silicon Valley that affects people at every economic level—particularly low- and moderate-income families. In 1988, Santa Clara County was the fourth most expensive metropolitan housing rental market in the United States (McLeod 1988). Unfortunately, this jobs/housing imbalance is expected to worsen in the decades ahead, impacting the social, environmental, and economic functioning of this metropolitan community (ABAG 1987; Rothblatt and Garr 1986; Brady 1989).

Finally, the bifurcated labor force characteristic of high-tech areas is split between the affluent white-male professional and managerial staff, and low-wage predominantly female ethnic production workers (Saxenian 1985). This pattern is spatially manifested by the increasingly socially separated residential areas in Silicon Valley (United Way of Santa Clara County 1987). When we consider that in Santa Clara County, the high school dropout rate for Hispanic youth approached 50 percent in 1985 (Santa Clara County Board of Education 1986), and that many of the entry level production jobs at jeopardy due to global competition are held by low-income minority workers, a disturbing picture emerges of widening economic disparities and growing social instability (Larimer 1987).

East Bay

Alameda and Contra Costa Counties, with a combined population of over 2,000,000 people, not only house many workers employed in Silicon Valley, but contain bedroom communities for commuters to San Francisco and San Mateo Counties. At the same time, there is much cross-commuting within and between the two counties—especially to Oakland and newly developed office centers in southern Alameda County and all along the I-680 corridor running from San Jose in the south to Walnut Creek and Concord and a heavy industrial complex on San Pablo Bay and the Carquinez Straits (ABAG 1989).

As in San Jose, there is talk in Oakland of a metropolitan area independent of San Francisco. A recent example is the assertion of Professor Edward Blakely, of the Department of City and Regional Planning, University of California, Berkeley, and founder of the University-Oakland Metropolitan Forum, that Oakland's economic health is no longer tied primarily to a declining San Francisco:

> Oakland should tie its future to the north and east, Contra Costa
> County and the San Joaquin Valley. He sees Oakland as the
> center of capital and transportation for the central valley, one of
> the fastest growing areas of the county (Daniel S. Levine,
> *Oakland Tribune*, May 11, 1991).

The increase in commuting from the central valley to Bay Area jobs has worried officials in adjacent Stockton and Modesto metropolitan areas. The mayor of Modesto and the Stanislaus County Council of

Governments have requested Bay Vision 2020, ABAG, and MTC to consider the effect of Bay Area policies on adjacent counties. Already, Bay Area workers are seeking affordable housing outside the Bay Area, and ABAG projects that by 2005, over 292,000 workers will have to commute into the nine-county San Francisco Bay Region (ABAG 1989). Five of the 10 Bay Area transportation subcorridors are in the East Bay. They are expected to generate during the 1990-2005 period 271,570 new jobs but only 236,200 new workers. The transportation facilities of these five corridors not only serve the East Bay, but also transport commuters to San Francisco and the Silicon Valley. Also, as jobs move from the Bay Area into surrounding counties, the corridors will have to transport reverse commuters as well as provide cross-community mobility within the Bay Area (ABAG 1989). If the proposed toll-road in eastern Contra Costa County connecting Silicon Valley with Interstate 80 in Solano County is constructed, a new major corridor of manufacturing, service, and trade centers could develop to serve not only the Bay Area (especially Solano, Contra Costa, Alameda, and Santa Clara Counties), but the adjacent central valley metropolitan areas.

The southern part of Alameda County and the central part of Contra Costa County have attracted large numbers of office jobs from San Francisco and related heavy traffic congestion. In the next decade, the fastest development of both jobs and housing will be in the eastern and southern parts of the two counties. At the same time, Silicon Valley will continue to import an increasing number of workers from newer housing developments in the undeveloped portion of the East Bay.

The East Bay firestorm in October 1991 destroyed over two square miles of houses and apartment buildings in the Berkeley and Oakland Hills. The fire only two years after the Loma Prieta earthquake is important not only for the lives lost, the thousands of homeless people, and the property damage but for the warning that uncontrollable natural forces, such as earthquakes, long periodic droughts, and hot high winds from the eastward central valleys, known as Santa Anas, are eternal dangers that must be faced in California. Governments, businesses, and the public will also have to face questions of response during the catastrophe, as well as longer range questions of land use, building and landscape controls, and water supply and conservation.

North Bay

The North Bay, consisting of Marin, Sonoma, Napa, and Solano Counties, is the largest in area and smallest in population. Its 1990 population of 839,408 constitutes only 13.9 percent of the Bay Area population. It is, however, growing very rapidly—one-fourth of the increase in population for the region between 1980 and 1990 was in the North Bay—equal to the growth of Silicon Valley (Santa Clara County). Its rate of growth has been consistently high—approximately 30 percent or more in each of the past five decades. ABAG estimates that between 1990 and 2005, the number of jobs in the three counties will increase by more than 132,000: 64,000 in Sonoma, 61,000 in Solano, and 7,100 in Napa. Population is expected to increase even more rapidly. ABAG projects an increase of over 291,000 persons, of whom 157,000 will be employed. It is estimated that net commutation into other counties will be approximately 13,000. This low net commutation rate indicates an expectation of a large increase in North Bay jobs (ABAG 1989).

In fact, the North Bay looks not only to the central Bay Area but part of it (Solano County) is also developing interdependencies with the large and fast growing Sacramento region in the central valley. Napa County is well-known for its wines and southern California tourists, its rural and agricultural lands in the north, and urban areas around the city of Napa. Between Vallejo and Fairfield in Solano County and the city of Napa, American Canyon voted in 1991 to incorporate as a municipality. Sonoma County, from Santa Rosa south, is developing as a small industrial economy and as a bedroom for commuters to jobs in Marin County and San Francisco. Santa Rosa in Sonoma County is developing into a major urban center. Just north of Santa Rosa, Windsor voted in 1991 to incorporate as a city.

The position of many North Bay residents is that they can neither live with nor without the Bay Area. The most often expressed view is that the mature high density communities to the south, now experiencing the inconveniences of a major metropolis, are determined to keep the North Bay in perpetual open space for their own enjoyment.

The Solano County Board of Supervisors refused to join ABAG for many years, and for several years Sonoma County withdrew from ABAG. It rejoined ABAG only after unsuccessful attempts to get the state government to recognize it as part of a north coast council of governments. At the same time, however, its municipalities were active members of ABAG. The attitude toward Bay Area regionalism of many residents and leaders of the North Bay is well expressed in a letter from the mayor of Calistoga to the Bay Vision 2020 Commission:

> . . . the County of Napa is an agricultural county. . . . Southern Napa County has many residents who commute to jobs out of the county, and is more linked to the urban centers. With that stronger link comes increased traffic congestion, pollution, housing difficulties, noise issues, and a myriad other urban concerns. The northern end of the county has a far different set of problems and concerns than does the south county. While the northern part of the county is still linked to the Bay Area, the problems confronting the Up-Valley and Pope Valley are different. . . . Small size and agricultural orientation make members of the City Council of the City of Calistoga fear that they will be overwhelmed by loud urban voices from more metropolitan areas.

The North Bay counties and their municipalities led the successful effort at the November 1991 general assembly of ABAG to reject endorsement of an earlier executive board resolution, modifying slightly the Bay Vision 2020 proposal to consolidate ABAG with MTC and the BAAQMD. They were, of course, supported by many municipal representatives from other parts of the Bay Area. In effect, the general assembly voted for ABAG to come up with its own proposal for regional governance to be presented to the general assembly in March 1992.

We include Marin County in the North Bay although it is more definitely a bedroom county for commuters to San Francisco than is any of the other three North Bay counties. The interdependencies between Marin and Sonoma counties are increasing as residents from the north commute to jobs in Marin County and along highway 101 to jobs in San Francisco. Political and other leaders in both counties are aware of intercounty dependencies—witness the unhappiness in the Marin County Board of Supervisors over the proposal for most of Marin County to share a state assembly district with San Francisco. The county supervisors prefer to be joined in a district with Sonoma County.

CURRENT CONCERN OVER GROWTH MANAGEMENT

Unlike previous efforts to create a multipurpose regional agency when Bay Area interests had to go it alone in the state legislature against opposition from the Central Valley and southern California, there is now statewide concern over traffic congestion, water supply and distribution, water quality, air quality, open space, preservation of agricultural lands, and natural resources.

Six bills have been introduced in the 1991 session of the legislature. AB3 by Willie Brown, a Democrat from San Francisco and speaker of the assembly, would establish a State Growth Management Commission and seven directly elected regional development and infrastructure agencies. The Bay Area region would consist of all of the nine counties except for the northern portion of Sonoma County. Each regional development and infrastructure agency, except in San Diego County, would be governed by a directly elected board of 13 members. In San Diego, the Regional Planning and Growth Management Review Board, established in 1988 by electoral approval of Proposition C and consisting of the executive board of the San Diego Association of Governments, would be recognized as the regional development and infrastructure agency. In any of the other six regions, locally developed plans for a regional agency could be substituted for the regional agency requirements of AB3. This was an open invitation to the Bay Vision 2020 Commission and its local governments, business, and environmental sponsors to use the Brown bill as the vehicle for legislative authorization of its proposal.

Similar to the Bay Vision 2020 proposal, but with significant differences, the Bay Area regional agency under AB3 would have three years in which to develop a plan for the consolidation of the Association of Bay Area Governments (ABAG), the Metropolitan Transportation Commission (MTC), the Bay Area Air Quality Management District (BAAQMD), and perhaps the Regional Water Quality Control Board (RWQCB). In the interim, the planning functions of all four agencies would be immediately merged, but nonplanning functions would remain with the respective agencies. Subregional planning agencies may be created for each county.

A 19-member State Growth Management Commission, appointed by the governor from nominees submitted by specified local governmental and water district associations, farmers organizations, building industry and realtors, State Chamber of Commerce and Manufacturers Association, labor, affordable housing organizations, and environmental groups would develop a State Conservation and Development Plan. It would negotiate rectification of inconsistencies between the state plan and regional and local plans, with final power of approval or disapproval vested in the state commission.

SB907, introduced by Senator McCorquedale, Democrat from Santa Clara County, authorizes with voter approval the creation of regional fiscal authorities. Section 54722.10 would instruct each authority to ascertain the effect of the present allocation of property and sales taxes on land-use decisions by local governments. If the result of current allocations were determined to result in an imbalance between jobs and housing, it could rectify the situation by offering the sharing of up to one-half the revenue from new developments as an incentive to rectify the imbalance.

Senator Bergeson's bill (SB434) would require the governor, through the Office of Planning and Research, to develop and maintain California growth management policies. Cities and counties would be authorized to create regional fiscal authorities "to implement planning and development on a regional basis consistent with California growth management policies." No regional fiscal authority could operate without the governor's certification that the regional authority is "likely to implement the California growth management policies" and develop boundaries within which development would be permitted, a tax sharing agreement, and a regional fiscal plan consistent with California growth management policies. State agencies would be required to give preference in the allocation of state bond money or other discretionary funds to regional and local projects found to be consistent with the California growth management policies.

AB76, introduced by Assembly Member Farr, Democrat (Monterey), would replace the Office of Planning and Research with two new agencies: an Office of Research to assist the governor and a State Planning Agency. Assisted by a State Planning Advisory Council, the State Planning Agency would prepare a biennial statewide planning report to the governor and the state legislature. A separate Department of Environmental and Plan Review would be created to review regional and local plans for their "conformance" with the State Planning Report.

SB929 (Senator Presley, Democrat, Riverside County) establishes 11 growth management policies to be incorporated into a state plan by a 15-member California Conservation and Development Commission. The commission would consist of nine state officials, three appointed by the governor to represent counties, cities, and regional agencies, three appointed by the speaker of the assembly to represent business, agriculture, and minorities, and three appointed by the Rules Committee of the Senate to represent housing, planning, and environmentalists.

The state commission would prepare reorganization guidelines for regional agencies, review proposed reorganization of regional agencies, and institute regional reorganization if regional agencies fail to develop an acceptable reorganization by January 1, 1996. The bill specifies that land be classified into six "tiers" and that regional and subregional plans stimulate growth in tiers suitable for redevelopment, facilitate planned urbanization in the remainder of central cities and in existing suburbs and rural towns suitable for planned urban growth, avoid premature urbanization, and prevent urbanization of agriculture, other productive resource lands, and environmentally important areas.

Finally, the Morgan bill (SB797), which originally embodied the recommendations of the Bay Vision 2020 Commission. It was designed as a holding operation and in May 1992 was completely amended as a result of extended negotiations among local governments and business and environmental groups.

All of these bills have moved from the house of origin to the other house of the legislature and thus are alive in the 1992 session. But Governor Wilson requested that all legislative action be delayed until he received in December 1991 the report of his Growth Management Council. Unlike his three predecessors, Governor Wilson is very interested in environmental protection and growth management. He is on record, however, in opposition to state-mandated regional agencies. His position has undoubtedly encouraged local officials in the Bay Area to push for stronger local government control over Bay Vision 2020's proposed regional commission. His official position, however, is still unannounced. It is unlikely that any action will be taken before 1993. State, national, and local election campaigns will dominate everyone's attention until after November. The new legislature, in which all members of the Assembly and half of the Senate, will have been elected or re-elected from newly drawn districts, will also face a huge budget deficit, re-organization of welfare and health-care systems, a declining or sluggish economy, ethnic unrest and the beginning of positioning for a gubernatorial election in 1994 and a presidential election in 1996. This is the context in which the Morgan bill will be debated and acted upon.

Local government officials, businesspersons, and environmentalists joined together in 1989 to create and support the Bay Vision 2020 Commission. The commission is composed of 31 members (none of whom were local government officials) appointed by its sponsors from all nine Bay Area counties. They are supposed to represent environmentalists, ethnic minorities, business, manufacturers, agriculture, labor, and

developers. The commission report issued on June 1, 1991, recommended the merger of the Association of Bay Area Governments, the
Metropolitan Transportation Commission, and the Bay Area Air Quality
Management District into a Bay Area Regional Commission (Bay Vision
2020 Commission 1991).

The regional commission would, under the Bay Vision 2020 plan,
consist of 60 percent elected local officials selected by and from mayors,
councilpersons, and county supervisors and 40 percent nonpublic
members selected by an *ad hoc* selection committee.

The regional commission would be an interim body like the original
Bay Conservation and Development Commission (BCDC) and the State
Coastal Commission. It would have three years in which to develop a
regional plan for transportation, air quality, open space, and other
regionally significant land uses. In the fourth year, the draft plan and
other recommendations would be submitted to the legislature and the
governor for their approval and for the enactment of legislation enabling
the regional commission to implement the regional plan. However, all
authority now exercised by MTC, BAAQMD, and ABAG would be
exercised by the regional commission.

After Bay Vision 2020 submitted its report in early 1991, it continued
in existence, but became inactive, except for occasional meetings to hear
reports on the Action Coalition's progress. Some of its members along
with its sponsors from local government, the Bay Area Council, and the
Greenbelt Alliance formed the Bay Vision Action Coalition to fine tune
the commission's recommendations and develop legislation for the 1992
session. The Action Coalition rewrote (or fine tuned) all the recommendations of Bay Vision 2020 except the basic one to consolidate the
Association of Bay Area Governments, the Metropolitan Transportation
Commission, and the Bay Area Air Quality Management District.

Early in its deliberations, it was decided that elected local officials
should make up two-thirds of the interim regional commission. Many
local officials are still insisting that all its members be mayors, councilpersons, and county supervisors. The ABAG executive board proposed
a regional board with 80 percent elected officials. However, this proposal
was rejected at the ABAG General Assembly November 1991, in April
1992, and again in October 1992. A resolution was passed demanding
that the regional board consist only of local elected officials (ABAG
1991g).

There are deep differences among local officials over representation
of cities and counties and of small suburbs and large cities. These

differences overlay differences over representation and regional policy among environmentalists, developers, and their allies among building contractors and labor, nongrowth and slow-growth proponents, various types of agricultural interests, farmers who wish to sell their land for development and proponents of open space, proponents of denser urban housing and cheaper, more spacious housing on the periphery and even beyond the Bay Area, proponents and opponents of restrictions on the use of automobiles, as well as of larger concentrations of ethnic minorities. Whether these interests can be satisfied by any representational scheme is yet unknown.

The Bay Vision Action Coalition must also develop a scheme for the orderly transition of the three agencies into a single regional agency. Of the three agencies, only ABAG has taken a formal position in support of consolidation. The Action Coalition now proposes in the Morgan bill that each of the agencies continue to exercise all their functions, except regional planning, for the first year. During this period, the regional commission would begin to prepare a regional plan and to negotiate the consolidation itself. At the end of the first year, it would assume all the authority of ABAG, MTC, and the Air Board.

The scope of its regional planning, as well as the relation of local, subregional, and other functional planning to regional planning will continue to be the major focus of disagreement. A major question is the extent of regional control over "regionally significant" (what is regionally significant?) changes in land use during the interim period while a regional plan is being developed and reviewed by local governments, the governor, and the state legislature. Some people fear that in the absence of such interim review, local governments would permit a flood of developments before the regional plan is adopted by the regional council and approved by the governor and legislature. However, to exercise such interim controls before regional plans have been completed and regulations adopted appears to many other people as *ad hoc* and arbitrary. Both the Bay Conservation and Development Commission and the State Coastal Commission regulated development while regional plans were being developed.

The Regional Planning Committee of ABAG has been debating regional growth management policies for several years (ABAG 1991d). These materials, as well as the report of Bay Vision 2020, have been used by a subcommittee of the Action Coalition to develop a recommended regional planning framework. The essence of the proposal is to draw urban growth boundaries around existing urban areas and to forbid development outside such boundaries that threaten agriculture, open space, and the natural environment. Within urban boundaries, development would be encouraged through public and private investment in infrastructure, affordable housing near jobs, new job-producing activities near housing, discouragement of long distance commuting, and development of alternatives to single occupancy automobile traffic.

A *San Francisco Chronicle* poll released in September 1991 shows strong popular support (74 percent) for the consolidation of ABAG, MTC, and the BAAQMD. An earlier poll showed that only 49 percent of the respondents favored creation of such a regional agency. However, "great unease" was expressed over regional control of housing development. A survey of local elected officials and other leaders conducted in 1990 by the League of Women Voters of the Bay Area while Bay Vision 2020 Commission was deliberating but before its report was issued showed strong support among local officials for regional air quality controls (73 percent), airport planning (66 percent), Bay fill (67 percent), solid waste management (62 percent), transportation (65 percent), water quality (69 percent), and water supply (51 percent). Only 21 percent favored regional zoning and land-use controls but 58 percent favored regional advisory land-use authority. Moreover, only 53 percent of nonlocally elected respondents favored regional zoning and land-use controls. Two-thirds favored mandatory regional growth management. Required fair share housing was favored by only 34 percent of locally elected officials and by 55 percent of other respondents (League of Women Voters of the Bay Area 1991b).

The Bay Vision 2020 Commission and the Bay Vision Coalition represent several strands of interest, ideology, temperament, and experience in Bay Area affairs—many of which are continuations or resurgences of positions held strongly enough to prevent legislative action only 15 years ago. One determinative division at that time that still exists today is over the proper or desirable role of cities, counties, and special districts in a multipurpose regional agency. Another example is the different emphasis placed by the Bay Area Council representing large industries and the Greenbelt Alliance on the importance—where they conflict as they frequently do—of suburban housing and the preservation of agricultural and other open spaces (Peter Lydon 1992).

There is then a renewed public concern with the condition of regional and local transportation, housing, air and water pollution, the homeless, open space, and recreational facilities (Viviano 1989a; Rapaport 1992a). Throughout the 20th century, there have been periodic efforts in the San

Francisco Bay Area to establish major regional special-purpose districts and to create some form of limited but authoritative multiple-purpose regional government.

While many special-purpose districts and agencies have been established, all attempts to create a multiple-purpose regional agency have been unsuccessful—from the efforts of the San Francisco Chamber of Commerce in 1910 to create a single regional municipality based on the borough system of Greater New York City, through continuous annual efforts, under the leadership of Assemblyman John Knox, between 1967 and 1975 to enact legislation to create an authoritative regional planning and land-use control agency (V. Jones 1973, 1974; M. Scott 1985; S. Scott and Bollens 1968; Wollenberg 1985). For almost a century, periods of intense activity have been interspersed with periods of recuperation, of acquiescence in the status quo, or of resort to incremental use of special-purpose agencies. As one staff member of the California State Office of Planning and Research stated, "the Bay Area, with a tradition of unification attempts, is quietly biding its time for a more propitious hour" (California Office of Planning and Research 1979). Has that hour arrived?

Whatever may emerge from these renewed activities, it should be recognized that the interdependent and many times conflicting interests that constitute the metropolis are still alive. For instance, no one interested in the governance of the Bay Area should forget how two lobbying groups (COLAB, the Coalition of Labor and Business, and the California Council for Environmental and Economic Balance) supported by construction contractors, labor unions, and other construction-related entities successfully persuaded ABAG through pressure on city councils and boards of supervisors to eliminate all land-use control measures from its Regional Environmental Management Plan (Huth 1977). Progrowth and environmental groups, such as the Sierra Club and the Green Belt Alliance, are engaged today in conflict not only with each other but with cities, counties, and special districts, as well as state and national agencies, over land-use controls. In fact, the issues are debated widely throughout the Bay Area not only as they impinge upon or are affected by land-use controls. There are many proposals, much discussion, and some decisions on transportation, water supply and distribution, sewage and waste disposal, water quality, air quality, environmental protection, and many other activities—private and public—that affect the lives and livelihood of over six million people, and constrain or encourage developmental uses of land (Rapaport 1992b).

The institutional capacity of local government should be considered in an interorganizational context. Whatever reconstruction of local government may be undertaken, the metropolis will continue to be governed by political and administrative actions of private, governmental, and quasi-public/quasi-private organizations in an interorganizational ecology of metropolitan regions (Rondinelli 1978; V. Jones 1979; Meltzer 1984; Self 1982; Chisholm 1989; Landau and Stout 1979; Landau, Chisholm, and Webber 1980; Hamilton and Landau 1991; Kirlin 1989).

THE PUBLIC SECTOR

Questions about the institutional capacity of local government must be considered in an interorganizational context of local governments, state and national agencies, and nonpublic profit and nonprofit corporations and associations. Whatever reconstruction of local government may be undertaken, if any, the metropolis will continue to be governed by political and administrative actions of private, governmental, and quasi-public/quasi-private organizations. The governance of the Bay Area is a mixture of public and private actions. Within the public sector, it is a mixture of federal, state, and local governmental actions. Within the local governmental sector, it is a mixture of actions taken by hundreds of local units—large cities, small cities, large and small counties, regional special-purpose agencies, subregional districts, and special suburban neighborhood governments called fire districts, sewer districts, police districts, etc. (V. Jones 1973, 1974, 1979).

There are hundreds of independent local government agencies in the Bay Area: 8 counties, 1 consolidated city and county (San Francisco), 100 municipalities, 383 independent special districts, and 180 school districts. Two new municipalities will be incorporated on January 1, 1993: Windsor, north of Santa Rosa, and American Canyon, southeast of Napa. In addition, there are 199 so-called special districts with county boards of supervisors acting as their governing body and 33 with city councils as governing bodies. The state of California and the United States are also involved directly and indirectly in the governance of the Bay Area. Both are as functionally and territorially fragmented as local government. Although, as in Canada, local governments are creatures of the state, home rule has been embodied in many constitutional and statutory provisions as well as in long-established practices and under-standings. The latter are important as political constraints. There are no significant constitutional constraints to hinder the legislature in creating more special-purpose agencies in consolidating or abolishing existing ones, or in establishing a multipurpose regional agency to exercise power over regional affairs (V. Jones 1974, 1988).

Home rule as an article of faith and practice is not held as tightly now by city and county officials as it was before the 1970s. This is partly due to learning from experience that many modern problems cannot be adequately managed by cities acting alone. It is also a pragmatic adjustment to the involvement of national and state governments in metropolitan affairs. As Kingsley Davis and Eleanor Langlois said 30 years ago: "The trouble with treating the Bay Area complex as an independent unit is that it is not independent. The Bay Area is an integral part of the state's and nation's economy" (Davis and Langlois 1963).

National legislation, with national agencies to formulate rules, provides some funding, imposes sanctions, provides incentives for compliance, and imposes basic constraints upon local governments. One need only mention the Clean Air Act, the Safe Water Act, the National Transportation Act, the authority of the Army Corps of Engineers over navigable waters (dredging and filling of the Bay). The present configuration of the region has been greatly influenced by the national interstate highway system, funds for local transit, provisions of tax law for deduction of interests on home mortgage payments, underwriting of mortgages, subsidies for sewage treatment works, and other facilities.

In many respects, the Metropolitan Transportation Commission and the Air Quality Management District are agents of the national government. In fact, they are good examples of a governmental agency serving all levels of government. It is a means by which authority and power are shared in our federal system. This is possible in the United States but not in Canada because American local and regional governments deal directly with the national government. However, current national policy is to deal increasingly through the state government as an intermediary. Nevertheless, MTC and the U.S. Department of Transportation deal both formally and informally with each other. MTC is the official regional transportation planning agency for both the U.S. Department of Transportation and the California Transportations Commission. All requests for national funds for local or regional highway or transit projects must be reviewed by MTC for consistency with the Regional Transportation Plan.

It is significant for informal relationships that San Francisco is the regional headquarters for federal agencies in California, Nevada, and Hawaii. Until 1980, a Federal Regional Council attempted to develop and oversee national government activities in the region and to establish and maintain liaison with states, metropolitan agencies, and localities. There is need for such a forum at both statewide and regional levels. Bay Vision 2020 did not concern itself with such intergovernmental relations.

In addition to the authority of the state over its local agencies, it is engaged in planning, promoting, and regulating many activities of Bay Area residents and organizations. The scope of state involvement is illustrated by the requirement in AB4242 that regional plans be consistent with the California Clean Air Act, state water quality standards, the Congestion Management Plan Act, the Integrated Waste Management Act, state housing allocation requirements, the proposed State Conservation and Development Plan, and the provisions of the California Environmental Quality Act (CEQA).

GENERAL PURPOSE LOCAL GOVERNMENTS

There are 100 incorporated municipalities in the Bay Area. Eleven are designated as central cities of the five primary metropolitan areas that make up the Bay Area portion of what the U.S. Bureau of the Census calls "the San Francisco-Oakland-San Jose Metropolitan Statistical Area." Only the three largest are popularly considered as economic and social centers, but the other eight as well as dozens of cities function as real "centers" for subregions. Unlike most metropolitan areas in the United States where the median size of municipalities is well below 2,500, in the Bay Area the median size is 27,500. The upper quartile runs from 54,000 to 750,000, and the lower quartile from 2,400 (excluding Colma, pop. 731, the site in San Mateo County of San Francisco cemeteries) to 8,700. There are 72 cities with populations larger than 10,000; 55 larger than 25,000; 27 in excess of 50,000, and nine cities of 100,000 or more population.

Not only are most municipalities large enough to play a full independent/interdependent role, but the position of most of them is enhanced by the fact that they were originally organized early in Bay Area history as distinctively and geographically *independent* entities. Only since the 1906 earthquake and especially during the postwar years have they been joined together by annexation of the rapid growth of their own suburbs and by incorporation of new municipalities (M. Scott 1985; James Vance 1964; Davis and Langlois 1963). Five were incorporated before 1860, 30 by the end of the century, and 56 by the end of World War II.

Central city-suburban relationships are not only important at the present time, they are likely to become even more important as the suburbs continue to increase at a rapid rate and the central cities continue to lose population or increase at a much lower rate. Reapportionment of legislative and congressional seats after the 1990 census has increased the proportion of suburbanites in the state legislature and in Congress.

Minorities are large enough and articulate enough to be a major political force in the Bay Area as well as in the cities where they are concentrated. Many of them are disadvantaged and their concentration creates the social disparities between central cities and suburbs that is coming to be recognized as a regional problem.

The mayor and councilmembers of Oakland, and especially the mayor and supervisors of San Francisco, considering the high stakes of their residents and businesspersons in regional developments, have played a relatively small role in ABAG. Only San Jose has attempted to develop a strategy for regional satisfaction of big city interests. There is a magnificent opportunity for central city and suburb to trade off interests in the development of regional policies. It appears that the central city has the most to gain and the most to lose through regional developments and accommodations. With the shift of population and votes to the suburbs likely to be accentuated in the coming decades, it seems appropriate, in fact, imperative, for the central cities to give up their traditional role of reacting to events and take the initiative in developing regional policies and organizing the regional accommodations necessary to adopt and implement them.

The regional conflict is not a simple dichotomous one of suburb versus central city. In the first place, no central city is homogeneous. Groups within central cities and in some suburbs often have mutual interests. Second, local governments and other groups within the three largest cities will often disagree. And in the third place, suburbia is divided among itself on any issue that may arise. This is why it is needless to fear, as some environmentalists have, that city and county officials will present a monolithic front on regional issues.

REGIONAL SPECIAL DISTRICTS

The most important regional and multicounty special-purpose bodies are the East Bay Municipal Utility District (1923), Golden Gate Bridge, Highway and Transportation District (1928), California Toll Bridge Authority (1929), East Bay Regional Park District (1934), San Francisco

Regional Water Pollution Control Board (1967), Bay Area Air Quality Management District (1955), Alameda-Contra Costa Counties Transit District (1955), San Francisco Bay Area Rapid Transit District (1957), North Bay Cooperative Library System (1960), Bay Conservation and Development Commission (1965), Bay Area Regional Water Control Board (1967), Peninsula Library System (1970), Metropolitan Transportation Commission (1971), Midpeninsula Regional Open Space District (1972), East Bay Dischargers Authority (1974), Livermore-Amador Valley Water Management Agency (1974), South Bay Cooperative Library System (1975), Bay Area Library and Information System (1978), Bay Area Dischargers Authority (1984), and Tri-Valley Water Authority (1986) (League of Women Voters of the Bay Area 1990a). There have been a few unsuccessful attempts to create other regional special-purpose agencies, the most notable being the failure in the '60s and '70s to create a Golden Gate Authority to manage airport, bridge, and harbor facilities, a regional planning district, and a district to regulate the conversion of open space to other uses. Under the Bay Vision 2020 proposal, three of these special-purpose agencies would be consolidated: ABAG, MTC, and BAAQMD.

Association of Bay Area Governments

The Association of Bay Area Governments (ABAG) was created in February 1961, largely in response to two perceived threats to cities and counties: Governor Pat Brown's interest in regional government and a bill in the legislature (supported by the Bay Area Council) to create a Golden Gate Transportation Authority (patterned after the Port of New York Authority) to manage regional ports, airports, and bridges. It was also recognized by some local officials that the physical, economic, and social well-being of the entire Bay region and of its individual communities required areawide cooperation and coordination of policies, plans, and services (V. Jones 1973).

The primary function of the association is to provide a framework for cities and counties to deal with regional problems on a cooperative, coordinating basis. The association is not in itself a "government," but it is a legal agency established by contractual agreement between member cities and counties acting under the authority of the joint Exercise of Powers Act. The act authorizes two or more governments, including state and federal agencies, to exercise jointly any power that they could exercise separately.

COMPOSITION OF GOVERNING BODIES
OF ABAG, MTC, AND BAAQMD

ABAG has a complicated governing structure: a large general assembly in which each member government has a single representative with a single vote (Metropolitan Transportation Commission 1991a; League of Women Voters of the Bay Area 1990a). Currently there are nine county representatives and 92 municipal representatives. However, on issues decided by a roll call there must be a majority vote among county representatives present and also among municipal representatives. The general assembly meets at least once a year to approve the budget, to amend the bylaws, and to act upon any other matter on the agenda or raised on the floor. The business part of the general assembly meeting is usually short and most of the session consists of a program of invited speakers discussing a stated topic. Sometimes, however, action at general assembly meetings is decisive as, for example, on the various Knox bills between 1969 and 1975 to create a regional agency and in 1977 to modify and approve a regional environmental management plan. The general assembly in November 1991 rejected the recommendations of the executive board with respect to the Bay Vision 2020 report (ABAG 1991e, 1991g).

The president and vice president of ABAG are elected by a secret ballot of all city councilpersons and county supervisors—an electoral college of over 500 local elected officials. An executive board of 35 members is appointed by and from elective local government officials: 20 from cities, 14 from counties, and one alternating between the "city of San Francisco," aka the mayor, and the "county of San Francisco," aka the board of supervisors (the legislative body of the consolidated city and county of San Francisco). The mayor's appointee may be an appointed official. The cities of Oakland and San Jose have permanent seats, three each. All other municipal seats rotate among other municipalities. They are selected by the mayors conference of each county and the county members by and from each county board of supervisors (League of Women Voters of the Bay Area 1991a). The U.S. Navy, Department of Defense, Region IX is a nonvoting member. Each county has at least two seats—one municipal and one county. Seats are roughly allocated by population, but the one county-two seats rule ensures wide disproportionality. For instance, the population equality index (a county's share of seats divided by its share of the Bay Area population) for Napa County is 317 and for Santa Clara County 80 (see Table 9.2).

Table 9.2. *Distribution of Seats on Association of Bay Area Govern-ments (ABAG), Metropolitan Transportation Commission (MTC), and Bay Area Air Quality Management District (BAAQMD): 1990*

County or Agency	Number of Members				% Distribution of Population, 1990
	ABAG	MTC	BAAQMD	Total	
Alameda	7	2	4	13	21.2
Contra Costa	4	2	3	9	13.3
Marin	2	1	1	4	3.8
Napa	2	1	1	4	1.8
San Francisco	5	2	2	9	12.0
San Mateo	4	2	2	8	10.8
Santa Clara	7	2	4	13	25.0
Solano	2	1	2	5	5.7
Sonoma	2	1	2	5	6.4
Association of Bay Area Governments		1			
Bay Conservation and Development Commission		1			
Total	35	16	21	70	100.0

[a]Numbers do not add up to total due to rounding
[b]Regional Average
[x]Combined ABAG and BCDC figure

ABAG, as stated in its name, is an association of local governments. It was created in 1961 through a joint powers agreement, which under California law can authorize two or more governmental units to perform jointly any function that they may perform by themselves. It is doubtful, however, that a joint powers agency can, without specific statutory authority, levy a tax, impose a fee, or regulate the use of property. This meant, for example, back in the 1960s, that the only means ABAG could use to regulate the filling of the Bay or the use of land on its shore was

% Distribution of Seats				Population Equality Index			
ABAG	MTC	BAAQMD	Total	ABAG	MTC	BAAQMD	Total
20.0	14.3	20.0	18.6	94	67	94	88
11.4	14.3	10.0	12.9	86	108	75	97
5.7	7.1	5.0	5.7	150	187	132	150
5.7	7.1	5.0	5.7	317	394	278	317
14.3	14.3	10.0	12.9	119	119	83	108
11.4	14.3	10.0	11.4	106	132	93	106
20.0	14.3	20.0	18.6	80	57	80	75
5.7	7.1	10.0	7.1	102	127	179	127
5.7	7.1	10.0	7.1	89	111	156	111
	0.1[x]						
99.9[a]	100.0	100.0	100.0	100[b]	100[b]	100[b]	100[b]

to persuade all counties and cities touching the Bay to enact a common ordinance to that effect. Assuming that unanimous action would have been politically possible, it would have taken months, perhaps years, to negotiate the terms of an acceptable ordinance and subsequent regulations. Since unanimity was required, a single city or a single county could have vetoed any proposed regional land-use policy for the Bay and its shoreline. This situation left the way wide open for the Save the Bay Association and other environmental groups to lobby successfully for the creation by the legislature of a state special-purpose agency, the Bay Conservation and Development Commission (BCDC).

ABAG was not created by the cities and counties of the region to be a government. It was designed as a forum for the discussion of matters affecting more than one city or county, for the development and analysis of information about interlocal problems, and for the development of recommendations to its members for individual or collective action to solve such problems. ABAG has gone through three planning phases. The first phase lasted only a few years while local planning officials were asked to contribute their time to pasting together on a map a mosaic of county and municipal plans. This phase ended around 1963 when local officials tired of the extra work and when it became clear that such a mosaic of local plans would be useless in the emerging transportation planning being developed, encouraged, and, in some instances, required by the United States government. ABAG agreed then to hire its own planning staff and to prepare a regional plan along the lines of a typical master plan document and maps. Comprehensive planning was the watchword (Kent 1963).

In 1970, the ABAG General Assembly approved a comprehensive regional plan. Much of the debate was about whether the plan, if adopted, would override inconsistent provisions of local plans. In fear that it might override local plans, the general assembly refused to *adopt* the plan but instead voted to *approve* it (ABAG 1970, 1986b; Hamilton 1965). As if it would make any substantive difference!

Two provisions were important and long-reaching (they are still being debated in 1991): a recommendation that 3,400,000 acres be kept permanently as open space and that growth be managed by directing growth into existing urbanized centers. Twenty years later (1990), these two provisions are the anchor points in the Bay Vision 2020 Commission's vision of the next three decades of growth management. (It should be pointed out that the 1970 regional plan anticipated much higher population growth than occurred: 6,200,000 by 1980 and 7,500,000 by 1990). Mel Scott evaluated the regional plan in these words:

Of paramount interest was the evidence of a dramatically changed perspective on the part of locally elected officials. . . . The plan of course embodied compromises made at the insistence of various local governments [and, it may be added, of various private interests working through local governments], and it had not been refined to the degree desired by the highly competent planning staff. Still the document presented more of a consensus than might have been thought possible a few years earlier. . . . It was . . . more a symbol of progress toward regional unity than a plan all communities in the region intended to consider seriously as they made controversial decisions on development proposals. Certainly there was no rush to alter local plans and local zoning ordinances to conform with the general scheme. . . . (M. Scott 1985).

The third and current phase of regional planning by ABAG began after Revan Tranter became executive director in 1972. In place of a single comprehensive plan, specific issues are examined as they arise and followed through to a policy decision by the executive board and the general assembly. Each major decision is explained in a document and assembled with analyses of other major policies in loose-leaf form under the title of the Regional Plan.

The current planning process (a kind of strategic planning) consists of four activities that are both consecutive and overlapping. The planning agenda arises from reactions to acknowledged problems or crises and from deliberate attempts to anticipate problems. Again, the agenda is developed formally and informally through a network of governmental and nongovernmental interests. Much of the agenda is dictated by the expressed or anticipated concerns of local, regional, state, and national agencies (ABAG 1980, 1986b, 1988a; Heitman 1982).

The second planning activity of ABAG is the collection of information and the analysis of data for use by ABAG, MTC, and the BAAQMD, cities, counties, special districts, and the public (ABAG 1985, 1988b, 1989, 1991a, 1991b, 1991c; Brady 1985, 1987, 1989; MTC, ABAG and California State Department of Transportation 1991). The centerpiece of this activity is the development of projected changes in population, households, jobs, and dwelling units for 5, 10, and 15 years. Projections are usually updated every two years. They are used by ABAG, MTC, and BAAQMD in developing transportation plans and air quality regulations. They also are used widely by local governments and the private sector. State construction in the Bay Area must be consistent with ABAG projections if approved by the Secretary of Environmental Affairs. No local conformance is required by state law (ABAG 1989).

ABAG's revision of its biennial projections now underway is especially important because of the availability of 1990 census data. Calibrations of projections with new census returns are especially useful in the few years after the decennial census and become progressively less useful as the decade unfolds. ABAG will also prepare special studies of the changes between 1980 and 1990. It will, as a census clearinghouse, make available at cost to public and private organizations recapitulations of census data by cities, counties, census tracts, and combinations of tracts into recognized and *ad hoc* subregions.

The third planning activity of ABAG is debate over regional issues leading to new or modified regional policies adopted by the executive board and the general assembly. Most of this debate, leading to recommendations to the executive board, is conducted in the Regional Planning Committee (ABAG 1988a, 1991d, 1991e; Binger 1991). The committee consists of local officials from each of the nine counties and public members representing business, economic development, environment, housing, labor, minorities, recreation/open space, special districts, and the "public interest." The presidents of both the Bay Area Council and of the Greenbelt Alliance, nonpublic sponsors, of the Bay Vision 2020 Commission, are members of the Regional Planning Committee. The debate is continued, of course, when a committee recommendation reaches the executive board or, occasionally, the general assembly.

During the past decade, the Regional Planning Committee has developed policies dealing with a regional system of trails, water quality, earthquake safety, air quality, hazardous spills, solid waste management, jobs and economic development, and housing. During 1991, the committee and ABAG staff have given primary attention to developing proposals and commenting upon the recommendations of the Bay Vision 2020 commission. This activity has quickened since the commission recommended that ABAG, MTC, and the BAAQMD be consolidated into an interim commission to draft a regional plan. The ABAG staff has supplemented the work of a small staff of the Bay Vision Action Coalition (the cosponsors of Bay Vision 2020) as it develops specific legislation for introduction in the 1992 session of the state legislature.

The fourth planning activity of ABAG is the effort to secure implementation of its general plan and specific policies. ABAG has no statutory authority to implement its policies, although under a joint exercise of powers agreement it could assume nonregulatory functions common to cities and counties. Examples of this are its Training Institute, Worker's Compensation agreements, Pooled Liability Assurance Network, Fixed-Rate Credit Pooling Program and its Health Benefits Trust (ABAG 1980; MTC, ABAG, and California State Department of Transportation 1991). These joint programs also generate additional revenue for ABAG.

Implementation must be achieved through persuasion, development, analysis, and dissemination of information. This is both a technical and political game. Preaching is not enough. Time, understanding of the situation and of the region, and collaboration with state and national agencies and with many persons, industries, and other organizations in the private sector are necessary. The nature of such demands on staff and public officials involved in ABAG is apparent from examination of one observer's (Rothblatt 1982, 1989) list of the characteristics of effective nonauthoritative planning:

1. *Openness.* Enable the various points of view of the major individuals, groups, and organizations (actors) involved with a metropolitan planning problem to be expressed to public decision makers.
2. *Broad representation.* Provide the professional skills and resources needed to assure that all actors involved are represented accurately, competently, and vigorously.
3. *Fairness.* Establish a system of inquiry that treats all actors equally, especially in terms of resources (including time) made available to each actor for research, planning, and presentation.
4. *Hostility reduction.* Provide a decision-making environment that would help to de-escalate the hostility and alienation that could develop between conflicting actors so as to enable each actor to consider more objectively the views of others.
5. *Provide information.* Present each view, together with supporting documentation and analysis, in a manner that helps clarify the issues involved and provide useful information for all parties concerned.
6. *Encourage broad citizen participation.* Expose the metropolitan community to the range of views on regional problems, and provide a means of registering their preferences for the resolution of these problems.
7. *Responsiveness.* Create a setting that would induce decision makers to really listen to, consider, and be responsive to the concerns and proposals of the actors directly involved, and to the metropolitan public.

An organization plays an authoritative role in a community through its goals, its ability to recognize problems and marshall its resources and those of others to deal with them, the quality and sufficiency of the information it collects and disseminates, the validity of analyses, its ability to develop consensus and to follow through by persuasion. ABAG can, without any statutory authority to force compliance with its policies, develop and orchestrate concerted action among a multitude of public and private agencies (often in conflict with each other) to: (a) define regional issues; (b) recognize their importance; (c) identify alternative ways of addressing problems; (d) consider the social, economic, and political advantages and disadvantages of the alternative solutions; (e) identify and weigh the likely impact in the short, intermediate, and long term of each alternative policy and program on other local, regional, state, and national goals and activities; (f) recognize and correct policies and programs when unintended consequences and other errors occur; and (g) support whatever measures are necessary to implement accepted regional policies by private parties and governmental agencies at all levels—local, regional, state, and national.

It is easier to order people, organizations, and governments to do or refrain from doing something than to convince and persuade them to cooperate. Frequently, however, the issuance of "binding" orders leads to a delusion of authority in the absence of effective compliance. The ritual of symbolic compliance is deeply imbedded in our culture. Therefore, as difficult and expensive as it may be, ABAG or any successor regional agency is more likely to be successful to the degree that its actions are convincing and persuasive, even though it may issue cease and desist orders. Even in hierarchial organizations, "to manage is not to control" (Landau and Stout 1979). In the complex Bay Area with myriads of independent but interdependent actors, whatever the structure, however hierarchical it may appear on paper, diplomacy must permeate the activities of a regional planning agency.

BAY AREA AIR QUALITY MANAGEMENT DISTRICT (BAAQMD)

If ABAG is able only to give advice and, perhaps, to persuade others to follow that advice, the Metropolitan Transportation Commission (MTC) and, especially, the Bay Area Air Quality Management District (BAAQMD) have authority respectively to determine how state and federal funds are to be spent and to regulate what people, governments, and businesses do if their behavior affects air quality. Both agencies, although they are governed by boards consisting of city and county officials, are in effect regional agencies implementing state and national programs.

The board of the Bay Area Air Quality Management District has a membership of 21. State law prescribes that counties with a population of under 300,000 (Marin, Napa) shall appoint one member; those between 300,000 and 750,000 (San Francisco, San Mateo, Solano, and Sonoma) two members; 750,000 and 1,000,000 (Contra Costa) three members; and over 1,000,000 (Alameda and Santa Clara) four members. Again, Santa

Clara County is underrepresented with a population equality index of 80, but the index for Contra Costa is even lower at 75.

The regional air control board has been implementing national Clean Air Acts since 1970, including its 1977 amendments. Congress has, after five years of debate, strengthened national requirements by passage of the 1990 Clean Air Act. It is considerably stronger than the earlier act, but no one knows exactly what its 500 pages require until EPA issues detailed regulations or guidelines. In the gap between the expiration in 1987 of the 1977 national Clean Air Act and the new Act of 1990, California enacted its own Clean Air Act. It is more stringent than the federal act. For instance, the national government standard allows 12 parts per hundred million of ozone as compared with a state standard of 9 parts per hundred million. The federal standard for carbon monoxide is 9.5 parts per million while the state standard is 9 parts per million.

The California Air Resources Board controls mobile sources of air pollution, largely through requiring installation, inspection, and repair of catalytic convertors on trucks and automobiles. All new motor vehicles sold in the state must meet higher standards than those required by federal law.

Regulating stationary sources of air pollution is the responsibility of regional and local air control agencies, such as the BAAQCD. This is done through the adoption of regulations to reduce nonvehicular pollution and implementation through the issuance of construction and operation permits. The BAAQCD also prepares a regional pollution control element, which, after approval by the state Air Resources Board, is incorporated into a federally required State Implementation Plan. The district, in collaboration with ABAG and MTC, adopted in October 1991 a new regional Clean Air Plan to replace the 1982 plan.

The district under the California Clean Air Act now has authority to regulate or mitigate emissions from any structure "which generates or attracts mobile source activity that results in emissions of any pollutant":

> The state Air Resources Board lists employment sites, shopping centers, schools, sports facilities, housing developments, airports, and commercial or industrial development as examples of indirect sources. According to the Air Resources Board, freeways are not indirect sources (Morrison and Foerster August 1991a).

This authority to regulate indirect sources has led some participants, mostly local government officials and the Bay Area Council, to insist that Bay Vision 2020's proposed regional agency would need no new authority to control land use. The ABAG Executive Board recommends that the powers of the interim regional agency be limited to those that the three agencies to be merged currently possess.

In fact, the 1991 Clean Air Plan that the BAAQMD adopted on October 30, 1991, was prepared under the direction of the three agencies Bay Vision proposes to merge: MTC, ABAG, and BAAQMD. Under memoranda of agreement, the Joint Air Quality Policy Committee (JAQPC) consists of the chair and two other members of each agency and is supported by an Inter-Agency Management Committee and a Joint Technical Staff. Some commentators question whether a formal merger of the three agencies would be able to accomplish anything the present collaborative groups cannot do (Hamilton and Landau 1991). Proponents of the merger insist that the legal responsibility for the adoption of a Clean Air Plan lies solely with the BAAQMD and that with new requirements to incorporate transportation measures and land-use controls into the Clean Air Plan make it desirable for ABAG and MTC, with their expertise and their constituencies, to be brought directly into a new regional planning and implementation agency. This is the core of the debate that is developing and is moving to the gubernatorial-legislative level in 1992.

State legislation now gives the BAAQMD, under supervision of the state Air Resources Board, authority to adopt both transportation control measures and land-use controls. Whatever it does will have to be acceptable to several state and federal agencies and probably to state and federal courts. Litigation has become a major policymaking process during the past 30 years (Kagan 1990).

State law authorizes BAAQMD to adopt and enforce acceptable transportation control measures (TCM) developed by MTC. The state Air Resources Board lists as "reasonably available" the following type of transportation control measures:

1. Employer-based trip reduction rules.
2. Trip reduction rules for other sources that attract vehicle trips.
3. Management of parking supply and pricing.
4. Regional high occupancy vehicle system plans and implementation programs (carpool and bus lanes).
5. Comprehensive transit improvements programs for bus and rail.
6. Land development policies that support reductions in vehicle trips.

According to the BAAQMD, the 1991 Clean Air Plan "includes indirect source controls" and all of the above "reasonably available" TCMs, plus other feasible transportation measures from the TCM task force process, as necessary to achieve the 1.5 average vehicle ridership target in the

California Clean Air Act (BAAQMD, June 18, 1991). Morrison and
Foerster report that:

> the District Counsel for the BAAQMD has advised the
> BAAQMD that it has the authority to limit parking spaces and
> indirectly impose parking fees as a TCM under the indirect
> source control program (Morrison and Foerster 1991b).

METROPOLITAN TRANSPORTATION COMMISSION

The third regional agency proposed by the Bay Vision 2020
Commission to be merged into a new regional agency is the Metropolitan
Transportation Commission (MTC). The governing board is composed
of 14 county supervisors and city councilpersons or mayors. Board
members have at times served on one or both of the other regional
agencies, sometimes simultaneously. MTC was established by statute in
1970 (D. Jones et al. 1974; D. Jones 1976). In all other metropolitan
regions of the state, the regional council of governments acts as the
regional transportation planning authority.

ABAG appoints one member who is also a locally elected official and
BCDC appoints one member. There are also three nonvoting members,
one each appointed by the California Business, Transportation and
Housing Agency, the U.S. Department of Transportation, and the U.S.
Department of Housing and Urban Development.

Santa Clara County has a population equality index of only 57 on the
Metropolitan Transportation Commission and Napa County again has the
most disproportionate share of seats with an index of 317. Two members
are appointed from Alameda, Contra Costa, San Francisco, San Mateo,
and Santa Clara Counties and one each from Marin, Napa, Solano, and
Sonoma Counties. ABAG and BCDC each appoint a member. The
ABAG appointee will always be a locally elected official. The BCDC
appointee could be a local official, but the current appointee is Angelo
Siracusa, president of the Bay Area Council (a regional association of
large businesses and a cosponsor of the Bay Vision 2020 Commission).

MTC is recognized by both the U.S. Department of Transportation
and the state of California as the metropolitan planning organization for
the Bay Area. Its principal purpose is to prepare a Regional Transportation Plan (first adopted in 1973), revise it annually, and direct and
monitor its implementation through review of applications for state and
federal assistance and the allocation of state and federal discretionary
funds:

MTC's transportation planning process can be simply defined as (1) identification of problems or concerns; (2) analysis of issues, alternatives, and recommendations of solutions; (3) adoption of recommendations as part of the regional planning documents . . . ; (4) allocation of funds; and (5) evaluation of results (MTC, ABAG, and California State Department of Transportation 1991).

In preparing the plan, MTC works closely with ABAG, BAAQCD, BCDC, the California Transportation Commission, the U.S. Department of Transportation, and the transit operating agencies in the Bay Area. The Regional Transportation Plan includes short- and long-range schedules of construction, maintenance, and operation priorities. Airport planning is conducted jointly with ABAG, BCDC, and airport operators; seaport planning with BCDC and seaport managers; air quality planning with ABAG and BAAQCD. Each of these planning activities has led to the development of joint institutional arrangements among the participating parties. For instance, the Seaport Planning Advisory Committee consists of members from MTC, ABAG, BCDC, Caltrans, the U.S. Corps of Engineers, the U.S. Maritime Administration, six Bay Area ports and two nongovernmental organizations, the Bay Area Council, and the Save San Francisco Bay Association.

The most significant joint institutional venture, in light of the Bay Vision 2020 recommendation that the three agencies be consolidated, is the nine-member Joint Air Quality Policy Committee, consisting of three board members from ABAG, MTC, and the BAAQMD. An interagency management committee known as the "troika" consists of top executives from each of the three agencies and directs a joint technical staff. These two joint committees have completed work on the 1991 Clean Air Plan that must be approved by the state Air Resources Board and the U.S. Environmental Protection Agency.

Two other joint arrangements among transit operators play a very important role in transportation planning and in implementing the integrative and coordinative provisions of the regional transportation plan: the Regional Transit Association representing seven major transit operators, and the Transit Operator Coordinating Council representing 11 transit operators. They advise MTC about allocations of transit funds and financial, coordination, and operational matters. The members of the two groups have established many informal relationships, thus mitigating some of the so-called disadvantages of multiple ownership and operation of transit services (Chisholm 1989). MTC is required by statute to evaluate the performance of operators and to analyze their budgets.

In 1991-92, MTC will review and negotiate desired changes in county congestion management plans (CMP). Projects in CMPs inconsistent with MTC regional transportation plans are ineligible for state or federal highway funds. County congestion management agencies are required in all urbanized counties (i.e., counties that contain or are parts of census designated urbanized areas) after voter approval of Proposition 111 in 1990. In Santa Clara County, the core of a congestion management agency was established even before Proposition 111 after extensive negotiations among city and county officials who were members of the County Transportation Commission and the Golden Triangle Task Force. In April 1991, the agency was converted into a joint powers agency. Proposition 111 requires a county congestion management plan approved by MTC before local governments in the county may receive gas tax funds levied in the proposition (Santa Clara County Congestion Management Agency 1991a, 1991b, 1991c).

The Santa Clara County agency says that its new approach is "multidisciplinary and multimodal" designed to provide "new transit facilities . . . , increased and more efficient transit services . . . , improved land use decision making . . . , reduced demand on the current system, as well as building additional roads" (Santa Clara County Congestion Management Agency 1991a). The governing board consists of 10 local officials representing cities and two county supervisors, one of whom also represents the county transit district.

The congestion agency functions as a subregion of MTC, thus serving as a prototype of the subregional bodies proposed by the Bay Vision 2020 Commission:

> In the light of current regional initiatives, there is an additional incentive to create an effective congestion management program. The transportation-related requirements of the California Clean Air Act (AB2595, Sher) will require that cities and counties implement transportation control measures (TCMs) to attain and maintain the state's air quality standard. Whether the final measures in the Clean Air Plan will reflect Southern California's centralized, draconian approach or reflect local initiative is largely dependent on cities and counties coordinated response to the draft Clean Air Plan. Coordinating this response through congestion management agencies wherever feasible will allow jurisdictions to tailor TCMs to the specific needs of the area rather than complying with multiple (and potentially conflicting)

requirements from different levels of government (Santa Clara County Congestion Management Agency 1991a).

The CMA not only becomes an intermediate planning and monitoring agency between local governments and MTC and BAAQMD with respect to transportation and air quality, but it is required to develop a program:

> . . . to analyze the impact of land use decisions made by local jurisdictions on regional transportation systems, including an estimate of the cost of mitigating those impacts (California Government Code 1991).

This provision will provide an opportunity for MTC and BAAQMD, in reviewing county congestion management plans to delegate their analysis and control of indirect sources of air pollution.

NONPUBLIC SECTOR

We will pay particular attention to the regional significance of the organization and activities of four nongovernmental associations: the Bay Area Council, the Greenbelt Alliance, the Santa Clara County Manufacturing Group, and the League of Women Voters of the Bay Area. However, there are thousands of other organizations, few of which operate throughout the entire Bay Area. They are actively engaged in its economy, in providing cultural outlets and social services, and in monitoring other private and public agencies as their actions affect the environment, consumer interests, or the ideological values of other Bay Area organizations. We have already mentioned COLAB, an alliance of construction industries and labor unions organized to fight the inclusion of land-use controls in ABAG's environmental management plan. Scores of public and private agencies involved in debate, bargaining, and decision making on a new airport, open space, and recreation facilities, low- and moderate-income housing, and surface transportation have been identified in the San Jose sector of the Bay Area (Rothblatt 1989). Lorri Fien (1990) counts 775 business, professional, and trade associations in San Francisco, Alameda, and Contra Costa Counties.

A 1982-83 survey by the Urban Institute identified 3,379 nonprofit human service agencies operating in the five central counties of the Bay Area (Alameda, Contra Costa, Marin, San Francisco, and San Mateo Counties). Annual expenditures were $1.2 billion. They employed 35,000 people in addition to the use of a large number of volunteers, making them collectively a major regional employer. Almost half of their funding came from governments. "Governmental support plays a particularly important role in the funding of agencies concentrating in the fields of employment, housing and community development, legal services, and social services" (Harder, Musselwhite, and Salamon 1984).

Greenbelt Alliance

Environmental organizations, such as the Sierra Club, were very active in the early '70s in supporting the creation of a regional planning agency. The Sierra Club, however, under Dwight Steele's leadership refused to alter its opposition to allow city and county officials to be on the governing board of such an agency. Significantly he has changed his position on direct election—saying frequently in Bay Vision 2020 sessions that it was a mistake in the 1970s to allow a division over the composition of regional governing board to defeat the Knox bills.

Today, the Bay Area's major land conservation organization is the Greenbelt Alliance (GA). Founded in 1958 as Citizens for Recreation and Parks, and then called People for Open Space (POS) after 1969 (People for Open Space, 1980, 1983, 1987, 1988), the Greenbelt Alliance is a merger in 1987 of POS and the Greenbelt Congress. It is a nonprofit, tax-deductible organization with over 2,000 members throughout the Bay Area and with offices in San Francisco and San Jose. With a 1988 budget in excess of half a million dollars, it receives the bulk of its funding from grants (46 percent), individual and organizational support (29 percent), membership dues (14 percent), and special events (8 percent) (Greenbelt Alliance 1988).

While preservation of open space has been its major objective, it has recently broadened its mission. It believes that an enduring Greenbelt can only exist successfully in harmony with a compact metropolis:

> . . . an urban framework that serves Bay Area residents' social and economic needs without perpetually expanding onto the region's open space. And more, we urgently believe it is the Bay Area's traditional urban structure—a tightly interwoven mesh of commerce and residence around and near the Bay—that serves these purposes far better than any other that they have uncovered (especially the featureless suburban sprawl that now threatens to blanket the region's precious landscape) (Greenbelt Alliance 1989).

The alliance presents a strategic plan to "revive and enhance the long-standing metropolitan structure of the Bay Area, ensuring that it does not overtake the region's ecological resources." To accomplish this, it proposes to establish permanent boundaries around designated open spaces, increase the density of residential, commercial, and industrial uses of existing urban areas, improve public transit, restrict the development of new water and sewer facilities, remove fiscal incentives that encourage local governments to favor industrial and commercial development over housing, and "devise limited-function governing mechanisms that enable Bay Area citizens to address regionwide problems" (Greenbelt Alliance 1989). It has also become directly involved in influencing local communities and decision makers to support policies protecting open space throughout the region, such as the 1987 general plan revisions in Contra Costa, Alameda, and Sonoma Counties. At the same time that the alliance has increased its visibility and general influence with the public and local decision makers, it has also become strategically involved in the policymaking processes of regional and state institutions concerned with Bay Area land use and transportation planning and development. For example, Larry Orman, the alliance's executive director, is a member of the Regional Planning Committee of the Association of Bay Area Governments and is active in the Bay Area Regional Issues Forum. He was a key participant in negotiations leading to creation of the Bay Vision 2020 Commission and is an important leader in the Bay Vision Action Coalition.

In addition, the Greenbelt Alliance has begun to develop cooperative efforts with some of the most influential representatives of the region's private sector, such as the Bay Area Council. Thus, the Greenbelt Alliance, with growing linkages to other organizations, support, and resources, and armed with its vision of the future will be a major actor in creating new regional development policy in the years ahead.

The Bay Area Council

The Bay Area Council (BAC) is a business-sponsored organization created "to provide a forum for consensus building and a platform for regional leadership" (Bay Area Council, 1988a). Most of the council's approximately 250 members represent major corporations in the Bay Area. BAC's million dollar annual budget is supported primarily from member dues that range from $600 to $28,000 annually. In addition, the council receives grants from other sources, such as the San Francisco Foundation, for special projects.

From the Bay Area Council's perspective, the consequences of metropolitanwide growth, such as mounting traffic congestion, declining supply of affordable housing, increasing deterioration of the environment, and expanding opposition to economic development, are serious impediments to continued economic growth (Bay Area Council 1988a). As Bay Area residents have perceived a decline in their quality of life, they have become increasingly negative about inefficient growth and the financing of community services (Dowall 1984). Consequently, Bay Area residents have approved most of the 48 growth measures proposed on local ballots during the 1980s (Viviano 1989). In 1986, San Francisco itself became the first major U.S. city to limit annual office space development.

The council believes that the deconcentration of jobs could be turned into an opportunity for expanding the economy, increasing the supply of housing, and opening access to recreation while lessening central city congestion (Bay Area Council 1988b). It proposes action to provide a better balance of jobs and housing; more focused development of housing and employment centers; increased funding for infrastructure; better coordination of infrastructure and land-use decisions; and improved fiscal incentives that will induce cooperative local development policies. Most important of all, BAC believes that a new framework should be established for dealing with regional growth problems that transcend the boundaries and resources of local governments.

For more than four decades, the Bay Area Council has served as both a booster for the regional economy and as a catalyst for finding solutions to problems affecting the Bay Area. However, in recent years, the council has come to advocate greater involvement of the private sector in finding solutions to regionwide problems.

Working through its influential members, BAC tries to bridge the gap between the public and private sectors. It also facilitates the cooperation of leaders in the private sector to work with others, including government officials, on issues, solutions, and strategies dealing with the perplexing concerns facing the future development of the Bay region. Bay Area Council's president, Angelo Siracusa, is a member of other influential organizations concerned with policy formulation for Bay Area development, such as the Regional Planning Committee of the Association of Bay Area Governments, the Metropolitan Transportation Commission, and the San Francisco Bay Area Conservation and Development Commission. In conjunction with the Greenbelt Alliance, the Bay Area Council cosponsored the Regional Issues Forum, a diverse assembly of public and private individuals concerned with growth-related issues in the Bay Area. The forum was an important factor in developing the consensus leading to the Bay Vision 2020 Commission.

In 1988, the council cosponsored with ABAG a 26-member group of the Bay Area's top government, business, and university leaders to frame and oversee an ambitious program to develop the regional economy. The forum recently published a report, *The Bay Area Economy: A Region at Risk* (1989), which analyzes the problems and long-term opportunities associated with the region's economic development.

The Santa Clara County Manufacturing Group

The Santa Clara County Manufacturing Group (SCCMG) was established in 1978 by leading high-tech corporations in the San Jose area (such as Hewlett Packard, IBM, and Lockheed) to deal with the emerging regional problems threatening the economic viability of Silicon Valley. Presently, SCCMG represents more than 90 companies employing about 200,000 people in Santa Clara County.

In the words of its chair, William Terry, SCCMG's major objectives are:

> . . . to identify issues that affect employees as well as the efficient management of business; to communicate these issues within member companies and to develop proposals for appropriate action; and to work with elected and appointed officials to form and influence public policy for the benefit of the people of Santa Clara County (Santa Clara County Manufacturing Group 1988a).

Transportation and the environment are perceived by the SCCMG to be the major problems in Santa Clara County. Its primary environmental concern is the reduction in the quality of drinking water in the valley as a result of excessive manufacturing and industrial activity.

The Manufacturing Group's approach has been to work with the local governments in identifying and generating solutions for specific problems, similar to the growing use of public-private partnerships employed in many urban areas in the nation (Goldstein and Bergman 1986; Weaver and Dennert 1987). By focusing attention on specific issues and developing a close rapport with both governmental units and major firms, the SCCMG has been successful as broker and mediator (Rothblatt 1989).

In 1984 SCCMG formed its own task force to study ways of funding needed improvements to heavily congested roads and successfully organized the movement for the county to tax itself to pay for highway improvements. Subsequently, voters in Santa Clara County passed Measure A, which is expected to raise an estimated $1 billion for highway improvements through a half-cent countywide sales tax increase. "A coalition composed of high-tech industry development interests and the Chamber of Commerce then waged a $641,000 promotional campaign, and voters endorsed the measure with 56% of the vote" (Whalen 1989). In the absence of federal and state highway support, Measure A became a model technique for generating funding for local or regional transportation projects. Indeed, since the passage of Measure A, two other counties in the Bay Area, Contra Costa and San Mateo, have passed similar measures.

The Manufacturing Group also believes that redressing the jobs/housing imbalance requires not only transportation improvements but related land-use policies that bring housing closer to jobs. Thus, after years of research and negotiations, the SCCMG helped to facilitate the agreement in 1986 of Santa Clara County and six cities (Santa Clara, Milpitas, Mountain View, Palo Alto, San Jose, and Sunnyvale) to establish a new multijurisdictional planning institution, the Golden Triangle Task Force. However, the city of Santa Clara has withdrawn from the task force, and two other cities, Fremont in Alameda County and Cupertino, refused to join.

Nevertheless, a Golden Triangle Plan was developed that limits industrial development and provides for about 65,000 much needed new housing units near existing employment centers (Santa Clara County Golden Triangle Task Force 1987). The Golden Triangle Task Force has also adopted policies on growth management, housing expansion, capital improvements, and transportation demand management. While many differences among the cities still need to be resolved before the plan can be fully implemented, this effort represents an important beginning in subregional planning in the Bay Area (Rothblatt 1990). Indeed, the cooperative work of the Golden Task Force provided the basis for Santa Clara County's highly developed Congestion Management Agency.

Since the major environmental concern of the SCCMG is the quality of the valley's drinking water, it sponsored the Santa Clara County Clean Water Task Force in 1984 to encourage and support activities by member industries in Silicon Valley to protect and conserve drinking water. With the help of SCCMG leadership, high-tech industry in Santa Clara County spent more than $175 million between January 1982 and July 1987 for the prevention and cleanup of groundwater contamination. They drafted with public officials the Hazardous Material Management Ordinance to mandate the correction of conditions that led to contamination. This ordinance has since become a model for state and federal regulations.

The large high-tech companies represented by SCCMG provide many of the jobs and much of the tax base that sustain local communities. This economic power has, of course, greatly enhanced the political influence of the Manufacturing Group on the public and private sectors in Santa Clara County. And since this county is a major engine of economic development for the entire Bay Region, generating nearly one half of the region's total employment growth between 1970 and 1980 (Schoop 1986), and more than 25 percent during the 1980s, the Manufacturing Group is also an actor of growing regional significance.

League of Women Voter's of the Bay Area (LWVBA)

The role of the LWVBA in the current debate and interorganizational negotiations over restructuring the governmental system of the Bay Area is as yet unclear. Its president and former president are on the Bay Vision 2020 Commission. There is no doubt that it will play an active and influential role in the debate and decisions of the next few years. It was a major actor in the Knox bills controversies in the '60s and '70s, at first holding out firmly along with the Sierra Club for a directly elected regional multipurpose agency. It finally, and reluctantly on the part of some active members, shifted its position to support a regional agency with half its members directly elected and half appointed by city and county officials (V. Jones 1974; Rapaport 1992a).

After several abortive attempts in the 1950s to create a regional league, the League of Women Voters of the Bay Area was established in 1961. Today all 23 local leagues belong. ABAG was created in the same year and the LWVBA has monitored and reported the meetings and activities of it and other regional agencies, first in the *Bay Area Observer* and now in the *Bay Area Monitor*. Six regional public agencies (Metropolitan Transportation Commission, Bay Area Rapid Transit District, East Bay Municipal Utility District, East Bay Regional Park District, and the Golden Gate Bridge, Highway and Transportation District) support the preparation and publication of the *Monitor*.

In addition to participation in the activities of these Bay Area agencies, LWVBA provides important regional information to the public. For example, it publishes an annual directory of public officials in the Bay Area and conducts a variety of studies (League of Women Voters of the Bay Area 1991a). One such study, the LWVBA Regional Governance Evaluation Project, was conducted in December 1990 to explore alternatives to the Bay Area's governance system and found strong support by Bay Area leaders for establishing a new Regional Umbrella Agency (League of Women Voters of the Bay Area 1991b, 1991c).

CONCLUSION

We can see now a widespread recognition among many public and private organizations that there are serious public problems with extra-local and, in many cases, regionwide ramifications and that we need some means of considering and acting upon the external effects of the action, or lack of action, of hundreds of particular organizations. The major private organizations are still committed to their particular interests (e.g., open space, affordable housing near jobs, economic development), but they are pushing for these objectives in a regional context and with a willingness to collaborate with each other and with public agencies. At the same time, local governments and regional special-purpose agencies operating through ABAG and MTC have abandoned the idealistic, but ineffectual, long-term comprehensive approach of the 1960s and 1970s for a strategic process of dealing with issues as they arise. In the real world, however, no issue arises in isolation from other issues and therefore cannot be kept isolated until it is resolved.

What will come from the private-public collaboration in the wake of Bay Vision 2020 in the years ahead and from the legislative and perhaps electoral struggles to follow is unknown. But the very process of collaboration will probably leave its mark. It may set the stage for more effective collaboration and metropolitan governance of the Bay Area well into the twenty-first century.

REFERENCES

Association of Bay Area Governments. 1966. *Regional Home Rule and Government of the Bay Area.* Berkeley, Calif.

_____. 1970. *Regional Plan 1970-1990.* Berkeley, Calif.

_____. 1980. *Regional Plan 1980.* Berkeley, Calif.

_____. 1985. *Jobs/Housing Balance for Traffic Mitigation: Interstate 680 and Interstate 580 Corridor Study.* Oakland, Calif.

_____. 1986a. *The Future: Is It What It Used to Be?* Oakland, Calif.

_____. 1986b. *ABAG 1961-1986: Emergence of a Regional Concept.* Oakland, Calif.

_____. 1988a. *David and Goliath: How Local Decision-Makers Are Confronting Bay Area Planning Challenges.* Oakland, Calif.

_____. 1988b. *Housing Needs Determinations.* Oakland, Calif.

_____. 1989. *Projections—'90.* Oakland, Calif.

_____. 1991a. *Residential Demand and Development Potential in the San Francisco Bay Region.* Working Paper No. 91-1, January.

_____. 1991b. *Changing Patterns in Retail Trade: Taxable Sales in the San Francisco Bay Area, 1970-1989.* Working Paper No. 91-2, January.

_____. 1991c. *Primary Central Business Districts in the San Francisco Bay Area, Spatial and Structural Shifts: 1981-1988.* Projections Working Paper 91-1, February.

_____, Regional Planning Committee. 1991d. A Proposed Land Use Policy Framework for the San Francisco Bay Area, July.

_____. 1991e. *Platform on Regional Growth Management for the San Francisco Bay Area.* Adopted by ABAG Executive Board, October.

_____. 1991f. *Position on Regional Governance.* Adopted by General Assembly, November 21.

_____. 1991g. *Proposed Budget and Summary Work Program: Fiscal Year 1991-92.* Oakland, Calif.

Bay Area Air Quality Management District, Metropolitan Transportation Commission, and Association of Bay Area Governments. 1991. *Draft Bay Area '91 Clean Air Plan: Implementing All Feasible Goals.* San Francisco, Calif.: April.

Bay Area Council and McKinsey & Co. 1986. *Corporate Restructuring: Profiling the Impacts on the Bay Area Economy.* San Francisco, Calif.

Bay Area Council. 1987a. *Bay Area Rental Housing: Will the Boom Continue?* San Francisco, Calif.

_____. 1987b. *The Future of Silicon Valley.* San Francisco, Calif.

_____. 1988a. *Annual Report: 1987-1988.* San Francisco, Calif.

_____. 1988b. *Making Sense of the Region's Growth.* San Francisco, Calif.

Bay Area Council and KQED. 1989, 1991. *Bay Area Poll.* San Francisco, Calif.: December.

Bay Area Economic Forum. 1989. *The Bay Area Economy: Region at Risk.* San Francisco, Calif.

_____. 1990. *Market-Based Solutions to the Transportation Crisis.* San Francisco, Calif.

Bay Vision 2020 Commission. 1991. *The Commission Report.* San Francisco, Calif.

Binger, Gary. 1991. *Land Use Policy Guidelines—Survey Results and Regional Planning Committee Recommendations.* Report to ABAG Executive Board, August 7.

Brady, Raymond J. 1985. *Perspective on a Region's Growth: Maintaining the San Francisco Bay Area Economy.* Oakland, Calif.: ABAG.

_____. 1987. *The Changing Structure of the Bay Area Economy: Interdependence Not Independence.* ABAG Working Paper No. 87-1, Oakland, Calif.

_____. 1989. *Final Employment, Population and Household Forecast 1980-2005.* Memo to ABAG Executive Board.

California Legislature, Assembly Office of Research. 1988. *California 2000: Gridlock in the Making.* March.

_____. 1989. *California 2000: Exhausting Clean Air.* October.

_____. 1989. *California 2000: Getting Ahead of the Growth Curve.* December.

California Code. 1991. Section 6089.

California, Governor Pete Wilson. 1991. *Shaping the Future of California.* California Chapter, American Planning Association. Sacramento, Calif.: October.

California Office of Planning and Research. 1979. Staff interview.

California Senate Select Committee on Planning for California's Growth and Senate Committee on Local Government, Hearings. 1988. *Growth Management Local Decisions, Regional Needs, and Statewide Goals.* Sacramento, Calif.

California, Senate, Office of Research. 1989. *Does California Need a Policy to Manage Urban Growth?* June.

Castells, Manuel, ed. 1985. *High Technology, Space and Society*. Beverly Hills, Calif.: Sage.

Cervero, Robert. 1986. *Job-Housing Imbalances As a Transportation Policy*. Berkeley, Calif.: University of California, Institute of Transportation Studies.

Chisholm, Donald. 1989. *Coordination Without Hierarchy: Informal Structures in Multiorganizational Systems*. Berkeley, Calif.: University of California Press.

Davis, Kingsley, and Eleanor Langlois. 1963. *Future Demographic Growth of the San Francisco Bay Area*. Berkeley, Calif.: University of California, Institute of Governmental Studies.

Deakin, Elizabeth. 1987. *Land Use and Transportation Planning in Response to Congestion Problems: A Review and Critique*. Berkeley, Calif.: University of California, Department of City and Regional Planning.

_____. 1988. *Transportation and Land Use Planning in California: Problems and Opportunities for Improved Performance*. California Policy Seminar, July.

Demoro, Harre W. 1991. Why Transportation Is So Bad—Bay Area Needed a Leader. *San Francisco Chronicle*, November 19.

Detling, Douglas, and Ann-Louise Bacon. 1977. Areawide Environmental Management: Six Decades of Regional Approaches in the Bay Area. Oakland, Calif.: ABAG.

Dowall, David E. 1984. *The Suburban Squeeze: Land Conservation and Regulation in the San Francisco Bay Area*. Berkeley, Calif.: University of California Press.

Elder, Rob. 1989. South Bay Cities Cautiously Reach for Regionalism. *San Jose Mercury News*, February 5.

Fien, Lorri. 1990. *The Directory of Bay Area Associations*. Bay Area Resource Exchange.

Fox, Kenneth. 1986. *Metropolitan America: Urban Life and Urban Policy in the United States*. Jackson, Miss.: University Press of Mississippi.

Freeman, Richard E. 1984. *Strategic Management: A Stakeholder Approach*. Boston, Mass.: Pitman.

Glaberson, William. 1988. Coping in the Age of Nimby. *The New York Times*, June 19, 3-1, 25.

Goldstein, Harvey A., and Edward M. Bergman. 1986. Institutional Arrangements for State and Local Industrial Policy. *Journal of the American Planning Association* 52: 265-76.

Greenbelt Alliance. 1988. *Campaign for the Bay Area's Greenbelt.* San Francisco, Calif.

_____. 1989. *Reviving the Sustainable Metropolis: Guiding Bay Area Conservation and Development into the 21st Century.* San Francisco, Calif.

Hall, Peter, and Ann Markusen. 1985. High Technology and Regional-Urban Policy. In *Silicon Landscapes,* ed. Peter Hall and Ann Markusen, London: Allen & Unwin.

Hamilton, Randy. 1965. *ABAG Appraised: A Quinquennial Review of Voluntary Regional Cooperative Action through the Association of Bay Area Governments.* Berkeley, Calif.: Institute of Local Self Government.

_____, and Martin Landau. 1991. Analysis of Bay Vision 2020. Report prepared for Alameda County Development Advisory Board, September.

Harder, Paul, James C. Musselwhite, Jr., and Lester M. Salamon. 1984. *Government Spending and the Nonprofit Sector in San Francisco.* Washington, D.C.: Urban Institute.

Harrigan, John J. 1993. *Political Change in the Metropolis.* Glenview, Ill.: Scott, Foresman.

Hartel, Terry M. 1985. Sisyphus Revisited: Running the Government Like Business. *Public Administration Review* 45: 341-51.

Hawkins, Robert B., Jr. 1989. Governance: The Case of Transportation. *California Policy Choices* 5: 211-26.

Heikkila, Eric. 1989. Impacts of Urban Growth. *California Policy Choices* 5: 99-122.

Heitman, Deidre A. 1982. The Association of Bay Area Governments: A Critical Look at the Bay Area's Regional Planning Agency, unpublished.

Hoerter, Darrell, and Michael Wiselman. 1986. *Metropolitan Development in the San Francisco Bay Area.* Working Paper No. 453, Berkeley, Calif.: University of California, Institute of Urban and Regional Development, December.

Homburger, Wolfgang S. 1990. *Transit System Reorganization in the San Francisco Bay Area.* Berkeley: University of California, Institute of Transportation Studies, June.

Hootkins, Susan G., and Chin Ming Yang. 1987. *Migration Patterns in the San Francisco Bay Area.* ABAG Working Paper No. 87-2, Oakland, Calif., November.

Huth, Ora. 1977. Managing the Bay Area's Environment: An Experiment in Collaborative Planning. *Public Affairs Report* 18. Berkeley, Calif.: University of California, Institute of Governmental Studies.

_____. 1992. See Peter Lydon.

Innes, Judith. 1991. *Implementing State Growth Management in the U.S.: Strategies for Coordination.* Working Paper No. 542, Berkeley, Calif.: University of California, Institute of Urban and Regional Development, July.

Jones, David W. 1976. *The Politics of Metropolitan Transportation Planning and Programming.* Berkeley, Calif.: University of California, Institute of Transportation Studies.

_____, Robert Taggart, and Edith Dorosin. 1974. *The Metropolitan Transportation Commission: An Innovative Experiment in Incremental Planning; A Cautious Experiment in Regionalism.* Palo Alto, Calif.: Stanford University, The Stanford Transportation Research Program and the Center for Interdisciplinary Research.

Jones, Victor. 1968. Metropolitan Detente: Is it Politically and Constitutionally Possible? *George Washington Law Review*, May.

_____. 1970. Representative Local Government: From Neighborhood to Region. *Public Affairs Report.* Berkeley: University of California, Institute of Governmental Studies, April.

_____. 1973. Bay Area Regionalism: Institutions, Processes, and Programs. *Regional Governance: Promise and Performance.* Advisory Commission on Intergovernmental Relations.

_____. 1974. Bay Area Regionalism: The Politics of Intergovernmental Relations. In *The Regionalist Papers*, ed. Mathewson Kent, Detroit, Mich.: Metropolitan Fund, Inc.

_____. 1979. From Metropolitan Government to Metropolitan Governance. In *Managing Urban Settlements: Can Our Governmental Structures Cope?* ed. K. G. Denike, Vancouver: University of British Columbia, Center for Human Settlements.

_____. 1988. Beavers and Cats: Federal-Local Relations in the United States and Canada. In *Meech Lake: From Centre to Periphery*, ed. Hilda Symonds and H. Peter Oberlander, Vancouver: University of British Columbia, Centre for Human Settlements.

Kagan, Robert M. 1990. Adversarial Legalism and American Government. Annual meeting of the Law and Society Association, Berkeley, Calif., May-June.

Kent, T. J., Jr. 1963. *City and Regional Planning for the Metropolitan San Francisco Bay Area.* Berkeley, Calif.: University of California, Institute of Governmental Studies.

Kirlin, John J. 1988. Building Now for the Future. Draft final report for Commission on County Government, County Supervisors Association of California.

_____. 1989. Improving Regional Governance. *California Policy Choices* 5: 187-210.

_____. 1990. Command or Incentives to Improve Air Quality. *California Policy Choices* 6: 147-74.

Kroll, Cynthia A. 1984. Suburban Office Markets and Regional Economic Growth: The San Francisco Bay Area's 680 Corridor. *Berkeley Planning Journal*, 112-130.

_____, and Efza Eurengil. 1989. *The San Francisco Bay Area Economy: A Profile of the Region As It Approaches the 1990s.* Working Paper 89-160, Berkeley, Calif.: University of California, Center for Real Estate and Urban Economics.

Landau, Martin, and Russell Stout. 1979. To Manage Is Not to Control. *Public Administration Review* 39: 148-56.

_____, Donald Chisholm, and Melvin M. Webber. 1980. *Redundancy in Public Transit.* Vol. I in On the Idea of an Integrated Transit System. Berkeley, Calif.: University of California, Institute of Urban and Regional Development.

Larimer, Tim. 1987. Gap Between Affluent, Poor Widening. *San Jose Mercury News*, May 29.

Le Gates, Richard. 1990. *Regional Housing Issues in the San Francisco Bay Area.* Report to the Bay Vision 2020 Commission, May.

League of Women Voters of the Bay Area. 1989. Regional Governance: Time to Revisit the Issue. *Bay Area Monitor*, March/April.

_____. 1991a. *San Francisco Bay Area Decision Makers: A 1991-1993 Directory of Regional and Inter-County Agencies.* Lafayette, Calif.

_____. 1991b. *Summary Findings of the LWVBA Regional Governance Evaluation Project.* May.

_____. 1991c. LWVBA Push for Strong Bay Area Government. *Regional Governance Network*, August/September.

Lewis, Sherman. 1990. *Managing Urban Growth in the S.F. Bay Region.* Hayward, Calif.

Lydon, Peter. 1992. Ora Huth and Yvonne C. San Jule: Conversations, Interviews, and Notes on Meetings of Bay Vision 2020 and Bay Vision Action Coalition.

McCreary, Scott T. 1990. *Governance and Natural Resources in the Bay Region—Air Quality, Water Quality and Land Use.* A briefing paper on current status and future trends prepared for the Bay Vision 2020 Commission, April 9.

McDowell, Bruce D. 1984. Regions at the Crossroads. *Journal of the American Planning Association* 50: 131-32.

McLeod, Ramon G. 1988. Bay Area Housing, Traffic: New Approach to Planning Urged. *San Francisco Chronicle,* October 19, A5.

Meltzer, Jack. 1984. *Metropolis to Metroplex: The Social and Spatial Planning of Cities.* Baltimore: The John Hopkins University Press.

Metropolitan Transportation Commission. 1988. *Regional Transportation Plan: 1988.* Oakland, Calif.

_____. 1990a. *At a Crossroads: 1990 Annual Report.* Oakland, Calif.

_____. 1990b. *Twenty Years Experience: Presentation to the Bay Vision 2020 Commission.* March 26.

_____. 1990c. *Transportation Control Measures for State Clean Air Plan.* June 27.

_____, Association of Bay Area Governments, and California State Department of Transportation. 1991. *Over-all Work Program for Planning Activities in the San Francisco Bay Area, 1990-1995.* Oakland, Calif.

_____. 1991. Land Use/Transportation Coordination Strategies—July 15, 1991 Meeting. Memorandum to Ad Hoc Regional Strategy Committee.

Morrison and Foerster. 1991a. Authority and Powers of Bay Area Regional Agencies: Response to Questions from Bay Area Council Bay Vision Action Task Force. August.

_____.. 1991b. ABAG, BAAQMD, MTC, SF Bay Regional Water Quality Control Board: Outline of Establishment, Relevant Authority and Funding.

O'Connor, Kevin, and Edward J. Blakely. 1988. *Suburbia Makes the Central City: A New Interpretation of City-Suburb Relationships.* Working Paper No. 485. Berkeley, Calif.: University of California, Institute of Urban and Regional Development, August.

People for Open Space. 1980. *Endangered Harvest: The Future of the Bay Area Farmland.* San Francisco, Calif.

_____. 1983. *Room Enough: Housing and Open Space in the Bay Area.* San Francisco, Calif.

People for Open Space/Greenbelt Congress. 1987. *The Bay Area at a Crossroads.* San Francisco, Calif.

_____. 1988. *Greenbelt: 1987, Annual Report.* San Francisco, Calif.

Radin, Beryl A. 1990. California in Washington. *California Policy Choices* 6: 279-300.

Rapaport, Richard, 1992a. Gridlock: Regionalism, Part 1—The Failed Dream. *San Francisco Focus* 39, 1: 44-49, 82-88.

_____. 1992b. Unlockicking Gridlock, Part 2—A New Approach. *San Francisco Focus* 39, 2: 76-77, 98-103.

Rondinelli, Dennis A. 1978. Policy Coordination in Metropolitan Areas: An Ecological Perspective. *Administration and Society*, August.

Rothblatt, Donald N. 1981. *Regional-Local Development Policy Making: The Santa Clara Valley Corridor.* San Jose, Calif.: San Jose State University.

_____. 1982. *Planning the Metropolis: The Multiple Advocacy Approach.* New York, N.Y.: Praeger.

_____. 1989. *Metropolitan Dispute Resolution in Silicon Valley.* Washington, D.C.: National Institute for Dispute Resolution.

_____. 1990. The San Jose Metropolitan Area: A Region in Transition. Working Paper No. 90-22. Berkeley, Calif.: University of California, Institute of Governmental Studies, April.

_____, and Daniel J. Garr. 1986. *Suburbia: An International Assessment.* London & New York: Croom Helm and St. Martin's Press.

San Jule, Yvonne C. 1992. See Peter Lydon.

Santa Clara County Board of Education. 1986. *1987 and Beyond: Choices for the Future.* San Jose, Calif.: The Center for Educational Planning.

Santa Clara County Congestion Management Agency. 1991a. *Draft 1991. Congestion Management Program for Santa Clara County.*

_____. 1991b. Analyzing the Impacts of Land Use Decisions on the Regional Transportation System. February.

_____. 1991c. The Relationship Between the California Air Clean Act of 1988 and Congestion Management Program Legislation. October.

Santa Clara County Golden Triangle Task Force. 1986. *Golden Triangle Strategic Plan: Phase I.* San Jose, Calif.

_____. 1987. *Golden Triangle Strategic Plan: Phase II.* San Jose, Calif.

Santa Clara County Manufacturing Group. 1982. *A Public-Private Record of Progress.* San Jose, Calif.

_____. 1987. *Chemical Dependency Treatment.* Santa Clara, Calif.

_____. 1988a. *Chairman's Report 1987.* San Jose, Calif.

_____. 1988b. *Public Policy Issues Affecting Santa Clara County Business.* Santa Clara, Calif.

Santa Clara County Strategic Vision Steering Committee, Advanced Planning Office, Department of Planning and Development. 1991. *Alternative Futures, Trends and Choices.* San Jose, Calif.

Santa Clara County Traffic Authority. 1988. *Annual Report for 1988.* Santa Clara, Calif.

Santa Clara County Transportation Agency. 1985. *Transportation 2000: Issues, Trends, and Projections Affecting Transportation in Santa Clara County.* San Jose, Calif.

_____. 1987. *Transportation 2000 Update.* San Jose, Calif.

Saxenian, Anna Lee. 1985. Silicon Valley and Route 128: Regional Prototypes or Historic Exception. *High Technology, Space, and Society*, ed. Manuel Castells, Beverly Hills, Calif.

Schoop, E. Jack. 1986. Major Factors That Will Affect the Future Economy and Quality of Life of Santa Clara County. Paper presented at the Conference on Silicon Valley: The Future. Santa Cruz, Calif.: University of Santa Cruz, October.

Scott, Mel. 1985. *The San Francisco Bay Area: A Metropolis in Perspective.* Berkeley, Calif.: University of California Press.

Scott, Stanley, and John C. Bollens. 1986. *Governing a Metropolitan Region: The San Francisco Bay Area.* Berkeley, Calif.: University of California, Institute of Governmental Studies.

Self, Peter. 1982. *Planning the Urban Region: A Comparative Study of Policies and Organization.* Alabama: University of Alabama.

Starsinic, Donald E., and Richard L. Forstall. 1989. *Patterns of Metropolitan Area and County Population Growth: 1980 to 1987.* Current Population Reports, U.S. Bureau of the Census, Series P-25, no. 1039.

Stein, Robert M. 1980. Functional Integration at the Substate Level: A Political Approach. *Urban Affairs Quarterly* 16: 211-33.

Stone, Daniel. 1940. *Organization and Transit Performance in the Bay Area: A Theoretical and Empirical Review.* Berkeley, Calif.: University of California, Institute of Transportation Studies, April.

Tranter, Revan A. F. 1984. Beyond Planning: A Call to Action. Oakland, Calif.: ABAG.

_____, and Raymond J. Brady. 1986. The Future: Is It What It Used to Be? Paper presented at ABA General Assembly Meeting, March 27.

Tietz, Michael B. 1986. California Growth: Hard Questions, New Answers. *California Public Policies* 6: 35-74.

U.S. Advisory Commission on Regulatory Barriers to Affordable Housing. 1991. *Not in My Back Yard—Removing. Barriers to Affordable Housing.* Washington, D.C.

U.S. Army Corps of Engineers, San Francisco District. 1991. *Long-Term Management Strategy LTMS for Dredging and Disposal: Study Plan.* March.

U.S. District Court for the Northern District of California. 1989, 1990. *Citizens for a Better Environment, et al., plaintiffs, v. Metropolitan Transportation Commission et al., defendants, orders.* September 19 and May 7.

Vance, James E., Jr. 1964. *Geography and Urban Evolution in the San Francisco Bay Area.* Berkeley, Calif.: University of California, Institute of Governmental Studies.

Vance, Jean. 1976. The Cities by San Francisco Bay in Association of American Geographers. *Contemporary Metropolitan America*, part 2: 217-367.

Viviano, Frank. 1989. New Regional Spirit Springs Up in Bay Area. *San Francisco Chronicle*, February 8, A1-5.

Wake, Jim. 1989. High-Tech's New Face. *San Jose Metro*, 16, 21 March: 13-15.

Weaver, Clyde, and Marcel Dennert. 1987. Economic Development and the Public Private Partnership. *Journal of the American Planning Association* 53: 430-37.

Whalen, John. 1989. The Valley Politech. *San Jose Metro*, 16, 22 March: 12-14.

Wollenberg, Charles. 1985. *Golden Gate Metropolis: Perspective on Bay Area History.* Berkeley, Calif.: University of California, Institute of Governmental Studies.

Chapter 10

Summary and Conclusions

Donald N. Rothblatt
San Jose State University and
University of California, Berkeley

While nearly every North American metropolitan area has some form of regional institutional arrangement to at least consider metropolitan issues (see Table 10.1), few of these institutions have the authority to govern. Our study confirms the view held by Goldberg and Mercer (1986) that Canadian metropolitan areas generally have more highly developed collective regional governance systems than their American counterparts. This seems to be true despite the great regional and developmental variations in Canada that have generated a rich diversity in political styles, from the more free wheeling resource-oriented province of Alberta, to the more established centers of Ontario and Quebec.

It is also true that even the most highly regarded Canadian metropolitan governments are not without their limitations. Clearly, Metro Toronto, established in 1954, has been one of the most effective two-tiered metropolitan governments in North America, rationally guiding development and infrastructure within its domain (Nowlan and Stewart 1991). Yet, most of the growth since the 1970s in the Greater Toronto Area (GTA) has occurred beyond the boundaries and control of Metro Toronto. Although the Toronto area, with its 1990 population of 3,752,000, does not have the large number of local governments found in U.S. urban areas, Frances Frisken in her essay observes, "the GTA has not entirely escaped local political fragmentation and administrative complexity." Metro Toronto is surrounded by four outlying regional municipalities containing a total of 24 municipalities making development decision making increasingly difficult within the GTA, especially when a number of these entities do not even have an agreed upon development plan. Indeed, as Frisken goes on to conclude about the Toronto region:

> What has become increasingly apparent is that Metro as a whole
> is in competition with its regional neighbors (and their member

Table 10.1.   *Sample Canadian and United States Metropolitan Planning Institutions*

Metropolitan Area	Regional Planning Agency (year created)
Canada	
Toronto	Metropolitan Toronto (1954)
Montreal	Montreal Urban Community (1970)[1]
Vancouver	Greater Vancouver Regional District (1968)
Edmonton	Edmonton Metropolitan Reg'l Planning Comm. (1981)[2]
United States	
Chicago	Northeastern Illinois Planning Commission (1957)[3]
Boston	Metropolitan Area Planning Council (1963)[3]
San Francisco	Association of Bay Area Governments (1961)[3]
Houston	Houston-Galveston Area Council (1966)[3]
Minneapolis-St. Paul	Twin Cities Metropolitan Council (1967)

[1]The Montreal Urban Community replaced the Montreal Metropolitan Corporation, which in turn replaced the Montreal Metropolitan Commission, which was established in 1921.

[2]The Edmonton Metropolitan Regional Planning Commission replaced the Edmonton Regional Planning Commission, which was created in 1950.

[3]Voluntary association of local governments.

municipalities) for population, economic investment and provincial funds for infrastructure.

In addition, Canadian metropolitan governments are not entirely autonomous within their own boundaries. The provincial cabinet, with its broad powers of providing social and infrastructure services and reviewing land-use decisions, still has the greatest potential to influence the character of public services and settlement patterns within a metropolitan region. This potential far exceeds the authority exercised by American states, which have usually given considerable deference to local governments, including home rule powers. Yet, in recent years the province of Ontario appears to have been reluctant to impose a clear development strategy for the Toronto area and has seldom overridden local planning preferences. The growing political influence of the expanding suburban areas and the concern of other portions of the province threatened by Toronto's growing economic power have directed provincial resources for infrastructure and community services away from Metro to other areas. Thus, while the province of Ontario took great initiative in establishing Metro in the 1950s and reorganizing it with some political consolidation and directly elected representation during the following three decades, the province has become primarily a regionwide and provincewide mediator and consensus builder in recent years.

When we examine Montreal, we see a similar pattern of provincial behavior to the Toronto case. As the second largest French-speaking city in the industrialized world, with a 1990 metropolitan area population of 3,068,000, and as the cultural and economic capital of Quebec, Montreal itself plays a distinctive role without parallel in the rest of Canada. Yet, the function of ethnicity and history in Montreal metropolitan politics are somewhat akin to those in the Boston region.

The regional government in the Montreal area, the Montreal Urban Community (MUC), was established in 1970 primarily to rationalize transportation and police services. Initially, there were hopes that the MUC, which now represents Montreal and 28 much smaller communities, would become a strong metropolitan government with broad powers to implement a vision for the region (Sancton 1988). However, because of the political tensions between Montreal and these other cities (many of which are primarily anglophone), and because of the community council's requirement for double approvals (by the council and the city of Montreal) for action, MUC's activities have been greatly constrained. As Marie-Odile Trepanier states:

> MUC's functions, except for police and transit, tended to be limited to noncontroversial technical matters such as sewage collectors or air pollution control.

From the outset, MUC boundaries were obsolete encompassing only about 71 percent of the metropolitan population in 1971, and dropping to 60 percent by 1986. The approximately 70 municipalities in the most rapidly growing part of the region, the outlying suburban ring, continue to increase their influence with the Quebec provincial government for public investment in infrastructure and other public services. For example, a major highway planned to link the Montreal area with the Ottawa region will be rerouted away from the city of Montreal to serve instead suburban areas (Simaerd 1989). Thus, like the Toronto case, the Quebec province seems to be involved in the politics of allocation and building a metropolitan consensus. As Trepanier put it, "the provincial role has become more of a facilitator than simply a mandator."

The Greater Vancouver Regional District (GVRD), established in 1969, also showed great promise as a metropolitan government. It not only had a mandated planning function for the Vancouver region comprised of 18 municipalities and 1.5 million inhabitants, but also delivered a wide range of services to the area, such as water supply and hospital facilities. GVRD's board of directors consists of 28 members representing municipal and incorporated districts that were initially free to "opt out" of a particular function of a district. Thus, the board in fact had a voluntary characteristic by functional activity.

During its first decade and a half of functioning with uncertain provincial support, the GVRD generated a sophisticated regional planning process to guide development for an extended regional area through its Livable Region Programme, which dealt with such issues as jobs/housing balance, employment, open space, rapid transit, and growth management. Yet, a series of conflicts with the provincial government as well as shifts to a more conservative provincial cabinet led to the removal of GVRD's regional planning authority in 1983. Consequently, the GVRD was left essentially as an elaborate service district, not a new level of government.

Still, the GVRD continues to have informal influence on regional development because of its past work, prestige, and ongoing leadership in such important planning activities as the 1990 update of the Livable Regional Plan, "Creating Our Future"—a set of broadly agreed upon policies for ensuring a more environmentally balanced metropolitan area. In this regard, Oberlander and Smith conclude in their essay:

> That the GVRD achieved such policy consensus without formal planning authority attests to the thesis that planning regionally has been established as a staple of governance in the metropolitan Vancouver region.

Thus, even without its formal authority, GVRD is the only institution in the Vancouver metropolitan area with the capacity to plan regionally, if not govern regionally.

As a newly developing resource oriented region, the Edmonton metropolitan area is more market oriented than our other Canadian study areas. Spurred by the post World War II petroleum boom, Edmonton's population increased five fold to 574,000 during the 1947-86 period, while the entire metropolitan area nearly quadrupled to 785,000. By 1990, its metropolitan area population reached 824,000 covering 1,599 square miles.

Like several emerging cities in America's sunbelt, Edmonton's growth was reinforced with vigorous boosterism and governmental reformism, which pushed for extensive annexation of surrounding areas. That is, there was a drive to create a larger central city that would increase the economic importance of Edmonton and rationalize metropolitan government. Thus, between 1947 and 1981 Edmonton grew from about 40 to 234 square miles in area. In fact, its last large annexation proposal, which was only partially approved (due to opposition of adjacent municipalities) by the province in 1981, would have increased Edmonton's size to 888 square miles. Ted Thomas describes this annexation showdown in his essay:

> The provincial government resisted all proposals for regional government, likely out of fears of the influence such a unified government in its own backyard might have on provincial politics. By emphasizing repeatedly its commitment to local autonomy of the communities within the region, the government was quite willing to accept the inefficiencies and redundancies which followed from the policy.

After more than two decades of rivalry between Edmonton and its neighbors over economic development and annexation issues, the Alberta cabinet established the Edmonton Metropolitan Regional Planning Commission (EMRPC) in 1981. EMPRC's boundaries include four rural and 15 urban municipalities in a 2,576 square mile area.

The commission's mandate is to "plan for the orderly development of the region . . . " (EMRPC 1987, 6). Its main functions are: prepare and administer a regional plan; provide advice and assistance to municipalities when requested; act as the subdivision approving authority for the region; provide advice and recommendations on annexation matters; and seek and encourage public participation in the planning of the Edmonton region.

As part of its ongoing operations, the commission often serves as a center for coordinating the planning activities undertaken by other levels of government. The EMRPC guides growth and development matters of local and regional significance. The commission works closely with municipalities by providing advice on land-use matters, but, except for subdivision approvals, serves in an advisory capacity only. The current goals and objectives of the commission concern enhancing the commission's role as an intermunicipal forum.

Yet, beyond its advisory capacity, the EMRPC seemed likely to run into major problems planning for the region. With the city of Edmonton possessing 73 percent of the region's population with only one-third of the votes, and the other rival municipalities having the remaining votes, it has been extremely difficult for the commission to build a consensus for effective action. As Ted Thomas concludes:

> The relationships between the regional planning commission with heavy representation from the smaller centers and the city were often strained as were the relations between the city and the provincial government.

In this respect the governance of the Edmonton area is again like those in American sunbelt metropolitan regions, such as the Houston area.

When we turn our attention to the American metropolitan areas, we find similar variety in institutional form, but far less success, in regional governance compared to the Canadian experience. The Chicago area, with its 8,066,000 residents in 1990 covering 5,660 square miles, brings the Canadian-U.S. differences into sharp relief. This third most populous metropolitan area in North America has, as Hemmens and McBride point out, "over 1,250 governments . . . making it one of the most intensely governed regions in the country." And while there are regional planning institutions in the Chicago area, such as the Northeastern Illinois Regional Planning Commission (NIPC) for general planning and the Chicago Area Transportation Study (CATS) for transportation planning, they have almost no authority to implement their plans. True, NIPC and CATS do provide useful information, technical assistance, and regional images and serve as vehicles for metropolitanwide cooperation. But few of their planning proposals have been accepted by the various cities, counties, and special districts that they serve and by which they are governed. Indeed, as Hemmens and McBride observe about the first long range CATS-NIPC transportation plan of 1962:

> Almost none of the plan's recommendations for freeway and transit network improvements have since become part of the region's infrastructure.

Established in 1957 with 32 commissioners reflecting regional and statewide interests, NIPC has no taxing authority and raises funds by contracting specialized planning services and through contributions of local governments in the region. In addition to CATS, NIPC's planning activities have to be coordinated with other influential regional special districts that provide important services, such as public transportation and sewers. At the same time, the city of Chicago and several subregional planning efforts in the form of outlying counties and suburban councils of government have also developed policies for major portions of the metropolitan area. These diverse public institutions coupled with private sector interests filtered through nonprofit organizations, such as the Metropolitan Planning Council, make regionwide consensus building very difficult but very important for almost anything implemented the area.

Major cleavages also exist along race and class lines that are reflected in the geopolitics of the region. Chicago, with its 1990 population 39.1 percent black and 19.6 percent hispanic residing in clearly defined minority neighborhoods, is perhaps one of the most segregated cities in the United States. Rivalry among the various neighborhoods for jobs, housing, and public services represents important controversies within the city, and competition between Chicago and the outlying suburbs for economic development, tax revenues, and public resources delineate major points of conflict within the region (Bennett, et al. 1987).

Thus, only the most crucial areawide problems are dealt with at the regional level, such as coping with excessive transportation congestion. For this reason, a considerable amount of cooperation was experienced by almost all parties concerned in the most recent NEPC-CATS sponsored transportation planning process (2010 TSP Plan) for necessary highway and transit improvements. Indeed, surveys undertaken in 1987 indicated that a majority of the regional population believe that transportation is the only problem that can't be solved by localities independently.

Yet, for most issues Hemmens and McBride characterize decision making in the Chicago area as "chaos, where there is no consistency in how issues are raised or resolved." And since potentially major actors, such as a regional planning institution and the state government, are unable or unwilling to provide leadership for the Chicago area to help resolve these issues, the result is usually inaction.

While representing the oldest U.S. metropolitan area in our study, the Boston region seems to experience governance problems similar to those in much of metropolitan America. With its 1990 population of 4,172,000 over 2,429 square miles, the Boston area has over 100 cities and towns, five counties, and dozens of school and special districts.

Despite numerous attempts to create some form of metropolitan government for the Boston region since the 1880s, none has been established. Instead, the Commonwealth of Massachusetts created the first American regional special district in 1889, the Metropolitan Sewer District, and many others over the years for such activities as parks and transportation. It wasn't until 1963 that the state established a regional planning institution for the Boston area, the Metropolitan Area Planning Council (MAPC).

With the arrival of Irish Catholic immigrants starting to dominate Boston's population in the mid-nineteenth century, the old line Yankee protestant population tried to control Boston and its metropolitan area from the statehouse and eventually from local suburban government. This political cleavage continues on today with perhaps even greater intensity with the emergence of a significant minority group population in Boston (25.6 percent black and 10.8 percent hispanic in 1990) in recent decades. Thus, it is not surprising that historically regional services were provided by state dominated special districts. It is also not surprising that MAPC, the first regional planning agency for the area, was established as an extension of state government requiring representation of all local governments in the region (now 101) and state agencies and special districts, and having purely advisory planning functions. As Mark Gelfand observes about the state in his essay:

It might have imposed metropolitan government upon the region, but chose not to do so because this would have created a major rival to its own authority.

After nearly three decades, MAPC finally developed enough of a consensus to adopt its first comprehensive regional plan *Metro Plan 2000* in spring 1990. However, it remains to be seen if the plan, which calls for more focused development and efficient infrastructive provision as well as a strengthened regional planning agency, will receive the support for its implementation by local and state government.

Clearly, the San Francisco Bay Area has a regional geography and settlement pattern quite different from those in most major North American metropolitan areas. While its development is dispersed around a 100-mile-long bay, the region is focused on three major central cities—San Francisco, Oakland, and San Jose—each competing for its share of political, economic, and cultural resources.

Yet, similar to many American metropolitan areas, it has a decentralized multinucleated political and physical settlement pattern. With its 1990 population of 6,253,000 over a 7,403 square mile area, it is host to 602 units of government including 100 cities, 10 counties, and hundreds of special districts.

The most comprehensive look at regional planning for the Bay Area has been undertaken by the region's council of governments, the Association of Bay Area Governments (ABAG). Created in 1961, ABAG's organization is provided by contractual agreement between member cities and counties acting under the authority of the joint Exercise of Powers Act of the state of California. Its membership includes 92 cities and nine counties, which send representatives and dues to the organization.

Jones and Rothblatt indicate in their essay that ABAG's primary function is:

> to provide a framework for dealing with regional problems on a cooperative, coordinating basis. The Association is not in itself a "government," but it is a legal agency . . . designed as a forum for the discussion of matters affecting more than one city and county.

In addition to providing information and a forum for regional concerns, ABAG has the responsibility to create a regional plan in concert with other regional institutions, especially the Metropolitan Transportation Commission (MTC). Its plan, produced in 1970 and amended in 1980, called for a "City Center Region" that would focus increased housing density development near existing urban areas and provide open space buffers between cities. However, in the absence of authority to implement these policies, ABAG's plan met with very limited success. During the 1970s and '80s, housing densities did not increase, and urban sprawl continued to consume open space and generate traffic congestion at an alarming rate. This process of metropolitan expansion was reinforced by the 1978 Proposition 13 tax change in California, which encourages inlaying local governments to capture the more fiscally desirable commercial and industrial activity and push service demanding residential development to the periphery of metropolitan areas. As a recent evaluation of ABAG's regional plan indicated (ABAG 1986, 3):

> Today, what remains of open space is increasingly under development pressures. Annually, regional growth is consuming close to 7,000 acres of undeveloped land. It is only a matter of time before the remaining buffers will disappear.

Another problem facing ABAG has been the drastic cutback of its federal funding that decreased from 85 to 13 percent of its annual budget during the 1976-86 period. As a result it has expanded its activities by providing many revenue-generating services to local governments, such as group liability insurance, credit pooling, and technical training. Indeed, nearly two-thirds of ABAG's staff work on these activities in order to support the remaining staff engaged in regional planning activities. Despite the revenues from these services, ABAG does not have the staff to fully conduct the comprehensive studies and persuasive planning required for traditional regional planning and implementation.

In addition, the expanding region has become more complex and difficult to plan for.

In order to economize on its limited resources, ABAG appears to have shifted to a strategic planning approach involving identifying specific regional problems and generating realistic solutions. Jones and Rothblatt observe this about ABAG's new approach:

> The current planning process (a kind of strategic planning) consists of . . . activities which are both consecutive and overlapping. The planning agenda arises from reactions to acknowledged problems or crises and from deliberate attempts to anticipate problems.

Meanwhile, the automobile-oriented transportation system continues to experience mounting near-gridlock conditions, such that recent surveys have identified traffic congestion as the leading problem concerning Bay Area residents. In the absence of an enforceable regional plan, many planning activities have been undertaken by numerous public and private actors at varying scales of operation: growth limiting regulations beyond normal land-use controls have been adopted by more than half of the region's local governments; several subregional organizations of local governments and counties have attempted to limit automobile use, through such measures as transportation demand management ordinances; Bay Area-wide organizations representing the private sector, environmental groups, and other interests, such as the Bay Area Council, the Greenbelt Alliance, and Bay Vision 2020, have been generating their own long-term comprehensive regional plans; and at the state level, legislation and initiatives have been passed to help reduce air pollution and transportation congestion.

What we may be witnessing in the Bay Area appears to be a new collaboration of public and private interests to cope with urgent metropolitan problems of broad concern. This collaboration may be setting the stage for effective regional management in the future. As the Bay Area Council President Angelo Siracusa expressed (Bay Area Council 1988, 1):

> Working with the Association of Bay Area Governments, the Bay Area Council formed an important new regional economic development effort aimed at the long-term health of the region's economy. Made up of the region's top leaders, from the public and private sectors, the Bay Area Economic Forum will provide a unique opportunity for the Bay Area to work towards regional consensus on public policy issues affecting our economy.

Thus, it appears that a new public-private partnership is likely to be the basis of any new regionalism in the Bay Area.

Like other American sunbelt regions, the Houston area has grown rapidly since the end of World War II especially with the rise in oil prices during the 1970s. By the early 1980s, the population in the metropolitan area had increased to 3.0 million, and Houston with 1.7 million persons became the fourth most populous city in North America in 1983. Growth has come from extensive annexation of adjacent areas as well as from migration and natural increase.

Similar to Edmonton, Houston was a newly emerging city located next to large tracts of unincorporated land when it launched its annexation drive. Employing its extraterritorial jurisdictional (ETJ) authority provided by the state legislature since 1963, Houston was able to control development beyond its boundaries and annex as much as 10 percent of its area annually. The growth of Houston through annexation has been dramatic. Houston's land area increased from 160 square miles in 1950 to 434 square miles in 1970, and to 556 square miles in 1980. And this geographic expansion enabled Houston to capture the lion's share of regional growth so that by 1980 Houston had a majority of the metropolitan population within its boundaries—the only central city of the 10 most populous urban regions in the U.S. to do so.

Houston's annexation process was also greatly facilitated by utility districts created by the state legislature to provide services for suburban development of nearby unincorporated land. Since the mid 1960s, this was especially the case with the state's creation of Municipal Utility Districts (MUDs) as they established a privatized mechanism to provide infrastructure for outlying residential and commercial development without burdening Houston with front end financing. Then, when all was developed, Houston would annex. Through annexation of these districts, Houston has been able to escape the plight experienced by other major cities surrounded by many incorporated suburban municipalities. Houston has maintained a sound tax base by annexing the fleeing middle class right back into the city.

Since the late 1960s, Houston's population growth has been matched by increments in the built environment. From 1970 to 1985, no less than 361 large office buildings were constructed, representing 80 percent of all existing buildings by 1985. Housed in Houston's major buildings are the white-collar staffs of the oil and gas companies and allied support companies such as law firms, accounting firms, and banks. Houston has been called the "oil capital of the world" because of the substantial investments of oil, gas, and petrochemical companies in the area.

Houston's growth has not occurred without conflict. Certain minority communities have suffered as a result of the growth plans of the predominantly white business elite. The initial decisions leading to destruction of minority residential communities were made by white leaders in the interest of business-oriented growth (Fisher 1990). In addition, the Houston area experienced a fiscal crisis in 1983. Houston found its expenditures rising much more rapidly than tax revenues. The crisis has been partially attributed to the oil/gas recession that hit Houston in 1982 and partially to the costs of growth. The Houston area faced possible service cutbacks, a situation brought about by the increased costs of services (and increased level of spending), and lack of planning by government officials.

However, the city was already experiencing problems by 1978. Because of the tremendous growth of population and land areas away from the inner city, Houston has been unable to maintain and upgrade the infrastructure of the inner city. In addition, when MUD's are annexed, the city often faces substantial expenditures to provide adequate facilities to replace poorly built, or poorly maintained, facilities previously constructed.

Another important constraint has been placed on Houston's annexation policies—a 1978 U.S. Department of Justice requirement to make its city council more representative of its minority population by shifting from an at-large to a partially district city council. This resulted in the election of some minority councilpersons who do not want their numbers further diluted by annexing predominantly white suburbs (Harrigan 1993).

The Houston-Galveston Area Council (H-GAC) is the regionwide voluntary association of local governments and local elected officials in the 13-county Houston-Galveston area (Gulf Coast Planning Region). It serves a vast area of 12,500 square miles, which contained over 3,700,000 people in 1985 (the smaller Houston PMSA has an area of 7,151 square miles and had a 1990 population of 3,711,000). H-GAC was organized in 1966 by local elected officials after authorization by state enabling legislation.

H-GAC's mission is "to serve as the instrument of local government cooperation in promoting the region's orderly development and the safety and welfare of its citizens" (H-GAC 1988, 4). H-GAC is the regional organization through which local governments consider regional issues and cooperate in dealing with areawide problems. In 1987, H-GAC's membership reached a record high of 147 local governments—all 13 county governments, 107 cities, 18 school districts, and nine soil and water conservation districts. Membership is voluntary, but all major general- purpose local governments in the region are members.

H-GAC is governed by local elected officials who are selected by, and responsible to, the local governments that are members of the council. Member local governments annually designate their representatives to H-GAC's General Assembly, which meets at least once a year. A 26-member board of directors (all locally elected officials) provides more specific guidance and policymaking through its regular monthly meetings. Member local governments pay annual dues based generally on population. These funds are supplemented by appropriations and grants from the state of Texas and contracts and grants from the federal government.

Currently, H-GAC's major activity is the establishment of a program to help local governments in their economic development efforts to diversify the regional economy. Another goal of H-GAC is to enhance the regional quality of life by helping local governments improve law enforcement, water and air quality, and transportation services. Like other COGs, H-GAC reviews grant and loan applications, determining the program's consistency with regional planning goals, and sends comments to the funding agencies.

Although H-GAC has no enforcement powers, the council does endorse or oppose federal grants to local governments, and this sometimes determines whether or not the governments will receive the grants. However, as a voluntary association of local governments, H-GAC was created to serve local governments, which retain the real decision-making power.

Indeed, Houston's political and business influence alone has had an overpowering influence on the metropolitan development. As Robert Thomas concludes about Houston's regional influence in his essay:

> The activities of government during the development of the Houston metropolitan area since World War II have generally facilitated the objectives of private economic interests. . . .
> Houston has dominated urban growth decision-making.

Time will tell, however, whether or not Houston will be able to maintain its dominance over the region. With annexation becoming increasingly unattractive, the balance of population growth and political influence may yet shift to the outlying suburban areas.

In many ways the Minneapolis-St. Paul metropolitan area is like most large U.S. urban regions. With its 1990 population of 2,464,000 over 5,049 square miles embracing 272 local government units, the Twin Cities region looks as politically complex as the next American metro area. In fact, having two central cities often in competition with one another as well as with the surrounding suburbs, the political structure of the Minneapolis-St. Paul area appears to be quite dispersed, American style.

Yet, upon closer examination, the Twin Cities area is the most Canadian of our U.S. study regions. With its relatively homogeneous population from publicly oriented northern European backgrounds and small minority populations (central cities had 10.6 percent black and 2.9 percent hispanic in 1990), its citizens seemed to arrive at a regional planning consensus more easily than most American metropolitan areas. Indeed, it is widely believed that it was this consensus-building character- istic that enabled the state of Minnesota to establish what is perhaps the most successful experiment in metropolitan governance in the United States—the Metropolitan Council of the Twin Cities.

Prompted by metropolitan area initiative, the council was created by the Minnesota legislature in 1967, replacing a largely ineffective advisory regional planning commission called the Metropolitan Planning Commis- sion. The Metropolitan Council's mission is to coordinate the planning and development of the Twin Cities area—a responsibility that has expanded over the years to include not just physical development and transportation issues but social programs, such as subsidized housing. However, the council is not truly a level of general government. The state legislature establishes the council's taxing power and responsibilities that usually are limited to functions that cannot be performed by city and county governments. In fact, regional services are provided by other metropolitan agencies, such as transit and waste control commissions. The council provides the regional oversight and coordination of these services.

Instead of representing local governments and special districts, as the previous Metropolitan Planning Commission had done, the governor of Minnesota appoints the members of the metropolitan council. In the beginning pairs of state senatorial districts were used for representation, but the Metropolitan Reorganization Act of 1974 redefined the districts, and now distinctive boundaries are served. The 1974 act also increased the number of council members from the original 15 to 17. Except for the council chair who was to represent the area as a whole, each member would represent, on a one-person/one-vote basis, a particular district.

Thus, the basic task of the council is to represent regional interests in certain designated areas over that of the more narrow local interests. To ensure that the council would not become the captive of local governments was one of the major reasons why council membership was not comprised of local government officials who might reflect only parochial viewpoints.

The Twin Cities Metropolitan Council has also made considerable contributions toward financial equalization. Legislation in 1974 passed the fiscal disparities law, and although the law is not directly related to the Metropolitan Council, without it there would be great difficulty in implementing regional land-use policies. This is because the law, by dividing the commercial/industrial tax base among the communities in the area, reduces the communities' incentive to compete for such development. Tax-base sharing requires each community to contribute 40 percent of its commercial/industrial tax base growth since 1971 into a metropolitan pool that is then redistributed according to each community's population and overall tax base.

Additional legislation further expanded the council's authority to review the metropolitan significance of major public and private projects, which meant it could block major development proposals that conflicted with its regional plan called the Development Guide. This authority included local applications for federal and state assistance.

Clearly, the regional gains for the Twin Cities area have been real and positive, and the following outcomes are directly attributable to the Metropolitan Council (Whiting 1984):

- resolving complex regional problems,
- distributing equitably regional tax revenues and social resources, such as subsidized housing,
- overseeing basic metropolitan services,
- generating a comprehensive regional plan,
- preventing such costly and unneeded capital undertakings as an excessively heavy rail transportation system,
- providing information about the region and its needs.

The council's success can be attributed to its broad role of policy-maker rather than being caught up in the details of a service provider. Also, with state-backed revenue and taxing authority, it is not dependent on the uncertainties and political pressures of voluntary local government membership. In addition, many of the council's powers were politically digestible in that they were awarded incrementally by the state legislature over a number of years.

Yet, the council has had its limitations. It was sometimes bypassed in the making of important facility decisions, such as the location of a domed stadium, shopping mall, and trade centers (Whiting 1984); and its development policies have not stopped the continued decentralization of the Twin Cities metropolitan area. Indeed, as Judith Martin points out in her essay:

> The council's authority extends only to the seven-county metropolitan area, but development pressures have expanded well beyond this point. . . . There is little or nothing that even the most sophisticated policy can do to control growth beyond the region's boundaries. So the Metropolitan Council has to live with the frustrating knowledge that the effective metropolitan area has outgrown its reaches, and that it is not at all likely that its own range of authority will be extended.

Nor has the council resolved serious problems in the Twin Cities region that exist elsewhere, such as suburban gridlock, increasing poverty and social tensions in the central cities, and central city-suburban competition. Thus, it is still an open question as to how well the council will handle the emerging increasingly diverse and less manageable metropolitan problems of the 21st century.

CONCLUSIONS

As the preceding summary indicates, a diverse pattern of metropolitan governance emerges in both countries reflecting the wide spectrum of regional and cultural qualities of these continental scale societies. However, the relative political dominance of the provincial government in local policymaking under the Canadian federal system (L'Heureux 1985) has caused more robust metropolitan governmental and planning institutions to be established in Canada than in the United States. And it seems likely that the importance of provincial authority and influence that has developed in the Canadian federation since World War II will continue, if not increase, because of proposed constitutional reforms in the foreseeable future (Smiley 1987, 1989; Fraser 1992).

At one extreme, the Chicago region with over 1,200 units of competing local government and no formal centralized metropolitan government with authority seems virtually unmanageable. Yet, Hemmens and McBride found that coalitions can be formed incrementally to build a consensus to deal with a critical problem, such as traffic congestion, and apparently enough adjustments are made to the system so that the region continues to function and grow.

At the other end of the spectrum, we have Canadian urban areas, such as metropolitan Toronto possessing one provincial office for the greater region, five two-tiered governments, and only 30 local municipalities. And while each province has some form of municipal fiscal equalization, Frisken and Trepanier found in Toronto and Montreal that there is increasing competition among Canadian local governments for economic development, population, provincial funds, and infrastructure despite the presence of metropolitan government.

How then can we explain these differences and similarities we've encountered? Are they the result of factors Andrew Sancton in his introductory essay hypothesized about the differences between the two countries: national and/or regional social, economic and cultural characteristics; and contrasting conscious public policies shaping urban development? Or are our findings due to global social and economic forces?

While more similar to one another than most western democracies (Birch 1986), it seems clear that there are significant longstanding differences in political culture between Canada and the United States. As Lipset (1990, 225) observed in his comparative study of values and institutions in both countries:

The United States and Canada remain two nations formed around sharply different organizing principles. Their basic myths vary considerably, and national ethoses and structures are determined in large part by such images. One nation's institutions reflect the effort to apply universalistic principles emphasizing competitive individualism and egalitarianism, while the other's are an outgrowth of a particularistic compact to preserve linguistic and provincial cultures and rights and elitism. Ironically, . . . the conservative effort has stimulated an emphasis on group rights and benefits for the less privileged; the liberal one continues to stress more concern for the individual but exhibits less interest in those who are poor and outcast.

No doubt some of these differences have influenced policymaking for, and the character of, metropolitan areas in both countries. As Goldberg and Mercer (1986) argue, the high degree of American metropolitan political fragmentation reflects the more individualistic market orientation of the American political ethos and makes centralized metropolitan planning and management more difficult in the United States than in Canada where there is a greater value placed on collective and government action. In addition, it's suggested that the greater racial homogeneity and tolerance of cultural diversity and the more supportive safety net of social and economic assistance for the disadvantaged in Canada has made its central cities safer and more livable for traditional families than those in the United States (Feldman and Goldberg 1987). Indeed, Canadian central cities have been shown to be more fiscally and economically viable (with provincial support), and have more compact development and better infrastructure, such as transit facilities, than their American counterparts (Goldberg and Mercer 1986; Artibise 1988).

Yet, while the general tendency of American fragmentation of local government is corroborated by our study (see Table 10.2), and that such fragmentation is nationally on the rise (see Table 10.3), there are striking variations. For examples, the Minneapolis-St. Paul area, which was found to be the most fragmented U.S. region (in terms of local governments per million population), has the Twin Cities Metropolitan Council—the most "Canadian-like" centralized metropolitan governance system of our American study areas; and on the Canadian side, Montreal, which was found to be the most fragmented of the Canadian regions, has the Montreal Urban Community—a well-established metropolitan government, which, by American standards, is quite strong.

And as cited earlier, despite fewer units of local government to coordinate and the centralizing authority of metropolitan government, Canadian central city-suburban conflicts over development and public resources have been increasing in recent decades. This is the case because during the past 20 years the bulk of metropolitan development and population growth has occurred in the outlying suburban areas, often beyond the boundaries of metropolitan governments—boundaries that provincial governments have been reluctant to extend because of concerns over the potential political influence of expanding metropolitan governments. In some ways, the central-city suburban competition could become more pronounced in Canada since the fewer governmental units are more populous and potentially more influential than those in the U.S. and some, like the regional municipalities in the Greater Toronto Area, may become more politically formidable than their smaller-sized American counterparts. And despite strong provincial resistance, Canadian local governments appear to be increasing their pressure for more autonomy and resources (L'Heureux 1985; Woodside 1990).

Table 10.2. *Sample Canadian and United States Metropolitan Area Charactertistics: 1990*

Metropolitan Area	1990 Pop. (Thous.)	Area (Sq. Miles)	Pop. Density (Pop./ Sq. Mile)	Local Govt.[a] (Municipal. & Counties)	Govt. Density (LGovt./ Mpop)
Canada (estimated)					
Toronto	3,752	1,445	2,597	30	8.0
Montreal	3,068	1,355	2,264	102	33.2
Vancouver	1,547	1,017	1,521	18	11.6
Edmonton	824	1,599	515	19	23.1
AVERAGE	2,298	1,354	1,697	42	18.3
United States					
Chicago	8,066	5,660	1,425	267	33.1
Boston	4,172	2,429	1,718	105	25.2
San Francisco[b]	6,253	7,403	845	110	17.6
Houston	3,711	7,151	519	100	26.9
Minneapolis-St. Paul	2,464	5,049	488	205	83.2
AVERAGE	4,933	5,538	891	157	31.8

[a]Does not include school and special disticts, and regional municipalities.
[b]Ten county U.S. Census definition of the Bay Area.
Sources: Canada, Statistics Canada, *Canada Year Book 1992* (Ottawa: Canada Minister of Supply and Services, 1991); U.S. Department of Commerce, Bureau of the Census, *Statistical Abstract of the United States: 1991* (Washington, D.C.: U.S. Government Printing Office, 1991).

At the same time, the fragmented, highly decentralized pattern of American metropolitan policymaking and physical development has come under increasing U.S. criticism as its heavy automobile dependency has been causing near gridlock congestion with a corresponding decline inenvironmental quality. As a result, a spate of subregional, regional, and statewide growth management efforts have emerged throughout much of the urbanized United States. Our own Chicago and San Francisco case

Table 10.3.   *Governmental Units in U.S. Metropolitan Areas: 1977-
               1987*

Type of Units In Metropolitan Area	1977		1987	
	No.	Per Metro Area	No.	Per Metro Area
General Government	11,069	40	13,259	47
Special Districts	9,580	34	12,690	45
School Districts	5,220	21	5,975	21
Total	25,869	93	31,924	113

Sources: U.S. Department of Commerce, Bureau of the Census. *1977 Census of Governments* (1978); and *1987 Census of Governments* (1988).

studies revealed the emergence of multijurisdictional subregional planning institutions to manage urban growth. In fact, during the 1970-90 period, no fewer than 14 states have adopted some form of growth management policies involving the improvement of transportation, environmental quality, and/or land development, at the local, regional, and state levels of government (DeGrove 1989; Chinitz 1990; Turner 1990).

With regard to social diversity, it does appear that Canada's relative social homogeneity has made collective action including spatial redistribution policies for such services as social housing more feasible in its central cities. Indeed, the only American study area with any metropolitan governmental success—the Minneapolis-St. Paul area—had the most homogeneous population of our U.S. study regions, during the 1960s when major innovations in its metropolitan governance system occurred.

Although Canada has long had a culturally diverse population regionally (Fallis 1990), it has become more racially and culturally diverse within regions, as recent immigration patterns have settled increasing numbers of newcomers from Asia, the Caribbean, and Latin America (Lipset 1990). Much of this settlement has occurred in Canada's major urban areas so that by 1986 substantial portions of the metropolitan populations were foreign born: Toronto 36.3 percent; Montreal 15.9 percent; Vancouver 28.8 percent; and Edmonton 18.4 percent (Malcolm

1990). As a consequence of this increasing diversity, groups have emerged to represent Canada's newest immigrants generating a new level of political divisiveness and social backlash in major urban areas (Lipset 1990; Malcolm 1990) and a recent study of all of Canada's CMAs reveal a "deepening residential segregation as measured by declared ethnic origin and by income" (Bourne 1989, 325). Thus, while neighborhood activism has been vigorous in Canadian cities, such as community involvement with housing, urban renewal, and highway projects in Montreal, Toronto, and Vancouver during the urban reform movement in the 1960s and early 1970s (Harris 1987; Leveillee and Leonard 1987; Caulfield 1988), this recent community action process appears to be more pronounced along racial and ethnic lines than in the past.

A strong indication of this growing Canadian urban divisiveness was the May 1992 rampaging of downtown Toronto by demonstrators protesting the fatal shooting of a black man by a white Metro Toronto police officer and the treatment of blacks in the Canadian justice system (Abbate 1992). In addition, serious confrontations have been developing between native Canadian groups and public authorities over land and water rights. In a recent outbreak involving armed Mohawk Indians near Montreal, a Quebec police officer was killed and a major bridge was blocked for several weeks. One observer reported that "some Indian leaders have compared the resort to armed defiance in Quebec to the rioting that swept black ghettos of America in the 1960s" (Burns 1990).

And while in the United States there is some evidence of a slight lessening of residential segregation in certain western metro areas, such as the San Francisco region (Miller and Quigly 1990), substantial inequalities persist in most American urban areas (Beauregard 1990). The Fainsteins (1989) argue that despite the emergence of black political leadership in many of the largest U.S. cities, the American black community is just as segregated as before and has actually lost economic ground with respect to the white population during the 1970s and '80s. Indeed, Wilson (1989), Downs (1991), and Galster (1991) suggest that, in the absence of appropriate programs to assist the most disadvantaged, the poverty in black ghettos could be perpetuated indefinitely in American central cities. Unfortunately, it took the recent riots, protesting the plight of disadvantaged minorities in Los Angeles and other American cities and resulting in dozens of deaths and over a billion dollars in property damage, to generate a renewed national interest in the problems of the central city poor in the form of new federal urban aid legislation (Krauss 1992) and an important 1992 electoral issue (Roberts 1992).

When we examine the policymaking process, it seems clear that provincial government has substantially moderated its support for metropolitan government. In each of our Canadian case studies, the provincial government has either not supported metropolitan government to the extent that its territorial authority kept pace with regional development, or, in the case of Vancouver, actually rescinded authority. Such constraints on metropolitanism placed by a senior level of government (the province or state) is similar to the long-standing plight of U.S. regional institutions (Wright 1988) and documented by Hemmens and McBride, Gelfand, and Martin in our Chicago, Boston, and Minneapolis-St. Paul case studies. This shifting of provincial roles has transformed each province into, as Trepanier stated, "a facilitator rather than simply a mandator," clearly reflecting the growing development and political influence of outlying suburban communities. Apart from changes in the Canadian political value system that might divert resources away from central cities as Frisken (1986) fears, the sheer weight of the growing suburban influence would divert provincial resources to outlying areas.

But some of Frisken's fears may be well founded. It does appear that in addition to growing suburban influence, there has been a rapid shift favoring the market mechanism in Canadian political values. The 1984 election of the Progressive Conservative government led by Brian Mulroney and the passage of the free trade agreement with the United States in 1988 are symptomatic of the Canadian movement toward Anglo-American political conservatism and the increasing market orientation of Canadian political values (Cooper, et al. 1988; Cannon 1989). In addition, the passage of the Canadian Charter of Rights and Freedoms in 1982 that encourages constitutional litigation about individual rights similar to that found in the United States. While rapid change on the part of the Canadian judiciary in land-use matters is not yet evident (Feldman and Goldberg 1987), in the long run judicial changes are likely to make "Canada a more individualistic and litigious culture" (Lipset 1990, 225).

Thus, our Canadian cases demonstrated that during the past decade provincial governments have been less willing to intervene in the political market place of their urban areas. However, it seems likely that provincial governments will not relinquish their potential authority to initiate strong metropolitan guidance, and will not completely abandon policies assisting the central city, such as municipal fiscal equalization and social services, since such policies clearly reflect the long-standing social equity values deeply ingrained in Canada's political culture. For example, recent policies within urban regions, such as Toronto and Vancouver, clearly demonstrate the ongoing Canadian commitment to strengthen the central city and limit suburban sprawl (Artibise 1988; Bourne 1992).

Of course, business and other interests have long urged provincial and municipal governments to encourage investment in the major economic centers—the central cities (Dyck 1986; Leveillee and Leonard 1987; Leo and Felton 1990). But as industrial and commercial activity began to decentralize (following residential development), the influence pattern has clearly been altered and directed more toward servicing outlying shopping centers, industrial parks, and office centers. Yet, with the possible exception of Montreal, there is little evidence in our Canadian case studies of private or nonprofit interests being directly incorporated into the broad regional planning process, that is, beyond lobbying as narrow special interest groups.

In contrast, in the United States there appears to be a growing tendency for public and private interests to collaborate on solving pressing metropolitan problems of great mutual concern (Weaver and Dennert 1987). In what may be a new form of American regional corporatism, the major private sector organizations appear to have become "public-like"—behaving more like public institutions than private firms with a telescopic lengthening of their time horizons and broadening of their views about regional development and the public good. For examples, the organizations representing major business interests, such as the Bay Area Council and the Santa Clara County Manufacturing Group in the San Francisco Area and the Metropolitan Planning Council in the Chicago region are heavily involved in metropolitan planning activities. A similar pattern has emerged among nonprofit environmental groups in the Bay Area in the form of the Greenbelt Alliance, which has joined with business interests to create a development strategy for the entire region, Bay Vision 2020 (1991).

At the same time, some of the American public regional institutions, such as ABAG in the San Francisco region and NIPC in the Chicago area, are marketing extensive services to communities while retreating from the idealistic, but ineffectual, long-term comprehensive approach for a more practical strategic planning process with shared local-regional responsibilities. Accordingly, these public institutions seem to have become "privatized"—behaving more like private firms than public institutions.

While these two sets of U.S. organizations are unlikely to become identical because of the differences in accountability between public and private entities, a substantial convergence of their views and methods is clearly underway. A question remains, however, whether this new public-private collaboration is a coalition created solely for the purpose of short-term crisis management in the absence of a viable metropolitan guidance system, or truly the beginning of a new institutional arrangement designed for conducting effective long-term regional planning.

As mentioned earlier, over a dozen American states have adopted growth management laws designed to rationalize land use, infrastructure provision, and protect the environment. Some of these policies, such as those in Oregon and Florida, have established new metropolitan planning institutions with local planning review responsibilities (DeGrove 1989; Bollens 1992). Although the full powers of these new regional institutions will be tested eventually in the courts, an American movement toward effective metropolitan guidance systems is clearly underway.

When we consider global social and economic forces impinging on the urban systems of advanced democracies during the past two decades, one overall pattern clearly emerges: decentralization of people and jobs (Hall 1990). Clearly, every metropolitan area we examined in our study in both Canada and the United States exhibited substantial decentralization of population, economic activity, and political influence to outlying areas. Even the urban regions having the most advanced forms of metropolitan governance, such as those in the Toronto and Minneapolis-St. Paul regions, were unable to contain and control this rapidly expanding growth. Indeed, studies of recent development of major urban areas throughout Canada, the United States, Western Europe, and Japan have clearly documented this decentralization pattern (Cherry 1984; Blumenfeld 1986; Bourne 1989; Garreau 1991; Zheng 1991; Maser 1992).

Many researchers of urban systems in the industrialized world agree that some form of evolutionary process may be at work (Rothblatt and Garr 1986; Dwyer 1987; Hall 1990; Alonso 1991). The theories suggest that the initial stages of development occur around a few favored growing areas that attract great concentrations of investment, population, and resources in order to create economies of agglomeration necessary for improved efficiency in the production, distribution, and consumption of desired goods and services.

As shown in Table 10.4, a model of metropolitan development emerges with the first stage representing "concentration," which involves

Table 10.4.   A Model of Metropolitan Development Stages

		Population	Change	Characteristics
Type	Stage	Core	Ring	Metropolitan Area
1	Centralization	+	-	+
2	Absolute Centralization	++	+	++
3	Relative Centralization	+	++	+
4	Relative Decentralization	-	+	+
5	Absolute Decentralization	-	+	-
6	Decentralization	--	-	-

Sources: Peter Hall and Dennis Hay, *Growth Centres in the European Urban System* (University of California Press, Berkeley, California, 1980), 229-31; and Norbert Vanhove and Leo H. Klaassen, *Regional Policy: A European Approach* (Allanheld, Osmun, Montclair, New Jersey, 1980), 180-90.

the "polarization effects"—the growth of large urban centers that dominate and drain the hinterlands of people, resources, and capital. Gradually, "trickling down effects" result from diseconomies of scale in large urban areas (e.g., traffic congestion, overcrowding, high land costs, pollution) and new investment opportunities in other regions, and government policies to redirect economic growth away from heavily developed areas overtake the "polarization effects" and a process of decentralization sets in. At first, decentralization will manifest itself with the growth and subsequent dominance of suburban rings, then with the decline of the central cities, and finally with population and economic dispersal away from the older or larger metropolitan areas to new growth poles in smaller urban regions and to outlying, less-developed areas.

According to this model, the United States is functioning around Type 5, Absolute Decentralization, and Canada is moving toward Type 4, Relative Decentralization. However, because the global economy is becoming more competitive and open, the metropolitan decentralization process may be accelerating. That is, as our urban markets expand and become more competitive, firms in these markets must not only become more efficient themselves, but also must function in a well-managed and supportive metropolitan environment. Thus, the slightest diseconomies in an urban region, such as increased traffic congestion and housing prices, begin to induce firms to move to less costly areas. In the advanced societies, the breadth of location and high quality of infrastructure can accommodate this decentralization while the reverse is true for the less developed countries or regions.

Some observers, like Bish and Nourse (1975), Chisholm (1989), and Parks and Oakerson(1989), argue that such a decentralized system of public service provision is more adaptive to rapidly changing conditions, and often more efficient in terms of local consumer satisfaction, than a centralized hierarchical pattern of urban development and authority. In fact, Peter Gordon and his colleagues (1989) found that this decentralization process has generated polycentric metropolitan structures that have enabled the largest urban areas in the United States to grow significantly in recent decades while actually shortening the average commuting times.

This process of metropolitan decentralization is likely to continue, not only because of global economic forces of dispersion and deconcentration, but also because of the emergence of what Manuel Castells (1990) calls the "Informational City"—the spreading out and restructuring of urban activities in space due to our increasing capacity of substituting communication of information for transportation of goods and people. In addition, this pressure for decentralization is being reinforced further by the large numbers of baby boomers who are still entering the low-density single family housing market (Dowall 1984; Moore 1991). Such housing preferences are often related to a desire for living outside the large central cities, in smaller communities where it is easier to control socially sensitive public services, such as schools and police (Rothblatt 1982; Oakerson 1989; Hughes 1991).

Finally, a competitive spirit also exists among the local governments vying to capture revenue enhancing commercial and industrial activities. In the absence of a metropolitanwide taxsharing mechanism, in the United States (excepting the Twin Cities area), and in the presence of a partial fiscal municipal equalization in Canada, it is difficult to convince many communities to forgo the potential revenues from commercial and industrial activity and accept the much needed, but less tax rewarding, residential development (Kitchen and McMillan 1985; Rothblatt and Garr 1986). Consequently, there is a tendency for in-lying local governments to try to capture the more fiscally desirable commercial and industrial activity and push service demanding residential development to the periphery of metropolitan areas (Dowall 1984).

In the face of these overwhelming forces of metropolitan decentralization, most of which are related to long-term global social, economic, and technological factors, much of the metropolitan development pattern may be beyond the control of regional or even national public policy. It therefore seems likely that settlement patterns of major metropolitan regions of advanced economies will become more similar as they continue to decentralize in a multinucleated fashion.

Yet, there are some policy choices available that can help to rationalize what appears to be the inevitable continuation of metropolitan decentralization. First, for each metropolitan area, there needs to be some overarching flexible institutional arrangement with the capacity to build a consensus for a comprehensive long-term shared image of where the region is, and where it should be going. This would require strong incentives for the broad participation of, and power sharing among, all interested public, private, and nonprofit organizations within the region. Second, it would be essential to involve the participation of the next higher level of government (province or state) so as to provide appropriate devolution of power, coordination, and administrative processes for dealing with the eventual expansion of development beyond the initial geographic boundaries of the regional institution. Third, this institutional arrangement should also have appropriate authority, resources, and incentives to help implement regionally approved policies. In addition to a council/commission decision process, this would need some built in procedure for dispute resolution leading to binding agreements, such as mediation and arbitration. Finally, it will be important to have some mechanism for metropolitanwide property tax and general revenue sharing so as to minimize interjurisdictional competition and public service inequities that can distort development patterns and undercut regional consensus building.

Clearly, the province or state has the ability to devolve the appropriate authority to a metropolitan institution and modify local government tax policies. Our study has shown that, while the Canadian metropolitan management system is far more developed along these lines than the United States, Canadian metropolitan areas are becoming institutionally out-stripped by the decentralization process, both in regional planning authority and in tax equalization policies (Frisken 1986). Consequently, Canadian provincial government may be moving toward more flexible regional planning institutions, with the ability to mediate between increasingly diverse communities and interests in expanding metropolitan areas, such as Ontario's Office of the Greater Toronto Area established in 1988 to foster regional cooperation in the GTA.

At the same time, there is a movement to structure the highly decentralized American settlement and authority pattern at the state or substate level with urban growth management policies. Recent efforts in the United States have already tried to centralize metropolitan policymaking, such as the 1985 Florida Growth Management Act requiring infrastructure provision (often with regional implications) concurrent with new local development, and compact urban expansion; and the 1990 measure (Proposition 111) passed in California requiring metropolitan congestion management plans from local communities in order for them to be eligible for state funding (DeGrove 1989; Fulton 1990; Bollens 1992).

In sum, it appears that the character of metropolitan development and each country's institutional response to it are converging. The trends we have observed do not represent the "Americanization" of Canadian urban public policy or the "Canadianization" of U.S. metropolitan planning, but rather the globalization of urban development and corresponding governmental adaptation.

To be sure, some differences exist between urban areas in both countries related to national character and conscious public policies as we hypothesized. For example, it appears that Canada has been better able to nurture more economically viable, safer, and livable central cities than the U.S. Yet, another Canadian-U.S. comparative study by Feldman and Goldberg (1987, 277) determined that:

> At the macroscopic level the systemic contrasts are as real as they are apparent. . . . Yet, microscopically, the powerful explanations gag at their foundations: Boston is more planned, controlled, even "governed" than Montreal. . . . And even with metropolitan government, Toronto is no more successful containing the urban fringe than officials in Oregon trying to preserve the Willamette Valley. The conventional wisdom comparing Canada and the United States, in light of findings here, needs long and hard rethinking.

Thus, while Lipset concludes that "Canadians and Americans will never be alike" (1990, 227), our study suggests that in the long-run the development and governance of their metropolitan areas may be.

REFERENCES

Abbate, Gay. 1992. Demonstrators Trash City Centre: Protest for Black Justice Turns to Looting. *Globe and Mail*, May 2, A1, 5.

Alonso, William. 1991. Europe's Urban System and Its Peripheries. *Journal of the American Planning Association* 57: 6-13.

Artibise, Alan F. J. 1988. Canada as an Urban Nation. *Daedalus* 117: 237-64.

Association of Bay Area Governments. 1986. *The Future: Is It What It Used To Be?* Oakland, Calif.

Barlow, I. M. 1991. *Metropolitan Government.* London and New York: Routledge.

Bay Area Council. 1988. *Annual Report: 1987-1988.* San Francisco, Calif.

Bay Vision 2020 Commission. 1991. *The Commission Report.* San Francisco, Calif.

Beauregard, Robert A. 1990. Tenacious Inequalities: Politics and Race in Philadelphia. *Urban Affairs Quarterly* 25: 420-34.

Bennett, Larry, et al. 1987. Challenging Chicago's Growth Machine: A Preliminary Report on the Washington Administration. *Journal of Urban and Regional Research* 11: 351-62.

Birch, Anthony H. 1986. Political Authority and Crisis in Comparative Perspective. In *State and Society: Canada in Comparative Perspective,* ed. Keith Banting, Toronto: University of Toronto Press, 87-130.

Bish, Robert L., and Hugh O. Nourse. 1975. *Urban Economics and Policy Analysis.* New York: McGraw Hill.

Blumenfeld, Hans. 1986. Metropolis Extended: Secular Changes in Settlement Patterns. *Journal of the American Planning Association* 52: 346-48.

Bollens, Scott A. 1992. State Growth Management: Intergovernmental Frameworks and Policy Objectives. *Journal of the American Planning Association* 58: 454-66.

Bourne, Larry S. 1987. Evaluating the Aggregate Spatial Structure of Canadian Metropolitan Areas. *The Canadian Geographer* 31: 194-208.

_____. 1989. Are New Urban Forms Emerging? Empirical Tests for Canadian Urban Areas. *The Canadian Geographer* 33: 312-28.

_____. 1992. Self Fulfilling Prophecies? Decentralization, Inner City Decline, and the Quality of Urban Life. *Journal of the American Planning Association* 50: 509-13.

Burns, John F. 1990. In Quebec, Yet Another Splintering. *The New York Times Week in Review,* July 29, 3.

Caiden, Gerald E. 1989. The Value of Comparative Analysis. *International Journal of Public Administration* 12: 459-75.

Cannon, James B. 1989. Directions in Canadian Regional Policy. *The Canadian Geographer* 33: 230-39.

Castells, Manuel. 1985. High Technology, Economic Restructuring, and the Urban-Regional process in the United States. In *High Technology, Space, and Society,* ed. Manuel Castells, Beverly Hills, Calif.: Sage Publications, Ch. 1.

_____. 1990. *The Informational City.* Oxford: Basil Blackwell.

Caulfield, Jon. 1988. Canadian Urban's Reform and Local Conditions. *Journal of Urban and Regional Research* 12: 477-84.

Cherry, Gordon E. 1984. Britain and the Metropolis: Urban Change and Planning in Perspective. *Town Planning Review* 55: 5-33.

Chinitz, Benjamin. 1990. Growth Management: Good for the Town, Bad for the Nation? *Journal of the American Planning Association* 56: 3-7.

Chisholm, Donald. 1989. *Coordination Without Hierarchy.* Berkeley, Calif.: University of California Press.

Cooper, Barry, et al., ed. 1988. *The Resurgence of Conservatism in Anglo-American Democracies.* Durham, N.C.: Duke University Press, Ch. 1.

Cullingworth, J. Barry. 1987. *Urban and Regional Planning in Canada.* New Brunswick, N.J.: Transaction Books.

DeGrove, John M. 1989. Growth Management and Governance. In *Understanding Growth Management: Critical Issues and Research Agenda,* ed. David J. Brower, et al., Washington, D.C.: Urban Land Institute.

Dolan, Drew A. 1990. Local Government Fragmentation: Does It Drive Up the Cost of Government. *Urban Affairs Quarterly* 26: 28-45.

Downs, Anthony. 1991. Obstacles in the Future of U.S. Cities. *Journal of the American Planning Association* 57: 13-15.

Dwyer, Dennis J. 1987. The Metropolis in Its National and Regional Context. In *The Metropolis in Transition,* ed. Ervin Y. Galanty, New York: Paragon House, Ch. 1.

Dyck, Rand. 1986. *Provincial Politics in Canada.* Scarborough, Ontario: Prentice Hall.

Edmonton Metropolitan Regional Planning Council. 1987. *Annual Report Fiscal Year 1986/1987.* Edmonton, Alberta.

Fainstein, Susan S., and Norman I. Fainstein. 1989. The Racial Dimension in Urban Political Economy. *Urban Affairs Quarterly* 25: 187-99.

Fallis, George. 1990. Housing Finance and Housing Subsidies in Canada. *Urban Studies* 27: 877-903.

Feldman, Elliot J., and Michael A. Goldberg, eds. 1987. *Land Rites and Wrongs: The Management, Regulation and Use of Land in Canada and the United States*. Cambridge, Mass.: Lincoln Institute of Land Policy, Chs. 1, 10.

Fisher, Robert. 1990. Urban Policy in Houston Texas. *Urban Studies* 26: 144-54.

Fraser, Graham. 1992. Fumbling on Both Fronts. *Globe and Mail*, June 8, A1, 2.

Frisken, Frances. 1986. Canadian Cities and the American Example: A Prologue to Urban Policy Analysis. *Canadian Public Administration* 29: 45-76.

Fulton, William. 1990. Florida's Growth Experiment. *Governing* 4: 68-74.

Galster, George C. 1991. Housing Discrimination and Urban Poverty of African-Americans. *Journal of Housing Research* 2: 87-122.

Garreau, Joel. 1991. *Edge City: Life on the New Frontier*. New York: Doubleday.

Gidengil, Elisabeth. 1989. Class and Region in Canadian Voting: A Dependency Interpretation. *Canadian Journal of Political Science* 23: 563-87.

Goldberg, Michael A., and John Mercer. 1986. *The Myth of the North American City: Continentalism Challenged*. Vancouver: University of British Columbia Press.

Gordon, Peter, et al. 1989. The Influence of Metropolitan Spatial Structure on Commuting Time. *Journal of Urban Economics* 26: 138-51.

Gottmann, Jean. 1989. The Great Urban Gamble. *Town Planning Review* 60: 89-94.

Hall, Peter. 1990. The Disappearing City. Institute of Urban and Regional Development, University of California, Berkeley, Working Paper 506.

_____, and Dennis Hay. 1980. *Growth Centers on the European Urban System*. Berkeley: University of California Press.

_____, and Ann Markusen. 1985. High Technology and Regional-Urban Policy. In *Silicon Landscapes*, ed. Peter Hall and Ann Markusen, London: Allen & Unwin, Ch. 10.

Harrigan, John J. 1993. *Political Change in the Metropolis*. Glenview, Ill.: Scott, Foresman.

Harris, Richard. 1987. A Social Movement in Urban Politics: A Reinterpretation of Urban Reform in Canada. *International Journal of Urban and Regional Research* 11: 361-81.

Houston-Galveston Area Council. 1988. *1987 Annual Report*. Houston, Texas.

Hughes, James W. 1991. Clashing Demographics. *Housing Policy Debate* 2: 1215-50.

Jones, Victor. 1976. Bay Area Regionalism: Institutions, Processes, and Programs. In *Metropolitan Areas, Metropolitan Governments*, ed. Gary Helfond, Dubuque, Iowa: Kendall/Hunt.

_____. 1988. Beavers and Cats: Federal-Local Relations in the United States and Canada. In *Meech Lake: From Centre to Periphery*, ed. Hilda Symonds and H. Peter Oberlander, Vancouver: University of British Columbia Centre for Human Settlements.

Kitchen, Harry M., and Melville L. McMillan. 1985. Local Government and Canadian Federalism. In *Intergovernmental Relations*, ed. Richard Simeon, Toronto: University of Toronto Press, 215-61.

Krauss, Clifford. 1992. Congress Comes Through with $1.3 Billion for Cities. *The New York Times Week in Review*, June 21, 2.

L'Heureux, Jacques. 1985. Municipalities and the Division of Powers. In *Intergovernmental Relations*, ed. Richard Simeon, Toronto: University of Toronto Press, 179-214.

Leo, Christopher, and Robert Fenton. 1990. Mediated Enforcement and the Evaluation of the State: Development Corporations in Canadian City Centres. *International Journal of Urban and Regional Research* 14: 185-206.

Leveillee, Jacques, and Jean-Francois Leonard. 1987. The Montreal Citizens' Movement Comes to Power. *Journal of Urban and Regional Research* 11: 567-80.

Lipset, Seymour M. 1990. *Continental Divide: The Values and Institutions of the United States and Canada*. New York: Routledge.

Magnusson, Warren. 1983. Introduction: The Development of Canadian Urban Government. In *City Politics in Canada*, ed. Warren Magnusson and Andrew Sancton, Toronto: University of Toronto Press, 3-57.

Malcolm, Andrew H. 1990. Beyond Plain Vanilla: Immigration Has Accentuated Canada's Diversity. *The New York Times Week in Review* 8: 2.

Maser, Ian. 1992. Learning From Europe. *Journal of the American Planning Association* 58: 3-8.

Metropolitan Toronto Planning Department. 1992. *Towards a Liveable Metropolis.* Toronto, Ontario.

Miller, Vincent P., and John M. Quigley. 1990. Segregation by Racial and Demographic Group: Evidence from the San Francisco Bay Area. *Urban Studies* 27: 3-22.

Moore, Dora J. 1991. Forecasting the Probability of Homeownership: A Cross-Sectional Regression Analysis. *Journal of Housing Research* 2: 125-44.

Northeastern Illinois Planning Commission. 1992. *Strategic Plan for Land Resource Management.* Chicago, Illinois.

Nowlan, David M., and Greg Stewart. 1991. Downtown Population Growth and Commuting Trips: Recent Experience in Toronto. *Journal of the American Planning Association* 57: 163-82.

Parks, Roger B., and Ronald J. Oakerson. 1989. Metropolitan Organization and Governance: A Local Public Economy Approach. *Urban Affairs Quarterly* 25: 18-29.

Popenoe, David. 1985. *Private Pleasure, Public Plight: American Metropolitan Community Life in Comparative Perspective.* New Brunswick, N. J.: Transaction Books.

Quesnel, Louise. 1990. Political Control Over Planning in Quebec. *International Journal of Urban and Regional Research* 14: 25-48.

Roberts, Jerry. 1992. Angry Americans Rock Political Boat. *San Francisco Chronicle,* May 6, A1, 10.

Rothblatt, Donald N. 1982. *Planning The Metropolis: The Multiple Advocacy Approach.* New York: Praeger.

_____. 1989. *Metropolitan Dispute Resolution in Silicon Valley.* Washington, D.C.: National Institute for Dispute Resolution.

_____. 1991. Silicon Valley's Independent Spirit Complicates Urban Planning. *Public Affairs Report* 32: 6, 7.

_____, and Daniel J. Garr. 1986. *Suburbia: An International Assessment.* London and New York: Croom-Helm and St. Martin's Press.

Sancton, Andrew. 1983. Conclusion: Canadian City Politics in Comparative Perspective. In *City Politics in Canada,* ed. Warren Magnusson and Andrew Sancton, Toronto: University of Toronto Press, 291-317.

_____. 1985. *Governing The Island of Montreal.* Berkeley, Calif.: University of California Press.

_____. 1988. Montreal's Metropolitan Government. *Quebec Studies* 6: 12-25.

Self, Peter. 1982. *Planning The Urban Region: A Comparative Study of Policies and Organizations.* Alabama: University of Alabama Press.

Sharpe, L. James. 1990. The Rise and Fall of the Metropolitan Authority. Nuffield College, Oxford, Research Paper.

Simaerd, Hubert. 1989. President, Montreal Urban Community Planning Commission, Interview, July.

Smiley, Donald V. 1987. *The Federal Condition in Canada.* Toronto: McGraw-Hill Reyerson.

_____. 1989. Meech Lake and Free Trade. *Canadian Public Administration* 32: 470-81.

Turner, Robyne S. 1990. New Rules for the Growth Game: The Use of Rational State Standards in Land Use Policy. *Journal of Urban Affairs* 12: 35-47.

Warren, Robert. 1990. National Urban Policy and the Local State. *Urban Affairs Quarterly* 25: 541-61.

Weaver, Clyde, and Marcel Dennert. 1987. Economic Development and the Public Private Partnership. *Journal of the American Planning Association* 53: 430-37.

Whiting, Charles C. 1984. Twin Cities Metro Council Heading for a Fall? *Planning* 50: 4-10.

Wilson, William J. 1989. The Underclass: Issues, Perspectives and Public Policies. *Annals of the American Academy of Political and Social Sciences* 501: 182-92.

Woodside, Kenneth. 1990. An Approach to Studying Local Government Autonomy: The Ontario Experience. *Canadian Public Administration* 39: 198-213.

Wright, Deil S. 1988. *Understanding Intergovernmental Relations.* Pacific Grove, Calif.: Brooks/Cole.

Yeates, Maurice. 1990. *The North American City.* New York: Harper and Row.

Zheng, Xiao-Ping. 1991. Metropolitan Spatial Structure and Its Determinants: A Case-study of Tokyo. *Urban Studies* 28: 87-104.

ABOUT THE AUTHORS

Frances Frisken teaches in the Urban Studies Program at York University, Toronto. Her interest in issues of metropolitan administration dates back to her postgraduate days at Case Western Reserve University in Cleveland, where she studied the area's A-95 Review and Planning Agency. Recent papers have dealt with "The Contributions of Metropolitan Government to the Success of Toronto's Public Transit System: An Empirical Dissent from the Public Choice Paradigm" and "Local Constraints on Provincial Initiative in a Dynamic Context: The Case of Property Tax Reform in Ontario." She is currently editing a collection of articles on *The Changing Canadian Metropolis*, to be published by the IGS Press in collaboration with the Canadian Urban Institute.

Mark I. Gelfand is Associate Professor of American History at Boston College, where he specializes in 20th century U.S. political development. He is the author of *A Nation of Cities: The Federal Government and Urban America, 1933-1965* (1975) and several articles on intergovernmental relations. He is currently writing a biography of Ralph Lowell, a Boston civic leader and pioneer in educational broadcasting.

George C. Hemmens is Professor in the School of Urban Planning and Policy at the University of Illinois at Chicago. His areas of specialization are the spatial structure of urban areas and urban social economy. At the time this chapter was written **Janet McBride** was a graduate student and research assistant at the University of Illinois at Chicago.

Victor Jones is Professor Emeritus of Political Science and Research Political Scientist at the Institute of Governmental Studies, University of California, Berkeley. He is coordinator of the Canadian-American Federalism Project of the Canadian Studies Program at Berkeley. His research interests include metropolitan governance, intergovernmental relations, federalism, and Canadian studies.

Judith Martin is Associate Professor of Geography and Director of the Urban Studies Program, University of Minnesota, Minneapolis. Martin has taught courses in urban studies, geography, history, architecture, American studies, and art history at Minnesota and universities in Munich, Amsterdam, and London. With a wide-ranging interest in things urban, her publications include *Past Choices/Present Landscapes* (with Tony Goddard), *Where We Live* (with David Lanegran), and numerous articles on topics such as comparative urban design and festival retailing.

H. Peter Oberlander, a graduate of McGill and Harvard, now teaches political science at Simon Fraser University after four decades of teaching and research in urban planning at the University of British Columbia, including founding its School of Community and Regional Planning and subsequently the Centre for Human Settlements. In the early '70s he served as Deputy Minister in Ottawa, inaugurating Canada's Ministry of State for Urban Affairs. For more than a decade he served on Canada's delegation to the U.N. Commission on Human Settlements. Oberlander has published extensively, including *Our Cities: Step Children of Canada's Constitution*, initially presented to the Policy Conference on Proposals for a renewed Federation, Vancouver, 1992; "Urban Policy: One Canada or Ten?" in *Canada on the Threshold of the 21st Century: European Reflections Upon the Future of Canada*, 1991; and *Land: The Central Human Settlement Issue*, 1985.

Donald N. Rothblatt chairs the Urban and Regional Planning Department at San Jose State University and is Research Associate at the Institute of Governmental Studies, University of California, Berkeley. A past president of the Association of Collegiate Schools of Planning, his most recent works include *Planning the Metropolis: The Multiple Advocacy Approach*, *Suburbia: An International Assessment* (as co-author) and *Metropolitan Dispute Resolution in Silicon Valley*. He has studied planning in the United States and abroad and holds the Ph.D. in city and regional planning from Harvard University, where he was on the planning faculty.

Andrew Sancton was educated at Bishop's University, Lennoxville, Quebec, and Oxford University in England. He is a member of the political science department at the University of Western Ontario, London, Canada, and from 1986-92 was director of its Local Government Program, which includes an MPA designed primarily for municipal managers. He is co-editor of *City Politics in Canada* and author of *Governing the Island of Montreal: Language Differences and Metropolitan Politics*. In 1991 the Intergovernmental Committee on Urban and Regional Research (Toronto) published his essay on "Local Government Reorganization in Canada since 1975." He is a member of the editorial board of *Canadian Public Administration*.

Patrick Smith is Associate Professor and Past Chair of Political Science at Simon Fraser University. He holds a B.A. and M.A. from McMaster

University and a Ph.D. from the London School of Economics. He is the co-author of *The Vision and the Game: Making the Canadian Constitution* (1987) and *The Almanac of Canadian Politics* (1991). Smith has written on local government, planning, public policy, global cities, comparative metropolitan governance, constitutional reform, ombudsmania, administrative discretion, democratic socialism, labor market policy, affirmative action, party organizations, and electoral reform in such journals as the *Canadian Journal of Political Science*, the *International Political Science Review*, *Planning and Administration*, and in related edited volumes.

Robert D. Thomas is Professor of Political Science and Director of the Public Administration Program at the University of Houston. He has written books and articles on state and urban politics, federalism, and intergovernmental relations including *Progrowth Politics: Change and Governance in Houston, The Forgotten Governments*, and *Public Policy Making in a Federal System*.

Ted E. Thomas is Professor of Sociology and Dean of the Division of Social Sciences at Mills College in Oakland, California. His major research has focused on the growth of Edmonton and Calgary, Alberta's two major cities, during the oil-boom decade and on comparative urban and social policy.

Marie-Odile Trépanier, a faculty member since 1980 at the University of Montreal's Institute d'urbanisme, teaches local government, urban law, regional planning, and open space management. Her research focuses on the evolution of urban planning legislation in Quebec, on regional municipalities and urban communities, and on open space preservation and management. She has also been studying metropolitan planning and institutions in several areas in Canada, the United States and Europe. Trepanier was a member of the Quebec Ecological Reserves Council (1981-88) and has actively followed recent planning endeavors in Montreal and the MUC through the submission of briefs during public meetings or as a research consultant. She has been chosen by the Minister of Municipal Affairs as a member of the Study Group on Montreal and its Region created in April 1992.